66-17430 (2-8-67)

Sparks

# The Time Between the Wars

## ARMISTICE TO PEARL HARBOR

JONATHAN DANIELS

1966   Doubleday & Company, Inc., Garden City, New York

Grateful acknowledgment is made to the following for permission to reprint:

*Little, Brown and Company*
> Excerpt from *A Pearl in Every Oyster* by Frank Sullivan. Copyright 1938 by Frank Sullivan. Originally appeared in *The New Yorker*. Reprinted by permission.

*Henry Cabot Lodge*
> Letter from Senator Henry Cabot Lodge to Edith Bolling Wilson. Reprinted by permission.

*Herb Reis Music Corporation*
> Lines from "Backwater Blues" by Dewey Bassett. Reprinted by permission.

*The Viking Press, Inc.*
> Lines of "Last Speech to the Court" by Bartolomeo Vanzetti, from *The Letters of Sacco and Vanzetti*, edited by Marion Denman Frankfurter and Gardner Jackson. Copyright 1928, 1956 by The Viking Press, Inc. Reprinted by permission.

*Mainstream of America Series* ★

*EDITED BY LEWIS GANNETT*

# The Time Between the Wars

## ARMISTICE TO PEARL HARBOR

# Books by Jonathan Daniels

# CONTENTS

## CONTENTS

# ILLUSTRATIONS

# THE TIME BETWEEN THE WARS

## ARMISTICE TO PEARL HARBOR

# I

## THE WOOD OF THE EAGLE

AT MIDDAY on November 7, 1918, Eleanor McAdoo, Woodrow Wilson's youngest daughter, found it a "thrilling adventure" to cross the little street between the great, gray Treasury Building, over which her husband presided, and her father's White House. Just turned twenty-nine then and pretty despite her strong Wilson chin, Nell was deliciously caught up in a whirlpool of men and women dancing, singing, shouting and celebrating that Thursday's premature report of an armistice ending world war. One enthusiastic man threw his arms about her and kissed her. Others, recognizing her, shouted her name. As she came gaily to her father's house for luncheon, she seemed "like a chip on the waves" to her stepmother, Edith Bolling Wilson, who in her opulent mid-forties was scarcely less excited.

As the day lengthened and the riot of rejoicing mounted, Edith Wilson could not resist having part in the happy tumult, too. She drove with her mother and sister to watch the celebrating swarm. Merry multitudes surged around them. In her big car Edith was more than a chip on the waves. Sometimes she had the air of a lady who could command them. In the midst of the celebration she ran to the study of the President, then a tired, tense man of sixty-one caught in one crowded week between home rebuke and world triumph.

Edith begged him to come out on the portico to greet the people. He rejected such a respite of rejoicing. He could not come. The report, as she knew, was not true. The German representatives were only then setting out on their journey to meet the implacable Allied commander, austere French Marshal Ferdinand Foch, in his saloon car on a railroad siding in the Bois de l'Aigle near Compiègne. Off east of that Wood of the Eagle, young Americans were still dying in the fierce drive to Sedan in the culmination of the Meuse-Argonne campaign.

Edith was disappointed that he would not go to the great porch where, fifty-three years before, Abraham Lincoln had spoken to just such a triumphant throng. Lincoln then disappointed the crowd by using the occasion, in the spirit of his recent Second Inaugural Address, to talk of restoration, not retribution, of charity without malice, of binding up a nation's wounds. As a historian, that earlier time was inevitably in Wilson's recollection. The triumph then had not been a part of his tradition. As an eight-year-old boy in a Presbyterian manse of the defeated South he had been far away when Washington went wild around the President's portico. Still he understood that America now was roaring in repetition of the same kind of high spirits and fulminations loosed when the news came of Rebel surrender in Virginia. The catcalls for the Kaiser recalled the readiness with the noose and the sour apple tree for Jeff Davis. There were fewer cowbells now and more auto horns. Long before Nell McAdoo was kissed, other girls were. The yells belonged to yesterday and tomorrow.

Wilson waited through that Thursday tumult as he knew he must. His task, as he solemnly conceived it, involved the wounds of the world. No assassin saved him from that improbable task. Lincoln, five months before victory, had asked his countrymen not to change horses in the middle of the stream—and barely reached the shore. Wilson in a similar appeal just before victory in 1918 was less lucky. Thirteen days before this first false armistice report he had asked the people to help him make the kind of peace he believed essential by electing a Democratic Congress. He put at stake more than political power at home. A Republican victory, he said, "would certainly be interpreted as a repudiation of my leadership."

However interpreted, that political repudiation came. Just two days before the premature cheering began, resentful Republicans, with the support of some who had never liked the war and more who were tired of its sacrifices and repressions, had won Congressional control. Ironically, on that same day, November 5, the Supreme War Council in Europe accepted the points Wilson had pressed as the basis for a just and lasting peace. As yet, there was no sound of home rejection in the roars of triumph which came into his study from the celebrants of the false report.

On Friday, Thursday's cheers were like the blown confetti, ticker tape and improvised banners which rejoicing crowds had left scattered upon the streets. However, expectancy stirred on Saturday. On Sunday the Wilsons attended church, services having been resumed now that the influenza epidemic, which had taken four times as many American lives as the Germans, was abating.

They went for a long drive in the afternoon. The red-leafed streets were quiet. But Edith Wilson remembered the excitement of waiting. After dinner guests were gone that evening, she set to work decoding messages. The long-awaited news came at three o'clock Monday morning. "The Armistice was signed!" she recalled. "The guns were still!" And outside, before the dawn, newsboys crying "Extra!" stirred the rise of cheers again.

Not on his customary small typewriter but with a pencil Wilson wrote a message to the American people. It was not a piece for delivery from a portico, but it said his purpose plainly.

"Everything for which America has fought has been accomplished. It will now be our fortunate duty to assist by example, by sober, friendly counsel, and by material aid in the establishment of just democracy throughout the world."

Then beyond midday he drove to the Capitol where Congress—though not the newly elected one—was in session. Beginning in a husky voice, he analyzed the problems of the politics of Europe and of victory everywhere. He spoke of the lava flow of Bolshevism from Russia, across Central Europe, to rioting and ruin in Germany. He mentioned famine which then, as the efficient, humanitarian Herbert Hoover said, was the wolf at the door of the world. The victors in their own interest would do well to lift the vanquished to their feet. The President did not minimize the problem. He described the dimensions of the victory.

"Thus the war comes to an end," he said.

"Armed imperialism such as men conceived who were but yesterday the masters of Germany is at an end, its illicit ambitions engulfed in black disaster. Who will now seek to revive it?"

Certainly, no one. Never, of course. So he rode back through more crowds and cheers to the White House. In the afternoon he reviewed a parade of the United War Workers. He went in his car down Pennsylvania Avenue with Edith to watch and share the continuing, tumultuous celebration. Certainly as he rode, often with his hat held high, there seemed no mere imitation of cordiality in his companionship with his countrymen. They showed no sense of remoteness from him. Only a forked feminine tongue could have spoken of Wilson in late 1918 as "showing his long teeth in that muscular contraction that passes for a smile."

Crowds, showing no signs that they had expended unjustified energy and emotion four days before, surged about his car to cheer and salute him. Secret Service men were overwhelmed by the joyous rioters. The President's car could not move for those who pressed about it to praise him. Only when smiling soldiers with locked arms made a protective ring about it could the car, under their escort, make its way back to the White House.

Similar crowds were celebrating in Europe and waiting to applaud him there. He was, said Colonel Edward M. House, his great friend and aide whom he had sent abroad to prepare the way for the kind of peace he proposed, "God on the Mountain." But even then at home and abroad not all approved his preparations and his plans. Great politicians were waiting for the cheers to subside. And before he sailed to his purpose a sharp-eyed and sharp-tongued woman in Washington wrote in her journal of his preparations "which exceed in grandeur those for the Field of the Cloth of Gold or the Queen of Sheba's visit to King Solomon. The apes and the peacocks alone are lacking and there are people unkind enough to say that they will go along in one form or another."

The possibility of such tartness after triumph did not mar the armistice celebration for Wilson. This was no time even to contemplate that the end of the war might release bitterness at home and in the world. Only good news seemed to come from the signing of the armistice document by Matthias Erzberger, whose name, hardly known then, was forgotten later. A stout son of a tailor in the village of Buttenhausen by the Black Forest in Württemberg, Erzberger had, like Wilson, begun as a schoolteacher before he moved into journalism and politics. Within the crumbling German citadel he had worked for peace. Now at forty-three, fat and strong, he had been entrusted, as the last secretary of state of the German imperial government, with the task of agreeing to the armistice. Through the lines of the disintegrating German armies, he and his colleagues had come with difficulty across the front to the Allied armistice train on the siding in the Wood of the Eagle.

Erzberger was shaken by the terms offered, which differed little from the "unconditional surrender" terms that Wilson's critics at home loudly insisted should be demanded. He protested—"haggled" as Edith Wilson put it later—remembered the chaos behind him, and signed. But he had risen at the last as the news of the end of hostilities was speeding to Wilson. He spoke of his country and the world around it, of hunger and revolution, anarchy and famine. Also he saved a little passage for his pride.

"A nation of seventy millions suffers but does not die," he said.

"*Très bien*," commented the frigid Foch. The session closed.

Erzberger returned to no cheers in Germany. Those old Conservatives, whom he blamed for the war, condemned him for the peace. He was slandered and assailed. But the great mass of his Catholic working-class support followed him in his proposals for new burdens upon capital and wealthy landed interests. Then the *Tägliche Rundschau* of Berlin, in allusion to Erzberger's rotund appearance, put a finger to its journalistic trigger.

"He may be round as a bullet," it said of him, "but he is not bulletproof."

So it was to turn out. As he walked with a friend in a lonely part of his native Black Forest two well-dressed young men, whom German and British newsmen believed were at least voluntary agents of the reactionary and military cliques, shot him down.

Information about other relatively obscure men involved in this autumn of victory was coming back to Wilson. On the early October day on which the President had first received overtures for an armistice, his friend, Ray Stannard Baker, on intelligence duty in Milan, had in elation watched a strong, articulate man speaking to crowds in the Piazza before the Cathedral and in the Galleria Vittorio Emanuele. He was urging the fainthearted to stay in the fight with their Allies until a dependable armistice had been achieved.

"I was too far away and the confusion was too great to hear what he said," Wilson's observer wrote, "but the vigor of the man, the rough power of his face, and the wild but vital way with which he flung his arms so impressed me that I inquired . . . about him as soon as I returned to the hotel." And Baker added, "I found that his name was Mussolini. . . ."

In Washington at the end of the day of elation Wilson's own ardor was not spent. Uninvited but with great doors opened wide to them, he, in white tie and tails, and Edith, in one of the costumes which matched her mounting sense of majesty, appeared suddenly at a ball at the Italian Embassy. The President lifted a glass to the health of the king whose birthday it was. He smiled at cheers for himself. When, with happy music behind them, they drove down Sixteenth Street at midnight, the tumult of celebration was quieting on the chill November streets. The portico of the White House stood high in the misty darkness. But, still excited, the President and his lady kindled a fire in Edith's room and talked until the peaceful day was about to dawn. Then, pious in victory, Wilson closed the day by reading a chapter in the Bible before they went to bed.

Messages poured in requiring no decoding by a lady. One which Wilson answered "with such emotion as you may imagine" came from tall, gaunt, scholarly Justice Louis Brandeis. His appointment to the Supreme Court, despite violent conservative opposition, had symbolized Wilson's readiness in peace before war to fight for the liberal cause of his New Freedom at home. Now the great Jewish jurist gave lofty homage to the meaning he saw in Wilson's victory in war. He sent him lines from Gilbert Murray's translations of Euripides which put a classic crown upon the cheers. The ancient poetry spoke of the Ruthless Will of proud men in their plots and plans, looking not to Heaven, but confronted at the last by the Strength of God, slow and still but failing never. Clearly the Zionist jurist, then as always concerned about the fate of his Jewish people, suggested that the Presbyterian President was an instrument in the purposes of power greater than man. The verse he sent concluded:

> *What else is Wisdom? What of Man's endeavour*
> *Or God's high grace so lovely and so great?*
> *To stand from fear set free, to breathe and wait;*
> *To hold a hand uplifted over Hate;*
> *And shall not Loveliness be loved forever?*

# II

## THE PASSOVER

PEACE in November, 1918, came as a private adventure and almost a military disaster for twenty-two-year-old Second Lieutenant F. Scott Fitzgerald. An almost girlishly pretty, green-eyed young man out of St. Paul, Minnesota, by way of Princeton, he got his overseas orders at Fort Sheridan in Montgomery, Alabama, late in October. With presentiments of death and frantic fear of losing his girl to many other military suitors in Montgomery, the slim soldier arrived with his unit early in November at Camp Mills, Long Island. Even second lieutenants then knew that peace was approaching. But the unit was marched on a grim camouflaged transport, then marched off again. If the army could not make up its mind, Lieutenant Fitzgerald made a decision of his own.

He slipped off bounds to New York, where he had often gone as Princeton playboy and where, as writer of skits for the Triangle Club, he had dreamed of sharing a garret in Greenwich Village with literary college companions who were overseas now. Other classmates had died at the front. Fitzgerald moved to the Knickerbocker Hotel on Times Square with its famous King Cole Bar painted by Maxfield Parrish in smooth golds and blues.

Wartime prohibition to save grain and protect young men in arms had been in effect for more than a year. Fourteen states had already ratified the Constitutional Amendment to make America dry forever. Lieutenant Fitzgerald was not deterred. He got very drunk. Then he sobered to the discovery that his on-again-off-again unit had been retrained for Alabama.

That, if ever, was the hour for his art of story-making. As he told it later, he hurried to Pennsylvania Station and with adequate impressiveness informed authorities there that he carried confidential papers for President Wilson which must not be delayed and could not be trusted to the mails. Perhaps the time's readiness for armistice's roaring relaxation made easier the acceptance of his tale. He was, so he said, provided with a special locomotive and rushed to Washington. There, in smoky yards near the marble Capitol, he found his unit and boarded its train. He was safely off to his girl in Alabama and the making of more profitable romances as a basis for their marriage.

Others were rushing in and out of Washington then with more or less likely excuses. The old genteel and garrulous city on the Potomac had jumped by sixty thousand in the first year of the war. Now many who had come then and later wanted to get home again quickly. Some dollar-a-year men scarcely signed the papers on their desks before they departed to start making more money and to confront labor, which had radical ideas about more money too. Resignations were as thick now as requisitions had been. The number of uniformed men diminished on the avenues, but equally militant suffragettes gathered to push their own Constitutional cause. Some of those who came for war jobs lingered; some were stranded. Also, shining young men passed each other coming and going.

Young Walter Lippmann of the Class of 1910 at Harvard left service in the War Department to help Wilson at the Peace Conference in Paris; and early in 1919 his classmate, the poet John Reed, was summoned to the capital for stern interrogation by a Senate committee investigating the Bolsheviks, who had succeeded the Kaiser in national fears. Another member of their famous class, Stuart Chase, was already engaged in work which seemed a sort of bridge between Wilson's New Freedom and Franklin Roosevelt's New Deal. Though liberal emphasis had lapsed with the hard preoccupations of the war, Chase was engaged in investigating the meat industry for the Federal Trade Commission. That odoriferous subject had drawn attention long before, when the journalists called "muckrakers" by Theodore Roosevelt had stirred up the stench of the stockyards. But not all time was devoted to reconstruction, revolution and research in the changing capital. Chase and other lively young people occupied a big house on Florida Avenue. They named the place "Hell House," gave gay parties, and somehow found, as Fitzgerald had, beverages which were supposed to be banned.

No roster was kept of their guests, but some were long remembered. Nearby lived young Dean Acheson, ex-ensign out of Yale and Harvard Law, and his pretty portrait-painter wife, Alice Stanley. Dean had come to be one of the brilliant legal law secretaries regularly chosen by Justice Brandeis. But the lively center of the "Hell House" gatherings was the tall, gawky, red-haired writer Sinclair Lewis, then thirty-five and already known as a writer of light fiction for the popular, conservative *Saturday Evening Post*. A Yale man from Sauk Center, Minnesota (one hundred miles from Fitzgerald's St. Paul), he had seemed to some of his college mates the poison variety in the Ivy League. Still, with two or three drinks in him at the parties on Florida Avenue he was an appealing presence. He could improvise hilarious, bawdy songs which delighted his hearers but would have fortified drys in their conviction about the conjunction of firewater and hellfire.

Unlike Fitzgerald, no haste after a hangover brought Lewis to or through Washington. When he arrived hangovers were presumably over forever. He sought with deliberation a place in which to write a serious book which, before he had begun it, he named *Main Street*. Lewis, though he used the capital for contrast, discovered there a "thick streak of Main Street." But he found also the possibility of unspied-on conviviality. He was not drawing, as it later seemed to some pastoral patriots, a disfigured foreshadowing for the age about to begin, but a satirical stereotype of the long-sentimentalized American home town from which so much of it emerged. He found in Washington and put into *Main Street* materials which later seemed almost the patented property of Fitzgerald. As items of a freedom not possible in Gopher Prairie, he described debutantes who clattered into Rauscher's Confiserie: "thin of ankle, soft under the chin, seventeen or eighteen at most, smoking cigarettes and with correct ennui talking of 'bedroom farces' and their desire to 'run up to New York and see something racy.'"

Lewis was pushing past the hundred-thousand-word mark as Christmas came in 1919. It did not bother him that outside the weather was terrible and that a special chill seemed to exude from Wilson's White House. The whole country was cold. Up in the Boston of Wilson's frigid adversary Senator Henry Cabot Lodge the season had been the snowiest in fifty years.

The redheaded novelist disregarded the cold. He had no time for politics. Peace was not his project. Though he had once casually carried a banner in a suffrage parade, the problems of women, insistent on the ballot and other evidences of equality, were their own. Also, though he had vaguely and briefly once considered himself a socialist, Red fears and beset radicals were not his business. His business was his book. When he could spare time, he could find his drink at "Hell House" or somewhere else. Others could formally note the legal arrival of national prohibition on January 16, 1920.

Others did. Legends grew about the event. One was that dying Republican boss Boies Penrose of Pennsylvania, hardly able to take any nourishment and able to have drinks only against his doctors' orders, sent word to his liquor dealer to double all his purchases in the past and send them to his Philadelphia house. Ships were carrying loads of liquor stocks to the salable safety of Havana. And visiting Admiral Jellicoe of the British Navy, twitted by genial, dry Secretary of the Navy Josephus Daniels for going there at the same time, solemnly admitted he had no alibi. Church bells rang. Glasses were passed and loud songs sung.

Few welcomes to the dry days ahead were more in contrast than those of the long-time great Commoner of the Democrats, William Jennings Bryan, and Assistant Secretary of the Navy Franklin D. Roosevelt. Certainly they were different men. Few in 1920 could visualize the balding Bryan as the young man who, twenty-four years earlier, had terrified the conservatives when in a real sense he began the progressive revolution in American politics. None imagined then that Roosevelt would be the man who would fulfill that revolution in his New Deal in 1932.

On the stationery of the socially exclusive and elegantly convivial Metropolitan Club Franklin wrote Eleanor Roosevelt: "Tonight we have a Class of 1904 dinner here to celebrate prohibition." The normally almost prancing Roosevelt needed something to celebrate. He was discouraged about politics. He spoke of "a Bryan" as a noun for political distaste. His cousin, Theodore Roosevelt, who had been interested in his plans for the future, had died just a year before. Wilson had been irritated by some of Franklin's cocksure claims about his militant role in the war and before it. The young Assistant Secretary had other troubles. A lovely young woman, to whom gossips had related his name, was to be quietly married within the month to a much older, rich widower. And Eleanor, to whom he remained safely attached, was busy getting out invitations to Navy teas. Their children were sick. He was hard up in the postwar high cost of living. And he was recovering from a late tonsillectomy. His chief, Secretary Daniels, who took an almost parental interest in all under him in the Navy, urged him to take care of himself.

"Do try to stay in until this beastly weather is over," he wrote. Sometimes to Franklin the Secretary seemed almost too protective, as he had seemed to some naval officers when he abolished their wine and liquor mess. That solicitude for the physical and even moral welfare of Navy men had increased as thousands of boys had been inducted in wartime. It did not keep Franklin in, however. And the Harvard dinner was certainly not one which Secretary Daniels, a teetotaler from a Southern agrarian background, would have prescribed. Obviously it was not a Bryanesque occasion. Before it occurred many of the members of the class and their friends had put in supplies for the drought ahead. Franklin could not afford to stock his cellar. He could and did lift a potent glass undisturbed by the possible disapproval of Josephus. And the prohibition eve dinner he attended was certainly less a solemn salute to a sober future than a gay farewell to good times past.

Daniels went to quite another celebration at the First Congregational Church and as the companion of Mr. Bryan. He had not urged Bryan to stay indoors when he arrived in cold Washington from Florida. Bryan had retreated there when he resigned as Secretary of State in 1916 in protest at the pace of the Wilson Administration toward war, which many other people thought too slow. Bryan's Southern movement then had been dictated by Mrs. Bryan's health. Perhaps it was hastened by the hostility of wets and war-makers in Nebraska who even refused to let him, as three-time Democratic Presidential candidate, go as delegate to the 1916 Democratic National Convention.

The change of residence brought him to Miami, then not much bigger than Gopher Prairie, the year after that resort town made its first $1900 appropriation for tourist promotion. Others were coming then from Western and Northern towns, many in the thousands of flivvers that other lover of peace, Henry Ford, was producing. In Florida the Bryans found as congenial neighbor a gentleman building a fifteen million dollar mansion. His fortune came from the International Harvester Company, one of the big trusts which had had Bryan's crusading opposition. About such matters the aging Commoner was apparently mellowing. Times were changing. On the land around a thousand country towns the International Harvester Company and other manufacturers were in the decade increasing the number of tractors from 4000 to 200,000. Bryan was changing. He was already prepared to turn his evangelical zeal to Florida real estate. But balmy Florida had not quieted his belligerence about peace, prohibition, rural virtues and the old-time religion. When he came north that winter, he "emerged from a conspiracy to ignore him," as Mrs. Bryan later said. The advent of prohibition provided him an opportunity to hail what he confidently regarded as an emerging millennium.

Bryan and his friend Daniels came in from the cold night to a front pew. Hymns were sung. Preliminary prayers of thanksgiving were offered. Bryan watched the clock as it ticked toward midnight. He had been given the honor of speaking last at the exact moment when, as he said, "the nation would be saloonless forever." He rose at the instant of "the passover from the old era to the new." He quoted a passage from the Bible. It was the language in which the angel assured Joseph that it was safe to take the young child Jesus back to Judea: "They are dead that sought the young child's life."

Bryan brought the tidings now.

"When you remember that King Alcohol has slain a million more children than Herod ever did, what language can more appropriately express the joy in the hearts of parents today than those words: 'They are dead that sought the young child's life.'"

He looked forward to the time just ahead when the Nineteenth Amendment would emancipate women by giving them the ballot. "Then on the mountain tops you will see the women and children, our allies in every righteous cause. We will not fail."

Bryan and Daniels went out into the night. The hour was late for such triumphant sons of the politically evangelical West and South, though the night was young for a Harvard Class of 1904 gathering in anticipation of the thirsty twenties. Bryan, as a man repeatedly disappointed personally, could still count for himself a leading part in the alteration of the fundamental American law to bring it closer to the aims of rural radicalism and the moral pattern, if not always the practice, of Main Street. He had helped alter the Constitution to provide for the popular election of United States senators and for the levy of a tax on incomes. Those two changes put the power of the poor closer to the pockets of the rich.

Now rich and poor would be protected from alcohol. And women, freed from shackles but keeping their places on pedestals, could help in the purification of politics. All seemed benign beneath the January skeletons of the shade trees. Bryan was not even troubled, as Daniels was, about the necessity for the kind of peace for which Wilson fought. It seemed to Bryan only necessary to make peace to possess and keep it.

The Great Commoner, wearing the fringes of his disappearing mane like a sort of frayed halo, went on to New York to a celebration not only of the new era but of his own sixtieth birthday on March 19. Eight hundred admiring guests acclaimed him about a great candled cake. Some of them had come to metropolis from a variety of Main Streets more happily remembered than the description of the one Lewis was finishing then. Bryan on March 26 was still in the city of the Tammany Hall he had fought and the Money Power he had defied. And on that day while Lewis in Washington still wrote and revised, ex–Second Lieutenant Fitzgerald published his first novel. *This Side of Paradise* suddenly— and to many shockingly—also hailed a "passover from the old era to the new." But it was called the Jazz Age.

Fitzgerald became its laureate. Actually, however, the Jazz Age had already been launched, to use a fitting nautical term, by Bryan's friend and companion at the church service, Secretary of the Navy Daniels. A man with much more humor than Bryan, he still seemed, with his long, strong upper lip and in his Quakerish clothes, an awkward harbinger of liveliness and blues. He did not dance. He could not carry a tune. Sometimes he seemed almost to court the caricature of those who did not care for either his moralistic or egalitarian ideas. He was interested in sanitation, not syncopation. As wartime chief of the Navy which had enrolled over half a million young Americans, he was acutely aware of his responsibility to them. Old-fashioned-appearing himself, he declined to take the old-fashioned quarter-deck view that sailors ashore should be left in their liberty to grog and the kind of girls which accompanied it in rough port areas.

He had found early an Old Navy attitude that the American sailor was a roughneck who could not be improved and neither wanted nor deserved protection ashore. He discovered that the kind of sailors he was trying to get did like schools on ships and he provided them. Sometimes to old salts among the old brass he appeared to consider sailors as schoolboys too. Certainly in wartime, as he went over the venereal disease statistics with his social hygienists, not yet equipped with penicillin, he insisted that, as far as the Navy could help it, boys not be made syphilitics in its service. The clear evidence was that there were more amorous casualties in New Orleans than losses on armed ships at sea. No man for half measures, Daniels called the mayor of the tolerant old town. He showed him the medical reports of the results of the visits of young Navy men to Storyville, the wide-open red-light district, where brothels flourished and nondescript little bands beat out strange lively music in the streets and halls.

Sadly the mayor, who had long presided over the city and lived in a section of it called Algiers where pirates and lusty boatmen had once congregated, regarded the reports. He expressed his regrets. But blood was hot and the young were young, he suggested. He shrugged. And sailors were sailors. An amiable puritan but an implacable one, Secretary Daniels coldly pointed out alternatives to the mayor.

Early in his administration, he recalled, he had sent young Franklin Roosevelt to the charming old city to inspect the rusting and deserted Navy Yard there. Franklin, with Eleanor, had been delightfully entertained. Eleanor remembered a dinner ending with café brûlé served in a silver bowl with only the light of its burning brandy illuminating the room. She was not as pleased with warm champagne served before any breakfast next morning. But Franklin recommended that the old yard be reactivated. Daniels put it back into service. Then with the coming of war the Secretary established a big naval training station close by. As both had been created, both could be closed if Storyville remained wide open. The mayor reflected Latin tolerance. He also represented his city's concern for prosperity and payrolls which was as strong along Canal Street as on Main Street anywhere. The district was closed.

The death march from Storyville moved to the music of its many small Negro bands which had so long added syncopation to sex. In a way the government which made their music mournful now had set them to playing in the first place. Military musicians, disbanding in New Orleans at the end of the Spanish-American War, had left many instruments in pawnshops. In the hands of proud black new possessors, they served the many marches of improvising, syncopating players to the ordinary funerals of girls found dead in rumpled beds and men knived in brawls. On such occasions they moved, blue moaning as they went, loud and lively as they returned to scenes of uninterrupted pleasure. But now there would be no return for trumpeting on the streets and in the dance halls for Storyville's fabled frolics.

The names of some of the sad musicians made a sort of music, too: Louis Armstrong, King Oliver, Wingy Manone, Pops Foster, Jelly Roll Morton, Kid Ory, Zutty Singleton, Sidney Bechet. They played against shut doors. The famous Mahogany House of the gifted Miss Lulu White, who "at an early age found out what the other sex was in search of," was deserted. Also to music, poorer black and white prostitutes departed, some of them carrying all their tawdry possessions on two-wheeled carts or in wheelbarrows. The dispersal was made memorable by the massed combination of all the Negro jazzmen of the now darkened red-light halls blaring and syncopating *Nearer My God to Thee*.

Perhaps, as Secretary Daniels undoubtedly felt, the movement was in such a divine direction. Some sailor boys were saved from disease and also from rough treatment by hustlers and pimps, gamblers and bums of the district. What happened to the girls and the madams is not regarded as a significant item in American cultural history. That history concerns itself with such details as the fact that Scott Fitzgerald came to New Orleans long after the hegira and was trying to write on Prytania Street when national prohibition arrived in America. New Orleans was "too consciously" a story town, he thought, but he found Sazerac cocktails there to take with him on a visit to his girl in Montgomery.

He was late for the earlier story of Storyville when hard times— and only hard times—came knocking at the shut doors of elegant whore houses and the closed cribs around which the bands had played. There was new reason then for blues among the Negro musicians. Some lingered in New Orleans. More moved sadly up the old lazy Mississippi River to Memphis, Chicago, San Francisco, New York, Minneapolis and St. Paul, possibly in passage even to Main Street. They carried their horns. And at the midnight moment when Bryan proclaimed "the passover from the old era to the new" there was an American generation already listening to their music. It was the overture to an age.

# III

## UNDER THE CLOCK

IN THICK fog in late February, 1919, the *George Washington*, a former German luxury liner, came with whistle moaning toward a symbolic Massachusetts shore. On board were two thousand home-coming troops, some lucky dignitaries, and Woodrow Wilson with his intimate circle. To him the precious part of the cargo was his Covenant of the League of Nations, a document, he believed, even more full of promise than the Mayflower Compact of the Pilgrims who had approached this same land in winter so long before.

Beyond the mists off the granite peninsula of Cape Ann was the rich man's resort of Magnolia. There the summer before on the estate of wealthy, aristocratic T. Jefferson Coolidge, Wilson, with the aid of his great friend, Colonel House, had drafted his proposed League of Nations. Now, little changed, that design for peace in the world had been approved by the high contracting parties at the peace conference in Paris.

The brief sunlit days at Magnolia were worth remembrance. But further down the shore like a stony finger in the cold sea was Nahant. It deserved attention as the beloved home of Senator Henry Cabot Lodge, who had no love for Wilson or his League and had taken no pains to conceal his distrust of both. This was the shore of promise and threat. But more immediate dangers than any senator or Senate were at hand.

This brief trip home by Wilson in the midst of the peace conference to attend to business at the conclusion of the Democratic Sixty-fifth Congress, which would be followed by the Republican Sixty-sixth Congress, had begun auspiciously on Valentine's Day just three months after the armistice. His decision to go abroad as chief

American negotiator of the peace had been decried as unprecedented and presumptuous by Republicans quick to emphasize to European statesmen that his party had been beaten at the polls. Republicans and some Democrats, too, resented the choice of his four colleagues on the American peace delegation. William Jennings Bryan, whose opposition to war had led to his resignation from Wilson's Cabinet, resented that he was set aside as "too utopian" in the making of the peace.

Lodge, soon to be chairman of the Senate committee which must consider any treaty, was not alone in condemning the selection of a delegation containing neither himself nor any other Republican except a popular career diplomat. "The President has appointed himself four times and Henry White," said Lodge. And to such mutterings at home were added predictions that Wilson as idealist would be unequal to sophisticated European statesmen scornful of his ideas of "peace without victory" at a time of opportunity for vengeance.

Yet on this Valentine's Day at the end of two months of pomp and parade, cheers and clamor, and of apathy and opposition, too, Wilson in black-coated dignity rose in triumph at a plenary session of the peacemakers in the Salon de l'Horloge of the Quai d'Orsay. Others had spoken. But he was given the honor of reporting the unanimous agreement of the high contracting parties on the League he sought as a part of the treaty. In fine voice he read the constitution of the world organization.

"A living thing is born," he said. "It is definitely a guarantee of peace."

The idea of birth permeated the room. So did fog, which came in off the shores of the Seine. In *L'Illustration* a week later a French journalist titled his report of the occasion *Sur un Berceau*. As a man at the cradle, he wrote: "In the emptiness and silence of this room called 'of the clock,' so ostentatious with its great drapes of red damask and brilliant gilding, three strokes resounded from the henceforth historic dial. And . . . the delegates began to file ceremoniously through the heavy fog which the high windows opening on the Quai d'Orsay permitted to penetrate the room. *Mon Dieu*, how opaque it was, that fog which surrounded the birth of the League of Nations."

Others present showed no sense of beginnings in a mist. Hope and excitement lit the room. The clock marked Wilson's hour and Mrs. Wilson's, too. As a decorative lady, whose high heels had been heard clicking in so many palaces as she moved in the gowns she later described in detailed pride, she was granted a special favor. Though no ladies were permitted at the session, she was allowed to tiptoe into an alcove and, through the red curtains, watch her husband's triumph. Then she slipped down into the dark courtyard to join him, tired but happy, in their limousine.

The triumph was clear. Henry Wickham Steed, who that month became editor of the *Times* of London, prepared a paean for publication next morning. Wilson had lifted the affairs of the world into new dimensions, he said. As a correspondent who had covered the complex affairs of Europe for nearly a quarter of a century, he wrote in exultation.

"The old dimensions of national individualism, secrecies of policies, competitive armaments, forcible annexations for selfish purposes and unqualified State Sovereignty, were raised, if only for an instant, to a higher plane on which the organized moral consciousness of peoples, the publicity of international engagements and of government by the consent of and for the good of the governed, became prospective realities."

Steed paused in his own enthusiasm.

"How long will the instant last?"

Then he wrote: "No man can yet say. All that can be said is that yesterday a sense that something new, something irrevocable, had been done, pervaded the Conference Hall. All the speeches were made in the tone of men who were not, indeed, afraid of their handiwork, but were obviously conscious of the boldness of attempting to frame a new charter for civilized and uncivilized humanity."

Even such sympathetic questioning about the "instant" seemed irrelevant. Certainly the hours on the day upon which it occurred had been crowded. Before the session, Wilson, who had too often appeared almost rigidly aloof from the press, let a five-minute interview, reluctantly agreed to, extend to an hour of exchanges with correspondents packed in a crowded room. That day, too, he faced pressure from pink-faced Winston Leonard Spencer Churchill, British Minister of Munitions.

For his part in the war, including disaster in the Dardanelles campaign, Churchill was regarded in Britain as a man of enormous vigor, industry, imagination and patriotism; but insufficient judgment and discretion. Wilson came to feel that he was pert and unreasonable. (Oddly perhaps, Senator Lodge had long felt an antipathy to Churchill, who, he wrote Theodore Roosevelt, was "undoubtedly clever but conceited to a degree it is hard to express either in words or figures. . . .")

Churchill now wanted greater Allied intervention in Russia against the Bolsheviks than his own government or the American President thought wise. Churchill was put off for the later dismissal of his ideas. Wilson was dealing with benign matters which seemed to him might have more revolutionary meaning for humanity. That day he prepared and dispatched a message about the League's success to the members of the Senate and House committees concerned with foreign affairs.

"I request that I be permitted to go over with you article by article the Constitution reported before this part of the work of the Conference is made the subject of debate in Congress. With this in view I request that you dine with me at the White House as soon after I arrive in the United States as my arrangements will permit."

The departure from Paris for the old port of Brest, which had welcomed so many American soldiers to its muddy camps, was a crowded, ceremonial occasion. France paraded its protocol. Silk hats glistened and gold braid shone in the lights when the Wilsons arrived at the railway station. For them a crimson carpet was spread from the street to the train with palms and evergreens beside it, making a plush path fifteen to twenty feet wide. There was, Mrs. Wilson recalled, much kissing of hands, clicking of heels. Bands played. Soldiers stood at attention. Wilson "looked happy, as well indeed he should," wrote Colonel House.

Others were happy, too, on the homeward-bound ship. The returning soldiers, many of them sick or recovering from wounds, were more than ordinarily anxious to go home even in a homesick time. And one old home-coming warrior was no soldier but David Rowland Francis, whose health had broken down as ambassador to Russia in the turmoil of revolution. He had moved his embassy from place to place, lived on trains, and to the last appealed to the Russians to stand by the Allies. But three months before, gravely ill, he had been taken by an American warship to London for an operation from which he now only hoped he was recovering.

He seemed still, to one fellow passenger, a kindly humorous man of latent strength despite the civil war, famine and plague behind him. He could tell Wilson, as a recent witness, of the starvation in eastern Europe. Some in Congress only wished American bounty to feed America's certain friends. Nonetheless, from the impartial hunger spread not only death but the danger that the contagion of Bolshevism might sweep across Europe—even the Atlantic. Fears built homesickness for an old America safe from both Hun and Red.

Nostalgia was not always so complicated. Young, ebullient Assistant Secretary of the Navy Roosevelt, who joined the *George Washington* at Brest with his Eleanor, had, according to a story told at the time, learned about that. He had been traveling, inspecting and souvenir collecting at the front across which American occupation troops had moved to the Rhine. Tall in his civilian clothes, which his cousin Theodore Roosevelt as Spanish War Rough Rider felt he should have changed for a uniform, Franklin addressed an array of marines. He tapped his pocket holding his passage home. He would gladly trade it for a marine uniform, he said. And a young leatherneck in the ranks shouted, "I'll swap!"

No such bargain was made. Instead, on the voyage the young Roosevelts lunched at sea with the Wilsons. There was light talk and storytelling. But Eleanor kept in faith and remembrance a Wilson statement about his League: "The United States must go in or it will break the heart of the world, for she is the only nation that all feel is disinterested and all trust." In spite of this she did not warm to the great man, perhaps betraying some of her sympathy for her militant Uncle Theodore who had cried for war long before Wilson made it and felt that the President had denied him a place in uniformed leadership. Uncle Ted had died only a month before. Eleanor did not share the heritage of hate for Wilson he had left. She was a little appalled, however, when the President, as confident civilian, disregarded naval etiquette and insisted that Mrs. Wilson and other ladies of his party go up the gangway of the *George Washington* before him. She believed stories that he trusted others too much. And: "He seemed to have very little interest in making himself popular with groups of people which he touched, though he had a wonderful sense of the psychology of people as a whole."

Perhaps it was in exercise of that sense or the lapse of it that he had decided to land at Boston. Capital of the state where his League plans had been polished, it was also the city which Senator Lodge regarded as his own. It belonged, also, as many old Bostonians regretted and resisted, to many Irishmen who hated Britain and any

American dealing with it in war or peace. From Massachusetts Wilson had received a petition from twenty-six Democratic members of the legislature urging him to come home from Paris to cut the high cost of living, "which we consider far more important than the League of Nations." Still, in Boston a well-organized movement for the League was under way headed by citizens who regarded themselves as the social, intellectual and political equals of Lodge.

The old city was a doubtful destination. The choice of Boston, it has been insisted, was not a studied affront to Lodge. The arrangements had been made long before. And from the ship as it approached the port came wireless word that the President only intended to speak briefly and that it would be "merely in the nature of an acknowledgement of a welcome home, reserving a discussion of the peace conference and its work for the meeting with Congressional leaders." Yet the very troubles of the voyage to Boston seemed portents of dangers ahead.

As the big liner turned its prow westward, influenza broke out aboard her. Relatively mild as it seems to have been, the outbreak recalled the horrors of the epidemic of the autumn before which, despite all the tumult of rejoicing, had brought America to armistice in the midst of much sickness and mourning at home. Rough weather was ahead. In it the convoying battleship *New Mexico* stripped one of her turbine engines and was forced to drop out of the escorting fleet. The mounting storm made it necessary for the destroyer flotilla to leave the line for a time. The *George Washington* proceeded alone.

Other ships were ordered to attend her. Then, as the liner approached the Massachusetts shore in thick fog, the *George Washington* lost her bearings. Suddenly the lookout on the escorting destroyer *Harding* saw land and surf only a thousand yards ahead. At his warning, the *Harding* gave five quick blasts on its whistle and swiftly swung across the *George Washington*'s bow. That great ship's engines were reversed so swiftly that passengers were shaken. Troops and passengers poured on deck, including the President with his Covenant secure in the pocket of his overcoat. He could see the rollers on the beach and the two lighthouses of Cape Ann. The liner's captain dropped anchor to make observations. The wind whipped up. Snow flurries came. Carefully in the thick weather the destroyer *Paulding* came alongside. As always, not all Americans showed concern in serious business. A picture show in the salon went on uninterrupted.

In history, visibility about the event has been as obscure as in the fog about the ship. Eleanor Roosevelt remembered that she was reading in her deck chair when the bells began to ring, the engines stopped and people began to run along the deck, one crying, "We are almost on the beach." She ran, she said, to tell Franklin who was below and found him already preparing to make for the bridge and fit into a later legend that it was he who saved the ship. Actually, when he reached the bridge he only guessed that they were in the vicinity of Marblehead, midway between Magnolia and Nahant— an area familiar to him as a small-boat enthusiast and golfer on the exclusive courses back of the beaches. News accounts of the event at the time did not contain any mention of Roosevelt. Mrs. Wilson in her *Memoir* barely mentioned the incident except to quote a sick soldier as saying that if they had gone ashore "it would be our own country." She chiefly recalled the "marvelous day" of the landing in Boston.

There was no doubt about the clarity and warmth of that welcome. Governor Calvin Coolidge came to the ship to welcome the President. He was neither the kind of man nor the kin of the rich Coolidge in whose house Wilson had worked on the League. Senator Lodge had once recommended to President McKinley that he make the rich Coolidge his Secretary of the Navy. Lodge later scornfully described Calvin Coolidge as the kind of man "who lives in a two-family house." Coolidge had risen from insignificance on the political escalator. Some who supported him also supported the League. Already noted for his austere caution and conservatism, the sharp-featured little governor had been elected the fall before in the campaign which Lodge hailed as repudiating Wilson's national leadership. But Coolidge, who escorted the President through the thronged streets, suggested no loss in the prestige of the President.

To a mixed audience of eight thousand idealistic intellectuals and still-loyal Irish Democrats in Mechanics Hall, Coolidge spoke as no tight-tongued Yankee. The Boston reception in which he joined, he declared in his nasal Vermont accent, was "even more marked than that accorded General George Washington, more united than any that could have been given at any time during his life to Abraham Lincoln."

Yet behind the oratory and the cheers, there was another Boston. Not only had the second-generation Irish taken political control of the city from old-time Bostonians, but also men of other and diverse national origins had filled its slums. Yankees as employers had welcomed the wave of cheaper labor which the immigrants provided. But, as Republicans who generally controlled the state though not the crowded Democratic city, they had kept the direction of Boston police in a state official. At their head now was Edwin U. Curtis, who as a younger man had been Republican reform mayor of the city. At fifty-eight, he had become, as a Boston historian said, a puritan martinet with supercilious eyes and a puffy, disdainful face.

Perhaps Curtis and other guardians of order were justified in the precautions taken on this occasion. The day before Wilson arrived, two members of the Grupa pro Prensa, a Spanish anarchist group at Philadelphia, were arrested by Secret Service agents for allegedly plotting the President's assassination. Nobody could be sure where danger lurked. Even such innocent-seeming people as a skilled edger in a shoe factory in nearby Milford named Nicola Sacco, and a fish peddler in the Puritans' Plymouth might turn out to be frightening Reds. And while the President had been sailing westward, prison trains had been moving east from Seattle and Fort Worth bringing scores of alleged alien anarchists, members of the International Workers of the World and "other undesirables" for deportation from Ellis Island in New York.

Boston was cheering and careful. Soldiers, sailors, state guardsmen and police lined the whole route of the Presidential procession, forming, as the papers said, "a guard of honor for the entire distance of the drive." Secret Service agents lined the roofs of buildings. Windows along the President's route were ordered closed. Because of the narrow way, it was said, no spectators were permitted to congregate in the block between Washington and Tremont streets. No unpleasant incidents occurred, though some militant suffragettes were locked up for loitering.

Certainly the Irish police seemed dependable. As good Catholics they were apparently as safe as possible from any communist or anarchist contagion. Radicalism seemed more likely at Harvard than in the old, crowded and dilapidated police stations of Boston. Indeed, that month a committee of the still Democratically controlled Senate in Washington was interrogating John Reed, graduate of the notable Class of 1910 at Harvard, which produced eminent poets, bankers, politicians, and publicists who would help shape the decades ahead. Reed, from gay, almost playboy beginnings, had turned his enthusiasm and his talents as a writer to the November, 1917, revolution of the Bolsheviks in Petrograd. While Wilson was still at sea, the tall, frail young man, under indictment for a seditious speech, had told the senators that he could not recall having said in Yonkers that "three million rifles are in the hands of three million Russian workmen and soon three million rifles will be in the hands of American workmen to do the same thing that is being done in Russia." Millions read the report that he said it. He also testified that he "couldn't imagine" himself saying in New York that he had started the Bolshevik movement in the United States and that there soon would be "something doing" in New York, Baltimore, Albany, Syracuse—and Boston.

He had not spoken, he said, at the meeting earlier in the month at Poli's Theater in Washington, which was largely responsible for the Senate interrogation. Some wives of congressmen had listened there when Reed's wife, Louise Bryant, described by a lady present as "a leggy, undeveloped young woman," had spoken then on "The Truth about Russia." Reed did not speak, he said, because he was "considered too disreputable," having been indicted for saying things that some anti-Wilson senators were also saying.

Boston police along Wilson's march that February were taking no part in the growing debate which ran between the extremes of Red and Right. They were only grumbling as they went about their duties. Their working conditions under their aristocratic commander were miserable. Their stations were old and dirty. Their wages, despite a small raise as living costs soared, were only a minimum (often a maximum) of $1100 a year out of which they had to pay for their own uniforms. They talked in their Social Club which, of course, was not a union and would never be allowed to be.

The great debate had already begun on the larger stage. At Wilson's request for a postponement of debate until he arrived in Washington, Lodge had remained punctiliously silent, though privately active. But able, independent Senator William E. Borah, of Idaho, had opened his attack. So had the fiery isolationist, Democrat James Reed, of Missouri. And Senator Miles Poindexter, of Washington, where this same month a general strike—the "Seattle Revolution"—had occurred, had made a violent speech comparing and relating the League and the Bolsheviks.

Their opposition oratory came to Wilson as clearly as the roars of acclaim upon the streets and in the hall. He was aware of Lodge's equal antagonism. Just the same, he began his address in the pattern of the postponement of discussion he had asked.

"I have not come to report the proceedings or the results of the proceedings of the peace conference," he said; "that would be premature."

The Associated Press, however, reported that he "had been on American soil not more than three hours before he threw down the gauntlet to those who distrust the proposed concert of governments based, he said, on the American ideals which had won the war for justice and humanity."

Wilson did not mention Lodge's name in Lodge's town. But in the face of such opposition as he knew was moving to meet him, he presented the American choice: "We set this nation up to make men free and we did not confine our conception and purpose to America, and now we will make men free. If we do not do that, all the fame of America would be gone and all her power would be dissipated. She would then have to keep her power for those narrow, selfish, provincial purposes which seem so dear to some minds which have no sweep beyond the nearest horizon."

Then he put his challenge direct: "Any man who thinks that America will take part in giving the world any such rebuff and disappointment as that does not know America. I invite him to test the sentiments of the nation." And when he said he believed he expressed the beliefs of his hearers, their applause, said a reporter, "leaped to thunder before the words were fairly out of his mouth."

Senator Borah, of the already determined "Irreconcilables" against the treaty, and Senator Albert B. Fall, a tall, bold-eyed New Mexican, refused to attend the dinner at the White House. Punctiliously Lodge "of course" accepted the invitation of the President. He sniffed, however, that it was "very characteristic" of Wilson to silence him as "an honorable man" while the President spoke in "my own city" to "a great mass meeting."

He sat next to Mrs. Wilson who again was the only lady present. In her often costume-cluttered *Memoir* she did not describe her dress that night. But descriptions of her regal peregrinations with her husband in Europe had already come to Senator Lodge from bitter feminine lips in his circle. Mrs. Wilson seemed more than ever presumptuous to the Washington society of which as the widow of a man "in trade" she did not quite belong before her marriage to Wilson. That had been little more than a year after the first quiet Mrs. Wilson had died and not long after Lodge's own wife had been suddenly and fatally stricken.

Edith Wilson was, a historian wrote, "beautiful and gay" that night. Certainly she seemed the forever answer to Theodore Roosevelt's dismissal of earlier gossip about Wilson and another lady. Then Roosevelt had said that no scandal would touch Wilson: "You can't cast a man as Romeo who looks and acts so much like an apothecary's clerk." One guest that night thought that the President was "never so human or so attractive." Handsome as she was, Edith Wilson was not at the dinner as tactful as she might have been. To Lodge she talked with the greatest enthusiasm—and "innocently" her husband thought later—about the magnificent reception the Senator's Boston had given them. Certainly in innocence she welcomed Lodge's bland statement that there would be no doubt of the ratification of the treaty "if the Foreign Relations Committee approves."

No tactlessness of Edith Wilson was needed to stiffen Lodge. The Senator sat in cold politeness while small, dignified Senator Philander C. Knox, of Pennsylvania, emerged from sullen silence to sharply question the President. He listened with masked appreciation when sharp-spoken, high-strung Senator Frank Brandegee, of Connecticut, Lodge's close friend, seemed almost to heckle his host. The President's performance, Lodge noted in a record made at the time, "under Brandegee's very keen and able cross-examination was anything but good."

He added: "The President answered questions for two hours . . . and told us nothing. . . . We went away as wise as we came."

Lodge and Brandegee came away together. They were not impressed by the charm of Mrs. Wilson. They complained to friends about the paucity of the cigars and the potency of the drinks. Brandegee described the occasion with a smirk.

"I feel," he told a reporter for the staunchly Republican New York *Sun*, "as if I had been wandering with Alice in Wonderland and had tea with the Mad Hatter."

No levity marked Senator Lodge when two days later he loosed his attack on the League in a speech which he had obviously been polishing while he was reduced to silence as an honorable man. He invoked warnings of George Washington against involvements abroad; he saw threats against the Monroe Doctrine. He spoke to fears that American boys under the League might be quickly pulled into the foreign wars of intriguing powers. Solemnly he insisted that there should be "consideration, time and thought," lest the United States be drawn "by any glittering delusions, through specious devices of supra-national government, within the toils of international socialism and anarchy."

Afterward, pleased with his performance, he drove up wide, tree-lined Massachusetts Avenue to the big, comfortable house in which he had lived long before Washington was occupied by Democrats headed by a proud professor whose pretensions had reached world-wide proportions. Washington, almost as much as Boston, had been Lodge's city. As a child Alice Roosevelt Longworth, daughter of the Senator's great dead friend Theodore, had thought the terraces of the Capitol were "Uncle Cabot's" private lawns. Lodge himself had some such idea about Republicans and the republic. He considered himself on guard for both.

# IV

## HERCULES OR ANTAEUS

THE MANSION, to which Senator Lodge came home from the Wilson dinner in the congenially carping company of Frank Brandegee, loomed high and handsome over Massachusetts Avenue. By day in the skeleton shade of old trees cast by cold late winter sun, the house appeared unaltered since the Senator in happier days had moved there from less pretentious Jefferson Place. On that smaller street he, as a rich, aristocratic young congressman, and his charming, violet-eyed wife, Anna Cabot Mills Davis, had been neighbors of the also young Theodore Roosevelts. Crowding company had filled their almost inseparable houses. Guests included politicians, writers, people who were just coming to build palaces in the so-long-almost-rustic capital. Both homes shared the friendship of erudite Lord Bryce, the British ambassador, and his gay subordinate, Cecil Spring-Rice, who brought witty poems to the adults and sometimes wild flowers to the children. Even then to outsiders Lodge had seemed remote and aloof carrying his head as high as his Boston Brahmin heritage. But there had been wit and laughter. Children had swarmed in liveliness in the happy Lodge and Roosevelt households.

Now Anna Lodge was dead. There could be no one to take her place. Also now even the Senator's grandsons were big boys. The only juvenile cries came occasionally from across the street in the limited yard of the Force School, public but serving an exclusive neighborhood. As the avenue ran northwestward to the palaced precincts about Dupont Circle there were now more motor noises and less of the clop-clop of horses upon it. Ladies, who once would have passed in broughams with coachmen before them, in 1919 flowed by enthroned in furs and operating their own electrics. Some bolder ones like Alice Roosevelt Longworth, who called the Senator "Uncle Cabot," drove their own motors by day and even by night. Change was clear. But at the Lodge house's big door old Hobday, the butler, was eternal. And the slim Senator in his library off the winter-brown rose garden seemed eternal, too. His curly hair was gray but the mustaches above his trim beard appeared more than ever luxuriant. By his books and his fire he sat as always, talking in his cultivated voice to many who came, listening politely, and habitually swinging his well-shod foot.

Yet even in a time of widespread American nostalgia for old times gone the Lodge residence, though snug and elegantly ordered, was a special sort of homesick house of a bereft and embittered man. That was never more so than in this late February and early March time. Reports which had preceded the Wilsons back from Europe had described them, often with snicker and sneer, as a pretentiously imperial pair making what they obviously felt was an almost apocalyptic pilgrimage.

Under any circumstances Lodge then might have listened, with lips curled under his mustache, to stories about Wilson, parson's son, professor, politician, accepting as his due cheers lifted to him almost as a messiah by European masses. Grief sharpened his resentment. On January 6, the President and his lady were rolling across Europe in a king's train attended by servants in royal scarlet. And on that same day Lodge's "dear Theodore," still hoping to recover to fight Wilson, whom he despised as Lodge did, died in his sleep at Sagamore Hill, the great, cluttered, comfortable home he loved on Oyster Bay. Eloquently but with controlled voice, Lodge, the "dear Cabot" of their relationship, delivered his eulogy to the Congress.

"Valiant-for-Truth passed over," said the Senator, "and all the trumpets sounded for him on the other side."

There seemed no trumpets left for Lodge. This March of the Sixty-fifth Congress's adjournment was an exact decade from the time when Theodore, almost as a dynastic gift, had turned the Presidency over to William Howard Taft. Of that day Roosevelt had remembered, as Lodge could not forget, that a warm item in transition was made when the Senator's tall, vigorous-seeming son, George Cabot Lodge, known universally as Bay, came "through the blizzard to say good-bye." That was the last time Roosevelt saw the much-loved young man whom he felt of all the men he had known well best deserved "the rare name of genius."

Bay had been for all to see everything that his father was not. After Harvard, he had become a spectacularly dressed poet wearing a great sombrero in the Latin Quarter of Paris. He came home to express his distaste for the "philistine-plutocratic" society of rich Americans which his father seemed defending against the menace of wild young William Jennings Bryan. Bay wrote a poetic drama called *Cain*, expressing eternal enmity to compromise. Yet he had fought as his heritage required in the war with Spain which his father and Roosevelt helped arrange. He had made a marriage eminently satisfactory in terms of family and wealth. Yet even afterward when he came up from the lonely island of Tuckernuck off the shore of Nantucket, where he wrote poetry by "the enormous solitude of the sea," he seemed the antithesis of his father. A tall, deeply tanned man in beach slacks with his collar open at the throat, he looked as he strode in Boston like a rebel at war with all the Brahmins on Beacon Hill. Some such Brahmins and their solid New England business associates must have been a little startled when, over the brandy and cigars at a banquet, they listened to Bay reading verses about the Pilgrims as "these rebellious men" who were not concerned with renown or power or merchandise.

Perhaps the evident contrast between them made the affection of the father and the son the stronger. On Tuckernuck in 1909, they had a beautiful time together. They rested. They read. The Senator, looking like a small triton with his beard drenched in the waves, joined his son in the surf. Then suddenly on the lonely island, Bay was stricken. No doctor was available. And alone with his desperate father, he died. Five years later, in 1915, Anna Lodge was taken in a similar swift attack.

Few ever gave any public sympathy to Henry Cabot Lodge. Except from those closest to him he would have disdained any display of sentiment as intrusion. And if he had been a man to show sorrow, there had been little time for it after Bay's death. He gathered together the collection of Bay's poems. In 1911 "Dear Theodore" wrote a gentle, glowing introduction. In many ways Theodore was like Bay. And Cabot was always captured in his almost impenetrable crustiness. As the book containing Bay's poems and Roosevelt's appreciative prose appeared, the Senator was beset. In a campaign in which he was abused and ridiculed for his chill, cultured voice, he barely squeaked through to re-election. The Progressive tide was rising which, with Roosevelt as its roaring leader, split the Republican Party, to which Lodge stayed true, and let Woodrow Wilson into the White House.

As a survivor of the disaster, Lodge was stunned, but his punctilious politeness was not impaired. Promptly, soon after Wilson's inaugural, he called, simply, as he said, to pay his respects to the new President. He gave no sign that his ulcers were acting up again. He had been troubled with the acid condition, which some thought a natural adjunct to his acid personality, as far back as the time when another Democrat had been in the White House in 1893. Then his flippant friend and often caustic critic, the much greater scholar Henry Adams, had noted with little sympathy that Cabot had "dyspeptic pains, caused, I presume, by the proposed tariff." Even as a hidebound protectionist, Lodge had greater cause in 1913 than any Democratic tinkering with the tariff.

In the White House, now swarming with Democrats or "odd beings," as Alice Longworth called them, Lodge could take some comfort by counting that in the election the year before, the combined votes of the divided Republicans had been a million more than Wilson received. There was no surcease for his acids in the clearer count that restless American liberalism behind T.R.'s Progressives and Wilson's Democrats had produced ten million more votes than the regular, conservative Republican ballots which he and others had cast for Taft. In the alien atmosphere of the White House he bowed to the new President.

"You do not, of course, remember me, Mr. President," he said, "but I had the pleasure of sitting next to you at the alumni dinner at a Harvard commencement."

Such a meeting on an academic occasion was a natural one for the two men, but Wilson as former president of Princeton had a longer memory and a happy rejoinder.

"A man never forgets the first editor who accepts one of his articles," he told the Senator. Lodge had been that man.

Lodge hurried from the call to his beautifully kept files. He had, indeed, as the twenty-nine-year-old editor of the scholarly *International Review*, in August, 1879, published an article on "Cabinet Government in the United States" by Wilson, then an unknown twenty-three-year-old recent graduate of Princeton living in Wilmington, North Carolina. The files produced a second Wilson ar-

ticle tersely marked "R.R.R." (received, read and rejected). The
Senator replaced the papers. He had introduced Wilson to the world
of scholarship in the same year in which he had departed from it
as a rich, literate young candidate for the Massachusetts legislature
who was sometimes described as the Dude of Nahant by less aristocratic voters to whom he had to appeal.

Wilson in the White House had not merely robbed Lodge of
distinction as "*the* scholar in politics." The thing went deeper than
that. Lodge, well able by inheritance to afford it, had abandoned
the gentility of learning and letters to accept the crude contacts of
politics. Wilson, as frail son of a Presbyterian parson of little means,
had found even the rough conflicts of law practice in Atlanta both
repellent and unprofitable. He had retreated to the academic cloisters.
Now at the end of their turning in different directions, Wilson, who
had withdrawn from the life of action, was President of the United
States. Lodge, who had turned to the heat and sometimes the hu-
miliations of politics, stood only on the slow moving escalator of
senatorial seniority as a member of the minority party.

The contrast and the irony, of course, did not alone cause the
increasing pain in Lodge's vitals. Indeed, in the Senate in 1913, he
showed no more than usual signs of acidity. He stood by the President on foreign policy questions important to him then. Even on
the domestic reforms the President was proposing as a program for
a New Freedom, Lodge only maintained his customary conservative
Republican positions. Quietly he left Washington in September suffering such a severe attack of his ulcers that a serious operation was
necessary at the Charlesgate Hospital in Cambridge.

He was still the scholar. That year he added *Early Memories* to
the fifty or more other works he produced in his life. It was a book
in many ways more remarkable for its reticences than its revelations.
There was no mention of Bay in it. He only mentioned Anna to
describe her lineage, which matched his own. But in it he paraded
like possessions the great figures in the flowering of New England
who had been familiars in the household of his youth: Emerson,
Whittier, Longfellow, Dr. Holmes, others.

"Hawthorne, I never knew, a misfortune I deeply regret."

Also he vividly described the great fire of Boston in November,
1872, a year after he married Anna. The conflagration which had
begun in the "tenements and houses of the poorer classes" was
stayed, he said, "just before it touched State Street . . . where the

safety vaults were situated." Obviously the God of proper and propertied Bostonians was on guard, but possibly ironical. In the month of the fire Anna conceived their flaming poet boy Bay.

As he recovered, Lodge got satisfaction out of his often erudite memories. But also as he convalesced he caught and clung to an error in scholarship which Wilson made. The President, who had first preferred the lectern to the stump, now seemed parading those contacts with the masses of men from which Lodge even in politics appeared to stand aloof. He spoke in October at the rededication of Congress Hall in Philadelphia. There Washington in farewell had warned against the insidious wiles of foreign influence. Wilson warned of the dangers of a leader's isolation in Washington. He counted it a fortunate circumstance that the windows of the White House opened upon America and not merely on Washington. The favor-seeking swarm there, he said, did not constitute the country. It was necessary to come away from the capital to renew contacts with the people. Then the President made his slip which the scholar in Massachusetts snatched in scorn.

"Unless a man gets these contacts," said Wilson, "he grows weaker and weaker. He needs them as Hercules needed the touch of mother earth. If you lift him up too high or he lifts himself too high, he loses the contact and therefore loses the inspiration."

Lodge later tartly annotated the allusion.

"I need hardly say that Hercules . . . gained no strength from touching the earth, but in his wrestling match with Antaeus, who was the son of Neptune and Terra, that is the ocean and the earth, he found that Antaeus gained strength every time he touched the earth and therefore, according to the story, Hercules held Antaeus in the air until the latter weakened for lack of contact with his mother Earth so that Hercules was able to crush him to death."

Lodge went on testily.

"The story is as popular as it is old," he wrote. "It is in every classical dictionary and in all the books which boys used to read about the Greek mythology. But as Macaulay says in one of his essays, 'I have no desire to detain my reader with this fourth form learning.' The point is that it seems incredible that Mr. Wilson should have made a blunder of this sort, which would not only be impossible to a scholar but, one would think, impossible to an educated man."

Lodge kept that memory across years of increasing animosity given Wilson and returned by him. The Senator himself, after war began in Europe, had proposed such an international organization to preserve peace and prevent aggression as Wilson's League provided. But he had scorned the "too proud to fight" pace at which Wilson moved toward war. He had charged him with readiness to submit to Germany's unrestricted submarine warfare and in Presidential language had been called a liar by Wilson. Before war began the President had declined to appear on the same platform with him even at the celebration of the anniversary of an old church. As early as February, 1915, Henry Adams noted the Lodge fury which was to mount afterward: "As for our dear Cabot, I think he is off his balance, and his hatred of the President is demented." Off balance sometimes he may have been, but demented he was not. Wilson's slip about the wrestling match of Hercules and Antaeus he kept almost as a design. He recalled it specifically six years later in the contest over the League.

Then sitting in his library talking, swinging his foot, he did not trouble such a fellow Republican as Senator James Watson, of Indiana, with classical allusions. Watson was no scholar. He was more comfortable in the company of Senator Boies Penrose who soon after Harvard had thrown away all early pretensions as a scholarly political scientist to become the physical and moral image of the political boss. Penrose was the strong arm of Republicanism as Lodge was its subtle, scholarly mind. But as the League fight began, Penrose's Gargantuan appetites for food, liquor, and women had reduced him to a physical wreck. Watson told his League fears to the impeccable gentleman from Massachusetts.

"I don't see how we are ever going to defeat this proposition," he told Lodge. "It appears to me that eighty per cent of the people are for it. Fully that per cent of the preachers are right now advocating it, churches are very largely favoring it, all the people who have been burdened and oppressed by this awful tragedy of war and who imagine this opens a way to world peace are for it, and I don't see how it is possible to defeat it."

"Ah, my dear James," said Lodge to his colleague whom every other politician called Jim, "I do not propose to beat it by direct frontal attack, but by the indirect method of reservations."

"Suppose the President accepts the treaty with your reservations. Then we are in the League."

Lodge's smile was very confident.

"But, my dear James, you do not take into consideration the

hatred that Woodrow Wilson has for me personally. Never under any set of circumstances in this world could he be induced to accept a treaty with Lodge reservations appended to it."

"That seems to me to be rather a slender thread on which to hang so great a cause."

"A slender thread!" cried Lodge. "Why, it is as strong as any cable with its strands wired and twisted together."

The old Senator was not quite so confident as he sounded that he had the cord which would hold Wilson above strength and reality till he could crush him and his cause. Not even a classicist then could be clear as to who was Hercules, who Antaeus in this match. As Republican leader of the Senate in the new Congress, Lodge would have only a majority of two. Even that slim margin contained Progressive men who had bolted the party in 1912 with Roosevelt. Some others had not shared Roosevelt's and Lodge's impatience with Wilson in the long time it took him to hand the Kaiser's elegant and elusive ambassador, Count Johann Heinrich Graf von Bernstorff, his papers and declare war on the imperial German government. Some even shared faith in Wilson's plans for peace in world organization. Others, like solid, liberal Hiram Johnson, of California, and independent, eloquent Borah, of Idaho, were more determined to defeat the League they earnestly feared than anxious to assure the triumph of the Republicans.

Even as Chairman of the Senate Foreign Affairs Committee, where the first fight must be made, Lodge had to pick—or pack, as some members of his own party said—carefully to make sure of a bare Republican majority of certain anit-League or anti-Wilson members. And outside the committee and the Senate support for the League was strong, possibly growing in enthusiasm to a new Wilson triumph which would be a Republican disaster despite G.O.P. gains in 1918. The League could be, as said small, intellectually strutting Senator Knox, whom Wilson hated almost as much as he did Lodge, "a plan to strangle and crush us." By "us" Knox meant the country. Neither he nor Lodge was unmindful of the Republicans. Though frontal attack might be dangerous, a strategic show of strength was required.

Four days after the White House dinner, Frank Brandegee provided a plan for that. The Sixty-fifth Democratic Congress was expiring on March 4. That same night Wilson, ending his trip home which had begun with ovation in Boston, was assured of similar enthusiasm in New York. Former President Taft was speaking with him at the Metropolitan Opera House there. Reports were that a hundred thousand people had applied for tickets. Watson's fears were justified; Lodge's confidence was shaken. Even determined Brandegee was disturbed when soon after breakfast on Sunday, March 2, he came from his own spacious bachelor's house on K Street to Lodge's residence. But he was exuberant, too.

Hobday let him in. Lodge listened as the high-strung younger man enthusiastically and persuasively outlined a clever scheme he had devised. Lodge listened. It was a bold idea, maybe a dangerous one. There was an element of the gambler in the younger man which a few years later would bring his ruin and his death. Yet now the more the excited and cynical Brandegee talked, the better the scholarly old Senator liked the idea. Wilson might have such ideas of the Sabbath that he had declined to attend on Sunday a special performance of *Aïda* given in his honor at La Scala in Milan, accepting only when a sacred concert was provided instead. But this Sabbath in Washington required Republican activity. Without delay the old Senator and the younger one set about it together.

One of Wilson's admiring biographers described Brandegee as Senator Lodge's "crony." The word somehow affronts both men and their relationship. Perhaps in Washington's exclusive eating-and-drinking Alibi Club composed of gay, top-drawer members of the only-less-fashionable Metropolitan, Brandegee, sometimes described as a "prime sport" of the Senate, had such relationships. Something of the sort may have marked his friendship with the wife of his fellow member of the Alibi, Congressman Nicholas Longworth. He and belligerent Alice sometimes seemed in the League fight the equal friends of Senator Lodge. They dared to tease and prod him when he assumed too much an air of statesmanship in the struggle with Wilson which the younger pair in their elegant toughness were ready to turn into a roaring wrangle. Lodge was not a "crony" man but he enjoyed the companionship, often the counsel and collaboration of the senator from Connecticut.

Supercilious, disdainful, sardonic and very good company, Brandegee fitted snugly into Lodge society and Lodge politics. Brandegee had been born to wealth and position in New London, gone down the shore to Yale and then across the seas to a gentleman's year in Britain and on the Continent. Like Lodge, he had taken his steps in minor politics before he came to Congress in 1902, and advanced to the Senate three years later. Like Lodge, also, the frictions of politics rubbed off none of his sense of superiority. He was inclined to show it with a snort as Lodge was with a sniff. They had much in common though the fourteen years' difference in their ages made Brandegee at fifty-four too young for easy equal embrace with Lodge and too old for any father-son relationship. Yet in politics Brandegee had more mutual concerns with the Senator than either Bay, the dead poet, or his other son, John Ellerton, curator of Asiatic art at the Boston Museum of Fine Arts.

Art was not Brandegee's forte. He wrote no rebellious poetry as Bay had done. He did not shape into drama his eternal enmity to compromise. Yet there was no more uncompromising man in the Senate. Noted there for his obstructive tactics, he had given sweeping opposition to election of senators by the people, parcel post, regulation of child labor, the income tax, prohibition, and woman suffrage. A critic who deplored his relentless "wrong-headedness" recognized in him "a consistent disregard of political consequences." He was always ready for frontal attack or undisguised nay-saying. So he approached the debate on the League.

"I shall never vote for it until hell freezes over," he said. "I am not to be buncoed by any oleaginous lingo about 'humanity' or 'men everywhere.'"

In the Lodge house he found caustic company. Alice, then thirty-five, was in and out of the house as she had been since childhood. Naturally present, too, was Constance Gardner, Lodge's daughter whose rich, polo-player husband, Congressman Augustus Peabody Gardner, had died in military service almost exactly a year before Alice's father passed to the trumpets on the other side. As bereaved women, they were not repining ones. Constance, when Alice feared and others suggested that her father wanted the League only safeguarded by his reservations, vigorously dissented. She herself was contemptuous of middle-class moralism, so much of which seemed arrayed behind Wilson. Alice's antipathy to Wilson and the League seemed a dedication after her father's death. Both women were members of a resentful old order who perversely already had set patterns for the new liberated woman only supposed to have emerged in the twenties. Despite disapproving dowagers Constance smoked constantly and calmly advertised in the Washington *Post* for a gold cigarette case she had lost in the gallery of the House. Alice got her name in the papers for discarding corsets long before other American women dared to follow suit. Both had claws. But Alice made history and wrote it in her reminiscences, *Crowded Hours*, sometimes with serpent's tongue in cheek. Senator Lodge and Brandegee in joking collaboration, she reported, had in the fight against the League designated her as Colonel of the Battalion of Death.

She was a natural coconspirator with Brandegee in the fight— and a decorative one. While her father was President she had learned to play poker with old, hard-bitten, and legislatively tyrannical Speaker Joe Cannon, who required a cuspidor by his card table. Also, a perceptive Washington diarist described Alice as "tossy and hoydenish" at a tea early in the Wilson administration, "whispering and snickering" among some ultrasmart associates who anticipated "a Wednesday-night prayer meeting atmosphere" in the new regime. On another occasion she was a handsome matron wearing "an electric-blue satin, flesh-colored stockings and gold slippers" who "held her very scant skirt quite high, and when the band played, kicked about and moved her body like a shining leopard cat." (The reference to the flesh-colored stockings was significantly sharp in a period in which decent women were expected to wear only black ones.) Leopard cat or not, Alice in the anti-Wilson fight was a feline figure and one often ready with talons in the company of Brandegee.

He had been among those planning her father's renomination in 1920. Also, even before Wilson sailed on his first trip to Paris in December after the armistice, he was one of those irreconcilables who, as Alice knew, were "mapping out their campaign to keep us out of the internationalism that we felt menaced our very existence as an independent nation." Though others thought Brandegee an indifferent speaker, Alice preferred him to anyone as he spoke in the Senate in deep earnestness "glinting with sardonic humor." Best of all she liked his audacity, which marked the anti-League plan which he brought to Lodge on the Sunday morning in March.

In Lodge's library Brandegee proposed that a round robin be prepared, signed by more senators and senators-elect than the third necessary to prevent ratification. This would make it clear, he said, that a league such as Wilson had proposed could not win the Constitutionally required approval of the Senate. There were dangers in the plan. Such a declaration if presented as a resolution would probably be defeated by the Senate. That would blunt its effect, even show that a majority of the Senate favored the League. It was necessary that it be presented in such a way and time that Democratic objection would prevent a vote on it but not prevent the listing, for all at home and abroad to see, of the names of those with voting power enough to kill the Covenant.

Lodge and Brandegee hurried to the home of Senator Knox not far from Brandegee's house. Knox approved the plan and undertook the drafting of the resolution. The three worked on it again later in the day. Then on Monday, March 3, a swift search for signatures began. Word got around about it and the Associated Press first reported that thirty-three signatures had been secured on Monday. The number rose to thirty-nine, two by telegrams. One of these was from Senator Fall in New Mexico, on his run-down ranch where back taxes were due. No Democrats were asked to sign, Lodge said, because the group did not wish to involve or embarrass them.

The collection of signatures proceeded in the midst of a Senate filibuster to prevent the passage of essential appropriation bills and so force the President to call a special session of the new Republican Congress. Ready to sign money bills which never passed, Wilson waited in increasing anger in his room at the Capitol. Alice Longworth sat in the Senate gallery purring approval as the filibuster droned on. Then just before the Sixty-fifth Congress expired at midnight Senator Lodge rose. He read the round robin which made certain the printing of the signed declaration in the *Congressional Record*. His voice was steady but, said the friendly New York *Sun*, his hand was perceptibly shaking.

"Its consideration was clearly out of order in the condition of the existing business," Lodge said later. But only an objection could point out that.

Quickly from Senator Swanson, of Virginia, came the Democratic objection Lodge had expected and required.

Lodge relaxed: "Our purpose . . . had been served. The declaration went out to the world."

"The plan worked out beautifully after Senator Swanson's objection," said the *Sun*. And it added, more in wish than fact at the time, "Woodrow Wilson's League of Nations died in the Senate tonight."

Lodge left the chamber quietly as soon as he had finished. Few in the gallery or on the floor seemed to appreciate what he had done. The Congress was adjourning in ill temper in the Senate and high spirits in the House. Alice left the Senate gallery and went to watch the terminal hilarity of "exhausted, frowzy legislators" in the House. A YMCA man was leading singing. Democrats and Republicans vied as to which best could sing "Keep the Home Fires Burning." The result was called a draw. Then two Irish congressmen sang "The Wearing of the Green" in celebration of a House resolution calling on the American delegation at the Peace Conference to use its influence for the independence of Ireland. Like Senator Lodge and Frank Brandegee, Alice went home content and filled, as she put it, with "malicious amusement."

# V

## CURSE AT THE GATE

NONE of them stayed content long. Wilson left Washington to return to Paris in anger and with a bad cold. But the ovation he received on the night of his departure from New York after his brief visit home equaled that of his arrival in Lodge's city of Boston. Also, suddenly there seemed a danger that Wilson would not be suspended by the cord of his antipathy to Lodge upon which, as Watson reported, that Senator confidently depended. The Massachusetts manipulator was startled when, before the President reached Brest, he received a cable from the one peace delegation Republican, Henry White. In it White, acting in his personal capacity, asked Lodge to send him "the exact phraseology of amendments modifying the League of Nations which Senate considers important."

"It is our desire," White cabled, "to meet the Senate's views as closely as it is possible to obtain acquiescence therein of other nations anxious for recognition of their own special interests."

Lodge balked. He had every reason to grant White's good faith and good intentions. But Wilson controlled the cables over which the message had come. He saw a possible Wilson trap to commit him individually though he could not speak for the as-yet-unorganized Foreign Affairs Committee or the Senate itself. He turned first for counsel, as he so often did, to Brandegee. Then he called Knox in Florida. Both were ready to suspect a Wilson maneuver. Even the moderate Elihu Root advised him to watch out for an "attempt to carry on the business in this kind of backdoor way."

"At all events," Root told him, "the net is spread in plain sight of the bird, and you are the bird."

White got no guidance. Wilson, back in Paris, faced a new sullen mood among the other Allied leaders at the conference and felt that in his absence Colonel House, whom he had left in his place, had been too acquiescent to their demands for a peace of vengeance and astronomical reparations. So beset in Paris and in the Senate at home, he both sought modifications and was forced into compromises. Once in despair he threatened to leave the conference and sail home. Idealists at Paris as well as isolationists at home damned his efforts to make possible a peace plan which would protect the world and be acceptable in the Senate. Then and afterward men differed as to how much he lost in the bargaining.

In the midst of the toughening debate, he was stricken in April with an illness never yet satisfactorily diagnosed for history. His physician, Dr. Cary Grayson, at first thought he had been poisoned, then described the trouble as influenza. Herbert Hoover, working to stem the ashen tide of starvation rolling in from war and revolution, heard from a source he considered authoritative that the President's ailment was an infection of the prostate and bladder. But many then and later believed he had suffered a stroke. There was a tic in his face when he reappeared.

Despite his physical depletion and the angers around him, Wilson worked on modifications which met—or he hoped would meet—objections in the Senate. Some held then and later that all of the concrete proposals made by Lodge were written into the revised Covenant. Others considered—or called—the revision a hoax. Certainly Senator Lodge showed no indication that his objections were answered. On the day the revised Covenant was published he wrote the Italians of Boston supporting their homeland's claims to more territory than Wilson in Paris thought they were entitled to. He supported a resolution by the industriously troublemaking Brandegee calling on the Peace Conference to take up the cause of Irish independence.

Others were stirring up the snakes: the Pope might rule America through Catholic countries in the League; losing its sovereignty under world organization, America might be overrun by a new, unrestricted immigrant horde; a domination of the League by "dark" peoples could impose racial equality in the United States. This was no mere anti-Negro fear in the United States. The Peace Conference had evaded Japan's demands for a declaration of racial equality. But the grant to that proud, pushing Far Eastern power of old German economic rights in the Chinese province of Shantung seemed almost as bad. The yellow press in America screamed of the yellow peril.

The jungle complexity of the world, where new nations came into being grasping and grumbling and old powers demanded geometrical reparations, only seemed strange to Americans. It was actually mirrored here. German populations in the United States, still galled by often-idiotic wartime repressions, shared the resentment in their homeland over Wilson's reluctant submission to demands which too much put his promises of a peace without vengeance aside. American workmen, including even policemen in Boston, felt mistreated and underpaid. Their restiveness seemed radicalism to the middle class above them caught in the high price of living, too. And at the top of the teeming heap, the rich groaned. They had paid no income taxes before the Wilson administration. Their share of the burden had risen precipitately in the war. And on February 24, 1919—the day of Wilson's triumphal arrival in Lodge's Boston—the President approved the postwar Revenue Act of 1918, passed by the expiring Democratic Congress. It increased the prevailing tax load by almost 250 per cent, with four-fifths of the burden on large incomes, profits and estates. The taxes on the largest incomes soared to 77 per cent.

Still, as the summer began, the ideals which Wilson had expressed in war seemed ready for flowering in domestic and foreign matters. Even the devices which had seemed sometimes repressive of freedom in war appeared to some to provide powers for a government stronger in its service and protection of the people in peace. His design for a better order in the world had raised expectations at home. They were advanced in a message he cabled to the special session he had been forced to call on May 18. In it he made vague but arresting proposals for "genuine democratization of industry" in America. He added that workers should share "in some organic way in every decision" which affected their welfare. To big employers those aims seemed already too much the intent of workers in demands for the nationalization of railroads and of mines and in the wave of strikes which had begun with the armistice and involved four million workers. Now it was evident that in the great steel industry workers were preparing to strike against inadequate wages and an average work week of sixty-nine hours.

Frank Brandegee hardly knew how well the situation was shaping to his purposes. Though Alice Longworth, at whose house he and his anti-League stalwarts met, said that the disdainful senator from Connecticut was "the one man who never lost confidence that the League would be defeated," he was troubled that spring. He arranged a very special meeting at his big bachelor house on K Street to talk of the "lamentably gloomy" outlook. Among his guests, one who came to call the group the "cabal," was George Brinton McClellan Harvey.

As a journalist from Peacham, Vermont, Harvey had attracted attention in New York and Chicago as the first American to wear horn-rimmed glasses instead of familiar gold and silver frames. They gave him an owl-like oracular appearance. He did nothing to dispel the impression. He forsook journalism in 1893 long enough to make a fortune on Wall Street and such rich friends as William C. Whitney and J. P. Morgan. He acquired his title as colonel on the honorary staff of a governor. Then as editor of *Harper's Weekly* after 1901 and as a would-be kingmaker his eye fell on Woodrow Wilson. Wilson, then pressing an idealistic educational plan at Princeton, was beset with trustee trouble, not unlike the Senate trouble he faced later. The editorial Colonel helped push him into politics as governor of New Jersey. A break came between them, some said because Harvey's rich backers thought Wilson too radical. Wilson actually made the break by frankly stating that Harvey's support was hurting him with liberals like Bryan. Certainly the break was bitter and complete. Now, in 1919, as editor of *Harvey's Weekly*, the pompous but pungent editor was aiming every shaft of satire, ridicule, and invective at the President and his League.

At Brandegee's house he listened to the talk of the necessity for an organized campaign to swing popular opinion against the international organization for peace. Senator Knox suggested that two of his Pennsylvania friends might help. Harvey, who had a special gift for reaching the checkbooks of millionaires, agreed to see if they would contribute. One of the rich gentlemen suggested was Henry Clay Frick, whose biographer Harvey became. Frick was then seventy, ailing and angry. In the restlessness of steel workers he had no difficulty convincing himself that Red revolution was at hand.

Not only was he one of those who had helped put the huge United States Steel Corporation together; also, before the turn of the century at Homestead, Pennsylvania, he had been the central figure in rough battles between his Pinkerton police and mobs of strikers and their women. In those troubled times he had been shot and stabbed by Alexander Berkman, a Russian anarchist. He recovered from his wounds but never from the bitterness of that struggle. Harvey described him as the kind of Republican who held that "the Democratic Party never was, is not now and never will be fit to govern the United States." Actually Frick had hailed Wilson's leadership at the beginning of the war though he had now completely recovered from this brief political relapse.

The other, slightly younger, rich man was Frick's lifetime friend, the diminutive, mild-seeming Andrew Mellon. Frick had introduced the chill-eyed, tight-mouthed Mellon to a high-spirited English girl whom he married but could not keep. Nothing interrupted his other accumulations in banking, steel, oil and aluminum. Despite his millions, at the time of the meeting in Brandegee's house few had heard of him outside Pennsylvania where Penrose and his machine welcomed his aid.

How much Harvey got from the two men was never known, but, as the editor reported in his biography of Frick, "the desired reservoir had been found and it was both deep and full." With funds from the reservoir, the League for the Preservation of American Independence was set up. The organization dispatched anti-League and anti-Wilson speakers to all parts of the land. To more Americans than Brandegee and Harvey or Frick and Mellon American security did seem already threatened by the menace of "international socialism and anarchy" of which Lodge had spoken in the Senate.

On April 28, the same day on which the revised Covenant was published, the peace was punctuated in the United States by the arrival in the mail of a bomb package addressed to Mayor Ole Hanson of Seattle, who had put down a general strike there in February. In days immediately following, thirty-five such packages were put in the mails addressed to a variety of rich men, officials and judges who in one way or another had aroused radical ire— one notably to A. Mitchell Palmer, Pennsylvania Quaker politician. Wilson had appointed him Attorney General during his brief visit home. Palmer had turned down appointment as Secretary of War in 1913 because of his Quaker pacifism. Now he seemed to bring a special belligerence to his often indiscriminate war on the Red menace in America. He had explosive grounds for his own fears.

The April batch of bomb packages had resulted in remarkably

little harm. Their character was detected before damage was done to the prominent intended victims. One bomb which did get through to delivery blew off the hands of a maid in a senator's house. Riots attended the celebration of May Day by some radicals. Mobs of servicemen crashed their halls and cracked some skulls. Palmer announced that a plot existed to kill high officials and force recognition of Soviet Russia. Then almost as if to prove it, a bomb blasted the front of his house on R Street in Washington.

Alice Longworth in her capacity as ever present historian witnessed the midnight scene: "The pavement in front of the house was matted with glass and leaves—the front wall looked as if it might fetch loose at any moment," she recalled. "Fortunately just before the explosion, the Palmers had gone to bed in the back part of the house. We went in to see Franklin and Eleanor Roosevelt, who lived just opposite. A leg lay in the path to the house next to theirs, another leg farther up the street. A head was on the roof of yet another house. As we walked across it was difficult to avoid stepping on bloody hunks of human being. The man had been torn apart, fairly blown to butcher's meat. It was curiously without horror. When we left a large number of pieces had been assembled on a piece of newspaper, and seemed no more than so much carrion."

There were other bombings in other places that night—in Boston; New York; Cleveland; Philadelphia; Pittsburgh; Newtonville, Massachusetts. No one was killed except the man or men (surgeons could not at once determine from the scraps whether the carrion had constituted one man or two) who bombed the Palmer house. Franklin Roosevelt and probably Alice, too, picked up some scraps of printed paper connecting the explosion with an anarchist group, not as the New York *Times* said with the Bolshevik or I.W.W. Such distinctions seldom were made. Anarchists, wobblies, Communists, Socialists, and some liberals were all daubed with the same red.

Such an event did not keep Alice at home at night. She rode on her appointed rounds trying, at Brandegee's request, to persuade Republican mild reservationists—" 'spineless creatures' was our kindest characterization of them"—to see the menace of the League. With Brandegee and the equally stalwart Medill McCormick, of Illinois, she drove "around and around the park in the cool of the evening, in Brandegee's high-swung, lumbering old car."

One of those she was trying to persuade may have been the

"somewhat staid, mild reservationist companion" who accompanied Alice on another night sortie in her anti-League activities. Then she went to spy on the President's strength. With elaborate ceremony the Versailles Treaty had been signed in the Hall of Mirrors on June 28. Edith Wilson, watching again, saw the German delegates as "uniformly stolid, uninteresting looking men" who had "continued to haggle about signing." But sign they did. The Wilsons turned finally homeward and Alice was on the edge of the crowd welcoming them back to Washington on July 8. She came with no cheers.

She parked in the shadows at the edge of the station plaza to see what sort of reception he received. Pleased, she reported that it was "a sparse crowd, of the sort to whom any man who happens to be President is a spectacle." On the hot summer night, the women wore light dresses and most of the men were coatless. There was very little cheering—"such as there was had a treble quality, as women predominated."

Still not satisfied, she hurried uptown to see how many people turned out to greet Wilson as he entered the White House grounds. She was happy to discover not more than two or three hundred there. On the curb, watching the Presidential party pass through the big gate into the grounds, she crossed her fingers making the sign of the evil eye. This was not new to Alice. Years before she had made the sign at William Randolph Hearst when he plagued her father. It was indeed, as she said, a reversion to the black magic of youthful days. But her companion was alarmed when she cried aloud a curse.

"A murrain on him, a murrain on him, a murrain on him!"

"Don't let anyone hear you," he kept saying, as if he feared the Secret Service might pick them up. He tried to look as if he did not belong with her. It would have displeased her to know that inside the big house the Wilsons were content. After "an exhilarating day" of tumultuous welcome in New York, they were feeling beyond palaces and ceremonies how good it was to be once more surrounded "by the simple dignity of the White House, spick and span with cool linen on the chairs and flowers everywhere."

Only the linens were cool that July in Washington. The city was deluged with hot rains periodically interrupted by steaming sunshine. Residents even along the fashionable street where the Palmer house had been bombed complained of windows so swollen with the damp that they could not be opened. More than ever Wilson was grateful that "almost all the windows of the White House open upon unoccupied spaces that stretch to the banks of the Potomac . . . and on to the heavens themselves." The windows and the doors in Washington between the White House and the Senate seemed swollen shut. When in his report to Congress Wilson spoke of the League as "the only hope of mankind" he was aware of sullen stubbornness in the Senate. There was no response on some of the faces before him when he demanded, "Dare we reject it and break the heart of the world?"

Afterward his son-in-law, William Gibbs McAdoo, wrote him that his splendid address was "like casting pearls before swine." Wilson agreed more than ever when he learned that handsome Senator Warren Harding, of Ohio, in his oratorical solemnity, which sometimes sounded like statesmanship, had said that the address was "utterly lacking in ringing Americanism." Wilson expected no more from Brandegee than his characterization of the speech as "soap bubbles of oratory and a soufflé of phrases."

Tempers were rising not only in the White House and the Capitol but in the hot streets between them. On July 19, ten days after the President's return, race riots in the streets stretching almost to the East Gate of the White House might have signaled to him that there was an ugly mood in America and not only in the Senate. There seemed almost a murrain on the land.

As a gentle Georgia woman, the first Mrs. Wilson, with no ideas of equality but with simple humanity, had been concerned about the conditions of Negroes in Washington. Many of them lived in old "alley slums" behind the great houses of smart people who thought she looked rather dowdy in the White House. In her brief life in Washington she had helped secure a law designed to eliminate or improve the slum conditions. It was passed just as she died in August, 1914, as war began in Europe. But it was as frail as she had been when American entry into the conflict shut off the immigration flow from abroad and labor needs not only expanded but exploded. The never-to-be-ended Negro migration northward began. Some moved to new hope. Others were sought and fetched by labor agents. In many cities they crowded close to equally disadvantaged foreign-born elements. At war's end whites saw them as competitors, often as strikebreakers. They were pitiful and opposed. "Covenants," not like the one Wilson brought back from

Paris, barred them from many neighborhoods. But in crowded ghettos they were readily identifiable targets for those who had not expended all their hate on the Hun.

Angry mobs of white soldiers, sailors, and marines moved on Pennsylvania Avenue, the street of great American parades. Historians later attributed the trouble to "inflammatory headlines" in Washington papers announcing assaults on white women by Negroes. Some of these attacks, they said, were shown to be false and some were "definitely invented as whips for the mob." At the time, however, the supposedly objective Associated Press spoke without qualification of "race hatred in the National Capital engendered by attacks on white women by Negroes." On July 22, when it reported that the bloody business had been confined to the "center of the black district" around Eighth and M streets, it declared that a white woman had escaped attack only after she had been stripped by an assailant.

Troops were called and home guards put on duty. Though deeply involved in his preoccupation with hopes of peace in the world, Wilson conferred with military officials about the violence at his door on the third day of rioting when seven persons, mostly Negroes, had been killed and eleven seriously wounded. Franklin Roosevelt, in the house across the street from Palmer's bombed house, thought more should have more swiftly been done to suppress the havoc.

Evidently not only some senators but some of the returning servicemen were also ready to lynch the League. Soon after the riots, Lodge spoke again, combining eloquence, acrimony, and perfervid patriotism in his attack. Uniformed marines in the gallery cheered him loud and long. There was noisy, angry approval, too, for the speeches of the senators sent in the Brandegee-Harvey-Frick-Mellon "educational" campaign. Anti-League sentiment was dispatched from the Senate "cabal," and poured back to the Senate, too. Wilson conferred with individual senators and tried to persuade even some who favored strict reservations about his League. Increasingly they told him that the treaty containing the League could only be ratified with at least some of the reservations proposed by Lodge. Jim Watson, to whom Lodge had spoken of the cord of hate upon which he depended, quoted Wilson as snorting in protest with fire in his eyes.

"The *Lodge* reservations! Never! Never! I'll never consent to adopt any policy with which that impossible name is so prominently identified."

The Massachusetts Senator apparently was right about the thread which was a cable. Still the President showed almost obsequious politeness, the chief White House usher thought, when he submitted himself to questioning by the Foreign Affairs Committee on August 19. Few, of course, noted that that was the tenth anniversary of the day when Lodge's son Bay died. He was imperturbable while the President was questioned and replied. Wilson stumbled occasionally under sharp cross-examination, but after the session was over the New York *Times* said that if the President's "straightforward replies to the questions of the Senators have not removed from their minds all reasonable doubts and misgivings, then evidently nothing can . . . and the country will be forced to the conclusion that their objections do not lie in the treaty or in the League Covenant, but somewhere outside. . . . The President has exhausted the resources of reasoning and exposition."

He had not satisfied the irreconcilables. Lodge moved in his plan to hold the matter in suspension with prolonged hearings. The Covenant was read word by word to an all-but-empty committee room. Then the room was filled by a procession of the disgruntled of every cause and kind. They piled protests, demands, angers, suggestions into the record. In the prolonged parade came Irishmen, advocates of independence for India, Negroes who wanted the League to do something about protecting the colored minority in the United States, Lithuanians, Latvians, Esthonians and representatives of the Ukraine. Movies of German atrocities were shown. More and more amendments were offered in the committee. Obviously the work of obstruction and confusion was in full tide.

So Wilson made his decision in terms of contact with the earth, with the people about whom he had spoken in 1913 when Lodge caught him in scholarly error.

"I will appeal to Caesar," he said.

Those who saw the President on the days before his decision to take his case to the country already were commenting on his frail appearance. His Cabinet, his doctor, his wife warned against such a trip. Friendly writers commented on the difficulty of his task. His own confidence in the response of the nation was not shared. R. L. Duffus, in the New York *Globe*, spoke of America's old "insular consciousness." To deepen it, he added, "a homesick army of three million men has poured back from France, irritated, disillusioned, and only too glad to shut the front gate and stay at home for a while."

Neither warnings about the nation's mood nor his own health deterred Wilson. Attended by many newsmen on his special train, he swung westward in his private car "The Mayflower." Through the state of Warren Harding he moved into the Middle West supposedly most ready for isolation. His audiences grew in size and seemed to increase in sympathy for his cause. His confidence mounted that nothing had changed the plain people, the good people, the ones whom he had said do not swarm in Washington but who "trust you without their personal counsel to do your duty."

His duty now was to counsel them. He had known, of course, that Senate opponents would follow him crying warning that he who had led America to victory would betray it in the peace. He was not surprised at their charges that he was ready to sell out American independence to make himself, under the League, the first president of the world. His Southern chivalry and his Presbyterian contempt were stirred by slurs which included Mrs. Wilson, too. A resolution was introduced in Congress calling for a "list of all presents of any kind whatsoever that were tendered" the Wilsons by "any King, Prince or Foreign State."

More significant than the auditorium applause he received or the partisan abuse which followed him was the turmoil in the nation to which he turned. Angry readiness for strike against low wages and intolerable hours was growing in the steel towns. Also growing was the charge built by steel managers, who declined to budge in any arbitration or conciliation, that the approaching strike sponsored by the American Federation of Labor was Bolshevik-inspired. That did not alter the very real grievances of the workers. Not even Wilson, who had recently proposed a more democratic economy, had time to understand the long-simmering troubles of the Boston police who were finally practically prodded by their reactionary commissioner into strike on September 10. Quickly from his train Wilson called this strike an "intolerable crime against civilization." His statement won him no such applause and profit as came to Calvin Coolidge, who had stood inert when he might have saved justice and safety in Boston, then became a national hero by his belated declaration that "there is no right to strike against the public safety by anybody, anywhere, anytime."

Wilson's train moved well south of Illinois with its irreconcilable senators and its Chicago *Tribune* thundering shut-in chauvinism. There, just the week before the President began his appeal to America, had occurred bloody race riots in which fifteen whites and twenty-three Negroes were killed, hundreds injured and a thousand families left homeless in smashed sections of the city. Pageantry, not turmoil, surrounded him. Bright-eyed children waving flags, well-dressed men and women cheering and applauding heard him make speech after eloquent speech for a safer, better-ordered world.

His train, as it zigzagged westward, passed on its way from St. Paul to Bismarck two Minnesota towns apparently too small to swing much weight in the great debate. One was Sauk Center, the model used for the portrait of Main Street. The other, a few miles away, was Little Falls, home of former Congressman Charles Augustus Lindbergh. Others like this sixty-year-old Farmer Labor politician, who had fought for Wilson's reforms, had been vilified and rejected in war. Wilson met resentments from workers who felt that he had let his war for democracy in the world serve the continuance of industrial oppression at home.

Trailed by speakers financed by Mellon and Frick, he was greeted in the West by angry workers whose fellows had been imprisoned or deported in the name—and sometimes only in the guise—of national security. There had grown in his idealistic war-effort, like a noxious weed among lilies, the tyranny of a Covenanter's state. There had been short shrift for dissenters. Pacifists were proscribed or quarantined. Resistance to regimentation had been heresy. Even to speak the German language had seemed sedition. The pursuit of radicals had become patriotism. Eugene Debs, who had polled nearly a million votes as Socialist candidate for President in 1912, was in the federal penitentiary in Atlanta for criticizing the arrest of workers for sedition. Tom Mooney, labor organizer who had been railroaded on the false charge that he set off the bomb beside the Preparedness Parade in San Francisco in 1918, was only barely escaping the noose in California.

Hate and anger had not been demobilized. Wilson, whose war government had fostered the fervors, faced resentments which resulted. At Seattle observers watched him shaken as an apostle of peace when he confronted those who regarded him as an apostate to the cause of people. His parade moved from cheering streets into a blocks-long passage where men in working clothes stood arrayed in silent scorn. Only placards on their hats demanding the release of political prisoners spoke to him. No eyes met his. And as his car moved through the tough stillness, Wilson's hand holding the hat he had been waving hung almost palsied at his side.

His fatigue increased. His headaches hammered as his train rolled down the West Coast. It moved close to Centralia, Washington. There the angers were already growing toward the celebration of its first Armistice Day in a bloody collision, ending in a lynching of an ex-soldier, when the new militant American Legion paraded by—or marched upon—the I.W.W. hall. More cheers greeted him from great friendly multitudes in California. But the headaches intensified as enthusiasm thickened around him. Those most devoted to his cause sometimes most crowded the hours in which he hoped for rest. In Los Angeles he set aside time for a luncheon with Mrs. Mary Hulbert Peck, whose name had been associated with his in whispers after the first Mrs. Wilson's death. It was an occasion on which he discovered how poisoned hate could become.

Her presence with Edith Wilson at the luncheon was the best evidence of the emptiness of the gossip about them and of his sympathy for the woman who had suffered by it. Mrs. Peck had come upon hard times. She was that day, Mrs. Wilson wrote later, "a faded, sweet-looking woman." Mrs. Peck found Mrs. Wilson "junoesque, but handsome, with a charming smile that revealed her strong, white teeth." Both women wrote bland memoirs of the occasion. At the luncheon Mrs. Peck said conversation was "gracefully diverted from subjects disturbing to digestion." That was not what in private talk she told a friend. Instead she said that at the luncheon the President spoke of how deeply he regretted the pain which must have been caused her by the gossip of his political enemies. Then Mrs. Wilson, apparently trying to be amusing in a strained situation, spoke up.

"Where there's so much smoke, there must be some fire."

The faded Mrs. Peck flamed in anger. She burst out with one of the horrid, ridiculous canards in the scurrulous whispering against the Wilsons.

"Then maybe you were von Bernstorff's mistress," she told her horrified hostess.

It is little wonder that Alice Longworth, looking back, wrote that some of the things said in that bitter year "were noticeably lacking in the Greek quality of Aidos—the quality that deters one from defiling the body of a dead enemy."

Wilson's cause seemed far from dead. But his skull-shaking headaches, his sleeplessness, his evident exhaustion were frightening his doctor and his wife. Behind him in Washington he felt betrayed by testimony before Lodge's committee that Robert Lansing, whom he felt he had lifted from the position of a clerkship to place as Secretary of State, had expressed strong doubts about the League. Fortunately only a few days remained of his eight-thousand-mile tour so crowded with speeches that when they were published they filled 370 pages of text. He looked faint before he spoke in a stifling auditorium in Salt Lake City. At Pueblo, Colorado, on September 25, members of the press and his party were shocked when he stumbled over a sentence, faltered in his speech. But though weak-voiced, he went on to final eloquence, making his appeal in the name of the young men he had sent to war.

"There seems to me," he said, "to stand between us and the rejection of this treaty the serried ranks of those boys in khaki, not only those boys who came home, but those dear ghosts who still deploy upon the fields of France."

Late that night as the train moved across Colorado and Kansas toward Wichita he was so seriously stricken that the remainder of the tour was canceled. When his speeding train with its curtains drawn arrived in Washington he was able to walk unassisted to his car. But five days later, while he was sleeping, he suffered a stroke which this time was unmistakable.

The last great gesture of American strength and unity in the war had been made in Washington while he was gone. There on September 17, the day when the President arrived so tired in Oakland, California, from the labor-disturbed Northwest, the War Department made a special final parade of the men of the First Division. Shortly before Alice Longworth had gone to New York to see that returning division, including three of her brothers, marching up Fifth Avenue with General Pershing at their head. In the capital in even more perfect array the division moved up Pennsylvania Avenue along which fifty-four years before the Union Army had moved in its Grand Review. To some who could remember the earlier parade Wilson's absence recalled the absence, too, of Lincoln in 1865. There would be no escape for Wilson from malice or little charity for him either. But even in a land tired of war and bored

with arms the division made a magnificent display. Since its horses
and mules had all been left in France or in quarantine, others were
brought for the occasion from posts in Texas and Kansas. With
their field guns, bands, trucks, rolling kitchens and ambulances,
twenty-four thousand men swung up the avenue. Airplanes soared
overhead. Observation balloons swung over the White House. After the four-hour march was over, the streets were left marked by
the deep gashes made by the caterpillar treads of tanks.

The scars were deeper than that in Washington politics. Little
more than two weeks after the parade and after the President's
collapse on the way to Wichita, Brandegee's publicist colleague in
the "cabal," George Harvey, in his *Harvey's Weekly* welcomed the
President home. Two entire pages of his paper presented the President as a dangerous, glowering, sinister figure. And Harvey wrote:
"In his unapproachable egotism he is quite capable of believing anything that he wishes to believe; even that his tour has been a triumphal march. . . . Undoubtedly he had the time of his life 'slang-
whanging' the United States Senate and insulting every American
citizen who ventured to disagree with him, in circumstances when
he was safe from direct reply. . . . He rushed about the country
like a howling dervish. . . . He uttered again and again what he
knew was untrue.

"He has had his say. He has shot his bolt. He has done his worst.
He is no more to be considered. Now let the Senate act."

The Senate was ready. So was Wilson, despite pleas from friends
in the Senate and outside it that he compromise. As the time of
voting approached, the sick, now white-bearded President wrote a
letter to his leader Senator Gilbert Hitchcock, of Nebraska. Despite
a suggestion from the Senator he said he would hesitate to offer
counsel to the Democrats in detail.

". . . but I assume that the Senators only desire my judgment on
the all-important question of the final vote on the resolution containing the many reservations of Senator Lodge. On that I cannot
hesitate, for, in my opinion, the resolution in that form does not
provide for ratification, but rather for nullification of the treaty. I
sincerely hope that the friends and supporters of the treaty will vote
against the Lodge resolution of ratification. . . .

"I trust that all true friends of the treaty will refuse to support
the Lodge resolution."

As the time of voting approached, Frank Brandegee reminded the signers of the round robin of their pledge in it. As for himself, he said, he would not vote for "this contraption," and would regard himself as "a candidate for the mad house" if he did.

The first vote came on approval of the treaty, with the Lodge reservations. The Democrats loyal to Wilson and the irreconcilables opposed to any treaty containing the League vote against this, defeating it 55 to 39. Then a vote on unconditional ratification failed 53 to 38.

In the Senate to watch the voting was the greatest crowd Alice Longworth had ever seen there. She spent most of the day and evening in the Senate gallery, leaving only occasionally for a bite or a smoke. In her recollections she blew a poisoned kiss of thanks to the President. "Thanks to him," she wrote, "his followers in the Senate never wavered. They persisted in their refusal, in Mr. Wilson's refusal, to vote for the Versailles Treaty with the Lodge reservations, and so the Wilson Democrats and the irreconcilables saved the country from the League of Nations."

(That was not quite so clear then. Four months later a second vote came after compromise conferences among senators in which Lodge participated. The irreconcilables then feared that he might be wavering. Alice, going to call on Lodge, had been halted at the door by Hobday who "opened the door not more than an inch." She waited outside and saw depart Republican senators suspiciously friendly to the League. Then she went in and Lodge "admitted that it was a conference of the mild reservationists." Long as she had loved him, she thought he was very highhanded about the whole matter. "He will have the irreconcilables to deal with," she said to herself. Quickly she reported the conversation to Brandegee. Brandegee was "greatly disturbed"; he hailed his friend Lodge to a meeting of the irreconcilables—Knox, Borah, Johnson of California, Moses, McCormick, and Poindexter. There they threatened to reorganize the Senate if Lodge budged. He would not be the majority leader a day longer. Lodge bowed or, as he said, assured the group "that there was not the slightest danger of our conceding anything that was essential. . . ." And on his side Wilson told his supporters that "practically every so-called reservation was in effect a rather sweeping nullification of the terms of the treaty itself."

The second vote came on March 19, 1920. Then on the question of ratification of the treaty with fifteen reservations, it came within seven votes of the two-thirds needed. If the Democrats who stood with Wilson to the last had voted for the treaty with reservations, America would have been in the League. Brandegee turned to Lodge.

"We can always depend upon Mr. Wilson," he said. "He has never failed us. He used all his power to defeat the treaty, because we would not ratify it in just the form which he desired."

"That is quite true," Lodge replied. "Without his efforts the Treaty would have been accepted by the Senate today.")

After the vote in November Lodge had said, "The door is closed." Certainly after that first vote there seemed reason for celebration. Alice sent word home by her Nick to have eggs ready to scramble for a late supper. Brandegee arrived dourly triumphant. The sharp-tongued Jim Reed, of Missouri, and the blind Thomas P. Gore, of Oklahoma, both Democrats, came. So did George Moses, who soon was to call some of the liberal, independent Westerners who joined him in the League fight "sons of wild jackasses" when they opposed reactionary domestic programs. Senator and Mrs. Medill McCormick brought to the party his big share in the robust Republican Chicago *Tribune* and her inheritance as daughter of the tough old-time Republican boss Mark Hanna, who had put McKinley in the White House and who was explosively distressed when Alice's father succeeded him. Also present was Senator Joseph Frelinghuysen, of the distinguished New Jersey family from which Bay Lodge's wife came. A special guest of honor was Senator Lodge, not averse to midnight celebration even at sixty-eight. It was a mixed group in the Longworth M Street house. Significant in recollection of the party were Senator and Mrs. Harding. Though he was the junior senator from Longworth's state of Ohio, Alice classified the Hardings as "people whom I never liked."

"From the time he came to Washington as Senator in 1913," she wrote, "he and Mrs. Harding came to our house a great deal, chiefly to play poker, a game to which he was devoted. Though Mrs. Harding did not play, she always came too, and the job of the 'Duchess,' as she was called, was to 'tend bar.' Harding and Nick and the others would say when they wished a drink, 'Duchess, you are lying down on your job.' And Mrs. Harding, who was watching the play of the hands, would obediently get up and mix a whisky and soda for them."

She added that "the Hardings never liked me." But this night of celebration all were happy companions in triumph.

"Mrs. Harding cooked the eggs," Alice reported.

The door was closed. And so were the gates in the high iron fence behind which Wilson lay, a sick man seldom seen and about whom rumors even of madness spread. Edward G. Lowry, a journalist who had served abroad in aviation and as an embassy attaché, came home to describe the White House scene before which recently the glittering First Division had moved with music in last parade. In a book, *Washington Close-Ups*, which he was writing then, he quoted (without noting error) Wilson's remarks concerning Washington in which he had made the slip Lodge caught about Antaeus and Hercules. Also he described Washington in the midst of the Lodge-Wilson struggle as a place in which the social-political atmosphere was "one of bleak and chill austerity suffused and envenomed by hatred of a chief magistrate that seemed to poison and blight every ordinary human relationship and finally brought to a virtual stoppage every routine function of the Government."

He went on:

"The White House was isolated. . . . Its great iron gates were closed and chained and locked. Policemen guarded its approaches." It "seemed to the sensitive local intelligence to exhale a chill and icy disdain for the chief subordinate figures and personages who under the President comprise the personnel of the Washington community. . . . It all made for bleakness and bitterness and a general sense of frustration and unhappiness."

Wilson remained as President for a year after the second vote on the League. Or, as some said, he held on to the office despite any true capacity to exercise it. Legends were made and historians have puzzled about the possibility that Edith Wilson, no longer moving decoratively in exalted society or sharing the cheers of multitudes, was not merely a fiercely feminine protector of her husband but almost a regent in his place. Certainly behind the great gates there was a shattered man and a shattered dream.

Not all the anti-Wilson folk were happy. Lodge had his victory. His daughter, the incessantly smoking widowed Constance, declared that "my father never wanted the Wilson League, and when it was finally defeated he was like a man from whom a great burden was lifted." But as a visitor at his Massachusetts Avenue house after the

League defeat, T.R.'s sister, Corinne Roosevelt Robinson, described him in his library as "with a very heavy brow."

"Just as I expected to get my Democrats to vote with my Republicans on going into the League," she said he told her, "a hand came out of the White House and drew back those Democrats, and prevented our going into the League with reservations."

It was not clear who was Hercules, who Antaeus. As the years passed both Lodge and Wilson were to seem less contesting wrestlers than collaborators for catastrophe. Even at the time Alice Longworth had a sense of foreboding. She had called at Lodge's house at Christmas time in 1919 nearly a year after the death of her father, who both had expected to run with valiancy for the Presidency again in 1920. On one of her many forays she came then from the darkness to the light and warmth of the Senator's library.

"The talk turned to politics," she wrote later, "and I recollect how miserable I was to hear him say that he thought the nominee would probably be Harding."

Massachusetts Avenue was bleak and silent when she strode out to her car from the tall, lonely house.

# VI

## SMOKED-FILLED SUITE

DECORATIVE and sharp-eyed but with a secret orphaned sense, Alice in July went to the Republican National Convention which, as its Presidential nominee was to say, would have chosen her father by "acclamation." She and her Nick traveled with Lodge, Harding, Brandegee and others as part of a "trainload of insects streaking out to merge with the convention ant hill." In hot Chicago, which had gone into the war with big-muscled fervor and come out of it fat with profits, she stayed at a mansion on Lake Shore Drive with the Medill McCormicks. They had shared the celebrative eggs Alice had served and Mrs. Harding had cooked when the League was first defeated in the Senate.

With them and other friends she ranged the crowded hotels, the bannered headquarters of candidates. She consorted, as she said, principally with Brandegee and George Harvey, roommates now in a Blackstone suite and impressively busy together at the cavernous Coliseum and in the clotted corridors of hotels. Often she was in the suite numbered 404. A little suspiciously she watched Senator Lodge presiding in chill dignity over the noisy, sweaty assemblage of roaring Republicans. But she joined in the prolonged cheering when in his keynote speech he spoke as an orator almost as she had spoken her curse in the dark at the White House gate the summer before.

"Mr. Wilson and his dynasty, his heirs and assigns, or anybody that is his, anybody who with bent knee has served his purpose, must be driven from all control of the government and all influence in it."

Since childhood Alice's nostrils had known the cigar-smoke smell of assembled politicians. She had shared her father's triumphs and disappointments at Republican conventions. She had been proud and excited at the rebel Bull Moose one at which he called his followers to meet at Armageddon and battle for the Lord. Now at this first in so many years at which his squeaky voice did not bring thundering response, she surveyed the situation with distaste. Her husband was a politician from Harding's Ohio; her aunt, Corinne Roosevelt Robinson, was seconding the nomination for her father's old friend, General Leonard Wood. Alice was an immobilized but not a mute spectator.

The Chicago about her had always been a city of excitement with its lake shore façade only carelessly concealing clutter, confusion, and corruption. Its smoke did not disturb her nor did the sullen steel towns nearby where troops and scabs had so recently smashed the strike. She was scarcely aware of or concerned about the amorphous, polyglot mass of the city where thousands of Negroes had recently joined as strangers, too, the swarm of Irish, Germans, Poles, Russians, Italians.

Not all the foreign-born then had stayed poor or forgotten. London-born Samuel Insull, who had come to Chicago over a quarter century before, was applying the knowledge of the mass public sales of securities he had learned in World War Liberty Bond drives to the building of his two-billion-dollar utility empire. Anton Cermak, a Bohemian-born real-estate man who had spent his first birthday on Ellis Island, was bracing himself after defeat for sheriff to begin his rise to political power which would take him thirteen years later to a seat beside President-elect Franklin Roosevelt and the assassin's bullet intended for F.D.R. The stockyards and the slums about them were not quite the stinking jungle they had been disclosed to be when her father was President and she was the Princess Alice. It was still, as its big Swede, Carl Sandburg, had written, a "city with lifted head singing so proud to be alive and coarse and strong and cunning." And it was almost secretly gentle too: as she tended the poor about Hull House, Jane Addams, who had supported T.R. in 1912, was keeping her peace sentiments which led both to her expulsion from the Daughters of the American Revolution and to the award to her of the Nobel prize for peace.

Alice's Chicago was less—and more—complex as a temporarily occupied political compound of determined Republicans from the whole nation. Her city ran by limousine from the mansion on Lake Shore Drive to the politically packed hotels, loud with conversation and band music, and to a decorated box in the intolerably hot convention hall. Still she looked under the trampled carpet of American political institutions. The campaign culminating in this convention, she wrote later, was "wormy with politicians—riddled with intrigue." Like a lady gathering her skirts—the hem was noticeably higher that year—about her lest she be bespattered, she was fastidious in recollection of it. But no one then knew better than she that hardly any politicians were so busy in intrigue as her old comrades in the League fight: Lodge, Brandegee and Harvey—the Senate scholar, the disdainful Senate sport and the goggle-eyed editor-manipulator. They had work to do.

Lodge, as chairman of the convention, appeared in his gray cutaway to be austerely above the battle for the platform and the nomination. Yet, as he managed the big, crowded hall, Brandegee and Harvey worked in their common causes. They mingled in the swarm on Michigan Avenue where some opulent visitors noted the "ever-depressing park" but were pleased to see that "fewer wretched tramps than usual were sleeping on the sooty patches of grass."

Harvey and Brandegee were not concerned about the landscape. Both were significantly present, engaged in their first order of business, at a conference called by Lodge's colleague, Jim Watson, chairman of the resolutions committee. He had assembled a small group to hear the demand of frail, earnest former Senator Murray Crane, of Massachusetts, that the convention now endorse the League which the Senate had rejected. Though Crane had retired from the Senate in 1912 because of ill health, he had pushed Calvin Coolidge forward in Massachusetts. Also he had recently had enough strength to force an endorsement of the League, in which he passionately believed, from the Massachusetts Republican Convention. He had accomplished that rebuke of Lodge at a midnight roomful of local bosses. Now he wanted similar action by the national convention. He was in a different room now. He was licked before he began. Senator Borah threatened to bolt if such a plank were adopted. But, according to Watson, it was Brandegee who in startling fashion broke up the conference.

Few had ever seen him show emotion before. This seemed an odd time for it. Still, as Watson recalled, "the tears rolled down his cheeks" as he denounced the Crane proposal. Perhaps he was drinking. In the Senate and elsewhere he kept, as Alice described it, a "supply." But his aims were not befuddled. The Indiana Senator

1. WOODROW AND
EDITH WILSON

2. RED LEWIS OF
MAIN STREET WITH
DOROTHY THOMPSON

3. JAZZ LAUREATE FITZGERALD AND FAMILY

4. JOHN REED
LAFAYETTE OF
BOLSHEVISM

THE GENTLEMAN FROM
MASSACHUSETTS

6.  THE PRINCESS ALICE

*Culver Pictures*

7.  MENCKEN AND NATHAN—THE KATZENJAMMER KIDS OF AMERICAN LETTERS

*Brown Brothers*

seemed to take the tears of his Connecticut colleague as signal. He turned quickly to Harvey. There were no tears behind his big, horn-rimmed glasses. Had he drafted, as already requested, a strong anti-League plank? He had. That would be it, said Watson. It was. Old Crane went home to die a few months later. Imperturbably Lodge at the convention chaired the delegates who were more concerned about candidates than ideas. But he joined Harvey and Brandegee, no longer visibly upset, at another more famous conference in the Brandegee-Harvey suite which has come down in history as presumably the model of the "smoke-filled room."

The legend about this term takes many forms. There are various versions of the manner in which it originated and how it was first started, though all go back to Harry M. Daugherty, who later scoffed at the smoke-filled manipulations he predicted. Daugherty was an able Ohio lobbyist and manipulator whose connections as politician extended far beyond the Buckeye State. As a long-shot gambler, he early saw in the picturesque Harding political possibilities which Daugherty could not hope for himself. At an Ohio county convention he saw just the material he needed as promoter in the handsome, easygoing, small-town editor. Harding's paper, the Marion *Star*, said some who minimized him, was then being pushed into prosperity by his older, strong-jawed wife. Years later Daugherty said, "I found him sunning himself like a turtle on a log, and I pushed him into the water."

The water seemed both deep and murky early in 1920 when the pusher-politician was hurrying about the country on the apparently improbable business of securing Harding's nomination for the Presidency. As he packed his bag in the old, ornate Waldorf-Astoria Hotel he was badgered by two unimpressed New York reporters. They could get no list of delegates from him to support his claim that his man would win. So, said one of the newsmen, he must expect to succeed by manipulation, after supporters of other leading candidates had beaten each other to a frazzle, by a small group of politicians "at 2 A.M. in a smoke-filled room."

"Make it two eleven," said Daugherty.

Certainly before the convention assembled, the phrase had been spread by press and tongue. Daugherty himself had made it more specific later by adding, "I will be with them and present the name of Harding. When that time comes, Harding will be elected, because he fits in perfectly with every need of the party and nation."

"Pure bunk," said Watson, who had quickly responded to Brandegee's emotion by taking Harvey's draft of an anti-League plank. Also, Watson pointed out that while coincidence might make Daugherty seem a prophet, when the fateful company gathered in the Brandegee-Harvey suite, Daugherty was not present and had not been invited to attend. Daugherty not only verified that, he sneered at Harvey and the meeting at which he played host. Those gathered there could not have changed fifty votes in the convention, he wrote. The tall tales Harvey told about it were a fable.

Certainly the greater probability is that any history which took place in the suite was only the culmination of plans hatched in other, earlier, smoke-filled rooms. They included Lodge's elegant library on Massachusetts Avenue, the very masculine quarters long occupied by Senator Penrose in the Willard Hotel in Washington, and even a Continental variety of rooms in which Daugherty worked in smoke. Certainly plans or plots for the nomination of Harding were made before the first cigar was lit in Suite 404.

Alice was not the only one who in the winter before the convention had been given intimations of the grand design. Then Henry L. Stimson, later in the Cabinets of both Hoover and Franklin Roosevelt, told the leading candidate, General Leonard Wood, that the gossip he got was that Harding was the opponent to watch. Jim Watson was present and participating when sick and cynical Penrose made his early promise to support Harding though the ailing old boss then said that the Ohio Senator, though a fine candidate, would make a President who would sag down in crisis. Harding was not only picked but pushed. He was content in the Senate and, one legend is, not anxious for the hard work of the Presidency. His wife had a presentiment of trouble in his candidacy. And Harding told Watson that his blood pressure was 185 and there were traces of sugar in his urine. Such details could be dismissed, it had evidently been decided.

One of Penrose's henchmen, who had long casually handled huge sums in cash from men like Mellon and Frick to munition Republican campaigns and candidates, furnished the press with information about big spending by General Wood in his almost military drive for the nomination. Indignant suggestions, not all coming from idealists, were spread that Wood and his chief contender, Governor Frank Lowden, of Illinois, were trying to "buy" the nomination. Neither of them nor Herbert Hoover, who had more popular than political support, promised to be Presidents who would "listen" as senators wished them to. Though T.R. had been forgiven, it was not forgotten that Hiram Johnson had run off with him in revolt. He was too much a man to lead rather than listen. And, as Senator Lodge had sneered, Coolidge, whom he was supposed to favor as the candidate from his own state, "was the kind of a man who lived in a two-family house." Who but Harding?

Yet the prospects of the Ohio Apollo seemed strictly limited as the convention began. Wood roared out ahead with 287 votes and climbed to 314½ on the fourth ballot. On that vote Lowden was close behind with 289½. Hiram Johnson had 140½. Harding was far behind with only 61½ votes. Obviously, with less than 30 votes dividing the top candidates an anticipated deadlock had been reached. Senators conferred around Lodge. A motion to adjourn was made, but Wood and Lowden forces, driving, pushing, some said ready with bribes, were anxious to continue. Lodge put the motion. Few ayes were heard. He called again. The noes resounded in the hall. Calmly Lodge announced that the motion had carried. The convention would reconvene in the morning. The time had come for the "smoke-filled room."

From the convention Lodge went to dinner with Harvey and Brandegee. Then, as the evening advanced, they and others gathered in the Blackstone suite. In history Harvey comes down as a sort of self-appointed master of the proceedings there. He did most of the talking about them, though he was not even a delegate at the convention. Before he broke with Wilson he had been a Democrat, and some considered him one still. He was not a man with any hesitancy about pushing himself. Obviously, however, he was working, as he had been, with Brandegee and Lodge. Certainly the group that convened in the rooms he shared with Brandegee was no such body of nondescript, even disreputable, cigar-chomping politicians as the "smoke-filled room" phrase came to seem to suggest.

The occasion as reported was a sober one. National prohibition was in effect and regarded as fixed and final even by those who evaded it. A rich cousin of the Longworths', who came as spectator in his private car, reported that in Chicago "the dry laws had shut up the interesting old places." Indeed, a historian of rackets there wrote that the dry laws had shut up fifteen thousand drinking places. Alphonse Capone, twenty-three, had just come to town as an "impecunious hoodlum" who covered his first operations under the vocational mask of a "secondhand furniture dealer." The town —certainly the convention—was not entirely arid, however. H. L. Mencken and his Baltimore *Sun* companions in the coverage of the convention had brought along a case of 100 proof stuff. Their quarters resounded with song.

There was no such hilarity in the Harvey-Brandegee suite. Brandegee generally had bottles for himself and friends. Harvey's grandiose airs were sometimes alcoholic airs, too. However, there were no suggestions that drinks went around at this assembly of decision. Probably in that pre-air-conditioned time the rooms were not even smoke-filled, since all windows were wide open in the bare hope of breezes from Lake Michigan. Mark Sullivan, in his history of the times, referred to those in and out of the rooms that night as "party elders." Daugherty sarcastically spoke of them as "the Sanhedrin of the Solemn Senators."

Although, perhaps because of his verbosity in vanity, the suite became known in history as Harvey's, those who assembled were not persons to gather at his beck and call. It was also Brandegee's suite and Brandegee was Lodge's colleague and coadjutor. The Sanhedrin assembled. Newsmen at the time got mixed reports as to what went on in the rooms and who was there. Various possible compromise candidates were said to have been discussed. An impression was apparently elaborately given newsmen that those conferring had no advance design but, as one patrician participant, New York Senator James Wolcott Wadsworth, put it, they were like "a lot of chickens with their heads cut off." That did not seem to be the case to another man present, Joseph E. Grundy, powerful tariff lobbyist of Pennsylvania and big Republican money raiser. As a Senate committee witness nine years later, he gave what the Associated Press called "the first detailed and authentic account of an occupant" of the supposedly smoke-filled room—or rooms—as to what went on.

First he emphasized just who was not there. Daugherty was not. Neither were such oil men as crude Jake Harmon, of Oklahoma, or richer, slicker Harry Sinclair. Though Senator Penrose was "very sympathetic" to Harding and had a private phone connection with a henchman at the convention, he was too ill in Philadelphia to participate in decision in person or by phone. The absent Daugherty did not agree with this. He wrote that he talked with Penrose who only at his request did not release in Philadelphia a statement for

Harding which Daugherty in Chicago thought might arouse boss-choice talk.

Those present could hardly have been more eminent in Republican councils or American society. With Wadsworth, son of a statesman and graduate of Yale, was his conservative colleague, Senator William M. Calder. Reed Smoot, Senator from Utah and one of the twelve apostles of the Mormon Church, and Senator Watson took part. Other leading figures in Harvey's rooms, Grundy said, were familiar, prominent figures in the "cabal" against the League: Senator McCormick, with whom Alice was staying at the time, Brandegee, and first and foremost, of course, Senator Lodge.

Lodge, according to Grundy, laid out the logic. As chairman of the convention, the curly-bearded Senator told the little group he was concerned about the trend it was taking. He had favored General Wood but he found the sentiment of the convention to be such that his nomination would be "ill-advised." He felt that Governor Lowden was unavailable for the same reasons. It was Friday evening of "the hottest week we have ever experienced anywhere." He doubted that the convention could be held over Sunday. The delegates were tired and their money was running out. Then, as Grundy reported, he went on saying ". . . that we should agree on a candidate and that the most available man was Senator Harding; that whether his friends would have spent the same large sums of money as friends of Wood and Lowden was not an issue because Harding's friends had not spent such sums to get the nomination; that it looked like the Democrats would name Governor Cox of Ohio; and that for these and other various reasons we should bring about the nomination of Harding as soon as we could."

Probably, as Lodge talked, he sat swinging his foot. Certainly he talked as the gentleman in politics. As Grundy reported the occasion, there seemed little debate. Harding "looked like a President." There was nothing bad about his senatorial record even if there was nothing good about it either. He was from strategic Ohio. He sounded when he spoke like a statesman even if superior critics regarded his oratory as the boom of platitudes. Less sensitive ears liked the sound of a phrase he had recently used that what this country needed was "not nostrums but normalcy." Accessible, not remote, he provided very folksy contrast to Wilson. He was regular. He would listen. Lodge's logic led to him.

Harvey, who did not minimize his own importance in doing most of the talking about the occasion later, reported that he summoned Harding. The Senator was ushered into a room where only the owlish editor and Brandegee were waiting to receive him. Then, Harvey said, occurred the dialogue which Daugherty later ridiculed as impertinent if not impossible. The Colonel told the Senator that "we" had decided to give him the nomination. "But—" said Harvey, "we want to put a question to you."

Solemnly he put it: "Is there in your life or background an element which might embarrass the Republican Party if we nominate you for President?"

Harding, said Harvey, was profoundly moved. (Daugherty, sneering at the story later, wrote, "God knows he should have been!") But Harvey reported the situation more reverently.

"Gentlemen," he quoted Harding as saying, "I should like to be alone for a little while with my God."

Whether this incident was almost apocalyptical as Harvey described it or entirely apocryphal as Daugherty suggested, there had been rumors circulated, abetted even by Harding's father-in-law who had opposed the marriage of his daughter, that there was Negro blood in the Harding line. That was a frayed tale. More lively and likely gossip tied Harding's name to philandering. Noticeably in the campaign that followed, a merchant in Marion declined to decorate his store front at the town's celebration for its famous son: the handsome Harding had been too attentive to his wife. But present in Chicago then, as she wrote later in *The President's Daughter*, was Nan Britton, a blond, kitten-soft girl from Marion who, from a schoolgirl crush about him, had become the Senator's mistress and mother of his child born in the fall before the convention. She was thirty years younger than fifty-four-year-old Harding. Their furtive affair, as she described it, read like the clandestine romance of a middle-aged floorwalker with his youngest ribbon clerk. But she wrote that during the hot, hectic days of the convention while he sought the nomination for the Presidency, he slipped off to see her twice at the apartment of her sister.

If so, Nan's image as well as his God must have been in the room of Harding's communion with his conscience for his party. However, according to the Harvey story, after ten minutes Harding emerged to assure Harvey and Brandegee that there was no stain on his record that the Republican party might fear. Word was passed that Harding was the man. His nomination was understood to be assured as the choice of the "smoke-filled room" and the elite and self-confidently patriotic group which filled it.

Nevertheless it took six more ballots and, many believed at the time, considerable skulduggery to swing the sweaty delegates to the choice of the gentlemen politicians in the elegant suite. Obviously the "party elders" needed much help. Essential were the votes of the Wood and particularly the Lowden men whom Daugherty had patiently and industriously persuaded to make Harding their second-choice candidate. Some promises had evidently been made to politicians who were less than impeccable. Some of them were more concerned with what they could get from the government than with getting Woodrow Wilson, his heirs and assigns out of the government. In hindsight William Allen White wrote that "oil controlled the convention of 1920. It worked through the Senate cabal, led by the irreconcilables who were so busy hating Wilson that they became easy victims of the greed for oil." Whatever forces were required were arrayed. And Lodge augustly, though not quite correctly, announced that Warren Gamaliel Harding was unanimously nominated. Actually his liberal, anti-League associate, Senator Robert M. ("Fighting Bob") La Follette, held back his Wisconsin delegates from this choice, unwilling as *La Follette's Magazine* said soon after to "accept the dictum of the secret choice at the Blackstone!" Once again Brandegee made dour comment on the decision as he had after the League vote.

"This year we had a lot of second-raters," he said. "Harding is no world-beater. But he's the best of the second-raters."

As a first-class poker player Harding declared, "We drew to a pair of deuces and filled."

There were still many who felt that the game in the smoke-filled room was played with a fixed deck. Alice referred to its occupants as "dealers." But Lodge with the help of Brandegee and Harvey was victorious once more. And the portrait of the gentleman from Massachusetts in triumph was gleefully drawn by a man in the press gallery who already was considered a sort of gadfly of American pompousness and moral pretentions. This time Henry L. Mencken, as reporter, seemed intoxicated by his own verbal exuberance in describing the icily sober Senator. He saw nothing pompous about Lodge. To such a proper commentator of American affairs as Mark

Sullivan, the senator on the podium seemed filled with "waspish malice." Mencken looked at him with delight. He had regarded his keynote as "bosh" but it was bosh "delivered with an air—bosh somehow dignified by the manner of its emission. The same stuff, shoveled into the air by any other statesman on the platform, would simply have driven the crowd out of the hall, and perhaps blown up the convention then and there. But Lodge got away with it because he was Lodge—because there was behind it his unescapable confidence in himself, his disarming disdain of discontent below, his unapologetic superiority."

Mencken went on in his description of the convention dominated by the man from Massachusetts.

"It was delightful to observe the sardonic glitter in his eye," he wrote, "his occasional ill-concealed snort, his general air of detachment from the business before him. For a while he would watch the show idly, letting it get more and more passionate, vociferous, and preposterous. Then, as if suddenly awakened, he would stalk into it with his club and knock it into decorum in half a minute. I call the thing a club; it was certainly nothing properly described as a gavel. . . . Supporting it was the Lodge voice, and behind the voice the Lodge sneer. . . . His delight in the business visibly increased as the climax approached. It culminated in a colossal chuckle as the mob got out of hand, and the witches of crowd folly began to ride, and the burlesque deliberations of five intolerable days came to flower in the half-frightened, half-defiant nomination of Harding—a tin-horn politician with the manner of a rural corn doctor and the mien of a ham actor."

Mencken wondered how such a man as Lodge could allow the nomination of Harding. The writer, who was as cocksure as he was sharp-worded, would have been more surprised if he had known that the part of Lodge in the nomination of Harding was at least as clear as his sometimes puzzling opposition to the League. Certainly, however, the Lodge who seemed so completely in control was shocked when delegates worn out with the dictation of the elders suddenly and spontaneously nominated Calvin Coolidge for Vice-President instead of another senator hand-picked by those who had occupied the smoke-filled room.

Mencken and many others of the press went on to more pleasant weather at the Democratic National Convention in San Francisco.

The Baltimore Bombastes disliked Woodrow Wilson as much as he admired Lodge but he could draw no venomed picture of him there, though sometimes it seemed that the President's paralyzed hand wished to dictate events there as Lodge apparently had in Chicago. Wilson, of course, was not at the cooler Democratic convention by the Golden Gate. He was seldom seen even in Washington.

Often behind his shut gates it was not clear whether men and affairs were more shut out or a greater bitterness was emitted. Not a chivalrous sick man but a bitter woman seemed behind demands from the White House that a minor British diplomat, said to have talked about Mrs. Wilson, be dismissed. Some of Wilson's Cabinet were appalled to learn that she felt that the President might have to run again. Certainly at San Francisco its old members constituted no "cabal" to bring that about. In a room filled with anger, if not smoke, they rejected an apparent purpose to set off an ovation for the sick President and bring off his renomination as a result. Men who loved Wilson most, most opposed this plan, which seemed mysteriously to come from the White House, that Wilson be re-nominated for the office many thought he was already mentally and physically incompetent to fill.

Democrats at San Francisco turned to Ohio, too. As Senator Lodge had forecast, they named James M. Cox, competent, un-exciting governor of that state. Then they snatched at the magic Roosevelt name of which death had deprived the Republicans in Chicago. With adequate tumult they picked as Vice-Presidential candidate young, tall Franklin Roosevelt, wearing the illustrious name and even more clearly related to the Roosevelt legend by marriage to Eleanor, T.R.'s niece and Alice Longworth's first cousin. Alice, who had gone into Franklin's house as congenial friend the summer before when the Palmer home was bombed, was not ex-hilarated by the event.

Later she was to say that this new Roosevelt was a maverick "not of our breed." Also, as she said later, she thought he had a marked resemblance to Wilson. She went along with Harding though she did not "purr" when Harvey undertook to placate her about him. If "they" were so strong, she wondered, why couldn't they have selected a man with higher qualifications for the Presidency. Har-ding would "go along," said Harvey. And as his and Brandegee's and Lodge's choice she did not need Harvey's assurances that Harding would be all right on the League. All the same she concluded that Daugherty's smoke-filled room prophecy was "painfully accurate" even if others had fulfilled it. And despite Daugherty's denial of the crucial part played by the "cabal" in the smoke-filled suite, Harding evidently believed it. Soon after the nomination he conferred twice and at length with Lodge and Brandegee. He went off for brief rest to the estate of their rich colleague Senator Frelinghuysen, of New Jersey. He had in mind rich reward for Colonel Harvey.

The campaign which went on to overwhelming Republican victory was not quite the clear and solemn referendum on the League Wilson had wanted made—and perhaps made by himself as candidate. Cox and Roosevelt rallied to his League cause. But distinguished Republicans who had supported the League were found to say solemnly that, despite the plank Lodge had wanted, Brandegee had demanded, and Harvey had drawn, entry into the League might somehow be served by the election of hand-picked Harding. Certainly before the avalanche of Republican ballots piled up in November the Wilson-Lodge story was over.

As Wilson approached the end of his term and was about to become a sort of legendary figure in a shrine to gradually growing crowds before his high house on S Street, Lodge moved as a figure in tradition. In December, 1920, he was the orator at the celebration in Plymouth of the three hundredth anniversary of the landing of the Pilgrims. He did not speak of them as "rebellious men" as his boy Bay had done to rich New Englanders years before. Instead, as some who heard him said, the words of the seventy-year-old Senator made a "masterpiece of sophistication and disillusionment." At his long-loved place at Nahant he wrote his venomed version of the League fight, remembering to the last Wilson's unscholarly slip about the wrestlers, Hercules and Antaeus.

Lodge was re-elected to the Senate by a slim majority in 1922, then only with the help of Coolidge in the precincts long controlled by Murray Crane. He was clearly growing frail in February, 1924, when Wilson died. He was punctilious still and the report that he refused to attend the funeral of the President he had fought was untrue. Perhaps in his behavior then he was most true to himself. A letter came to his Massachusetts Avenue house with a request for an immediate reply. It read:

*My dear Sir:*

I note in the papers that you have been designated by the Senate of the U. S. as one of those to attend Mr. Wilson's funeral.

As the funeral is private and not official and realizing that your presence would be embarrassing to you and unwelcome to me I write to request that you do *not* attend.

> *Yours truly*
> Edith Bolling Wilson

The Senator sent his reply written in his own hand:

*My dear Madam:*

I have just received your note, in which you say that the funeral services of Mr. Wilson are to be private and not official and that my presence would be unwelcome to you. When the Senate Committee was appointed I had no idea that the Committee was expected to attend the private services at the home and I had supposed that the services at the church were to be public.

You may rest assured that nothing could be more distasteful to me than to do anything which by any possibility could be embarrassing to you.

I have the honor to be

> *Very truly*
> *yours,*
> H. C. Lodge

Lodge himself then had only nine more months to live. In July he was taken to the Charlesgate Hospital in Cambridge where he had been operated on for his ulcers as Wilson began his Presidency. He recovered sufficiently to go back to Nahant. In October the word came that the bristling Brandegee, caught in financial difficulties due to unfortunate investments in real estate—or "on the decline to a reckless bankruptcy," as the sharp chronicler Samuel Hopkins Adams put it—had killed himself by inhaling gas in his big K Street house where five years before the anti-League "cabal" had often convened. A week later Lodge himself was operated on again in the Cambridge hospital. On November 9, 1924, a stroke brought his end. Few trumpets sounded for him anywhere.

# VII

## BACKWATER BLUES

EVEN by Greenwich Village standards the quarters of Harold Stearns in the basement at 31 Jones Street were dingy. A writer for intellectual journals and a notorious deadbeat, he lived below the apartment of a lady novelist on the top floor and under the first floor rooms of a gay village couple who gave lively parties fortified by "bathtub gin" coming into favor under prohibition. Above him feet tapped to loud music. Then sentimental song whispered through the floor. And sometimes from such parties came the bittersweet cry of the blues just beginning to slip into white consciousness from phonograph records first designed to bring the hard and homesick song in "race recordings" to Negro buyers. Already the mood of many whites and Negroes met the cry, crack, and moan of the blues as big Bessie Smith of Chattanooga sang them:

> *Backwater blues done cause me to pack my*
> *things an' go, . . .*
> *Backwater blues done cause me to pack my*
> *things an' go, . . .*
> *Cause my house fall down and I cain't live*
> *there no mo', . . .*

In his basement the small, brown-eyed Stearns had a similar feeling about his country falling down. Maybe it was time to pack things and go. So in inverse homesickness in 1920 he confidently proposed a critical contemplation of his native America to be called *Civilization in the United States—an Inquiry by Thirty Americans.* At its inception he called to his basement Van Wyck Brooks as his first counselor and contributor. Brooks, critic and literary historian, had written since his days at Harvard, a little before Stearns's time there, much on the thesis that Puritan materialism had crushed American culture. Now when many moralistic patriots were feeling that Senator Lodge had saved American civilization from foreign entanglements and alien contaminations, he brought forward the Senator's dead poet son, Bay, to testify that that civilization was scarcely worth saving. In the big, thick book which grew from discussions in Stearns's unkempt and smoke-filled basement, Brooks quoted Bay, the hardly remembered Brahmin rebel, in words like a banshee cry from the grave.

"We are a dying race," this Lodge had written, "as every race must be of which the men are, as men and not accumulators, third rate."

Bay Lodge went on: "Was there ever such an anomaly as the American man? In practical affairs his cynicism, energy and capacity are simply stupefying, and in every other respect he is a sentimental idiot possessing neither the interest, the capacity, nor the desire for even the most elementary processes of independent thought. . . . His wife finds him so sexually inapt that she refuses to bear him children and so driveling in every way except as a money-getter that she compels him to expend his energies solely in that direction while she leads a discontented, sterile, stunted life. . . ."

Certainly the accumulators, sexually inapt or not, seemed in command in 1920. Intellectuals were suspect and radicals were on the run—or had better be. Many of the poor were restless or sullen and headed for defeat or despair. And behind the accumulators and the politicians who served them the guardians of public morals were watching books as well as bootleggers. Perhaps Greenwich Village, where freedom had flourished and was faded, was the proper place for the planning of a sort of pessimistic philosophical photograph of America circa 1920.

Already then Greenwich Village had become much more than the name of an old New York neighborhood around Washington Square. It was a label in the American language for a Bohemia, fascinating or repellent, seldom anything between. Here was the delightfully dilapidated home of free spirits providing poetry, drama, ideas in a stuffy land. Or it was the noxious warren of twisting streets around Washington Square, where males wore their hair long, females theirs short, and both were persons of doubtful means, morals and manners. Though the increasing troop of tourists did not realize it, its heyday was passed.

The good days, beginning around 1912, when low rents had attracted so many of high spirits in arts and ideas, were gone. John Reed, who had come with three Harvard classmates as an ebullient poet on his way to swift journalistic success, described it then in the spirit of his striding liveliness. It was a place, said Reed, not even dreaming then of a destiny which would come from dissent, where people "dared to think as Uptown would not dare." He sang of the area:

> Policemen walk as free as air,
> With nothing on their minds but hair,
> And life is very, very fair,
> In Washington Square.

The already evident passing of the horse made possible the transformation of stables into studios. The decay of old mansions provided low-rent rookeries for artists, writers and radicals. The ingathering around Washington Square coincided with the surge in spirit of a nation grown rich and self-critical and marked by the Progressive insurgence of Roosevelt and the New Freedom of Wilson. It attracted the angry, the aspiring and the gay, exhibitionists, eccentrics and some who just came for the roaring ride. It had its cliques and contentions, its favorite bars where ideas and glasses sometimes both clashed. Such a rich woman as Mabel Dodge Luhan maintained in a nearby mansion a true salon where no variant ideas were barred. In it could be seen Lincoln Steffens, the famous "muckraker" journalist, and his protégés Reed and Walter Lippmann of the famous Class of 1910 at Harvard. (That class also contained Alan Seeger, T. S. Eliot, Heywood Broun and others of a glittering array.) Present often were angry, one-eyed Big Bill Haywood, leader of the I.W.W., such socialistic writers as Max Eastman and Floyd Dell, playwrights and scenic designers who were to become famous at Provincetown on Cape Cod, and on Broadway. In the company would be Vassar girls and vagabonds, many who came for the talk and some who came only for the food.

Everything that grew there held in perfection but a little moment. Pretenders piled in on the poets. And if the Village's swiftly spreading reputation attracted eager boys and girls from Minnesota and

Mississippi, it shocked and irritated protectors of genteel literary and accumulative traditions. The *Saturday Evening Post* began almost a campaign of ridicule in a process of condemnation. Sinclair Lewis, once a resident himself, wrote of the Village as Hobohemia. Irvin S. Cobb jibed at Hallroomania and the table-d'hôttentots there. Even some able and radical residents, feeling dispossessed, moved to a sort of suburban substitute at Croton-on-Hudson. Dell, one of them, said the Village had become a tinselly peep show for tourists who regarded it as one of the "sights" of New York like "imposing Wall Street and teeming Harlem." With the coming of war and its inhospitality to dissent, policemen and federal agents, too, around Washington Square had a good deal more on their minds than hair.

When Stearns and Brooks talked down beneath the blues in 1920 of the big book to be, the Village had become less a precinct of freedom than a sort of focal point for war-stiffened repression. Old frequenters of the neighborhood Big Bill Haywood and Emma Goldman had been packed off first to prison, then deportation. Theodore Dreiser's German name seemed to make more certain the charges of obscenity against him. Even such a non-Villager as one of the contributors to Stearns's book, Mencken, got reflections on his patriotism in supposed literary criticism of his writing. Such essential Villagers as Eastman, Dell and Reed who considered the conflict a "traders' war" were indicted for sedition and their socialist magazine *The Masses* suppressed. Reed had holed up in the neighborhood in 1919 to write *Ten Days that Shook the World*, his classic story of the Bolshevik revolution which he had observed and approved. In 1920 as true expatriate with the police behind him he escaped to Russia on a forged passport as a stoker.

There were no radicals in the group of essayists Stearns summoned to his assistance in the preparation of *Civilization*. Theirs was only a rebellion of distaste. Stearns organized quite a Thirty. The Katzenjammer Kids of American letters, Mencken and George Jean Nathan, of *Smart Set* followed by *American Mercury*, wrote respectively of politics and the theater. Mencken was concerned with the ignoble fellows from parochial places who largely composed the Congress. Nathan chose the Boston of his friend's admired Senator Lodge to damn a hypocritical culture which ignored or suppressed honest drama but crowded to slick smut and leg shows. Lewis Mumford said of the American city, "Today more than one-half the population of the United States lives in an environment which the jerry-builder, the real estate speculator, and the industrialist have created." He used the word "suburbia" for outskirt areas where, he said, life was carried on without the disciplines of rural occupations and without the cultural resources of the city.

Conrad Aiken and Walter Pach found poetry and painting in healthy condition. But of music Deems Taylor reported that Americans squandered millions every year "upon an art that we cannot produce." He did not note that George Gershwin, though then only twenty, was already shaping the music he had heard in Harlem into sophisticated cadences. In general, disenchantment was repeated in essay after essay. Ring Lardner wrote in sardonic humor of spectator sports. Joel E. Spingarn, whose interests ranged across the whole board of American ideas and causes from comparative literature to the advance of the Negro, flatly stated that "no great work of classical learning has ever been achieved by an American scholar." John Macy condemned the "tediously uniform" American press. Stearns himself, writing of the intellectual life, found it dominated for "enforced dull standardization" by those who would keep it "a spiritual prison."

The book, when it appeared later, attracted no such absolutely opposite acclaim as made best sellers at the time of the pessimistic *The Mind in the Making* of the native historian James Harvey Robinson and the panegyric autobiography, *The Americanization of Edward Bok*, by the long-time editor of the *Ladies' Home Journal* and husband of the daughter of its publisher. Robinson was contemplating a race between education and catastrophe. Bok was looking back on his rich life in a happy America as a Dutch-born boy with all the conventional American virtues. But the smaller Stearns, in person and not merely as editor, made his *Civilization* a sort of Book of Exodus or a kind of philosophic passport for expatriates. Certainly he undertook to make himself their model when, later, reporters gathered about him at the French Line pier to hear his not-so-fond farewells to the country he was leaving, so he said, forever. In response to chiding by contented patriots, he said they were right in depicting "the younger generation as in revolt against right-thinkers and forward lookers."

"It is in revolt," he declared, "it does dislike almost to the point of hatred and certainly to the point of contempt, the type of people who dominate our present civilization, the people who actually 'run things.' . . ."

In his basement Stearns and his twenty-nine fellow Americans had only brewed testiness in a teapot compared to the true tempest in the caldron of American life that year. His basement even when music was loudest above it was a cloister. His contributors seemed not only erudite but remote from muscular revolt of any kind. Macy, in his essay on the press, did mention its antilabor bias in reporting the steel strike. An anonymous writer on medicine referred to "the now extinct Wilson." Jeremiah Chafee, Jr., writing of the law, noted that "when other peoples judged the Covenant of the League of Nations as an expression of broad policies and aspirations of a hundred years . . . we went at it word by word with a dissecting knife and a microscope as if it had been a millionaire's will or an Income Tax Act." There was mention of the rising Ku Klux Klan.

But there was little tumult in the book's pages. There was little sweat or smoke in it, no pain, little stress, none of the participation in protest which John Reed had brought to his reporting of civilization or the lack of it in the United States. They seemed ineffectual, almost inaudible, compared to other men whose ideas of civilization were completely different but just as strong. Such men in action and not merely literary composition set out to save it.

Attorney General Mitchell Palmer most dramatically—hysterically, some thought; and for his own political purposes, others believed—cried the great Red danger. The bombing of his house the summer before gave him personal basis for concern. Now with the help of a ready press he built a panic fear of revolution.

"Like a prairie-fire," he told his countrymen, "the blaze of revolution was sweeping over every American institution of law and order. . . . It was eating its way into the homes of the American working man, its sharp tongues of revolutionary heat were licking the altars of the churches, leaping into the belfry of the school bell, crawling into the sacred corners of American homes, seeking to replace marriage vows with libertine laws, burning up the foundations of society."

So believing, on New Year's Day, 1920, Palmer, who was pleased to be called the "Fighting Quaker," sent his agents swooping down on the headquarters of unions, the halls of radical societies and private homes. Suspected radicals and especially foreign ones were arrested without any legal fastidiousness about warrants or the rights of search and seizure. Little distinction was made between degrees of radicalism. In Palmer's roaring view Red was Red. Though the supervision of aliens was the responsibility of the Department of Labor, the Attorney General did not bother to consult in advance its officials, who afterward regarded his raids as part of a "deportation delirium." His men rounded up and packed into jails six thousand individuals. Some other people were arrested merely because they came to jails to see their captured friends.

It was soon evident that the whole business was a furious fiasco. No arsenal of revolution was discovered. Only three pistols were found, no explosives at all. Only one in ten of those seized were found guilty of crime or subject to deportation. Also, perhaps, as many believed afterward, Palmer's agents in their mass arrests missed two dangerous radicals, Nicola Sacco and Bartolomeo Vanzetti, who were arrested that spring for the murder of a paymaster and guard of a shoe factory in South Braintree, Massachusetts, on April 15. Still, Palmer was the hero of many patriots. Certainly he and his eager agents helped build the mood in which the great steel strike collapsed in the same month as his raids.

Working for bare subsistence wages for an average of sixty-nine hours a week, men in the steel mills had flocked to the organizing efforts of the American Federation of Labor. Around 343,000 men struck in the Chicago area; others walked out in other places. The United States Steel Corporation pulled in Negro strikebreakers, protected them with troops and refused to negotiate any grievances. The company undertook to stir up trouble between Italian and Serb strikers. At Gary, Indiana, alone, eighteen strikers were killed in futile rioting. The smoke from the stacks of operating mills rose by cold houses.

So, herded by hunger and hostility, sullen men left bitter women in their homes to go back to the mills. They had won nothing they had sought. When they were allowed to come back at all, they received only the old, low wages they had received for inhuman hours at hot, hard jobs. Their union was, of course, not recognized. They would have to wait fifteen years for that. Little sympathy attended their defeat. With only limited dissent, the "tediously uniform" press had helped the steel managers convince the country that revolution was behind their protests.

Indeed, it did turn out that their leader, William Z. Foster, would run for President on the Communist ticket four years later. Some believed that only bitterness after the strike pushed Foster, an old I.W.W. man, to the Communist line. In contrast with him, Judge

Elbert H. Gary, steel chief who had declined arbitration or conciliation, was evidently a Christian gentleman. A humorless, almost foppishly dressed man of seventy-three, Gary said that he believed "all" of the Bible, "not a little piece here and a little piece there." Such a man and other sound men naturally called the new antiunion program they instituted "the American Plan." To it presumably all the virtuous could repair. No scruples and possibly no suspicions troubled Judge Gary when at Warren Harding's request he gave a job to the Senator's friend Nan Britton.

It would be good riddance if such folk as populated basements and garrets in Greenwich Village left for France. It was a sanitary measure to ship subversive strangers off to Russia. American decency was otherwise served when, in the month the Reds were raided and the steel men were starved back to work, the muscular evangelist Reverend Billy Sunday could cry, "Hell is for rent," as national prohibition went into effect. Also at that time in New York, John S. Sumner, executive secretary of the New York Society for the Suppression of Vice, seized the plates and all the copies of *Jurgen* by James Branch Cabell. Like Judge Gary, Sumner was a true American. Son of a rear admiral and a member of the Sons of the American Revolution, he had taken leave of his vice job to serve, as he put it in *Who's Who*, in "the St. Mihiel and Argonne offensives" as a YMCA secretary.

Other confidently American persons had spoken up for the protection of American traditions. One was Congressman James F. Byrnes, later to become Senator, Supreme Court Justice, chief World War II aide of F.D.R., Secretary of State, and Governor of South Carolina. He called for the strict application of the Espionage Act in the South lest Negroes turn it into "another Russia." Such dangers were met by lynchings, sometimes even of "uppity" Negro soldiers still in uniform, and not only in the South but even in such a place as Omaha. The pattern of black dangers seemed perfected in the back country around the little village of Elaine, Arkansas, the fall before Stearns began to assemble the materials of his discontent. An essay in his *Civilization* did mention almost in passing that the Ku Klux Klan organizing in Atlanta, where Eugene Debs was in prison, claimed a membership of 100,000 in 1920. No sheeted mobilization had been reported in Elaine. There, apparently, Negro sharecroppers had been bold or foolish enough to form a union. Cotton prices were still high. In some parts of the South planters grumbled about labor agents luring off their "niggers." Negroes grumbled, too, when they heard of the pay old neighbors who had gone North were receiving. Some of their cabins were falling down, and not only in songs about the backwater blues.

What happened at Elaine was pogrom or revolution, absolutely the one or the other depending upon the teller. Some whites were shot but more than a hundred Negroes were killed. Only the buzzards could count the bodies in the swamps. After the shooting was stopped, eighty-seven colored people were sentenced to the penitentiary and twelve to the electric chair. All those found guilty were finally freed on appeal. But by the cottonfields and the bayous in the South and in the packed slums of Northern cities Negroes in despair as dark as their skins wished for a place where they could pack their things and go. The blues were not new. Music historians seeking their origin found Negroes in New Orleans born as early as the Civil War who said, "The blues was here when I come." But in the aftermath of World War I in dispersal and disappointment the hope for a home that would not fall down was more than something in a song by Bessie Smith.

They wanted to pack their things and go, but were without hope of satisfying destination. Joel Spingarn, while he wrote the essay on "Scholarship and Criticism" in Stearns's book, was active as one of the founders and directors of the National Association for the Advancement of Colored People. Then he was trying not so much to advance as protect them from savage mistreatment as well as segregation. Slavery then was less than a man's lifetime behind.

The nation as it moved to war had seen with roaring approval the first great modern film, *The Birth of a Nation*, in which the Negro had appeared as the brute to pursue and the Klan true knights in spotless robes. Its influence was not offset by the fact that in 1920, as one of Stearns's essayists said, Eugene O'Neill, emerging from Greenwich Village and the summer playing of Villagers at Provincetown, had created in his *Emperor Jones* perhaps the first "strong, upstanding black man" in American literature. From Negro musical influences George Gershwin had made beginnings in the sophisticated jazz he produced later in "Swanee" sung loudly by Al Jolson in *Sinbad*. Adventurous, artistic, and literary folk had begun to visit the night spots of Harlem which another old Villager, Carl Van Vechten, lightly and sympathetically described later in his novel *Nigger Heaven*.

It was no heaven to the packed and exploited tenants in the streets behind the cafes where black musicians blew jazz from their horns and black and yellow women sang the blues. Certainly it was not the promised land which labor agents had described and war wages at first seemed to prove. A new Moses was required. He appeared in the person of Marcus Garvey, an eloquent Jamaican, who was ready to lead panicky possible expatriates out of their fears and frustrations. Perhaps he was, as Frank Freidel concluded, only a "persuasive charlatan"; maybe he was, as E. David Cronon said, "personally honest and sincere" but inexperienced and irresponsible. White friends of the Negro and educated Negroes, too, distrusted him. Certainly he was a sort of minstrel-show messiah who appeared when one was desperately required, and the NAACP seemed intellectually remote from the jungle of black poverty.

Garvey produced no book describing the faults of civilization in the United States. None was required by his dark listeners. What he proposed was something in the nature of a black Zionism, a "Back to Africa" movement or at least a rediscovery of Negro dignity and pride. Probably few of the poor and ignorant who listened to his militant black chauvinism really wished or planned any flight to Liberia. But behind them in the South were rope and fagot; about them in Northern cities, crime, crowding, contempt, the poorest pay for the worst jobs. Out of their meager earnings, laborers and domestic servants invested in Garvey's grand schemes, a Black Star line of ships, a Negro factories corporation, all the glittering plans of his Universal Negro Improvement Association. In Harlem he purchased Liberty Hall and there on August 20 he gathered about him the greatest assembly of supposedly would-be expatriates in America.

Garvey's movement only led to a new, deeper frustration among his followers. It took him to prison for mail fraud. Perhaps it was well, as better-educated Negroes felt, to get such a figure of fantasy out of the way on the road to true advance for colored people. Certainly, however, as crusader or charlatan, he served to voice the deep yearning of a people who now cried through old sweet spirituals with the sharper blues. They made the music of men and women eager for deliverance from an Egypt of captivity but with a moaning affection for the scenes upon which they had suffered.

Explosion, when it came the month after Garvey's great meeting and far from the Negro ghettos, seemed destructive to no purpose.

Shortly before noon on September 16, 1920, a horse-drawn wagon drew up before the granite building of the J. P. Morgan Co., at the corner of Wall and Broad streets in New York City. Horse-drawn wagons were not uncommon then. One attracted little notice. The street at the hour was thick with brokerage employees and tourists, too, visiting the financial center as they visited Greenwich Village and Harlem. Suddenly the wagon disintegrated in a terrific explosion. People at windows six floors from the ground were badly burned. Fragments of metal in the wagon spread like shrapnel. Thirty-eight people were killed. Hundreds were injured, fifty-seven badly enough to need hospital treatment. Damage to property was estimated between half a million and two million dollars. Little was left of the horse but a shoe. The driver was never identified. Police assumed but were never sure that it was an act of radical terrorism. Others suggested that it was the work of a criminal maniac. No great oppressive capitalists were killed. Those who died were generally innocents with little stake in the Money Power. Certainly, however, whoever was the killer, he had no affection for American civilization.

In such an explosive time not much sympathy would have been expected when the report came a month later from Moscow that John Reed, once the gayest of the Villagers, was dead of typhus. His place in the Russian revolution may have seemed to its makers that of a sort of Lafayette. He was certainly the tall young figure of hated Red revolution in America. Yet a certain respect attended the news of his death. Some echoed the wonder of Claire Sheridan, the British sculptress, who saw him three or four days before he was taken ill. She saw him as "a well-built, good-looking young man, who has given up everything at home to throw his heart and life into the work here."

"I understand the Russian spirit," she wrote, "but what strange force impels an apparently normal young man from the United States."

Even Russian peasants and soldiers were full of wonder, wrote Reed's wife Louise Bryant, who in strange coincidence was to become the wife of the first American ambassador sent to the Soviet Union in 1933. They came to his grave by the Kremlin wall, she said, took off their hats in the cold and spoke very reverently.

"What a good fellow he was!" said one. "He came all the way across the world for us."

Certainly he had gone all the way across the world from America. Yet, his portrait, painted by his friend of the Class of 1910, Robert C. Hallowell, was hung at Harvard. And another classmate, Edward Eyre Hunt, who served as economics expert under Harding and Hoover, later wrote of him in the records of the class, which contained so many bankers and businessmen, Brahmins and reactionaries, as well as poets and publicists. He spoke of Reed as "an outlaw" but: "The soul of this man whom we knew and loved goes marching on in the garments of a Soviet saint, and in his name in our own land little struggling clubs of painters and writers attack the foundations of the existing social order."

Reed's revolt had no relation to Stearns's revulsion. Explosion to Stearns and some of his associates in the examination of American civilization seemed less serious than the erosion of the spirit which, as they saw it, had produced the "discontented, sterile and stunted life" Bay Lodge had described for them in advance. And not all of them were repelled to the point that they sought lands of greater artistic promise or intellectual comfort elsewhere. Mencken was the most mocking of the stay-at-homes. He remained "on the dock, wrapped in the flag, when the Young Intellectuals set sail." In America he had at hand the targets which his delight in lambasting required: ". . . here more than anywhere else that I know of, the daily panorama of human existence . . . is so inordinately gross and preposterous . . . that only a man who was born with a petrified diaphragm can fail to laugh himself to sleep every night, and to awake every morning with all the eager, unflagging expectation of a Sunday-school superintendent touring the Paris peep-shows."

Mencken did go abroad briefly. In Germany he enjoyed the Pilsener he often praised. But that land, which in wartime he had seemed to some patriots to like too much, confused him. He wrote home: "Outwardly everything looks serene (the Communist outbreaks reported are chiefly no more than drunken fights) but every intelligent man looks for a catastrophe. If it comes, there will be a colossal massacre of the Jews." He hurried back to his country which at the moment seemed to him to promise more comedy than catastrophe.

Stearns was neither early nor eminent in exodus. The procession of literary expatriates had moved since the early days of the American republic. John Howard Payne had written "Home, Sweet Home" in Paris. Oddly, as it may have seemed, in the twenties one of the greatest expatriates, Henry James, had set the scene of an American novel of domination by the elders in Washington Square near Stearns's basement. When Stearns cut the umbilical cord of his nativity, Gertrude Stein had been abroad for twenty years, Ezra Pound for more than a decade. Ernest Hemingway, after war service and war wounds, was already a reporter in Paris. Before he came Alan Seeger had made his rendezvous with death at Belloy-en-Santerre in the Battle of the Marne. In 1920 T. S. Eliot had already become schoolmaster, bank clerk, and poet in England. Scott Fitzgerald who, with his Zelda, became almost the frenetic models of flight not only from America but reality, did not move to France until 1924.

The artistic spirit did not seem stifled behind Stearns in America, nor the free spirit either. The barriers of prohibition were not impenetrable. The tall, disheveled Heywood Broun and others were joining Mencken in the forays against censors and were pricking at the pompous, including even patriots. Will Rogers, a sort of grinning puritan among the lovely bare-legged girls of Florenz Ziegfeld's Follies, was swinging his lariat, chewing his gum and making cracks at politicians so shrewdly witty that not even the discomfitted could complain. More and more Americans were approving and sharing the satire of solemn pretension by Don Marquis in his column characters, archy the lower-case cockroach, and his friend mehitabel, queen of the alley cats, whose motto was "Wotthehell!" In Harlem and on the Chicago South Side, cold lonesome Negroes formed block-long queues to buy copies of the latest blues recordings of Bessie Smith and her older associate in throbbing song, Gertrude "Ma" Rainey. The time was coming when, looking back across the Atlantic, American culture would be considered in such a work as "Deux Grandes Chanteuses de Blues, Ma Rainey et Bessie Smith" by François Postif, in a French magazine called *Jazz Hot*.

Harold Stearns did not carry the blues, the creative spirit, or much of anything else to Paris. His fame as he sat at his favorite sidewalk cafe, the Select on Montparnasse, grew as borrower, deadbeat, race-track tout, and at best as horse-race writer for the Paris edition of the Chicago *Tribune*. Hemingway portrayed him in *The Sun Also Rises* as a befuddled character often sprawled drunk over his cafe table. Many Americans who came in bigger, faster, more luxurious liners to look at the Left Bank as other tourists had looked at Greenwich Village saw him there. Some, who had read the thick book he had begun in his basement, regarded the potatory expatriate and made the comment, "There lies civilization in the United States."

That was good for a laugh. Few of the laughing considered that at home as abroad, a nation like a man might go on a prolonged binge.

# VIII

## PRO PATRIA AND PRO PELF

At the end of the ride to the Capitol with the haggard Wilson, Warren Harding got out of the big car and vigorously walked up the steep steps, waving his shining silk hat. Without the least intent to humiliate, he left the retiring President, who had measured every step he would have to take to enter by a little-used, ground-level door. Wilson walked to an elevator with his walking stick tapping the old, cold stones. The new President mounted the flag-decorated platform. The air was clear and invigorating; so was the country's mood. Harding—handsome, vigorous—spoke to it.

In blithe spirit, to the great crowd before him, with disabled veterans in its front rows, he reiterated opposition to American involvement in Old World affairs. This was not aloofness; it was "patriotic adherence to the things which made us what we are." And at home he called for "an end of government's experiment in business, and for more efficient business in government administration." He basked in the applause.

Harding was among friends and the country was in friendly hands. "Joy at seeing the heels of the Democrats was keen," said Alice Longworth, who herself, as wife of one of its congressmen, was part of the Ohio restoration which only later was to be referred to as the Ohio gang. Now it represented sound government by solid men. Austerity and Presidential autocracy had gone off with its tapping cane. Warmth succeeded chill.

Portents remembered later seemed only amusing then. Fat, jolly former President Taft passed on to his newspaper friend, Gustav Karger, correspondent of the Cincinnati *Times-Star*, as only diverting gossip "a curious little story" about Mrs. Harding which he had heard from "one right close to the throne."

"The tale has it," he wrote less than two months after the inauguration, "that she is a believer in 'High Class' clairvoyance and that for a long time it has been her custom to consult one of the Washington elect of the esoteric circle. Some time before Harding was nominated this soothsayer, grasping at the obvious, informed Mrs. Harding that her husband would be nominated and elected President of the United States. That was very nice, and easy and comfortable to believe. But it is reported that she has consulted the prophet again, since the inauguration, and that the oracle this time indicated that the President would not see the end of his term."

Others heard similar reports. Ike Hoover, long-time chief usher at the White House, wrote that Mrs. Harding "believed in fortune-tellers and used to slip away with her spooky housekeeper to consult them." That was not so strange at the time. World war had been followed by rising interest in spiritualism. The following year, with one of its own editors writing sympathetically about it, the *Scientific American* offered a $2500 prize for any objective demonstration of psychic phenomena and named a distinguished committee to investigate the matter. Stories went around about J. P. Morgan taking tips from an occult adviser. The Ouija board, spelling out messages under the fingers of amateur mediums, had become a popular plaything in thousands of homes.

There was nothing occult about Taft when he wrote his gossip. He was, however, a corpulent symbol throwing light on the group of politicians accompanying Harding to Washington. Certainly Taft did not regard the election of a man from Ohio as an ominous portent. He had heard such talk around his own portly person when as a Cincinnati man he reached the White House. During his administration Henry Adams, watching Washington from his house across the square from the Presidential mansion, had spoken of Ohio politicians with disdain.

"The longer I live under this Cincinnati regime," the old historian said, "the cheaper and commoner and fatter I find it. John McLean is about its measure."

Not all regarded John R. McLean as a bad measure. He not only owned the *Enquirer* in Cincinnati but the Washington *Post* as well. Also in Washington he owned the gas company, the street railway system, and one of its leading banks. His dainty sister had married

Admiral George Dewey when he came home a hero from Manila. McLean himself married Emily Beale, of a distinguished family, and even Adams regarded her as "reigning empress" of Washington society. Her sister was the wife of George Bakhmeteff, the last ambassador of the czars. She rode in Washington with a Cossack on the box of her carriage.

Despite revolution in the world the Taftian ties which ran from Cincinnati to the czars were not greatly altered in 1920. Taft himself had chosen Harding as the man to nominate him for President at the Republican National Convention of 1912. Daugherty had been useful to Tafts in state and national politics. The anatomy of the relationships was perhaps best shown when a rich man seeking federal pardon hired Daugherty as the Ohio lawyer who might best reach Taft's ear. Shrewdly, Daugherty had not gone directly to the President. He sought executive mercy through the good offices of his and Taft's mutual friend McLean. Soon after Harding's inauguration he named the delighted Taft (on Daugherty's recommendation, so Daugherty said) to be Chief Justice of the United States. And elegant welcome to Washington society was provided at the huge downtown McLean mansion.

Old John R. was dead but his son Edward Beale, or Ned, as Harding and associates called him, had succeeded to much of his wealth. As a wedding present Ned had given his wife, Evalyn Walsh, whose father by her own account had "struck it rich," the Hope diamond. The great stone was no more noted for its value than for the legends of bad luck to its owner which attended it. It was glittering only at Harding's inauguration. In insistence on plain folksiness the Hardings had vetoed an elaborate inaugural ball. The McLeans provided a better one. Alice Longworth, who of course attended it, reported that visiting statesmen, new officials, Washington society "came in full force and revelled throughout the night."

The Hardings were not quite newcomers to such society. According to Nan Britton who, of course, only reported from shadowed trysts, Senator Harding had regarded such people as the McLeans with awe. He was much impressed by their "pile of money." Also when Nan was sensitive in pregnancy in 1919, he had mentioned with admiration that he had seen Evalyn McLean at a reception she had given a month before her child was born, her slim figure showing no sign to the roving Harding eye that she was soon to be delivered. The McLeans had been "very lovely" to Mrs. Harding.

She was grateful as a woman both determined and not quite sure of herself. There is the butler's eye report of Ike Hoover that Mrs. Harding was "wild and anxious, but so constituted that she could not be a social success."

Harding sometimes seemed socially overeager to Hoover. William Allen White, whose opinion of Harding ran in his writing like a fever chart from low to high to low, wrote at the last that the President was "Main Street in perfect flower." Sinclair Lewis, abetted by H. L. Mencken, had made it fashionable then to speak of Main Street with contempt. And undoubtedly Harding's Marion (population 27,891) differed in its most famous son from Emporia (population 11,273). But the Main Street picture in 1920 was the same as the "log cabin" image earlier required of Presidents.

Harding, according to White, had as newspaper publisher been making fifteen thousand to twenty thousand dollars when he came to the Senate in 1914—more when he entered the White House. Also, White said that as early as 1916 Harding had his clothes made by a Fifth Avenue tailor. Certainly the surfaces he showed were eminently acceptable. As daughter of a wealthy man, Mrs. Harding's remark that they were "just folks," which later was used by critics as an addition of snobbishness to scorn, was her shrewd way of saying that austerity and aloofness would no longer mark the occupants of the White House. She did sometimes seem pushy even to many of the President's friends. He was quoted as saying that "Mrs. Harding wants to be the drum major in every band that passes." Some other Presidents have so spoken in bewildered affection. The Hardings were welcomed as seeming what America wanted. Perhaps their tragedy came from being what America was.

Despite the use of the word "revelry" by Samuel Hopkins Adams as the title of his lurid novel about the Harding days, more than revelry at the McLean mansion or anywhere else faced the new administration. But social friends did help. The President's first friend, Daugherty, and Daugherty's first friend, Jess Smith, both from Washington Court House, Ohio, soon were in the *Social Register* and listed there as members of the exclusive Metropolitan Club. They rented a house on H Street from the McLean estate. Mrs. Daugherty, as a sufferer from serious arthritis, was often absent. The Hardings came to dine. But the house was largely used for business, Daugherty said, though of course, he and Jess, with no official status, had offices in the Justice Department. Later, sinister suggestions were made as to the sort of business conducted in the house. Daugherty denied them. Also he insisted that so far as he was concerned there never was the slightest basis for such "myths," as he called them, which grew later lushly about a much publicized "little green house on K Street." He said he never entered this house where Jess was supposed to reign.

That house, at 1625 K, occupied by two of Daugherty's acquaintances, one of them from Ohio, was strangely located as any place of misbehavior and malfeasance. It sat squarely in the precincts of pride and respectability. Mrs. George Dewey lived at 1601; Mrs. George Vanderbilt at 1612. The houses of Senators Brandegee and Knox were only a block away. The street was studded with the residences of those who regarded themselves and were regarded as eminent in American society. If the house was, as afterward reported, a sort of Ohio outpost as Washington brothel and bistro, pay-off house and private gambling den, no complaints from neighbors proved it.

There were few complaints from the nation as the Harding administration moved forward. Charles Evans Hughes was presiding in bearded dignity over the State Department and giving equal rebuffs to the League of Nations and the Soviet Union. Andrew Mellon as Secretary of the Treasury was more and more regarded as "the greatest Secretary of the Treasury since Alexander Hamilton," a sobriquet which Daugherty claimed to have originated while recommending him to Harding. With Harding's approval the Pittsburgh plutocrat pressed for repeal of wartime excess profits taxes and cuts in the surtaxes on large incomes.

To applauding capitalists it seemed almost impertinent when Senator Bob La Follette declared that "brazenly and impudently" rich Mellon had demonstrated that "wealth will not and cannot be made to bear its full share of taxation." As Secretary of Commerce, Herbert Hoover proved that he was not merely the open-handed humanitarian some of the Old Guard had feared. Facing hard times soon after taking office, he described the slump in business and agriculture as "the necessary reaction from the foolish post-war boom." Both Hoover and Mellon opposed the bill backed by Farm Bloc senators to create a Farmers' Export Finance Corporation. And Harding himself spoke of the unemployed as the "parasite percentage."

A special session of Congress, quickly called, began its hatchet work on liberal and idealistic ideas of government. As an emergency, tariffs were raised. Immigration was strictly limited with special attention to Orientals. By a simple resolution, skirting all settlements and aspirations, war with Germany was terminated two and a half years after the fighting had stopped. But the unpredictable, old irreconcilable Senator Borah finally succeeded in attaching to the naval appropriations bill a call for an international conference on the limitation of armaments. After hesitating, the Harding administration seized it as its own. Even the call to conference from withdrawn America was a world sensation. The burden of arms and the threat of war might be averted. And at the same time, more quietly, work was being done, as they insisted, by Attorney General Daugherty to save the country from the Communists and by Secretary of the Interior Albert B. Fall to protect it from the Japs.

Looking still like a lank prospector and rancher with blue eyes of direct, level gaze, Fall began to work first. On May 10, 1921, he and bald, obtuse Secretary of the Navy Edwin Denby had a brief conversation with the President. There had been preliminary talks before. Now as the first cigarette smoker in the Presidency, Harding lit one as he listened. The two Secretaries had agreed on the transfer from Navy to Interior of naval oil reserve lands set up under Roosevelt and Taft and guarded by the Wilson administration even during the emergency of World War I.

Fall did most of the talking. It was good administration to put all public lands under one department. Denby, as the decent, dull former congressman from Michigan whose appointment as Secretary of the Navy had been something of a surprise, agreed. True, some of his officers had warned him that the oil would be lost forever, if control passed to Interior. They had hardly said, "and to Fall" of the powerful new Cabinet officer from New Mexico. Some feared him. Many knew Fall's views on conservation. Some shared his ideas about free enterprise development of the public domain. Secretary of Agriculture Henry C. Wallace, with strong and opposite ideas, stubbornly and successfully resisted Fall's efforts to get the national forest lands from him. That was a bagatelle which Fall could dismiss.

Oil was something else. Not only was the Navy making the clean shift from coal to oil, but also motor vehicle registrations in the United States had increased from 468,500 in 1910 to 9,239,161 in 1920. Despite his pacifism, public demonstration of an amazing ignorance of history and energetic anti-Semitism, Henry Ford was becoming almost the national folk hero. His affectionately called "tin lizzies" crowded to service stations which had begun to meet demand as early as 1907. Behind mounting oil uses, search and grab for oil fields mounted, too. Eager gentlemen lined up at Fall's door anxious for possession of the naval reserves. Some undoubtedly had shown their eagerness earlier in political contributions, some to both parties, as it turned out. Certainly oil had been said to surround if it did not touch the "smoke-filled" room in Chicago. Fall, however, carefully avoided getting a legal opinion on the constitutionality of his oil dealings from Daugherty, who had received most Harding contributions.

The Secretary of the Interior was engaged, he insisted later, in a patriotic enterprise much of which, without any nonsense about competitive bidding and the like, had to be conducted quietly as a military secret. First he was going to save the Navy oil from being drained away by privately owned wells on the margins of the reserves. But more important than that, the tall New Mexican with the bold eyes was working to protect America from its new menacing enemy in the East—stirring, ambitious Japan. That nation was far from satisfied with its war gains of German economic rights and territories in the Pacific. It had renewed its alliance with Britain. And the British were soon to be fortified in their suspicion of American selfishness by bespectacled George Harvey. Rewarded as Harding's Ambassador to the Court of St. James, he had in "a spirit of combined supernationalism and subalcoholism" told a Pilgrims Dinner in London that America in World War I fought only for its own hide.

Britain, struggling to maintain its place as mistress of the seas, was already murmuring under the load of its war debts to the United States. It felt, as Chancellor Stanley Baldwin stated to Harding's debt negotiators, that every cent of the money borrowed in a common cause had been spent in America to the profit of farmers, workers, capitalists and the taxes on their profits had gone to the U. S. Treasury. So it had enriched the U. S. to help pay for the protection of the U. S. hide.

America's hide did not seem entirely invulnerable in 1921. Anti-Japanese expressions in California and elsewhere received bitter answer in Tokyo. And new American insistence on the open door in China seemed to Japan designed to slam the door on its ambitions.

Not only disturbed Americans but angry Japanese read a popular book, *The Rising Tide of Color Against White World-Supremacy*, by Lothrop Stoddard. It presented an almost panic picture of peril, brown, yellow and black. Its overwrought prose seemed no fantasy when at the same time the Japs were launching the powerful battleship, *Mutsu*, the most formidable fighting ship ever built up to that time. Its prow seemed almost pointed at the Philippines.

Some Navy men were more nervous about war than oil. Fall put them together. The Navy had long been seeking oil storage tanks from Congress. Now officers wanted immediate provision of oil storage depots at the Pearl Harbor base in Hawaii. Fall suggested that if the naval reserves were leased the Navy could take its royalties not in cash, which would go into the Treasury, but in oil certificates with which it could build depots.

On May 31, 1921, the transfer from Navy to Interior was signed by Harding. Later in defense or defamation or merely sprightly journalism, William Allen White published the report, "probably apocryphal," that the President signed "when he was drunk." However obtained, Fall's patriotic reasoning about the leases already seemed shaky. Ten days before the transfer, on May 21, Congress adopted Borah's call for a disarmament conference. Fall might have been more disturbed if he had known that the suspicions of Senator La Follette had been aroused by a seven-line story on an inside page of the Washington *Star* which seemed all the space the news of the transfer justified.

Generally the public paid no more attention to this item than to a social note that Secretary Fall was a guest of Harry Sinclair on his private car at the Kentucky Derby. More people then knew of Sinclair as owner of such a horse as Zev, which won the Derby two years later, than as tycoon of the Mammoth Oil Company. Few had even heard of another friend of Fall's, Edward L. Doheny. That rich oil magnate only got press attention when he made such statements as one early in 1919 proclaiming as many others were doing that America was endangered by "socialism and Bolshevism."

Though some have suggested that Harding once considered naming Fall as Secretary of State, he had, of course, no part in the Washington conference for the limitation of armaments when it convened in Washington in November. Dramatically, its sessions began on November 12, the day after America with pomp and ceremony, mourning and pride, entombed the Unknown Soldier on the third anniversary of the armistice. Then in the exciting advance of electronics Harding's voice had been heard by a hundred thousand people covering acres in the Arlington Cemetery and by thousands more in Madison Square Garden in New York and the Plaza in San Francisco. But unamplified he spoke to the world's heart and hopes when he addressed the distinguished statesmen convened in the hall of the Daughters of the American Revolution. He invoked the great symbolic funeral of the day before in urging an end to costly preparations for war.

"Whether it was spoken or not," he said, "a hundred millions of our people were summarizing the inexcusable causes, the incalculable cost, the unspeakable sacrifices, and the unutterable sorrows; and there was the ever-impelling question, How can humanity justify or God forgive? Human hate demands no such toll; ambition and greed must be denied it. If misunderstanding must take the blame, then let us banish it."

Historians have differed about the quality of the speech. Emporia's itinerant White wrote that it was "rather insignificant." Frederick Allen dismissed it as "profuse." Oddly Harding's most caustic chronicler, Samuel Hopkins Adams, stressed its simplicity and beauty. At that moment he saw Harding standing at "the shining apogee of his career."

The conference did not always work in the glow in which he left it. Solemnity was attended by much entertainment. The Ned McLeans showed the delegates the popular Gish sisters, Dorothy and Lillian, in *The Orphans of the Storm* after a dinner in their enormous house. Britain's Arthur Balfour on a less formal occasion complimented Alice Longworth on the "home brew" beer she served him. Still, under the guidance of Secretary Hughes, significant work was done. Intermission was ordered in battleship building. In the agreements reached Japan seemed curbed behind Britain and America in the 5–5–3 ratio of battleships permitted the leading powers. Agreements were reached in Pacific differences, giving America rights it wished but forbidding defense installations in the Philippines and on Guam. In effect the disturbing Anglo-Japanese alliance was terminated. In an enthusiastic country such an eminent journalist as Mark Sullivan could announce, "Naval competition was ended, a naval holiday was ordained, and offensive naval warfare was made impossible."

Mr. Fall did not share the elation. His sense of urgency was not eased. He was both bankrupt back in New Mexico, where he had not been able to pay his taxes for a decade, and swashbucklingly disturbed about increased peril in the Pacific. The ratio of naval power granted Japan would still leave the Japs more powerful in the Pacific unless the United States concentrated its sea strength there. The Philippines could sit open to Japanese imperialism. But the oil depots he proposed at Pearl Harbor would double the effectiveness of the American fleet in the wide sea between our coast and Japan.

Fall proceeded pro patria and pro pelf. While the disarmament conference was in session he was negotiating with his old friend of early prospecting days, Doheny, for the lease of the Elk Hills reserve in California. And on November 28, while the statesmen talked, all lease details having been worked out, Fall telephoned Doheny in New York that "he was prepared now to receive that loan." It was brought to him—$100,000 in cash—in what became famous later as "a little black bag." In April Doheny got his lease, which obligated him to build the oil tanks at Pearl Harbor. In the same month Sinclair secured the lease to Teapot Dome and, as only a first payment in appreciation, sent the Secretary $168,000 in Liberty bonds.

Secrecy about the leases in Washington did not quiet gossip about oil drilling in Wyoming and Fall's new opulence in New Mexico. In the month the leases were made Senator La Follette asked for an investigation. But action and interest were stilled by Harding's statement that Fall's leasing policy had been submitted to him "prior to the adoption thereof, and the policy decided upon and the subsequent acts have at all times had my entire approval." The nagging of insurgent senators was dismissed.

Even more patriotic in his announced purposes was Harry Daugherty, or so said Harry Daugherty. Already rumors had been growing about strange goings on in his department. Gossip said that William J. Burns, detective out of Columbus, Ohio, whom the Attorney General had made chief of the Federal Bureau of Investigation, was running a strange shop of which the innocent might be more afraid than the guilty. Burns had as his most notorious assistant Gaston B. Means, who had already been tried for murder and had served as a German espionage agent. Close to the Attorney General's office, genial Jess Smith seemed to have his fingers in some very strange pies. And in June, 1922, two months after Fall had made his leases, the Attorney General was accused of failing to prosecute war profiteers including Charles W. Morse, whose pardon for violating banking laws Daugherty had secured from Taft through John R. McLean.

At the time, as Daugherty related later, he was engaged in saving America from revolution in the guise of strikes which he said Lenin's collaborator, Grigori Evseevich Zinoviev, had in April ordered in America. Strikes had attended the hard times that summer. Miners in Illinois, where men were laid off and wages cut, had blazed in resentment which culminated in the murder of twenty strikebreakers in the "massacre" in June, 1922, at Herrin. Local sentiment was such that after several trials the cases were dropped. Red agents had bored into the organizations of miners, said Daugherty. Reds inside the Shopmen's Union called the railroad strike, he wrote. The strikes of more than a million men, he declared, "threatened the foundations of the Republic." Harding was condemned for weakness in crisis. Mrs. Harding, the Attorney General said, was driven to illness by the criticism.

He acted though he—and Harding, so he said—believed his life was in danger. In Chicago before James H. Wilkerson, a friendly judge whom he had recommended and Harding had named, he secured an injunction which forbade interference by the strikers in any way with strikebreakers and outlawed even peaceful picketing or inciting others to picket. Though in the Cabinet Hughes, Hoover, even Fall, denounced the sweeping antilabor injunction, the strike was promptly broken. That was the beginning, Daugherty declared, of a Red conspiracy in the country and in the Senate to get rid of him. Senator Borah was against him, he charged, because he had opposed the Idaho statesman's proposal for recognition of Soviet Russia. Also, he boldly declared that Senator Burton K. Wheeler, of Montana, later active in investigations, was "the Communist leader in the Senate, picked for attack."

Harding stood by his old friend. The President was clearly on the business side against labor. His administration began the decade in which, under the "American Plan" for open shops, union strength was to be reduced from 4,000,000 to 2,700,000 members. On September 21, 1922, he signed the Fordney-McCumber Tariff Act, setting the highest rates in American history. Protected by this act the aluminum interests of Mellon, who was already getting more in tax cuts than Fall got from oil loot, pushed up prices to ensure, so

Democrats said, an annual profit of $10,000,000 on an $18,000,000 investment. Perhaps the President deserved the praise of J. P. Morgan for his "extremely courageous action" in vetoing the soldiers' bonus. The farmer, Harding wrote in the fall of 1922, "throve mightily at the height of war inflation, and he invested as a rule, no less highly, and generally with the average farmer's usual lack of good judgment." In the war prices of farm land had gone up more even than farm products prices. Much land had been bought and mortgaged at values the land could not support as war prices declined.

Still, behind the applause of the business community not all in the summer of 1922 was idyllic in Harding's house or among the members of his "poker Cabinet" who trooped to it. There were reports of quarrels between the President and his wife. Though unsympathetic Nan Britton wrote that Florence Harding seemed always ailing, her illness that summer was serious. Yet, also according to Nan, the President's concern about his wife was not so serious that he did not amorously receive her as younger woman in the White House itself that summer. The monumental liar Means wrote that as FBI man he served as Mrs. Harding's secret agent in affairs involving her husband, including that with Nan. A better witness, Ike Hoover, suggested that Mrs. Harding was a suspicious, worried woman as well as a sick one. She was, he wrote, the first President's wife to whom a Secret Service agent was assigned "and he acted as messenger, special watchman, general handy man, and at times almost as a lady's maid." Rumors spread almost as widely as recollections were broadcast later.

No rumors, wrote Alice Longworth years afterward, could exceed the reality. One evening while a big White House reception was in progress, she said, she was taken upstairs to Harding's study, which was filled with cronies: "the air heavy with tobacco smoke, trays with bottles containing every imaginable brand of whiskey stood about, cards and poker chips ready at hand—a general atmosphere of waistcoat unbuttoned, feet on the desk and the spittoon alongside." Alice on this occasion apparently did not put this scene beside another recollection of hers that even during her father's administration she had learned poker from old Speaker Joe Cannon who also required the cuspidor by the card table.

Still the public image of the White House seemed erect and unstained as 1922 advanced. If rumors could be disregarded, however, the election returns could not be. Republican strength in the House dropped from 296 to 227, a loss of seventy seats; in the Senate from 60 to 53. Not even the slim Republican majorities could be depended upon. In the Senate, Republican Progressives—La Follette, Borah, Johnson, Brookhart, Norris, Howell, Norbeck, Capper, Ladd, Frazier and Shipstead—held the balance of power. They met with men of similar sympathies in the House to shape a program of liberal legislation all aimed at driving "special privilege out of control of government." Regular Republican politicians and editors described them as demagogues "organizing for a raid on wealth." Harding could not forget an exchange with La Follette as he was leaving the Senate to become President.

"Now, Bob, be good."

"I'll be busy," said the Wisconsin Progressive, "making you be good."

Obviously the election was a signal that even gossip could not be disregarded. Harding could not fail to listen when his personal physician, Dr. Charles E. Sawyer, whom he had brought from Marion and made a brigadier general, came to him with disturbing tales about the newly organized Veterans Bureau presided over by the President's dashing friend, Charles R. Forbes. Sawyer had been given duties in the Veterans Bureau, too. Now he reported amazing transactions in the purchase of medical supplies at high prices and their quick sale as surplus at low ones; in the selection of sites for hospitals; in deals by which speculators got sheets which sick veterans needed. Unneeded supplies were bought in vast quantities. Harding could not have known then that Forbes, a charming companion and a light of Washington society, had at one time been a deserter from the Army. That detail was hidden and forgotten when Harding first met him as a debonair veteran of World War I in which he had risen to the rank of colonel. Daugherty, who did not like him, said that he had the "enthusiastic backing of the American Legion" when he was appointed to the top Veterans' post. In the Veterans Bureau Harding had, in addition to Sawyer, another trustworthy man, Charles F. Cramer, who, on coming to Washington, purchased the house in which Harding had lived while senator.

The President listened reluctantly to Sawyer's tales of graft by Forbes. He felt, it was said, that they represented the doctor's personal dislike of the companionable Forbes. Also Sawyer, who at sixty-one had become "the suddenest brigadier general in all history," was more Mrs. Harding's favorite than the President's. She believed he had saved her life. The medical general was small and apparently vain but his abilities and reputation were by no means as limited as some suggested. *Who's Who in America* had given him a place in its pages and he had become a Fellow of the American College of Surgeons before Harding put him in the White House.

His reports were troublesome. So on November 22, 1922, Harding ordered a stop in all sales of supplies at a big depot near Washington. Forbes hurried with assurances to the White House. In December the President declared the charges to be an "abominable libel" and lifted the embargo. The graft went on. It was not until the late winter next year, according to a story heard by Samuel Hopkins Adams and Will Irwin, that an unexpected visitor came into a White House room to find a livid Harding choking the handsome Colonel.

"You yellow rat!" he was crying. "You double-crossing bastard. If you ever—"

Certainly the blithe spirit seemed subdued as the new year began. Mrs. Harding's ill health continued. When that month Nan was slipped in to see the President in the White House offices he had such a cold that she spoke her doubts that Dr. Sawyer was properly treating him for it. It was on this occasion, she wrote, that the President mentioned that his wife was older than he "and very probably will pass on before I do." In that event, he assured her, he would adopt their child "and make her a real Harding." Despite his cold he seemed very charming dressed in knickers, then popular with such devoted golfers as himself.

"That was the last time," she wrote, "I ever saw Warren Harding, my sweetheart."

Not long after, in generosity or precaution he sent her money and his approval for her sailing to Europe on a tour which would include six weeks of university study at Dijon, France. She was to sail on June 21, 1923, a day after Harding was planning to begin a transcontinental speaking tour.

Nan's whole trip was to cost only $525 including passage on the *Roussillon* of the French Line which was then carrying so many restless Americans to Europe. Her destination in Dijon brought her, apparently without her noticing it, to the city where American literary expatriates had secured the printing of *Ulysses* by James Joyce after serialization of that work in the *Little Review* in America had brought that avant-garde publication into conflict with the postal and other authorities on the grounds of obscenity.

Such conflicts with puritanism seemed far from Harding's concerns then. His interest in printing related exclusively to such matters as the publication of his Marion *Star*. For talk about that he saw William Allen White, who had advanced from the idea that Harding's nomination would be a disgrace to the party to the feeling that as head of a "sweetly progressive" administration he might become "one of our great Presidents." At this time, early in 1923, the Emporia man was certainly far from his later conclusion that Harding was a "he-harlot." Happy to be welcomed in the White House, he listened to the President talk as a friendly, garrulous fellow publisher. Much later the Emporia editor quoted the Marion publisher as a man loud in complaint.

"My God, this is a hell of a job! I have no trouble with my enemies. I can take care of my enemies all right. But my damn friends, my God-damned friends, White, they're the ones that keep me walking the floors nights."

Even White reported this as "serio-comic" talk. Also he reported in his memoirs that as he left the President's office that day he met Secretary Fall, who seemed to him "a cheap, obvious faker" about whom no one should be fooled. Some were. When Fall resigned to retire to his bigger, richer ranch on March 4, 1923, Herbert Hoover wrote him that in his recollection the Interior Department had never had "so constructive and legal a leadership as you gave it."

"I trust the time will come," Hoover said, "when your private affairs will enable you to return to public life, as there are few men who are able to stand its stings and ire, and they have got to stay with it."

The stings and ires were already evident. Two days before Fall retired a Senate investigation of the Veterans Bureau had been ordered. Shock was added when twelve days later, Cramer, counsel of the bureau and apparently an honest man, killed himself in the house in which the Hardings had been so happy while he served in the Senate.

One of Burns's FBI men, as came to be almost routine, was quickly on the scene. Samuel Hopkins Adams reported "the story" that he found there letters addressed to the President which Harding refused to receive. As rumors spread then, legends multiplied later. At the time of the investigations which ultimately sent Forbes to prison, Will Irwin estimated that graft out of veterans' funds cost the nation $200,000,000; in 1965 Andrew Sinclair, in a biography of Harding, put the loot at $2,000,000,000.

Other gossip was growing. Malodorous stories came from the office of the Alien Property Custodian, Thomas W. Miller, a Yale graduate and member of the best clubs, who later also went to jail for accepting money to influence an official action. Harding wrote to Daugherty in this connection of "commercial and financial vultures." But the juiciest stories and most amazing suspicions were directed at Daugherty's friend, Jess Smith, and those he joined for reported frolic and finagling at "the little green house on K Street." Reports surrounded him of illegal liquor withdrawals, protection to bootleggers, pay-offs by tax chiselers, sale of jobs, and suppression of cases against corporations and individuals. He was said to be blatant about his activities, going around crying, "My God, how the money rolls in!"

That certainly was not quite evidence that it was rolling into Jess's pockets. Others were singing this old ditty. It had been revived to be sung along with such songs of the times as "Makin' Whoopee" which Americans were chanting that year in the new prohibition-inspired night "clubs," apparently not yet generally called speakeasies. One verse ran:

> *My father makes book on the corner,*
> *My mother makes synthetic gin,*
> *My sister makes love for a dollar,*
> *My God! How the money rolls in!*

While many were looking askance at a generation which would sing such a song, Jess could have been as innocent as many others who sang it. Even Daugherty at last reluctantly admitted he was not so innocent. But he was no obvious rascal. In the pictures most often preserved of him in a sort of rogue's gallery of remembrance, he appears a flabby, flashy, wide-jowled, disagreeable-looking fellow. A more charitable and possibly more accurate photograph shows him as a handsome, happy man sharing the kind of eminent company he loved at a baseball game with the President. Evidently he was, as Daugherty wrote in a sad recounting of his story, a "social success" in Washington. He counted a wide variety of friends, including not only politicians and gay companions at the Metropolitan Club but even Wayne B. Wheeler (another Ohio man), general counsel of the Anti-Saloon League. One of his admirers, the journalist, Mark Sullivan, liked Jess in these days. But the amiable Ohio man also had some friends of whom Daugherty did not approve. One was the Attorney General's own FBI employee, Gaston B. Means. Daugherty "couldn't endure" Means, he said, and "never saw him but twice." J. Edgar Hoover, then assistant director of the FBI, who became the director in 1924, regarded Means with a sort of adverse admiration as "the greatest faker of all times."

Jess loved the bright lights, prominence, display. Evidently he enjoyed the supposed dazzling dissipation so enthusiastically described later as taking place at the "little green house." Whatever the pace, he could not stand it. In May, 1922, he went back to Ohio broken in health and was operated on for appendicitis complicated by diabetes. He came back to Washington, but not for long. In the spring of 1923 Harding abruptly told Daugherty to send him back to Ohio.

"I am informed," the Attorney General reported the President as saying, "that he is running with a gay crowd, attending all sorts of parties. And you should know too that he is using the Attorney General's car until all hours at night."

The decree of exile also dropped Jess from a place in the company on a trip to Alaska already being planned by the President. Jess departed for unexciting Washington Court House. But Daugherty, who had been ill, agreed to let him return to see a few friends and wind up his business. One piece of business was to make his will, leaving his estate to five persons including Daugherty and his brother. They had moved then to the new, fashionable Wardman Park Hotel. Daugherty did not spend the night of May 29 at the apartment but at the White House. He sent one of his assistants to stay with Jess, who never liked to be alone, particularly after dark. During the night Jess industriously destroyed all Daugherty's house accounts and personal correspondence. Then in the early morning his companion in the apartment heard a shot. Jess, who hated pistols, had sent a bullet through his right temple. Burns, head of the FBI, who lived in the same hotel, was called. He notified authorities and sent word to the White House. The President, Daugherty said, was "shocked." He had had a date to play golf with Jess and Ned McLean this day.

Though gossip galloped from the death scene, apparently the public was not aroused. Newspapers emphasized the ill health which all agreed had led Jess to suicide. Only later did thunderous, maned

Senator Tom Heflin of Alabama, "the blatherskite of the Senate," as Daugherty called him, rise to declare that Jess was murdered and to hint that the Attorney General was party to the crime.

Softer voices followed Jess to his grave in the cemetery at Washington Court House where some said he had secretly buried millions in loot. Will Hays, who had resigned as Postmaster General to watch over the morals of the movies, wired Daugherty, "Your grief is mine." Mark Sullivan wondered why Jess of all men should have taken his life: "He was such a wholesome, optimistic fellow. . . . It is a queer world and the tragedy of it is all mixed up with the pleasures of it."

Certainly Jess as crushed clown or flashy crook seemed to deserve some such revealing epitaph as those Edgar Lee Masters was writing then on the imaginary tombstones of the frustrated and frolicsome dead in his *Spoon River Anthology*. Spoon River and Washington Court House were similar little Middle Western towns. And they were as much America as Main Street or Pennsylvania Avenue. Jess was a character common to both.

# IX

## PRODIGAL SON

THREE weeks after they put Jess Smith in his grave, Harding left on his continental speaking tour, which he called a "voyage of understanding." He had achievement on which to base prestige as he set out. After much negotiation his administration had secured British agreement to repay American war loans. This was not only a financial but a moral triumph: "a recommitment of the English speaking world to the validity of contract." As he talked of this and other matters, there seemed a new strength and purpose in his manner. Also he spoke in new appeal to the people. Since Daugherty, in the March in which Fall departed and Cramer killed himself, had announced that the President would seek re-election, the trip became inevitably one of Presidential politics as well as Presidential understanding. Harding, who, as he said of his speaking, loved to "bloviate," had looked forward to it. Certainly he appeared to have no premonition of trouble in connection with it.

He did appear to be getting his house in order. As he prepared for his trip he sold the Marion *Star* for $550,000, a price some thought was a good deal more than it was worth. He asked Daugherty to draw his will. Neither in it nor in the discussion about it, the Attorney General said, did he mention Nan Britton or her child by him. He had, she wrote, sent her money and she found a tender letter from him awaiting her on shipboard when she sailed on the *Roussillon* as he set out for the West.

Amazingly—considering the schedule arranged—some, including Nan, thought it was to be a trip of rest, relaxation and escape from worries. Harding needed it. He was in debt on a brokerage account. He looked "mortally tired" to some who saw him depart. He took few cronies with him. The "poker Cabinet" was not on board as the train rolled out of the station on June 20. Refreshments were absent. He had shortly before given newsmen an almost official announcement that he would set an official example in a dry land by drinking no more. His chief associates on the trip which would take him to Alaska were the three members of his Cabinet concerned with the territory's problems: Secretary of Agriculture Wallace, Secretary of Commerce Hoover, and the new Secretary of the Interior, Hubert Work, a Colorado physician whose specialty had been mental and nervous diseases. All were happy that Mrs. Harding was well enough to make the trip. Others included Dr. Sawyer; young Dr. Joel T. Boone, of the Navy; and inconspicuously and inconsequentially rich, dissipated Ned McLean.

Without any pressure of a great cause behind him, Harding, in his private car, *Superb*, moved westward almost along the route Wilson had followed in the League fight four years before. Some afterward made the trip seem less a voyage than a flight. Herbert Hoover in his memoirs related that the President took him aside and asked him an ominous question.

"If you knew of a great scandal in our administration, would you for the good of the country and the party expose it publicly or would you bury it?"

But when Hoover advised publicity and began to ask questions, Harding, he wrote, "abruptly dried up and never raised the question again." Emporia editor White, riding as a welcome passenger on a brief part of this trip, remembered Harding moaning again about his "friends." And White recalled, too, that at about the same time Harding had been closeted for an hour at the Muehlebach Hotel in Kansas City with the wife of Secretary Fall who was then in Russia seeking Soviet oil concessions for Harry Sinclair and other oil men. Harding emerged from the conference "obviously frustrated, worried and excited." Samuel Hopkins Adams added the touch that Mrs. Falls was "an elderly woman, veiled and furtive."

There was nothing veiled, however, about the country stretching far and wide about Kansas City, its troubles, and the wish of its people for Presidential reassurances. Missouri's misfortunes were typical of those in all states in the middle American country. Harding's Secretary of Agriculture Wallace said that from 1920 to 1923, 10 per cent of the farmers of Missouri lost their farms or held them only through the leniency of creditors. Symbolic was the experience of a twenty-nine-year-old man there at the time of Harding's visit, one Harry S. Truman, recently elected county judge.

He had gone into the haberdashery business in 1919 when wheat was selling at $2.15 a bushel; he had gone out of it busted the September before Harding came when wheat had fallen to 88 cents. In his troubles Truman had assigned a 160-acre farm which in mid-1921 he had acquired with $5000 plus the assumption of a mortgage of $8800 on it. Perhaps he should not have been surprised at trouble. This same $13,800 farm had been sold, mortgage free, in July, 1909, for $2250. In Truman's shop, shirts, which in the war boom had become a symbol of overpaid labor and opulent farmers, were marked down for sale below the prices he and his partner had paid for them. Many veterans like himself had lost the exuberance which had made Kansas City even in 1921 the founding place of muscular mischief by still young veterans at the national conventions of the American Legion.

There was exuberant welcome for Harding. Crowds greeted him everywhere as he crossed the continent. He got to the people. To the people not even economic troubles seemed so important as Harding's impression as a small-town man himself who represented the farmers and townsmen at a time when many of them felt that their status was threatened by new urban powers in polyglot and poly-faith cities later to be embodied in such a figure as slum-born, wet, Catholic Alfred E. Smith of New York. Old-stock Americans saw in the man from Marion a replica of themselves. He was a sort of son of the old middle border which, as described in ethical romanticism by Hamlin Garland, was in these days receiving almost as much nostalgic attention as the sterile stereotype Sinclair Lewis had made of frustration, hypocrisy and smugness on Main Street. Such nostalgia could be hard as well as homesick. Harding moved westward after the Ku Klux Klan had spread there. That hooded organization seemed good, not evil, to many disturbed and defensive small-town folk. It was active in Kansas before the President passed through. The following year editor White was to run for governor "to free Kansas from the disgrace of the Ku Klux Klan"—and to run a poor third. The supposedly Southern organization had sprawled continentally from beginnings in Atlanta in 1915, up from 100,000 members in 1921 to 5,000,000 in 1924.

Joiner that he was (Elk and Shriner and others), Harding was no Kluxer. His "affidavit face," as Jim Watson described it, seemed never masked. Certainly the press reported nothing concealed or portentous about his journey. There was a little flurry among those who, like Taft, had heard of Mrs. Harding and the fortunetellers, when he told friends on the trip that he felt a "conscious spiritual influence." He had seen no Madame X or any other figure of such ghostly gossip. It was only in the irresponsible riot of supposed rememberance later that *Liberty Magazine* published a piece about one Madame Marcia called "When an Astrologer Ruled the White House."

The President seemed earthy and in the prime of his powers. Fourteen major speeches were delivered by him, many minor talks. At St. Louis to a gathering of Rotarians, whose booster spirit had been satirized by Sinclair Lewis in *Babbitt*, he had spoken for his plan for entry into the World Court hedged to meet the protests of his old irreconcilable, anti-League opponents. At Hutchinson, Kansas, in a blazing sun he told farmers better days were coming and proved his rural sympathies by driving a binder and shocking wheat. At Denver, with no show of chagrin about Veterans Bureau scandals behind him, he told veterans at the Army hospital that he would "keep everlastingly at it" to assure full justice to their wounded and needy comrades. He went further: in any other war, if he had anything to do with it, the government would draft money as well as men. Also at Denver, in a veiled reference to such Democrats as those in New York who, under Governor Al Smith, had recently repealed the state dry enforcement law, he stood squarely politically, and evidently personally, for prohibition.

In Utah, home of his "smoke-filled room" supporter Senator and Mormon Apostle Reed Smoot, he advised his listeners to "keep your eye everlastingly upon those who administer your government units for you." That word "everlastingly" cropped up repeatedly in his "bloviate" vocabulary. He went sightseeing along the way. He proposed to cut costs of living and taxes.

At Helena, Montana, happy reception was not marred by any anticipation that the state's two senators, Thomas J. Walsh and Wheeler, would soon be leaders in energetically uncovering scandals which only a few suspected in 1923. Instead, in that capital city long plagued by labor unrest and fears of the I.W.W., he gave assurances that his administration was no enemy of labor. One of his critics had said earlier that he would open his pocketbook to a destitute man, then vote for legislation to exploit the poor. Perhaps that was first shown when he pardoned the Socialist leader Eugene Debs, whose doubtful crime of "sedition" in wartime Wilson had declined to forgive. And Harding had moved the pardon forward so that Debs might spend Christmas with his family. Yet he had approved Daugherty's sweeping strike injunction. He was a smiling contradiction in feeling and philosophy, difficult for labor to approve, hard to hate. When he spoke in Helena, as one of his real achievements he had put uncharacteristic and unexpected pressure on his old friend Judge Gary and his associates to end the twelve-hour day in the steel mills. He was nobody's enemy, except perhaps his own.

His train rolled on to Seattle, close to the northwest forests where protectors and exploiters, lumber barons and lumberjacks had long met in argument and anger. He talked about conservation. What he said would have interested, perhaps reassured, his recently retired Secretary of the Interior, Albert Fall. The President argued against locking up the public domain "as a treasure house of potential wealth" on the grounds that such action would prevent it from being ready for use when needed. As, for instance, though he did not mention it, in oil depots at Pearl Harbor.

Bands played as he sailed from Tacoma to Alaska. Suspicions had preceded him there as to the disinterestedness of his administration in the development of the territory. The President himself seemed uncertain as to policy with regard to it. He had announced that upon his return from Alaska he would decide whether "to call on Congress for further appropriations to open up the territory or to throw open the resources of the country to private development." Conservationists were not hopeful as to which decision he would make. In February, 1922, his Secretary Fall, while explaining that the administration did not favor the government operation of the Alaska Railroad, or railroads anywhere else, seemed to welcome all to riches he was secretly grabbing for himself.

"Help us liberalize the laws and open up Alaska that the boys back from the War can do what their forefathers did in California in 1849," Fall said. "Oil has been flowing into the Arctic Ocean at Camp Fleming for years, perhaps centuries. What is believed to be one of the greatest oil fields in the world is in the Arctic near the Aleutian Islands."

Though this sounded like an invitation to a big barbecue, Fall was apparently diverting attention to a dry hole. Twenty years later Alaska was still securing most of its oil by imports from the states. Harding with his party looked into the territory's resources. They enjoyed its scenery. The President drove a golden spike to mark the completion of the government-built Alaska Railroad. But in Alaska, also, post-mortem diagnosticians of his decline set tragedy on its way. There he received, it was said, a long message in code brought by airplane. Neither the contents nor the sender was revealed. But after reading it, Samuel Hopkins Adams reported, "he suffered something like a collapse." The Associated Press correspondent did not notice it. There is clearer and more credible evidence of physical disturbance among members of the whole company on the way back.

"During our last day at sea," said Secretary of the Interior Work, himself a physician, at the time, "many of us were attacked by a temporary indisposition, not seasickness, but due to an item of food put up in a can. I will not say what the item of food was. The indisposition was temporary."

Evidently it was not with Harding, though when Work spoke none thought he was seriously ill. He returned to one of "the busiest days of his trip," as the Associated Press described it. At Seattle, the fleet which he had limited passed in review before him. Then he rode in an auto parade, attended a boys' picnic, and stood two hours bareheaded in the July sun receiving an overwhelming welcome. He made three separate speeches to crowds totaling more than a hundred thousand people. To them, though little noticed at the time, he apparently showed a greater change in his mind than in his health.

Significantly, as an Alaskan historian wrote, "he surprised his associates and the public by announcing a policy of thoroughgoing conservation." Fall's proposal to discontinue government operation of the Alaskan Railroad was postponed. And for those who needed it there was rebuke in the President's words. We must, he declared, "regard life in lovely, wonderful Alaska as an end and not a means." It was time to reject the policy of "looting Alaska as the possibility of profit arises." He was, he announced, opposed to "turning Alaska over to the exploiters."

That could have been a determination for America, too. But next day the first hint of serious illness came in the newspapers. Plans were changed to give the President two whole days of rest before resuming his speaking tour. He had then made eighty-five public speeches; as

Daugherty wrote later, "an average of more than two a day through the hottest days of one of the hottest summers on record."

Only afterward was Harding pictured as a man driven, sleeping little, keeping his companions day and night in almost compulsive, endless games of bridge. Herbert Hoover, who intermittently held a hand in such games, served this picture of distress when he recalled that those on the trip "came to know that here was a man whose soul was being seared by a great disillusionment. We saw him weakened not only from physical exhaustion but from great mental anxiety." But Dr. Sawyer, as the train moved from Seattle, only reported that the President had had a slight attack of ptomaine poison, a diagnosis afterward disdained in some literary post mortems despite Work's contemporary corroboration of the illness of many on the ship who had eaten something from a can. Fortunately, Dr. Sawyer added, the "bowel condition" was improved.

Then on Sunday, July 29, word came that his entire California program had been canceled, indicating, the Associated Press man on the train wrote, "that Mr. Harding's condition was worse than had been generally believed." Alarm rose when it was announced next day from his headquarters in the Palace Hotel in San Francisco that he was "gravely ill with broncho-pneumonia." He "battled for his life," headlines said. Dr. Sawyer did not delay in calling in other physicians. In addition to young Dr. Boone, Dr. Work was in attendance. Also called into consultation were Dr. Ray Lyman Wilbur, later president of the American Medical Association and Secretary of the Interior under Hoover, and significantly, as the press reported at the time, Dr. Charles M. Cooper, a heart specialist. Full reports about his condition were released. Mrs. Harding, who had been expected to be the invalid, joined the nurses. Sick as he was, Harding was cheerful. A joke reported from his sickroom seemed a sort of testimony in defense later.

"Mr. President, we would like to make an X ray of your chest."

"Come on," he said, "for I have nothing to conceal."

Tuesday he was better. The crisis was over, Sawyer told reporters. He was "entirely out of danger." And on Wednesday the doctor only spoke of a "tedious" convalescence. Mrs. Harding urged Daugherty, who had come to join them in San Francisco, to see the President. He said he did not wish to disturb him, "everything is all right at Washington." Fall, who might have disturbed him also, was in New York where on his return from Russia he told newspapermen that the situation there was not as bad as it was painted. He looked forward to the recognition which Daugherty had vigorously opposed.

Such problems were excluded from the President's sickroom. A new air of hopefulness permeated it. Tirelessly Mrs. Harding attended him. On Thursday evening she was reading to him a *Saturday Evening Post* article praising him as a "calm man" in the White House, by Samuel Blythe, who had been writing of Presidents since McKinley's time. It was good, Harding said, read on. Then without warning at 7:35 P.M., August 2, he slumped and died, "instantaneously and without warning," as the five doctors reported.

Nan Britton insisted that there was warning in a dream to her in far-off Dijon. She had read the first disturbing news of the President's illness, then the reassuring dispatches. But on the night of August 2, at a time when her clock told her it would be seven o'clock in San Francisco, she had a dream:

She was conscious of "something above me, to the left. It seemed to be floating through the air. It was shrouded about with white clouds which seemed not to hide it from view but rather to protect it in its slow mount upward." It was "a coffin draped with and trailing about it, American flags, and heaped with red, red roses! A coffin, ascending on my left, rising so slowly that it seemed suspended in mid-air, yet ever moving upward and away from me. How blood-red were the roses! And the crimson stripes of the trailing flags stained the clouds! The whole mounting majestically, lifted by an invisible force, upward, onward, protectingly shrouded by white, white clouds!

"So he had come to me! He had come in this way that I might be the first to know he was leaving this earth!"

Yet by her own account, not even Nan then believed the dream. Next morning, looking for the gayest she could find, she bought herself a cerise dress in which to go to a dance for foreign students. The day was half over when another student casually told her the news: Harding was dead. She walked half blindly down the street. "But," she wrote, "strangely enough, I did not cry. I could not cry." She was as dry-eyed as reporters in San Francisco were reporting that Mrs. Harding was.

Unconcerned with the supernatural, correspondents quickly dispatched the facts. Two nurses were in the room with Mrs. Harding when the stroke of "apoplexy" occurred. Doctors were nearby. Reporters as close as they could get to the room noted the quick panic in the corridors. All described Florence Harding as "the bravest member of the group" about the President. She was strong, contained. Only long afterward was the story made that in the room with two nurses in attendance and with sharp-eyed, honest doctors nearby, Harding's death was suicide or murder by his wife. And only afterward, when scandals were not whispered but broadcast from Senate hearing rooms, did the event seem, as Adams called it, "the timely death of President Harding."

Yet apparently sinister suggestions about the President's death came swiftly. Alice Longworth, though she dismissed them, wrote that she heard "the rumors about the manner of his death" when she returned from a trip to Europe soon afterward. Certainly there were whisperings long before the great liar Gaston Means put them into print in 1930. Mrs. Harding had poisoned the President, Means strongly suggested in *The Strange Death of President Harding*, because of his affair with Nan Britton. That young woman had published her book, *The President's Daughter*, in 1927 despite the efforts of John S. Sumner of the New York Society for the Suppression of Vice to prevent it. Such an authority as Allan Nevins accepted her claim of parentage as authentic. Andrew Sinclair, in a biography of Harding written thirty years after his death, wrote that "Miss Britton proved to all except the most charitable that she was the mother of Harding's daughter." Yet a federal court jury in Ohio refused to accept her story as basis for claim on the Harding estate.

Certainly some historians gave credence to the Means story on the basis of the Britton claims. Frederick Lewis Allen in his *Only Yesterday* wrote that "both the suicide theory and the Means story are very plausible." Oswald Garrison Villard in *Fighting Years* not only leaned "to the belief that there was foul play in his death" but intimated that a year later Mrs. Harding may have killed Dr. Sawyer in the same way. This insinuated that the doctor was dispatched because he knew too much, one rumor being that Mrs. Harding and Sawyer had conspired to "save the unsuspecting victim from his own black future." The Means book was later repudiated by his collaborator. She happened to be the sister of Thomas Dixon who helped Daugherty write his *The Inside Story of the Harding Tragedy*. Even such a historian as James Truslow Adams was puzzled. In *The March of Democracy* this more objective Adams wrote that "without accepting the most sensational stories of his death, it must be admitted that the mystery of it has never been cleared up."

Actually there was no mystery about Harding's death. No more eminent physicians ever signed a death certificate. Even suspicions are based only upon two books, both of which are suspect. Mrs. Harding did not permit a post mortem. No need for one seemed indicated. During the year she lived after he died, she did unsuccessfully undertake the destruction of her husband's personal letters. But if Nan Britton dutifully destroyed her love missives from him, Mrs. Carrie Phillips, wife of a Marion merchant, did not. They came to light years later.

Perversely the shadow over the Harding story was most darkened by Daugherty, who undertook to make himself the guardian of his memory. Three years after Harding's death he was called upon to testify before a New York grand jury investigating charges about his malfeasance in office. Then he invoked his close relationships with the President and Mrs. Harding as preamble to the statement:

"I refuse to testify and answer questions put to me because:

"The answer I might give or make and the testimony I might give might tend to incriminate me."

And by clear suggestion might tend to incriminate the friends he presumed to protect.

Majesty and grief, not mystery and suspicion, attended the last journey of Warren Harding to Washington and then back to little Marion for burial. The casket was placed at window level so that all could see it as the funeral car passed. Thousands waited as the train moved by them on its way over the mountains, the desert, the plains, through cities and green countrysides. Children tossed flowers before the locomotive. People stood without seeking shelter when rains fell upon them and the mourning train. A great concourse waited at the station in Washington and lined the streets as his catafalque moved by. At the services at the White House the heat was so intense that several marines standing in the guard of honor fainted and fell. About them in the opened grounds hundreds perspired and wept.

Moist-eyed officials and their wives came out to join the procession which would move his body back to Marion—to Ohio and American Main Street. Mrs. Harding, however, asked that no Senate delegation accompany the remains to the grave. Jim Watson, who remembered that, as one who would have gone, gave no reason for the request. Other senators in no requiem spirit followed Harding's story—an obituary of obloquy—from his inauguration to his death. Two months after the great transcontinental funeral procession, persistent Senator Thomas J. Walsh of Montana began to look hard at the oil leases. Other investigations followed.

The business was a political prying, some protested. It was a Red effort to destroy faith in American government, declared Daugherty, who was to evade conviction but not public disgrace. That did not bring him any sense of shame. With evidently adequate means, he lived to enjoy years of companionship with many friends in Columbus, Ohio, and Florida. Fumbling Fall wrapped the flag about him. He invoked Pearl Harbor as a defense against his infamy. But not even that nor his tremulous ill health saved him at last. He went old and broken to jail for taking the bribe from Doheny while Doheny who had given it escaped punishment.

Sinclair similarly escaped conviction for the rape of the reserves, though he served short sentences for contempt of Congress and for "shadowing" the jury trying him. He had done that with the aid of William J. Burns, Daugherty's chief of the FBI. But on the day after the oil magnate went on trial for this attempted jury tampering he was unanimously re-elected to the board of directors of the American Petroleum Institute.

Playboy Ned McLean, who had welcomed Ohio friends to Washington, played a clown's role in the maze of mischief and malfeasance. He attempted to lie for Fall until his friendly fable, that the money Fall had taken as a bribe had actually been a loan from him, fell fantastically apart. Not even this experience with fabrication was to warn his wife Evalyn, wearer of the Hope diamond. She later listened to and trusted with large sums on a supposedly noble errand, Gaston Means, who when her Ned was caught lying, had already been indicted for having arranged the illegal withdrawal of liquor from government warehouses. Means went on lying in wholesale and retail fashion, by word and by book until his death in a federal prison in 1938.

Others were soiled by oil, some only by its almost promiscuous spattering, like Democratic Presidential aspirant William G. McAdoo, who as lawyer had served Doheny in matters unconnected with the oil leases. Harding, of course, was not heard but he was ever present like a dead man at his posthumous trial. The dis-

closures were the "Harding Scandals." The dedication of a marble
memorial to his memory in Marion was long postponed. Then
Hoover spoke his praises in such careful phrases that Daugherty
behind him on the platform stirred in restless resentment.

Not Harding's death but Harding's life remains much a mystery.
The two and a half years in which he served did make, as Samuel
Hopkins Adams labeled it, an "incredible era." But in it so many
incredible things occurred that even many truly incredible things
have been believed. Certainly every material of melodrama surrounded his living and his dying from the report of his birth in a
heritage of miscegenation to his death as murder in a room which
all the world watched. Perhaps history only owes him such dismissal
in disdain as Alice Longworth, whose elegant friends helped make
him President, gave him at the last.

"Harding was not a bad man," she said. "He was just a slob."

History has written his story in much the same spirit. His times,
however, could hardly quite disassociate themselves as disdainfully
and confidently as Alice did from the man. Small Emporia's peri-
patetic White, whose varied views across the times make him seem
in history a sort of weather-vane reporter, saw that clearly at last.
Brand Whitlock, a writer too, who as Wilson's ambassador had
become a hero of Belgium when it was overrun, watched the un-
folding Harding story from retirement in Europe. He suggested
that White write a book about Harding. The Emporia editor was
enthusiastic about the idea but this time clear-eyed as well.

"It isn't Harding's story," he wrote; "it is the story of his times,
the story of the Prodigal Son, our democracy that turned away
from the things of the spirit, got its share of the patrimony ruth-
lessly, and went out and lived riotously and ended it by feeding
among the swine."

Harding, of course, had not lived even to the possibility of coming
home to his "Father's house" which, along with "Babylon," White,
always lavish with metaphors, put also into this paragraph to his
friend abroad.

# X

## CONTENTMENT SELDOM SEEN

ON THURSDAY, August 2, 1923, Calvin Coolidge, who had been wearing almost burlesque bumpkin clothes as he tended an ailing sugar maple, told reporters in Plymouth, Vermont, that he and Mrs. Coolidge were leaving next morning to visit two of his great friends who had pushed him forward in politics. The stiff Vice-President and gracious Grace Coolidge were motoring to fashionable Swampscott on the Massachusetts shore to stay awhile with rich Frank Stearns, Boston merchant. On the way on Friday night, August 3, they were stopping in Peterborough, New Hampshire, at the estate of Guy Currier, wealthy, aristocratic and powerful Massachusetts politician whom one of Coolidge's biographers described as an American samurai. Before her marriage his wife had been a well-known Shakespearean actress. For the Coolidge visit she had arranged a presentation of *Romeo and Juliet* staged out of doors in the extensive Currier gardens.

A little delay in the death of Harding that evening might have brought Coolidge to the Presidency before the backdrops of plutocracy. They would have been as appropriate as the rustic stage set Plymouth provided. Certainly neither Stearns nor Currier suggested the scandals in Washington from which Harding's death permitted Republican escape. Both were decorously above the revelry in the nation which in this year, as Scott Fitzgerald wrote, brought the unrestrained twenties into full swing. By 1923, he said, the elders of the flappers and their hip-flask escorts "tired of watching the carnival with ill-concealed envy, had discovered that young liquor will take the place of young blood, and with a whoop the orgy began. . . . A whole race going hedonistic, deciding on pleasure." But not Stearns, not Currier. Certainly not Coolidge.

Neither plutocracy nor hedonism had reached Plymouth, Vermont. Its name recalled the Pilgrims. Almost a chromo of Puritan democracy was made there when by the yellow flickering light of a kerosene lamp, the small, blond, solemn Vice-President took the oath on the worn family Bible as Harding's successor from his father, John Calvin Coolidge, crossroads magistrate and notary public.

Lacking telephone or telegraph, reporters and other messengers had hurried with the news of Harding's unexpected death from the nearby town of Ludlow. That little-larger village had survived in the manufacture of shoddy, or wool reworked from old rags. Plymouth had declined as better-educated boys like Coolidge or merely hopeless ones had moved away. In the new President's lifetime it held in its environs only 400 people where once 1400 Yankees had found it possible to make a living from soils thin over granite hills. Those who remained or returned needed to be thrifty and industrious. On the day before the tremendous news came, as on other days, Mrs. Coolidge had been helping with the housework. Their boy, thirteen-year-old Calvin, had been working as a hand in a Connecticut Valley tobacco field. The Vice-President, with his face puckered in the way which led Alice Longworth to say that he looked as if he had been weaned on a pickle, was working with the ailing tree. Now he was called to the leadership of a secretly sick republic.

"I think I can swing it," he told a country friend.

The impression that he could poured out in dispatches from the lamplit scene in a pattern of antique integrity. The picture of him as "Silent Cal" pleased many in a time when there was too much loose language. To describe him as penurious was to praise him when extravagance seemed too prevalent. The country welcomed the picture reporters got from his neighbors that he was "thin and sharp as a scythe," a solemn man, without humor, without emotions. There was no room then except among the utterly irreverent for the suspicion that his simple ways and twangy terseness were parts of a sustained political pose. Those who suggested that, his neighbors said later, were "deluded by their own sophistication." Certainly at the time, the country wanted the picture of a man as conventionally American as the Fourth of July on which he was born fifty-two years before.

Too many people were trying to tear down. Without even waiting for a decent period of mourning, Senators Walsh and Wheeler began probing into the possibilities of scandals under the dead President. Walsh was meticulously meddling with the matter of oil leases by Fall. Wheeler was assiduously seeking to substantiate suspicions about Daugherty. Not alone, Coolidge regarded them as Democratic troublemakers. The always loyal Republican New York *Tribune* called the Senators "the Montana scandalmongers." The impeccable New York *Evening Post* described them as "mud-gunners." The New York *Times* referred to them as "assassins of character."

Even when the stupidity of Secretary of the Navy Denby and the venality of Fall and Daugherty were astonishingly apparent, Coolidge, who had moved with a pedestrian pace about the whole business, seemed still a reassuring presence. Fall was gone; Denby had resigned; Daugherty had been late and reluctantly fired. About the White House now was the enduring image of old-fashioned no foolishness. Much of the impression was justified. No men in unbuttoned waistcoats with cuspidors beside them played poker in its rooms. Grace Goodhue Coolidge was a simple and charming first lady. No rumors of resort to soothsayers attended her. Some felt, as the legends of Presidential silence grew, that perhaps she was protected in her charm by the fact that she had once taught in a school for the deaf and dumb. Her two boys, John and Calvin, were proper boys strictly reared but much loved.

Oddly, however, as Harding came to seem almost the mirror of his era, Coolidge became quickly almost the mask of his. Observers then, as historians later, saw the pleasing contrast of his "thrift, caution, honesty, industry and homely sagacity" with the "materialistic, extravagant and unprincipled tone of the times." Yet it was apparent that in economic and political philosophy he might better have taken his accession stance in the halls of Currier and Stearns than in the little Plymouth parlor which only later observers described as "small and mean." His democracy was as thin as the soils about Plymouth; his plain ways reflected no sympathy for miners, farmers and textile workers who were not sharing in improving business. No moral fervor moved him. He was, like a preacher whose sermon he described to Mrs. Coolidge, "against sin." But he was above the battle when as he entered office the scandals of intolerance and crime, corruption and racketeering mounted in the land.

Perhaps as President his duty was done when, in October, 1923, he called governors to a conference on law enforcement in Washington. As one of those present, Al Smith, who in his second term as governor of New York had shown his wet sentiments, said he had never heard such eloquent speeches in his life. But, said Smith with little truth and less tact, he was one of only two governors who did anything about it. Speakeasies were spreading then in Manhattan and other cities, and, behind them, the violence and corruption necessary to their supply. Sometimes in other areas law enforcement became illegal intolerance. Gangs and the Ku Klux grew coincidently. Good wets deplored the gangs while they drank the booze they brought. And good drys condemned the Klan, the stiff moral pretensions of which at least were the same as their own. City people damned sheeted, intolerant rustics often armed with rope and fagot. And rural regions were horrified by city hoodlums often equipped with "typewriters" or Thompson submachine guns with "ukeleles," as their drums containing fifty or a hundred bullets were called. They made murder a fine art or at least a mass activity. Above them the White House never seemed more silent and serene.

A month before Coolidge assumed the Presidency the flourishing Ku Klux Klan held possibly its greatest national meeting in Kokomo, Indiana, on the Fourth of July. In this small industrial city James Whitcomb Riley had published in the *Dispatch* some of his first poems, which sang of the still cherished virtues of rural and small-town life. There also had been built the first mechanically successful spark-ignition automobile. Nostalgia and new mobility made Kokomo an ideal place and time for the meeting. More and more people had moved to towns like Kokomo as agricultural prices fell and machine farming on the worn soil became too expensive for small farmers. Many of them brought their old rural ideas and prejudices with them. Some felt menaced in change.

So bumper-to-bumper cars loaded with Klansmen poured into Kokomo. Some were hung with placards: "America for Americans," "The Pope Will Never Rule America," "Trade with Klansmen." Flags waved. Patriotic and religious songs were sung. Bands played. Though its own Nathan Hale Den of the Klan had only been established two years before, Kokomo that day was the resounding center of those who recognized their task as the protection of America from foreigners, Catholics, Negroes, Jews, from sin and syncopated change. When the hoods were lifted many of the faces were as grim as those Grant Wood, Iowa artist, was already seeing for places in his picture "American Gothic." A huge American flag carried by a dozen men on each side was used as the collection plate. It sagged in the middle as coins and bills, rings and watches were flung into it. Afterward it was announced that fifty thousand dollars had been collected.

The host at this assemblage, which had originally been planned only as a tri-state konklave of Klansmen from Indiana, Illinois and Ohio, was David C. Stephenson. A thirty-two-year-old Texan, he had settled in Evansville, Indiana, after the war in which he served as a second lieutenant without overseas service. From organizing veterans he had gone into politics, first as a wet Democrat. But when the Anti-Saloon League beat him he became a dry Republican and joined the new Klan. Before this day in Kokomo he had become Klan organizer for twenty-one states, mostly Middle Western. At the time of the Kokomo konklave he was, as a reporter of the occasion said, well on his way to his first million dollars. He seemed even richer than that when in a gilded airplane he arrived in a meadow surrounded by a whole landscape of men in white. A bulky man in a robe and hood of purple silk, he spoke on "one hundred per cent Americanism." Also he apologized for being late, saying that he had just come from a conference with the President of the United States. No doubts seemed to meet that statement though Harding was in the Pacific Northwest and not even golden airplanes then moved swiftly from Indiana to the West Coast.

There was no question about his Klan position. The speaker he had called to the occasion was no less a man than Dr. Hiram Wesley Evans, former Dallas dentist, now robed in eminence as the Imperial Wizard of the national order. A pudgy, blue-eyed man in his early forties, Evans' geniality seemed more dependable than that of Stephenson who, a Catholic who watched him from a safe distance said, "could be as hearty as a country drummer, and as cold as a hangman." Evans spoke on "Back to the Constitution," but before he talked of the dangers to it from "foreign influences" he amiably commented on the transfer of Klan activities from Atlanta to Kokomo. Pleased Midwestern Klansmen listened to his injunction that they vote for officials who would make sure that "Americans be born into the American heritage." The great day ended when weary, rumpled Klansmen watching the burning of the "fiery cross" sang the Klan anthem, "The Old Rugged Cross." Fundamentals in theology, patriotism and morals seemed safe even if many of their guardians marched away with aching feet.

Evans, with the aid of Stephenson, had only taken command of the Klan in the November before. It had been founded in a ceremony on top of cold, wind-swept Stone Mountain near Atlanta, in 1915, by William Joseph Simmons. Simmons, who affected the complimentary title of Colonel, was a lanky, pince-nezed former teacher, revival preacher and recruiter for fraternal orders with a taste for boxing matches, horse races and a not too occasional drink. He claimed that the idea of reviving the post–Civil War secret society came to him in a vision when he was twenty in 1900, but actual organization coincided with the first really big motion picture, *The Birth of a Nation,* in which the sheeted order of post–Civil War times was melodramatically arrayed. The new order faltered at the outset. "A traitor in our ranks" pilfered its small treasury. Simmons mortgaged his house to keep it alive. Then, in 1920, when the market for bitterness was growing in postwar hysterias, he took in two promoters, Edward Young Clarke, an Atlanta newspaperman and fund raiser, and his more-than-associate, pretty, widowed Mrs. Elizabeth Tyler.

Now, as the song went, "My God, how the money rolled in" from initiation fees, dues, purchases of regalia. Simmons drew a thousand dollars a month as salary and unlimited funds for expenses. Grateful Klansmen gave him a thirty-three-thousand-dollar home and two big automobiles. Clarke, as Imperial Kleagle, drew as much as forty thousand dollars a month and mounting memberships justified it. Unfortunately for him, as the New York *World* discovered later, on a tip from Clarke's estranged wife, he and Mrs. Tyler had been arrested for misconduct together before they joined the Klan. Also, after he joined the order, Clarke had been guilty of violation of the White Slave Act in Texas. These incidents were not known when, in September, 1921, the *World* began its crusade against the Klan, charging that its hooded members had caused a mutilation, a branding with acid, twenty-seven tar-and-featherings, forty-one floggings, five kidnapings and four murders. With such newspaper charges, for which Simmons denied Klan responsibility, he said the Klan really began to grow. And when in October, 1921, a fruitless Congressional investigation followed, Simmons declared, "Congress made us."

Evidently the prosperity was too much for the "Colonel." In

March, 1922, fearful of a nervous collapse, he took a six-months' leave of absence from his Klan duties. Then, in November, 1922, at a Klonvokation in Atlanta, Stephenson of Indiana, accompanied by a former New York pier detective who had become chief of the Klan's internal secret service, woke Simmons in the night to tell him in effect that a palace revolution had decided upon his removal and the elevation of Evans. In final arrangements Simmons got $146,500 for all his rights, titles and interest in the Klan. Unsuccessfully he tried to establish similar organizations, then retired to Luverne, Alabama, where he took much solace from the bottle. Behind him Evans set out to "reform" the Klan. Hoods were to be worn only on ceremonial occasions. More scrutiny was to be given to the character of members (though apparently not to that of such a man as Stephenson). Evans undertook to make his "band of twentieth century knights, without fear and without reproach" a power in politics for God, for country and morality—and, incidentally, for profit.

Certainly the dentist from Dallas seemed to himself as Imperial Wizard and to his 4,000,000 Klansmen (500,000 in Indiana) as different as possible at this time in America from Al Capone who made his headquarters just across the Illinois line from Indiana's greatest Klan concentration. He was different. He was Klan chief in the nation. Al Capone, even when his liquor trucks ran from Canada and his rackets extended to Florida, was more a local symbol of a national phenomenon than the national commander of anything. It took a lot of killing to maintain his control even in Chicago. Other gangsters, though none with so glamorous and gory a name, struggled for control in New York, Boston, Philadelphia (where a marine general was brought in to clean up the town until Philadelphia decided it would rather have the gangsters than the overdramatic general). Gangsters were not new in America nor was the municipal corruption which attended them. Capone, when he came to Chicago in 1920, was also a product of the Five Points Gang in lower Manhattan. That gang had furnished such killers as Gyp the Blood and Lefty Louie, in 1912 in New York, when Police Lieutenant Charles Becker, fearing exposure of his operations in graft, had arranged the murder of the too-talkative gambler, Herman Rosenthal.

There is some question as to whether Capone when he arrived in Chicago already qualified for the nickname "Scarface Al." One story is that the scars on the left side of his face were made by shrapnel while he served in France as a member of the Lost Battalion of the Seventy-seventh Division. Another is that he got them in a knife fight in the tough Four Deuces joint at 2222 South Wabash Avenue where he began his Chicago career. There were plenty of characters about ready to slash or plug his hide as he rose in a dynasty of vice lords from James Colosimo to Johnny Torrio to his own ruthless and uneasy power.

Prohibition did not make gangs but it gave a gangster like Capone vastly expanded opportunities. He and Torrio went early into illicit breweries. They pleased many of the poor by putting them into the home industry of cooking poisons out of industrial alcohol at earnings they could not hope for in honest occupations. And in wet Chicago, Torrio and Capone were less harassed by implacable police than by competitors as ready as they were to kill in an almost feudal struggle for monopoly operations. In the jungle were such forces as the Unione Siciliana, and the Mafia ready to go after the rich even of their own breed. This was no mere Italian struggle, however. Two of those ready to put an end to Capone were Dion O'Banion, Irish graduate of Chicago's newspaper circulation wars, and Earl Hymie Weiss, who was credited with much of the ingenuity in the motorization of murder and who sometimes killed for passion and not merely, as Capone did, for profits. Weiss was a furious operator; O'Banion as a man who loved flowers happily masked his operations as a florist.

Uneasy as was the crown he was already reaching for in 1923 when the Klan converged on Kokomo, Capone was already putting crime and corruption on an efficiency basis. That year he already had an organization of seven hundred tough characters at his command. He was disbursing twenty-five thousand dollars a week in payrolls in the booze traffic alone and was on his way to operations which would bring him millions a year. He was no longer the gorilla gangster. He was a well-dressed personage said to be pleasant to meet except by persons who were buying somebody else's beer. At police headquarters, at which he sometimes complacently appeared, he was respectfully addressed as "Mr. Capone." He was moving toward the day when, as Westbrook Pegler reported, deferential ex-heavyweight boxing champion Jack Dempsey, as host at a prize fight, dusted off the seat he had reserved for Mr. Capone.

A year after the Klan showed its strength in Kokomo, a hundred

miles away Capone, by favors and force, took over the Chicago
suburb of Cicero in an election in which four people were killed
and forty wounded. From such a municipal stronghold, which he
packed with speakeasies, honky-tonks, gambling houses and brothels,
Al directed his underworld empire, which extended from liquor
trucks crossing the Canadian line to rackets in Florida. And with
Cicero in his pistol pocket and Chicago as a huge, corrupt and
thirsty market nearby, Capone did not have to be concerned in the
politics of the nation then being called beyond national governmental scandals to keep cool with Coolidge.

With Coolidge embodying the rural virtues the Klan presumed
to defend, Imperial Wizard Evans and such supporters as Stephenson in Indiana might have stayed out of national politics, too. But
the time had come for a display of Klan strength. Also there were
the Democrats and among them the wet, Catholic, Tammany, urban
Al Smith seemed a threat not only to dry, Protestant William Gibbs
McAdoo but an aid to everything the Klan feared including the
Pope. Though Evans, attended by Grand Dragons, set up headquarters in the Statler Hotel in Cleveland, Ohio, at the Republican
National Convention in the summer of 1924, the Klan played no
great part there. Obligingly the Republicans adopted a plank reaf-
firming devotion to liberty but containing no unkind mention of
the Klan. The significance of any Klan support of Coolidge was
submerged in his nomination on the first and only ballot by a vote
of 1065 to 44, of which 34 went to La Follette, who was already
planning as Progressive to run on an independent ticket.

Dr. Evans moved on to New York where a very different convention of Democrats assembled on June 24. With his Dragons he
established headquarters in a suite in the McAlpin Hotel sufficiently
close to big Madison Square Garden. All Democrats roared enthusiastically and hopefully when speakers indignantly described
Republican derelictions. But early it was clear that country-city
cleavage had almost been designed. Even then Franklin Roosevelt,
though supposedly at the end of his own political career as a result
of a polio attack in 1921, was watching that. Long before the decision to hold the convention in New York had been made, Roosevelt, who later became Smith's manager, had told William Jennings
Bryan that the effort to hold the convention there was the work of
"hopeful idiots who think that the Democratic platform will advocate repeal of the Eighteenth Amendment."

As the time for the convention approached, the crippled New York's man Friday, Louis McHenry Howe, told him that Tammany was demanding thirty-five hundred seats in the galleries "and the plan is to pack the house when the psychological moment arrives with Smith rooters." Under such galleries the New York *World* estimated that there were three hundred dues-paying Klansmen among the thousand-odd delegates on the floor, all for McAdoo despite disclosures that he had been employed by oilman Doheny. Between gallery roars and country delegate resentment on the floor, Roosevelt's biographer, Frank Freidel, wrote, "Rural nativism and urban rowdyism clashed head on."

It seemed worse than that. McAdoo, who had a Progressive record as Wilson's Secretary of the Treasury and had much appeal to labor because of his treatment of workers during his management of the railroads in wartime, was not only unduly smeared with oil; also he was practically hooded as a Klansman himself. And Smith, who had emerged from Tammany to give New York government which pleased intellectuals and humanitarians alike, was dressed in back-country imagination as a puppet of the Pope and a figure for the old Tammany Hall image of politics for graft and corruption. The galleries roared when bands played his special music, "The Sidewalks of New York." That old song was revived in joyousness and sentimentality out of the 1890s when the now brown-derbied Al had been one of the boys and girls who danced the light fantastic on the sidewalks of New York. Many grim Democrats only recalled the gay nineties as times of depression rather than gaiety. Then Tammany let Republicans carry the town against the rural revolt of Bryan while its leaders were presiding at prodigious profits over police extortion and blackmail. Tammany was still the name for political Babylon. Songs of the city's sidewalks set back-country Democrats to snarling of guttersnipes.

The Tammany behind its rather puritanically Catholic candidate was insistently altered and changed. Perceptive as he was debonair, Smith had helped to teach the Hall that new social legislation was needed to serve the poor who once had been kept loyal by summer picnics and winter scuttles of coal. He had kept his sympathies for the poor as he rose among and above them. But his old city had not become an entirely moralistic metropolis. Stanley Walker, of Texas, soon to become the youngest city editor the old *Tribune*, or the new *Herald-Tribune*, ever had, wrote that 1924 in New York had begun "wet and noisy." Actually it was adding sophistication to what seemed only loudness to many. That year Sinclair Lewis, famed now for his portrait of American Babbitts in booster cities as well as for his picture of the sterility of Main Street, regarded the music of Paul Whiteman, wearing a questionable crown as King of Jazz, as "noise and nothing much else." But Whiteman, in February, had first played George Gershwin's "Rhapsody in Blue" in the cultured precincts of Aeolian Hall. Euphony and cacophony seemed combined at the year's beginning when Mencken and Nathan launched their decorously printed *American Mercury* with equal cracks at rural boobs, Ph.D.'s and the "press agents and dishwashers" of J. P. Morgan. Their magazine was prophetic in its scorn of supposed American serenity—"the doctrine that the interests of capital and labor are identical—which is to say that the interests of landlord and tenant, hangman and condemned, cat and rat are identical." Town and country might have been added.

As Gotham prepared for the assembling Democrats, Walker wrote that there was "a great pother about drying up the city before the delegates, most of whom were dry but wild for the bottle in the big city, could gather for their quadrennial hippodrome." It was not quite dried up, as he admitted. The New York *Times* had written of the development of "clubs" which had no more right to that name "than the Waldorf-Astoria." Still no liquor lord had yet risen to match the Capone position in Chicago. Owney Madden, later master of so many of its rackets, had only emerged from a period at Sing Sing the year before. Even in his supremacy as a lean, catlike gentleman Madden disliked killings and dodged the publicity which Capone sometimes seemed to relish. And Arthur Flegenheimer (better known as Dutch Schultz) was at twenty-two only a bully boy not yet controlling the beer business in upper Manhattan and the Bronx. Lesser characters were already appearing. There was Larry Fay, who like many other such persons, came from Hell's Kitchen and died by the bullet. He opened a nightclub called El Fay with boisterous, charming Texas Guinan as a hostess. As she moved on to other "clubs," she enlivened the language as she greeted customers, Democrats or Republicans, with a cheery "Hello, sucker." It was she who invented the name "big butter-and-egg man" for ready spenders. Hearty la Guinan, pretty, dreamy Helen Morgan and Florence Mills, whose burnished charm and voice of unlimited range carried her quickly through the color line to Broadway, were the toasts of the town in this hot summer and afterward.

As Walker wrote, some liquor seeped into rooms in the Waldorf at Thirty-fourth Street and Fifth Avenue where the best-heeled Democratic delegates were staying. There was plenty to drink within a block's walk from the hotel in any direction. And New York's wide-open hospitality served, depending upon the point of view, impressions of both hypocrisy and hoodlumism.

Some country drys did drink to the scorn of some wet Smith men. And some drys visited nightclubs and saloons—even some Southerners went for dark-skinned entertainment to the Cotton Club and Connie's Inn in Harlem. They came away not only fortified with bootleg spirits but fortified also in the belief that corruption and protection attended the free flow. Wild images grew in wet-dry, town-country, Catholic-Protestant antagonisms. The convention contest seemed not merely between Klan and Tammany but between hooded hypocrisy and the kind of prowling politics which produced the Al Capones. The equal exaggerations certainly did not diminish the equal antagonisms.

Oddly, at this convention the two most universally applauded men pointed the absurdity of the furies behind the divisions. Senator Thomas J. Walsh, of Montana, who had uncovered the oil scandals, presided as permanent chairman over the raucous assemblage with a sternness and composure which pleased all. He was Irish, Catholic and dry. And Franklin Roosevelt, who came forward gallantly on his crutches to nominate Al Smith, was a Protestant of the oldest American stock who insistently maintained a country or at least a country-squire image of himself.

He had fought the Tammany whose idol he now served. In his speech nominating Smith, in which he first called Smith the "Happy Warrior" (a title suggested to him by a New York Jew), he spoke without interruption save for applause. But the packed hall gave the McAdoo nominating speech such "noise, inattention and disorder" that Chairman Walsh had to intervene. Nevertheless McAdoo's demonstration, conducted by delegates on the floor, ran seventy-seven minutes. The Smith rooters only carried on for seventy-three minutes, but electronic horns, strategically placed in the galleries, made it the more vociferous.

The greatest uproar, however, came before the voting on the candidates when on the fifth day, June 30, the row broke as to whether the convention should go beyond the diplomatic verbiage of the Resolutions Committee and condemn the Klan by name in its platform. After Bryan, cartooned in the New York press as a molting mountebank in an alpaca coat armed only with a palm-leaf fan, spoke in pious opposition against splitting the party by putting the three little words "ku klux klan" in the platform, the voting proceeded in pandemonium. Demands were shouted that delegations be polled. Fist fights started in some of them. State standards were broken. Chairs were overturned. Yells came incessantly from the galleries. ("Attaboy" was a word frequently put into the formal record.)

In retrospect many aspects of the voting seem strange. The list of those states voting solidly to condemn the Klan by name was led by Alabama, followed by Maryland, New Jersey, New York, North Dakota, Rhode Island and Vermont. As expected, among those solid against it were such Southern and Southwestern states as Arkansas, Louisiana, Mississippi, Oklahoma, South Carolina and Texas, but they were joined by Kansas, Idaho, Nevada, Oregon and Washington. The final vote as announced was $542\frac{7}{20}$ to name and $543\frac{3}{20}$ not to name—a difference of less than one full vote in the whole clamoring convention. Even then a loud delegate from Chelsea, Massachusetts, which had gone $35\frac{1}{2}$ to $\frac{1}{2}$ to name the Klan, claimed that a vote in his delegation had been changed by intimidation. Intimidation was certainly rampant on both sides of the issue. But the vote stood. After it, at nearly two o'clock in the morning, Franklin Roosevelt moved to adjourn. Despite cries of "No" the motion was carried. Delegates poured out on the dark, hot sidewalks of New York.

Obviously the convention was completely and neatly split. Persons listening on the new, wonderful radio heard ballot after ballot begin with the Southern-accented shout, "Alabama casts twenty-four votes for Oscar Underwood." Only priority on the roll calls gave prominence to that wet and anti-Klan senator from the South. The balloting began on June 30 with McAdoo receiving $431\frac{1}{2}$ votes to Smith's 241. Days later on the sixty-ninth ballot, on July 4, McAdoo rose to 530 votes to Smith's 335. But on the eighty-sixth ballot Smith, on July 7, nosed ahead 360 to $353\frac{1}{2}$. The next day Roosevelt, with his man ahead, offered to break the deadlock by withdrawing his candidate if McAdoo would do the same.

Some McAdoo men felt that the gangs were moving from the

galleries. The chairman did "firmly direct" the officers of the convention to keep unauthorized persons from intruding into the delegate space. McAdoo ran ahead again on the ninety-fourth ballot. But he was only a half a vote ahead on the ninety-ninth. To both hisses and applause a McAdoo letter was read saying that while he would not withdraw his name in this fight against "reactionary and wet elements in the party," he wished to leave his friends free to vote as they would. On the hundredth ballot McAdoo was down to 190, Smith up to 351½, but the signal for compromise, arranged behind the scenes in rooms filled with smoke and despair, was the mounting vote given to John W. Davis.

Named on the one hundred third ballot, Davis had been Woodrow Wilson's Ambassador to the Court of St. James and was attorney for J. P. Morgan. He was as well dressed as an undertaker managing rites in a cathedral and some felt that was the sort of party role assigned to him in the steaming, cluttered hall. That seemed more than ever the case when compromise went on to the nomination as Vice-President of Charles W. Bryan, Governor of Nebraska, whose greater brother had so long damned Tammany and Wall Street together.

Broke, bruised, and bewildered, the Democratic delegates who had come confidently to New York sixteen days before (it seemed sixteen weeks) adjourned sine die to cries of "Good" from the galleries. They dispersed to the sidewalks of New York and the railroads to the country. A few like Senator Wheeler, of Montana, spoke disgust. He accepted nomination as Vice-President on the Progressive ticket headed by Senator La Follette, who offered the only choice available to liberals. That was a choice without much chance. La Follette did have behind him, though in inadequate numbers, farmers, union members, Negroes, intellectuals. They made a combination which would have to wait to prove its capacity for such peaceful revolution as no one could have believed then was only eight years ahead. Davis and Coolidge competed with each other in denouncing La Follette as a dangerous radical. La Follette, of course, denounced the Klan. So did Davis. Coolidge remained silent as usual in his campaign, which was waged under the slogan, "Coolidge or Chaos." The only surprise in November was the lopsided dimension of his 382 to 136 electoral vote victory. Certainly any urban-rural collision which had disrupted the Democrats was obscured by the overwhelming choice of a man with the pursed personality of a Vermont hill farmer whose philosophy of government and business served city plutocrats symbolized at their best by Frank Stearns and Guy Currier.

In that sweep it was absurd for Imperial Wizard Evans to "admit" that there was truth in the claim or the charge that the Klan had both brought on the Democratic debacle and "the defeat of Mr. Davis that followed." Evans was unexpectedly lucky, however, when difficulties and irritations grew between him and Grand Dragon Stephenson, who had been able to say with much truth, "I am the law in Indiana." As a result of their differences Evans read Stephenson out of the Klan, though he could not keep him from carrying on with power in his own realm.

That made it possible for Evans to deny Klan association with Stephenson when the latter fell in criminal and obscene scandal. "Steve" owned one of the show-place houses in suburban Indianapolis, maintained a suite of hotel rooms in the city, kept a fleet of cars, his golden plane and a yacht on Lake Michigan. By a bust of Napoleon, which he kept in his quarters, he indulged himself with power and pleasures. But in drunken megalomania he determined on the possession of a spinsterish woman clerk in a state office. He kidnaped her, raped her. She took bichloride of mercury and while slowly dying dictated all the details of her mistreatment to a prosecuting attorney who was one of the few officials in the Indianapolis area Stephenson did not control. When he went to prison, the miracle was that the Klan anywhere survived.

The worst aspects of city rowdyism had no moralistic pretensions for scandal to wipe away. In Chicago, just a week after the national election, tough Dion O'Banion, still gloating over carrying his wards Republican, was happily engaged in the florist shop which served as the cover for his lucrative bootleg activities. Almost impishly he had been uncooperative with Capone's growing power. Already "Scarface Al" was becoming Mr. Capone when addressed in person. He was applying to the underworld an executive ability almost equal in its field to that of Samuel Insull in the utilities business in the same city. Insull, coming up from almost as obscure beginnings as Capone's, had worked with Thomas A. Edison and, his biographer Forrest McDonald believed, had been as important in the development of the economics of electric supply as Edison was in its technology.

Now Insull was bringing about a "customer ownership" of utilities with great corporations "owned by anonymous millions and therefore owned by nobody" but operated by a noncapitalistic managerial class of which Insull was the high-powered example. Capone worked in the economics and technology of the liquor supply in an industry requiring equal inventiveness. Insull in his operations declined to be dominated by the New York establishment of finance and made enemies in the process. In determination to run his show, too, Capone could not depend upon the finesses of finance. But in the business of liquor supply he was the manager, only anonymous when his operations required murder.

This November, O'Banion was, in the language of the time, "too sick to live," though evidently he didn't know it. He whistled in his shop from which he went by nights to tend to his other, underworld activities. Sympathetically he accepted a $750 order for the funeral of a president of the Unione Siciliana who by some strange chance in his position had died a natural death. O'Banion clipped the chrysanthemums; carefully he shaped the big arrangement. And though he always wore guns in holsters under his coat, he came out cheerfully and carelessly to greet three men who came for the flowers. One shook his outstretched hand—and did not let it go. The others gave him six bullets and left him sprawled among scattered petals. He was laid out in a ten-thousand-dollar coffin. Blue-chinned, tailored hoodlums and their befurred and bejeweled women passed by it. A newspaper woman wrote of O'Banion's "graceful hands which could finger an automatic so effectively," but no more. Other florists provided the fifty thousand dollars' worth of flowers which in twenty-six trucks followed him in the great model for gangster funerals to his grave in Mount Carmel Cemetery. One great basket of roses bore the message "From Al."

Even in the purple-prosed journalism of the time, however, O'Banion's obsequies got no such attention as the roaring stock market boom which immediately followed Coolidge's election. The Associated Press described it as "one of the most impressive buying demonstrations in many years," which took prices to "new peaks." Crimes in the bootleg boom were becoming commonplace. True, space was given in the week after the election to the death from poisoned liquor of ten men at the Elks National Home at Bedford, Virginia. At the beginning of Coolidge's first year in the White House after Harding's death, a United States senator from his own pastoral state of Vermont had been shot in midtown Washington in an exchange of fire between bootleggers and prohibition agents.

Even the Jazz Age seemed past its crest. In April, 1924, it had apparently been rejected by its laureate, Scott Fitzgerald. He and his Zelda, with her bobbed hair and short skirts, had sailed off to the French Riviera to escape "from extravagance and clamor and from all the wild extremes among which we had dwelt for five hectic years. . . ." To many, as the mid-twenties approached, such a view seemed only more of the clamor and extravagance of literary heretics and some political radicals. Actually Fitzgerald had written his best book in *The Great Gatsby*, published in 1925. Main Street and Wall Street, too, bankers and Babbitts moved confidently toward the inauguration at which the President could report a "state of contentment seldom before seen."

That seemed one of his typical, twangy understatements to his well-dressed audience which expected him to be economical with his words, emotions and everything else. Oddly, beyond the first Presidential image of his lamplit integrity, disparaging Democrats had helped build the appeal of the pinch-faced little Yankee. The summer before, their great brawl with its nationwide radio audience had helped make him seem to millions even more a sort of reticent man-next-door with homely virtues deserving emulation but also subject like all to sorrows which entitled him to sympathy.

As the nation listened then, fascinated with its feuding, the Democratic Convention had paused on July 7, between its seventy-eighth and seventy-ninth ballots "to offer to our President and Mrs. Coolidge our sympathy in this hour of anxiety at the bedside of their dear son, Calvin, Jr., who lies critically ill in Washington." So the attention of more than the politically commiserating delegates was brought to that bedside.

On Wednesday, July 2, as the convention proceeded from its thirty-first to its forty-second ballot, the young naval doctor, Joel Boone, who had attended Harding, came to the White House for a prearranged tennis game with the Coolidge boys. John Coolidge told him his brother was not feeling well. Boone went to the quarters of the boys, known as the Lincoln Room. Young Calvin was lying on his bed fully dressed. A very blond boy, at sixteen he had swiftly grown to the awkward, skinny, knock-kneed height of about six feet. Listlessly he was listening while his mother played to him on a grand piano which she had placed there so that she could

8. MARCUS GARVEY—BLACK MESSIAH

*Freelance Photographers Guild*

9. THE LAST DAYS OF
WARREN G. HARDING

*Brown Brothers*

10. CHIEF CALVIN

*Culver Pictures*

11.   ALFRED E. SMITH AND FRIEND

12. WILL ROGERS

13. SPEAKEASY

14.   ERNEST HEMINGWAY AND BRUCE BARTON—THE BOYS FROM SAINTS' REST

entertain her sons when they were home from Mercersburg Academy in Pennsylvania.

John thought he had picked up a cold. But Boone found he had a high fever. His throat was not inflamed. Examination showed no signs of an inflamed appendix. But in the boy's groin the doctor found some enlarged glands which made him suspect an infection. Laconically young Calvin answered his questions. "Yup," as a result of tennis play three days before, he had a small blister on a toe of his right foot. He had soaked it and put iodine on it. But Boone found faintly appearing streaks up his leg toward his knee. Immediately concerned, the doctor sent a culture to the Naval Medical School laboratory.

Calvin had a restless night and on Thursday morning was definitely a very sick boy. The naval laboratory reported that Staphyloccus aureus organisms had been found in the culture. In mid-1924 this report was somewhat reassuring, because of greater concern then about streptococcic infections. There were then no antibiotics available even for a President's son. The Swiss-born Italian, Daniel Bovet, who was to discover sulfanilamide, was then only a seventeen-year-old student at the University of Geneva. In Britain, Sir Alexander Fleming had not yet made even his laboratory discovery about penicillin which was to lead to its therapeutic possibilities in 1940.

As the boy became sicker and sicker there were consultations with physicians from Washington, Philadelphia and Baltimore. On Saturday, July 5, he was taken to Walter Reed Hospital. Surgical procedures were resorted to to see if there was spread of the infection. At the time a variety of dyes were coming into vogue for intravenous administration. One of the best authorities in the nation on the use of them requested that he be permitted to inject one of the dyes. Though a severe reaction was predicted, in the boy's desperate state it was authorized. There was no reaction, nor was there any help to the patient. Then an autogenous vaccine was grown and injected. There was a response for an hour or two but the benefit was only transitory.

"Each day Calvin lost ground," his helpless physician recalled later. "It seemed as though his decline could be likened to a prairie fire. He could not develop for himself any defensive forces, nor could we physicians produce any for him. He developed an ileus on Monday afternoon and died that evening, exactly one week from the day he rubbed the blister on his toe."

(Forty years later Dr. Boone said that it would be only surmise to say that the President's son would have survived if the drugs later available to any boy had been developed. "But, we should reasonably feel, with the existence of various antibiotics available in our armamentarium, that most, if not all, lives in such circumstances as Calvin's could be saved.")

Helplessly the President and Grace Coolidge watched their boy die. One day the President, remembering his boy's love of animals, coaxed and captured a small brown rabbit on the White House grounds. He carried it to the sickroom where it brought a brief wan smile to the boy's face. Mrs. Coolidge sat steadily by the boy. The President and young John came hour after hour. In delirium the sick boy fought imaginary forces and at the last called to his nurse to join him in "surrender." His battle was over.

A physician looking down from the hospital saw the President as a small, hurt man, holding the hand of his other son, John, and looking up at the window of the room in which Calvin died. Coolidge was to write later of his lost boy: "When he went the power and the glory of the Presidency went with him." Reticent as he seemed, he spoke to others of the boy's death more than Grace Coolidge did. She was outwardly contained and charming, moving in an evident sense of duty to show a gracious, amiable face to all as first lady, with her head up, smiling. But in November, 1924, after her husband's great victory, she commenced to mark the days ahead in the great White House to which they had come to so great a loss. With the domestic craftsmanship she had learned in her own Vermont girlhood, she began to crochet a bedspread. It was to be eight squares long and six squares wide, one square for each of the months they would have to live in the White House in this term to which her husband had been elected to serve.

# XI

## LISTEN, THE WIND

"WE ARE all a lost generation," young, dapper Ernest Hemingway quoted the earlier expatriate Gertrude Stein as saying on a fore page of *The Sun Also Rises*, which he published to the delight of some and the shock of others in 1926.

He seemed an unlikely one to be lost. He had come to writing among Left Bank expatriates in Paris, through reporting and war, from the Chicago suburb of Oak Park, long-time prohibition stronghold known as Saints' Rest because of its many churches. Oak Park adjoined Cicero, which Al Capone had recently appropriated as his own malignant municipality.

The contrast between the two towns was no greater than that between some of Oak Park's rising sons. Hemingway's manuscript, which contained some short dirty words, had troubled editors at Charles Scribner's Sons, but they had turned down as more shocking the book of another bright Oak Park product. Bruce Barton, thirteen years older than Hemingway, had soared from a Saints' Rest parsonage to high place in the advertising business as partner in the formidable firm of Batten, Barton, Durstine and Osborn, which helped make Madison Avenue a name for advertising as Wall was the street of finance.

The two streets were happily almost equal parts of the gilded business community in the twenties, and both were content under the business administration of Coolidge. Barton, in *The Man Nobody Knows*, undertook to set up a sort of doctrine of the divine right of business in his biography of Jesus as a master salesman. Admiringly he described the Son of God as one who "picked up twelve men from the bottom ranks of business and forged them into an organization that conquered the world." If the solid old firm of

Scribner's was aghast at such an idea, bankers, salesmen and advertising men were not. A less sensitive publishing house sold over 400,000 copies of the book to businessmen eager to share places in the new theology.

Certainly such businessmen and book buyers saw nothing symbolic about themselves in a Hemingway hero whose war wound left him with desire but the inability to satisfy it. The America in which they occupied presiding places had no sense of hopeless, aimless wandering like that of the characters in his tale. There was at least a spectator sense of lustiness symbolized by the combat that year of Jack Dempsey and Gene Tunney when 130,000 people paid close to two million dollars to see Dempsey lose his heavyweight crown. Certainly there was nothing hopeless or aimless about the thirty-one touchdowns in twenty games of Harold E. ("Red") Grange, who had turned pro and been presented to Coolidge the year before, or any desultory wanderings through strange scenes in the dash to goals of the "Four Horsemen" backfield of Notre Dame.

The kind of European travel which excited the mass of Americans was that of Gertrude Ederle, who on August 6, 1926, became the first woman to swim the English Channel. Her swim from Cap Gris-Nez to Kingsdown Beach for most people in the United States was not even on the way between Stein, Fitzgerald, Hemingway, *et al.*, in Paris, and Ezra Pound and T. S. Eliot in Britain. Though it had been published four years before, most of his countrymen were unaware of Eliot's long poem *The Waste Land*, and had no sense of the despair of the postwar period which he expressed in it. They preferred the sugary certainties of Edgar A. Guest, who in reverse expatriate passage had come from Birmingham, England, to Detroit, Michigan, where the auto business was booming though there were troubled suggestions that so swift was the pace of America that Henry Ford's first, famous, popular Model T was obsolete.

On April 1, 1925, not quite a month after the inauguration of Coolidge, the Wall Street banking house of Dillon, Read & Co. had announced that it had bought the Detroit automobile company of Dodge Brothers for $146,000,000, the largest single cash transaction in American industrial history. The Dodges had started with Ford, sold out their stock in 1920 for an estimated $25,000,000, and branched out for themselves. Now the Dodges were dead, their widows took big profit and Dillon, Read began to sell to the already stock-hungry public around $160,000,000 in securities.

Evidently the "money trust," if any, did not feel part of any lost generation. Even the old enemy of the House of Morgan and all the other supposedly predatory plutocrats, Mr. Bryan, though in political shadows himself, enjoyed the sunny optimism about him. Appreciative crowds of other newcomers from lands like his own old Nebraska made it necessary for him to move the Bible class he had begun from the First Presbyterian Church in Miami. Under the palms on Biscayne Bay he expounded the old-time religion to more and more people coming to Florida in Fords—and in the increasingly competitive Chevrolets and Plymouths. The number of eager listeners to the old faith in the new land grew. In 1922 his lessons went out over the air from one of the country's earliest radio stations.

His booming voice and the developing Florida boom seemed made for each other. Soon he was dividing his preaching between his Bible class and daily promotion lectures for Coral Gables, "$100,000,000 development" it was called, from a platform over the waters of its Venetian Pool. For this service to "Miami's Master Suburb," he was said to receive $100,000 a year. When he had appeared so obnoxiously obsolete to anti-Klan wets at the Democratic Convention of 1924 his voice and his investments had made him worth a million.

Still, though he used other language to describe it, he was concerned about the danger of a "lost generation." Lack of old-fashioned faith, especially among college students, he decided was due to the teaching of evolution which shook the whole Bible as it cast doubts upon the story of creation set out in Genesis. As early as January, 1922, he addressed the Kentucky legislature in support of a ban on teaching evolution in state-supported schools. Despite his oratory, the bill lost there in the House 42 to 41. But a similar law went into effect in Tennessee on March 21, 1925. In April, almost as a joke or a publicity stunt, defiance of the law by a young schoolteacher, John T. Scopes, was arranged at a drugstore symposium, in the small town of Dayton, close to the poor mountains and the still undeveloped Tennessee River. In May wires and letters sped to Bryan asking him to join in the prosecution of the case. He could not refuse and he was brought into classic conflict with another man who in his own different way had been concerned for a fee with true specimens of a "lost generation."

Thirty years before Bryan and Clarence Darrow had been on the same political side, which Darrow thought "represented the disinherited." Then, while not quite trusting Bryan's golden oratory, he believed that they were defeated by an "enormous fund" of reactionary Republican money. Giving up railroad clients, Darrow had fought in a succession of great labor cases. He spoke, he said, "for the children of the poor." Also, along the way he defended fifty persons charged with first-degree murder, only one of whom was executed. But in a famous bombing case in California he lost the faith of labor leaders and was himself unjustly charged with criminal misconduct. His future seemed bleak. Then in 1924 he was asked to take his most famous case.

With no motive save a sadistic sense of superiority, two intellectually brilliant Chicago boys, Nathan Leopold, Jr., and Richard Loeb, both in their late teens and sons of well-to-do respected families, decided to commit a perfect crime. On May 21, 1924, they kidnapped thirteen-year-old Bobby Franks, child of another rich family, killed him, left his naked body in a culvert, then demanded ransom for the safe return of the already dead boy. Far from perfect, it was a bumbling crime. Detectives quickly traced it to Leopold and Loeb and an outraged country was confronted with the case of two incomprehensible young monsters.

In the midst of public outcry against them, Darrow took the apparently hopeless case. He had no defense. Though alienists whom he called in found both boys "decidedly deficient in emotions" and Darrow regarded them as "incipient paranoiacs," he did not plead innocent by reason of insanity. Carefully he weighed the prospects as "brutal and abusive" mail piled up in his office. He made his decision. Only two criminals of the age of these boys had ever been put to death in Illinois. Also the judge before whom the case was tried had earlier shown enlightened modern ideas in helping create a juvenile court. Avoiding a jury, Darrow entered a plea of guilty in the hope of life sentences.

As he spoke to the judge he was, after nearly forty city years, still a persuasively rural-appearing personality plausibly presenting modern ideas of sin and psychology much popularized in this period by almost faddist attention to the ideas of Sigmund Freud and others. In his autobiography afterward Darrow devoted much attention to the training and troubles of children which, he thought, should be "free of all fable and superstition." Those ideas flowed in his plea for clemency. In the face of what he called the "mob hysteria outside the court," he won, though the victory only meant for Leopold and

Loeb, he wrote, life behind "stark, blank stone walls." (Leopold was murdered by another convict in prison; Loeb was paroled as a middle-aged man after nearly forty years in prison.) Darrow emerged from the trial regarded as an almost Mephistophelean advocate of young demons for a big fee. Also he was more than ever recognized as an able adversary of "mob hysteria" whether stirred in demand for implacable punishment in Chicago or for the protection of Fundamentalist faith in Tennessee.

Mencken, who more and more delighted in his role as clowning picador plaguing puritans, took much credit for the Scopes trial melodrama in the Tennessee hills. According to his biographer, William Manchester, he met Darrow at this time when he and novelist Joseph Hergesheimer were visiting James Branch Cabell, author of the once suppressed *Jurgen*, in Richmond. Darrow came to call. The Baltimore *Sun*, with which Mencken was still connected, had gone on Scopes's bond. Mencken insisted that Darrow join Arthur Garfield Hays, of the American Civil Liberties Union, and Dudley Field Malone, eloquent advocate of prohibition repeal and other liberal causes, in the defense of Scopes—or in the chastisement of Bryan and all he represented.

"Nobody gives a damn about that yap schoolteacher," Mencken said. "The thing to do is make a fool out of Bryan."

Darrow's own recollections of his entry into the case suggested no such manhunt for the old Commoner. By his account, not needing persuasion, he volunteered his services for the only time in his life because of long antipathy to Bryan's grim Fundamentalist efforts to save the children from the supposed infidelity of teachers and professors.

Mencken went to Dayton accompanied by three *Sun* reporters and a cartoonist. The whole case was cartooned as the "monkey trial." Scores of other reporters came to the rather attractive little town which was even by Menckenesque accounts by no means so bigoted as it was made to seem. A variety of dour Fundamentalists who believed the Bible from "kivver to kivver" did arrive. They were no more part of the spectacular intellectual carnival than some of the imps of impious penmen, village atheists and the like. All in the pummeling heat which brought the case out of the stifling courthouse to the shaded lawn made a great show. Darrow, playing his role as sharp intellectual masked as a drawling county-seat lawyer in rumpled, rural-looking costume, described Bryan. The old Commoner sat "fanning himself, looking limp and martyr-like between assaults upon the flies that found a choice roosting place on his bald, expansive dome and bare, hairy arms." Bryan left no memoirs as to how Darrow looked to him. They collided sharply. To Bryan, Darrow was using a Tennessee court to cast slurs on God. Darrow examined Bryan on his "fool ideas that no intelligent Christian in the whole world believes." The outcome of the case was to be expected. Darrow, lifting the trial out of the farce the press was making of it, said later that "it was evident that Scopes was trying to do for Dayton, Tenn., what Socrates did for Athens. And so why should not Dayton, Tenn., do to Scopes what Athens did to Socrates." Even with the Chicago lawyer's help the cases did not quite compare. Scopes was given no hemlock. He was fined $100 and on appeal that punishment was set aside.

Shock came into the side show at Dayton five days after the close of the trial. Then, on July 26, 1925, Bryan, apparently healthy, went to bed for a nap after a hearty midday dinner. When they went to awaken him he was dead. Darrow wrote that he was sorry that Bryan could not have seen the devotion shown by great throngs of people at his funeral and along the slow journey of his funeral train to the grave. The lanky lawyer only showed some obituary testiness in his statement about "the irony of fate—a man who for years had fought excessive drinking lay dead from indigestion caused by over-eating." It was not quite that simple. Darrow himself died of heart disease though at an advanced age. The brutal epitaph was made by Mencken.

"Well," he said, "we killed the son-of-a-bitch."

Perhaps it was well that Bryan died in Dayton, not to return to his Villa Serena in Florida. Not only did the infidels seem derisively increasing in a world which was no Sunday-school class. Also, thirty years later a play was written about the farce and tragedy at Dayton called *Inherit the Wind*. Bryan escaped greater wind than ever blew in Dayton.

No one could take his place on the real estate promotion podium over the Venetian Pool at Coral Gables. Had he lived, his voice there would not have sufficed. During 1925 when he battled and was battered at Dayton, once-barren land six and eight miles outside Miami sold for twenty to twenty-five thousand dollars an acre, choice parcels bringing as much as forty thousand dollars. During the year, too, 971 subdivisions were platted and 174,530 deeds and purchase papers were filed by the county clerk. Building operations required four hundred miles of awning material, seven thousand carloads of lumber as 481 hotels and apartments were built in a year. Million-dollar deals became commonplace. In this year of high carnival in real estate 2,500,000 people came to the state. Income from the pioneer Halcyon Hotel was $519,000 for the year ending April 30, 1926. No one dreamed that in 1934 the hotel itself would sell under the hammer for $333,600.

Yet the spring beyond Bryan's death marked the beginning of the expiration of the Florida boom. Toward the close of 1925, Federal Reserve banks stiffened for the time at least their rediscount rates. Some banks tottered. Income tax troubles beset some who had been counting their profits only on paper. But there were no signs of danger in the paved streets still being pushed through the scrub palmettos and in the buildings still rising sometimes too quickly and too shoddily beside them.

Then the wind came. On September 14, 1926, telegraphic reports were received of a tropical disturbance about two hundred miles northeast of St. Kitts in the Antilles. On the sixteenth the storm passed Turks Island with winds of 150 mph. Reports were inadequate. There were no unusual meteorological conditions to mark the storm's approach in Miami. With "great suddenness," according to the weather man in charge there, the center of the storm passed over the central and southern portions of the city. Then in downtown Miami the deceptive winds dropped to ten miles an hour. In the lull people poured into the streets to see the damage of the storm which seemed to have passed. Thirty-five minutes later the stronger side of the hurricane suddenly struck.

This was the greater blow with winds of 135 miles an hour. Storm tides rose. The roar of the wind was accompanied by the crash of buildings, flying debris, breaking plate glass, and the sounds of the sirens of ambulances and fire equipment. Rain came in sheets as dense as fog. Torn power lines hissed and flashed. More than two hundred people were killed in Florida and property damage amounted to $111,775,000. Nonetheless, in the storm's aftermath the Associated Press reported less than a week later that "Miami boosters turning from the serious struggle of the past few days radiated happiness over the triviality of the damage when it might have been far worse." They announced that every trace of damage would be removed from hotels and apartments by November when the winter tourist season will be under way.

That was a whistle by a hurricane. Old-timers had hardly remembered a storm like this one. Newcomers had not believed such a blow possible. Their discovery that it was, made the season when it came one of bitterness and disappointment. The stream to Florida became a trickle. Those who did come were appalled by the scars that remained. The boom had passed with the storm.

It seemed only an incident to many in America. The dead in Florida had been only mortuary statistics beside the death less than a month before—and almost the apotheosis—of Rodolpho Alfonzo Raffaelo Pierre Filibert Guglielmi Di Valentina d' Antonguolla in Manhattan. Drugs which might have saved young Calvin Coolidge were also not available for this dark and glamorous gentleman, known to his thousands of panting feminine admirers as Rudolph Valentino. "The great lover of the silver screen" died of a combination of peritonitis and pneumonia. Weeping crowds followed the body covered with a cloth of gold to the funeral parlor at Broadway and Eighty-sixth Street. More gathered to view the body which was prepared for eternity "by the same special process used after the death of Enrico Caruso, a process insuring perpetual preservation." Plate windows were smashed by the mourning multitude. A god was gone who in the height of fashion wore bracelets and other trinkets and was making a million dollars a year. Will Hays, the protector of Hollywood movie morals, and Mayor "Jimmy" Walker, whose own morals some censured, served as honorary pallbearers. In the attention paid to his passing there was little room to note the coincident death of ninety-two-year-old Dr. Charles W. Eliot, former president of Harvard, who in his lifetime had built a provincial college into a great university. History has been more considerate of Eliot. Yet his memory has been attended by nothing so dramatic as the recurrent and much publicized visits of "ladies in black" to Valentino's grave on the anniversaries of his death. It was suggested that such ladies, masked by their weeds, were noted beauties of the time. The veiled visitors only ceased to appear when movie columnist Hedda Hopper undertook to expose them as models in a hoax by florists designed to promote the sale of memorial flowers.

Other events attracted attention. While Florida cleared its cluttered streets, papers published an exclusive interview with Calvin Coolidge as the embodiment of the American virtues and the solid

American scene by Bruce Barton. The mutual satisfaction of interviewer Barton and interviewed Coolidge was easy to understand. Trading on the New York Stock Exchange had doubled between 1923, when Coolidge came to the Presidency, and 1926, when they talked while Coolidge petted his collies, Rob Roy and Prudence Prim. And the average price of twenty-five representative industrial stocks had risen from $108 to $166 a share, or about 54 per cent. Even so, the big boom had not set in. Business was only responding to the salubrious economic climate which attended Mr. Coolidge's feeling that "the business of America is business." To the Yankee watchman on the nation's tower all seemed well. In the March before Barton's glowing interview the New York *Times* had reported that the family of Coolidge's Secretary of the Treasury Andrew Mellon had made $300,000,000 in the market on aluminum and Gulf Oil alone. Wind seemed only filling the sails of fortune's fleet.

It was to be a decade before Anne Morrow Lindbergh would write, in an entirely different context, her book *Listen, the Wind*. Few were listening in 1927. Anne Morrow, daughter of a partner in the great House of Morgan, was just graduating from Smith College. She had, of course, never met her future husband Charles A. Lindbergh, Jr. But Americans, more concerned with soaring than storm, were ready to have as symbol not merely Mr. Coolidge, whom Barton had set up as saint in his advertising man's theology despite the fact that some, like the radical heretic cartoonist Art Young, called him a "slit-mouthed Puritan." Even before they heard of Lindbergh, people were prepared to take him to their hearts as the shining figure of the era—certainly not one of a lost generation.

This tall, blond, deceptively self-depreciatory, young man of twenty-four appeared almost ironically to play his role in the Coolidge era. Young Lindbergh's father, Congressman Charles A. Lindbergh, had died in 1924 when he had hoped to be recouping his political fortunes by election as governor of Minnesota. His son had flown to scatter his ashes over the family homestead at Little Falls, Minnesota, a small town on the shores of the Mississippi.

The old man had been listed as early as the Taft administration by "Fighting Bob" La Follette as one of the "pioneer House Insurgents" whose successors under Coolidge formed the Farm Bloc, which held an irritating balance of power in the Congress with which Coolidge dealt. La Follette had died June 18, 1925. Others, however, notably Senator George Norris of Nebraska, were pressing for economic and agricultural reforms. Also Norris was seeking government development of a wartime powder-making plant on the Tennessee River at Muscle Shoals which would later, as the Tennessee Valley Authority, bring greater light to towns like Dayton than Mencken, Darrow and all the so-called modernists were able to do in the Scopes trial. Insurgents like Norris were called by Republican regulars "sons of the wild jackass." The elder Lindbergh would have qualified as one.

He had in his Congressional days from 1907 to 1917 fought for a variety of reforms. Notably he had introduced the resolution in 1912 which set up an investigation of the "Money Trust" and brought even the massive J. Pierpont Morgan to interrogation. Also, as war approached, Lindbergh, Sr., had denounced propaganda and profiteering. He had spoken prophetically of himself when he cried in the clamor for war that "the man who reasons and exercises good sense today may be hung in effigy tomorrow by the jingoes."

He was defeated in a race for the Republican nomination for U. S. senator by Frank B. Kellogg, who under Coolidge became Secretary of State. Two years later, running with the support of the radical Non-Partisan League, he was defeated for governor. This Lindbergh, wrote a Minnesota historian, "was of the type to whom statues are erected only after the lapse of years." He was probably only futilely fighting in the lag of agriculture behind the prosperity of Wall Street in the year in which he died. His Farmer-Labor associates, scorned and ridiculed by conservatives, in the campaign which followed his death voted for La Follette, but the state went for Coolidge.

The agricultural depression had begun in 1920 when foreign demand ceased sharply. Net total farm income dropped from $10,061,-000,000 in 1919 to $9,009,000,000 in 1920 and to $4,138,000,000 in 1921. A slight rise in 1922 brought it to $5,081,000,000 but it continued to lag far behind the supposed general rising prosperity and its rising prices on the things farmers required. The Farm Bloc's efforts to aid agriculture culminated in 1924, the year of Lindbergh's last candidacy and death, in legislation called the McNary-Haugen Bill, designed to provide government assistance to farmers in disposing of surplus crops abroad and in raising prices in the domestic market. Violently opposed by Eastern Republicans and by Coolidge, it was defeated in the House on June 3, 1924, a month after the elder Lindbergh died.

His son then was no mere gangling Main Street boy. Young Charles's father wrote as well as fought. His mother was a science graduate of the University of Michigan. And much of his boyhood was spent in Washington, where his father served in Congress from the time he was five until he was fifteen. There he attended the fashionable Friends School. His was by no means a sheltered childhood, however. At sixteen he was driving his father in his wild, bitter, losing, 1918 campaign for governor. Later, in the early twenties, he flew campaign literature and speakers for his father and once got his father to fly in his plane.

The elder Lindbergh did not care for the flying business. Perhaps young Charles's fascination with it caused him to drop out of the University of Wisconsin after three semesters. He enrolled in a flying school in Lincoln, Nebraska. Within four years he had made a reputation in flying circles in the West. He enlisted in Army aviation the spring his father died. In 1926, with a reserve commission as captain, he went to work flying air mail between St. Louis and Chicago. Already he had a longer trip in mind.

As early as May 22, 1919, Raymond Orteig, exuberant operator in Greenwich Village of the Lafayette Hotel, patronized by more gourmets than impecunious poets, had offered a $25,000 prize "to the first aviator who shall cross the Atlantic in a land or water craft (heavier-than-air) from Paris or the shores of France to New York, or from New York to Paris or the shores of France, without stop." For seven years the prize had gone unclaimed for lack of an engine which could be depended upon for such a distance. But in 1926, new 220-horsepower, air-cooled Wright Whirlwind engines had carried U. S. Commander Richard E. Bryd over the North Pole. Flyers began to contemplate the Atlantic flight. The least promising among them seemed Lindbergh, who had put his own savings and borrowed money together, totaling about $14,000, for a single-engine monoplane equipped with the Whirlwind engine. He seemed only a gawky boy eating many hot dogs as he waited in May, 1927, for good weather at Roosevelt Field on Long Island where other aviators were preparing to take off. He attracted attention, but bets were on his better-known competitors—Byrd, Giuseppe Bellanca, Clarence Chamberlin. Then suddenly on the morning of May 19 he was airborne and Europe-bound.

A nation which had been giving much of its attention to the tawdry trial of a corset salesman named Henry Judd Gray and Ruth Snyder for the murder of her husband lifted its eyes and its hearts to the skies. At a prize fight between Jack Sharkey and Jim Maloney spectators were called to a moment of silence and prayer for the boy in the skies. Word came as he passed Ireland. And his flight seemed most threatened by *tout le monde*, which crowded, cheering, about the runways as "We," the man and the plane, landed at Le Bourget Field in Paris on the evening of May 21.

His modesty matched his accomplishment. He was brought home on a cruiser to Washington for accolades from crowds and from Coolidge. It seemed irrelevant and immaterial for one newspaper-man at the time to inject the sour note that he was the "son of a man who was driven from public life by the same political forces which placed Calvin Coolidge in the White House." No one apparently noticed that the first official in Coolidge's Cabinet was Secretary of State Kellogg, who in person had pushed his father from the Congress.

No ironies were stressed in the tumultuous rejoicing. And Coolidge did not let the tumult interrupt the even tenor of his ways. On the day after he welcomed Lindbergh home, promoted him to colonel and gave him the nation's thanks, he set off for a summer sojourn in the South Dakota State Game Lodge in Custer Park in the Black Hills. Despite the name of the park, Coolidge gave no indication that he had chosen it for a last stand. His year had come to a political and economic peak high as the mountains in the park.

Early in 1927, the Federal Reserve Board in Washington appeared to be trying to curb the speculation in Wall Street. But Coolidge issued a statement predicting that the year would be "one of continued healthy business activity and prosperity." His statement stimulated the market. Secretary Mellon followed with more assurances a few days later. J. P. Morgan the younger lunched at the White House in February. By March the New York *Times* reported that "the main advance has been resumed" on the Stock Exchange. And later that month when Secretary Mellon sailed for Europe he noted that "the stock market seems to be going along in an orderly fashion, and I see no evidence of over-speculation." In the month in which Lindbergh returned and the Presidential party left for the Black Hills, Coolidge again stressed the sound business situation. At that statement, according to his biographer William Allen White, the market jumped twenty-six points.

And to bounding prosperity was added the promise of peace. Already in gestation when the President went to the Black Hills was the Kellogg-Briand Peace Pact to outlaw war. Wily French politician Aristide Briand had first suggested only an agreement between the United States and France renouncing war as an instrument of national policy. Kellogg, known in the Senate as "Nervous Nellie," had been, with the nation's troubles extending from Nicaragua to China, unenthusiastic at the outset. Coolidge's interest was not increased by the activities for peace of Senator Borah, who definitely was not docile on the regular Republican reservation. About this time the President made one of his straight-faced witticisms which belied the legend of his humorlessness. Observing the Idaho Senator on a bridal path in Washington, he commented, "There goes Senator Borah horseback riding and both he and the horse are going the same way."

Lindbergh's flight to Paris, however, had made Franco-American friendship almost a love affair which Kellogg could not disregard. He and Coolidge found a way to satisfy peace demands and avoid an appearance of an entangling alliance with France. Ultimately the proposed treaty was broadened to include any and all agreeing nations. Sixty-two nations, all the great powers, signed. War was against the law. The achievement was to bring Kellogg the Nobel prize in 1930. In 1927 in the Black Hills hardly anybody, including the summer sojourner at Custer State Park, was concerned about an obscure, furious politician named Adolf Hitler who had been sent to jail for treason in the fall Coolidge became President of the United States. For the "outlawing of war" there was universal acclaim.

Also nearer at hand Coolidge's old Amherst classmate and Morgan partner, Dwight Whitney Morrow, was doing much as ambassador to Mexico to quiet differences between that country's revolutionary government and the Roman Catholic Church and to improve relations between Mexico and the "Colossus of the North." As an aid in Morrow's work, in came Lindbergh flying as a goodwill visitor welcomed by tumultuously friendly Mexicans. Friendship was ruling the affairs of nations. It appeared almost a part of the scheme of soaring civilization that Lindbergh should meet not only Mexico but the Morrows. Not only could nations renounce war;

love, when all skies were fair, could bind the Morgan princess, Anne Morrow, to the old, battered, anti-Wall Street insurgent's son.

The times did not seem rose-tinted to all. Though peaceful and beautiful, the Black Hills seemed an odd choice as the site of the summer White House in 1927. Custer State Park had been established by Senator Peter Norbeck who, as a long-time progressive Republican, was active in the support of farm legislation which Coolidge was testily opposing. No grandeur attended the quarters the Presidential party occupied. A rambling, pine board, paper-lined building, the State Game Lodge was hot at midday despite breezes from the surrounding mountains. Certainly Coolidge did not look imperial when he let himself be photographed there in an elaborate cowboy outfit presented to him by welcoming South Dakotans. His spurs clanked on the steps as he displayed himself for the new sound pictures which were that year being introduced not only in newsreels but in such a film as *The Jazz Singer* starring black-faced Al Jolson.

All seemed serene during Coolidge's first days in the hills though some incidents irritated him. It was about this time that he began to speak in twangy sarcasm of his Secretary of Commerce Herbert Hoover as "the wonder boy." Pressed by governors of flood-endangered states in the Mississippi basin, he had sent Hoover there earlier in the summer to take charge of the emergency in the great deluge of 1927. Putting on his old relief hat, Hoover made the most of his opportunity in the overflow of the big river which beyond broken levees sometimes spread 150 miles wide from Cairo, Illinois, to the Gulf. In a special Pullman car with water often above its axles, Hoover in steaming weather circled inundated towns. He rode ahead of the waters with warnings often regarded with incredulity in towns about to be flooded. He raised millions in relief funds, for, as he said rather tartly later, "at this time we all believed in self-help" and it had not occurred to citizens that the federal government should pay for the job.

He made himself, however, a symbol of federal help and beneficence. He set up tent towns, hospitals, commissaries. He called in the Coast Guard, the Weather Bureau, the Army Engineers, the Red Cross to deal with the situation in which 1,500,000 people were driven from their homes, two million acres of crops and thousands of animals were lost and property damage amounted to $355,147,-

ooo. He built boats and borrowed more. He rented one thousand outboard motors; and discovered when time came to return them that river fishermen, thrifty even in flood time, had carried off for their own uses all but 120. Hoover, looking back, recalled other amusing incidents. But at the time he was a publicized hurrying hero, mentioning that at least in part due to his efforts only three lives were lost in the whole catastrophe—one of them that of an overcurious sightseer.

Hoover in his report on the flood to Coolidge made recommendations. He proposed higher levees, spillways and bypasses on the lower river. Nothing in his report suggested such upstream control of waters as Senator Norris of the Farm Bloc was already envisaging in his plan for the public development of the Tennessee River. That stream poured its waters from a wide Appalachian region, past already forgotten Dayton, Tennessee, into the Ohio and Mississippi rivers building flood to the Gulf. Upon it in World War I the government had begun at Muscle Shoals a great power plant for the production of nitrates for explosives. Now private companies, with both Coolidge and Hoover behind them, wanted the great resource. Certainly expanded utilities wanted no public competition in power.

Most exciting to the popular and the Republican imagination was an offer by Henry Ford to lease the plant for a century at $1,500,000 a year. He would, he promised, produce cheap fertilizers and build a city seventy-five miles long on the shores of the Tennessee River. His proposal met the mood of boom. Puffed by his proposition, real estate speculators (some of them refugees from Florida collapse) were buying up the river shore and selling lots from plats at hawkers' booths on Broadway and elsewhere like tickets in a grand lottery.

The river rolled on and Hoover's flood was less remembered than a song made about the big Mississippi at the time. In the year when the waters spread so wide, Florenz Ziegfeld turned from his *Follies* and the beautiful long-legged girls who danced beside lariat-swinging, gum-chewing Will Rogers. He made a musical play from Edna Ferber's novel *Show Boat*. For it Jerome Kern and Oscar Hammerstein 2d wrote a song for the voice of the Negro basso Paul Robeson. "Ol' Man River" took its place in hearts and voices like none since Stephen Foster's melodies. Even a prosperous country could delight in this nostalgic wail from its lower depths of the weary, the oppressed and the poor, "tired of livin' an' feared of dyin'" beside the relentlessly rolling river.

Streams ran clear and quietly in the Black Hills where that summer not only was a Sheep Mountain rechristened Coolidge Mountain but in definite improvement a Squaw Creek was renamed Grace Coolidge Creek. Life was pleasant though news was in short supply for the twenty-five press correspondents at Custer Park. Then, on August 2, the big story came. On that day, the fourth anniversary of his accession to the Presidency, the President distributed to newsmen a ten-word statement he had dictated to a confidential stenographer. It read:

"I do not choose to run for President in 1928."

He declined to amplify or explain. The words said what they said. Yet there seemed no such finality about them, even to Herbert Hoover resting from his flood labors at Bohemian Grove in California, as an announcement next day by Governor Alvan T. Fuller of Massachusetts, from the office Coolidge had once occupied. Fuller and a distinguished advisory committee he had named unanimously agreed, he said, that the trial of the shoe edger, Nicola Sacco, thirty-six, and the fish peddler, Bartolomeo Vanzetti, thirty-nine, for murder had been fair and their guilt proved.

The roar of protest, which had been rising about the supposed prejudiced prosecution of these two poor, oddly eloquent, Italian anarchists and atheists, reached the point of scream. The crime of which they had been convicted was the murder of a shoe factory paymaster and guard seven years before on April 15, 1920. Many believed that their conviction at the height of the Red Scare then had come not from proof of their guilt but prejudice against them as radical foreigners. Beyond multiple appeals and motions, by 1927 they had become almost sacred symbols of reactionary oppression to many intellectuals, liberals, writers, some aristocratic Boston women of good works and fellow Italians. Sensitive folk who had been offended by Bruce Barton's story of Jesus as a businessman themselves turned quickly to the images of Calvary in writing of Sacco and Vanzetti. The critic and poet, Malcolm Cowley, referred to them as "dago Christs."

There was a roar also for their blood. Governor Fuller in the Irish stronghold of Boston had earlier in the year declined to commute the sentences of three Irish-Catholic ex-servicemen guilty of a holdup similar to that with which Sacco and Vanzetti were charged. The two Italians had been draft dodgers. Governor Fuller seemed to hesitate. He had risen from a bicycle mechanic and a dealer in plush Packard cars to become one of the richest men in Massachusetts. He was new to Back Bay society but he had Back Bay advice in his advisory committee headed by Abbott Lawrence Lowell, not only president of Harvard but one of those Lowells who in the Massachusetts hierarchy spoke only to God. Fuller heard, too, from other solid citizens who felt that cries for clemency struck at orderly judicial process in general and in particular at the jurist who tried the case, Judge Webster Thayer, and in manner to make him seem worse than Pilate. Governor Fuller was a great admirer of Coolidge. Some felt that he thought that the political lightning which had struck Coolidge after the police strike might come his way, too.

Coolidge was a far way from the roars. As long as he could as governor he had remained in the background during the lesser tumult of the police strike in 1920, even if to many he had seemed to emerge as its hero. Now in Dakota he had no inclination to become involved in the riotous sounds of protest around the world which impinged on Massachusetts. August advanced in anger and despair. Reds from Buenos Aires to Calcutta demanded mercy. They were joined by royalists in France. Even Benito Mussolini diplomatically tried to intervene. Coolidge was keeping cool in Dakota.

Certainly it was cooler and quieter there on Sunday, August 21, two days before Sacco and Vanzetti were scheduled to die. On the East Coast around Boston defense lawyers were frantically seeking intervention by a variety of reluctant judges. One tried unsuccessfully to get help from Chief Justice Taft in Canada. Then, as pickets gathered about the State House in Boston, 150 of them to be carted away by the police, frantic efforts were turned toward Dakota.

A telegram begging Presidential intervention came to the White House. It was not answered. A clamorous telephone call from Boston was taken by a member of the President's staff. He refused to give his name to the telephoning lawyer. The President could not be disturbed. There was no federal question involved. He listened while the lawyer in Boston offered to fly to the Black Hills. Firmly he told him that if he did come, he would not be received.

So Sunday ended in Dakota and in Boston. More petitions and petitioners poured into Coolidge's old capital. Fiorello La Guardia, then a member of Congress, came by chartered plane to plead with the governor who had been a congressman, too. Edna St. Vincent Millay, seeming almost too frail to hold the fire within her, came to speak as one of a long list of concerned writers: John Dos Passos, Dorothy Parker, Heywood Broun (soon to lose his job on the New York *World* for too great vehemence in the case), Walter Lippmann, H. G. Wells as one of many Europeans, Zona Gale, Katherine Anne Porter, many more. That morning before the execution impending in the night ahead, Miss Millay had published her poem, *Justice Denied in Massachusetts*, in the New York *Times*. In the muted metaphor of a New England more like Plymouth, Vermont, than Boston, she shaped a sense of something more than the death of men. She wrote of a land grown sour to the fruitful seed where men were left to till the blighted earth with a broken hoe.

But the resounding poetry in the case, still heard across the years, came from the two condemned men. Though members of the working class in Massachusetts, both came from substantial rural folk in Italy. Both were anarchists in a group of which some members were arrested and deported in the Red Scare of 1920, the year in which they were arrested. And both, working in limited English, spoke and wrote like poetic characters in the drama their story became. Vanzetti's prose, attended by the misspelling and the lyric reshaping of words, sometimes sounded to ordinary ears like the often baffling writing of Gertrude Stein. But beauty came through. Just after his seventh Christmas behind bars he wrote of "the words and deeds of Massachusetts black gowned, puritanic, cold-blood murderors." Yet there was a sort of poetic nostalgia in his remembrance of his father's garden at Villafalletto in northern Italy.

. . . so beautiful, unspeakably beautiful it is . . . the singing birds there; black merles, the gold-finches, the green finches, the chaf-finches, the neck-crooking, the green ficks; the unmachable nightingales, the nightingales over-all. Yet, I think that the wonder of my garden's wonders is the banks of its path. Hundreds of grass, leaves of wild flowors witness there the almighty genios of the universal architecture—reflecting the sky, the Sun, the moon, the stars, all of its lights and colors. The forget-menot are nations there, and nation are the wild daisies.

He was lyric, too, about the flowers some well-to-do ladies of liberal faith sent to his cell: "My window here is peopled of recipients, it is a riot of blissing colors and beauties forms: a giranium

plants a tulipan plant from Mrs. Evans. White flowers, pink carna-
tions, roseate peaches, buds, and flowers, bush-yellow flowers. . . ."

But so powerful was the poetry in Vanzetti's speech at the time
of their sentence to death that eleven years after he was dead, it
appeared, set down like lines of verse, in Selden Rodman's *A New
Anthology of Modern Poetry*. Speaking as perhaps "more witful"
than Sacco, "a better babbler," he addressed Judge Thayer whom
the less talkative Sacco had called a "gowned cobra." Sacco's name
would be remembered in gratitude, Vanzetti said, when the bones
of judge and prosecutor would be "dispersed by time;

> when your name, his name, your laws, institutions,
> and your false god are but a dim rememoring
> of a cursed past in which man was wolf
> to the man. . . .
>
> If it had not been for these things
> I might have live out my life
> talking at street corners to scorning men.
> I might have die, unmarked, unknown, a failure.
> Now we are not a failure.
> This is our career and our triumph. Never
> in our full life could we hope to do such work
> for tolerance, for justice, for man's understanding
> of man, as now we do by accident.
> Our words, our lives, our pains—nothing!
> The taking of our lives—lives of a good
>       shoemaker and a poor fishpeddler—
> all! That last moment belongs to us—
> that agony is our triumph.

They died while some wept, some cried in helpless anger, and
some said loudly that it was good to have the dagos dead. And the
debate about their guilt after their deaths did not subside. It went
into books, poems and plays. Ferris Greenslet, noted Boston publisher, answered a question, "Is immortality desirable?"

"I almost think it is, if only to get at the truth of the Sacco-
Vanzetti case."

Thirty-five years after their death, Francis Russell, in an exhaus-
tive study, *Tragedy in Dedham—The Story of the Sacco-Vanzetti
Case*, reached a conclusion of his own. In their trial he recalled
that an attorney had felt that if he gave up on Nicola Sacco he had

a chance of persuading the jury to acquit Bartolomeo Vanzetti. He put it up to Vanzetti.

"What shall I do?"

And Vanzetti answered, "Save Nick, he has the woman and child."

In his trial by investigation Russell came to the conclusion that Sacco was either guilty or knew who was. He was convinced of Vanzetti's innocence.

Many never had any doubts. The Reverend Billy Sunday, conducting one of his strenuous revivals designed to save a lost generation from the fate of Sodom, at Tremont Temple in Boston hoarsely cried his convictions about the doomed men and those at home and abroad who clamored for clemency.

"Give 'em the juice," he shouted from his pulpit. "Burn them, if they're guilty. That's the way to handle it. I'm tired of hearing these foreigners, these radicals, coming over here and telling us what to do."

The crowds about the State House dispersed after word came from the death house. Sometimes in following days the Common was as quiet as Camp Custer in South Dakota. When the Coolidges returned to the capital, murmurings in curiosity among politicians about that word "choose" were muted in uncertainty hardly louder than cricket cries. The music welcomed was the sound of stock tickers ever counting higher and of factory machines turning out more and more gadgets and goods.

Henry Ford turned from the grandiose dreams he had stirred about development of a Southern river. And nobody was disturbed because weeds grew in the empty city lots on the Tennessee shore which hucksters had sold to suckers. Whatever happened to the river, Ford had to keep his cars rolling on the roads. For him prosperity meant competition, too. Richer people wanted to ride in more elegance and comfort. Other automobile manufacturers, notably General Motors, for whom the Danish immigrant W. S. Knudsen developed the Chevrolet, and Walter P. Chrysler, were building better cheap cars. New paints were adding color to automobiles. The old, light, tough, dark Model T Ford, the much-loved Tin Lizzie of many jokes, seemed in trouble on the many better roads to more and more filling stations. Ford reluctantly turned to eager designers in Detroit and advertisers on expanding Madison Avenue where Barton equally communed with Christ and commodities.

In the spring of 1927, the auto magnate closed down his big shops, scrapped his Model T, and put the country in suspense with the announcement that he was producing a new car. Interest mounted across the summer and the fall. Stories about it got space in newspapers even in competition with the Sacco-Vanzetti case, the Lindbergh flight, the I-do-not-choose statement, and the lurid Hall-Mills murder case, which was covered by far more reporters (including poets, columnists, revivalists and philosophers) than had gone to Dayton for the "monkey trial." In secrecy Ford's builders produced the Model A and the advertisers presented it in explosion. Its unveiling on December 2, 1927, was heralded by a five-day series of full-page advertisements in two thousand daily newspapers at a cost of $1,300,000. That sounded like a lot of money then, though mathematics indicates it was only an average of $650 per paper or $130 an advertisement. Obviously the advertising business had some heights to climb and was climbing in this decade after Bruce Barton had entered it at the end of World War I and on Forty-fifth Street, not Madison Avenue. The advance of advertising as an art form was perhaps indicated by the fact that even as the decade began Barton was living at Great Neck, Long Island, where his neighbor, Scott Fitzgerald, said he couldn't live on less than $36,000 a year.

The advertising on top of the suspense paid off for Ford. A million people—so the New York *Herald Tribune* estimated—tried to get into the New York showing. More mobs of the eager poured to the displays in Detroit, Cleveland, Kansas City, other places. And they added orders to eagerness. With a new choice, including Niagara Blue roadsters and Arabian Sand phaetons, they pushed Ford to new leadership in the decade in which the number of cars was to be almost quadrupled. In the same period sales of radios were to go up from nothing to annual sales volume of $842,548,000 a year.

It seemed incredible that Coolidge could choose to remove himself from this Coolidge era. Politicians who wanted to be on a band wagon, any band wagon, began to look around, and Mr. Hoover, who wanted to create one, was uncomfortable. Coolidge would not talk to him. Politicians, in a time when all were seeking stock market tips on a sure thing, might have got their tip from the story of the bedspread Grace Coolidge was said to be crocheting with a square in it for each month of the Coolidge term—and only one term. If she was so crocheting she gave another reason for her husband's intent to retire, according to Dr. Claude M. Fuess, who became the President's official biographer. Always a woman to smile at her husband's silences and his occasional testiness, too, she listened while some guests were seeking to get more from Coolidge than his simple "not choose" statement to the press. Why had he done it? Grace Coolidge supplied the answer.

"Poppa says there's a depression coming."

Perhaps that story was true even in this time of a rain of riches. Once in real rainy weather someone had murmured to Coolidge a question as to whether he reckoned the rain would ever stop.

"It always has," he said.

Few expected any change in the weather now. Those who suggested it were disregarded or considered somehow untrue to Bruce Barton's new theology. Winds came. Men rode the wind. Angers arose. Rivers rolled on. Certainly no one paid much attention to the verses from Ecclesiastes which Hemingway had put down on his fore page under Gertrude Stein's line about the lost generation. It is doubtful that Hemingway put them down as prophecy.

> One generation passeth away, and another
> generation cometh; but the earth abideth forever
> . . . The sun also ariseth, and the sun goeth
> down, and hasteth to the place where he arose . . .
> The wind goeth toward the south, and turneth about
> unto the north; it whirleth about continually,
> and the wind returneth again according to his
> circuits. . . . All the rivers run into the sea;
> yet the sea is not full; unto the place from
> whence the rivers come, thither they return again.

The poetry America preferred was that heard in the tremendous upward surge of the stock market in 1927. Brokers' loans increased from a little over $3,000,000,000 in January, 1927, to $4,500,000,-000 by the end of the year. The volume of shares jumped from 451,000,000 to 577,000,000. And all were sure that the sea of speculation was not yet full.

# XII

## THE SUN ALSO SETS

THOUGH Sinclair Lewis could not recall it later, others remembered the dark prophecy he made in August, 1928.

Rich in the land he lampooned, well groomed for his new wife, the brilliant journalist Dorothy Thompson, he stood in the high offices of the publishing firm of Harcourt, Brace which his books had enriched, too. At a window he looked down at the canyon of Madison Avenue. Buildings loomed about him filled with the plush offices of other publishers and of expanding advertising firms staffed to stimulate new, dazzling salesmanship.

Their promotions ran across America from door to door, from Babbitt to Babbitt, to Main Streets and less certainly to rural roads, though sometimes along the way the big advertisements in fat newspapers and magazines were only used to chink the cracks in weather-beaten walls. By radio the most popular entertainers, saved from the decline of vaudeville, attracted the customers clustered at home as once they had been collected at the tail gates of medicine peddlers' wagons by boys with guitars. Now great strings plucked Buy! Buy! Buy!—on the installment, on the margin, from the increasing chain stores and from all the more and more importunate producers of everything.

Lewis watched the street below him swarming with shoppers, clerks, stenographers, models, copywriters, salesmen, all the company of a gilded age. He shook his graying red head.

"Within a year," he said, "this country will have a terrible financial panic. I don't think, I know. Can't you see it, smell it. I can see people jumping out of windows on this very street."

On a less than wholesale scale such a thing had already happened on this very street. A block or so away at the Biltmore Hotel, where now Democrats had offices in the raging Smith-Hoover Presidential campaign, the hostelry's builder in a spell of depression years before had thrown himself from a high window to the street. That irrelevant incident was long forgotten. Now the hotel not only lodged politicians hopeful though bitter about back-country bigotry. Also, beside swarming Grand Central Station, it was the place where commuters stopped for a last look at the stock ticker about the rising securities they had bought on margin, then burrowed to trains waiting to carry them to mortgaged homes in spreading suburbs.

"Under the clock at the Biltmore" was a favorite meeting place for such young folk as girls from Vassar and boys from Yale and other assorted schools and colleges. Throughout the twenties they served as not-too-much caricatured models for the lively drawings of John Held, Jr., in *Life*, *Judge* and other humorous magazines. Not all regarded Held's flat-breasted, short-skirted flappers with their shingled hair and his Joe Colleges with hip flasks under their coonskin coats as figures in a proper portrait of America. They gathered for whoopee and the Biltmore was convenient to a good share of the 32,000 speakeasies the city provided then, many of them as decorous as the old brownstone mansions they occupied, and serving in an air of exclusiveness liquor which had to make no prohibition apologies. Parking was still no great problem and some of the young drove to similar bibulous places in the country in sporty Stutzes (price $3570) provided by papas watching tickers in the quieter elegance of the Waldorf-Astoria at Thirty-fourth Street and Fifth Avenue. There, with the famous maître d'hôtel Oscar Tschirky still rationing his smiles by his well-understood rank of the guests, it seemed improbable that there could be any truth even in this explosively expansive year that the Waldorf was obsolete and would have to come down that a greater tower with higher windows might be put up.

Few shared Lewis' sense of coming danger—or his anticipation of the dramatic spectacle of falling men. Six months before he ominously viewed this Madison Avenue of manufactured eagerness, on March 3, 1928, the stock market had entered upon its most exciting movement. Harvard economists had been talking about declines. The New York *Times* had been speaking of investor hesitation. But General Motors began a swift advance. Radio Corporation showed even greater strength, jumping 12¾ points in one day alone. Word got around that John J. Raskob and others who had made money in motors and the markets were now buying in huge quantities. They figured that with Ford delayed in meeting his orders for his new Model A, General Motors was in for a big year. Equal expectations attended Radio Corporation of America. In 1928 total radio sales were rising to $650,550,000, ten times the total of its infant year of 1922. Radio Corporation's 1928 low was 85½. With the push of Raskob and company and their expectation of the trooping of thousands of smaller margin buyers behind them, it was off toward a 1929 high of 549.

Mr. Raskob was even more clearly behind a boom in politics that year. He was only standing in the political wings when ebullient, able, brown-derbied Al Smith advanced toward the Democratic nomination for President despite acre-big precinct meetings of protest in what Mencken had called the Bible Belt. While thousands cheered, other delegates in hot Houston listened charmed but reluctant when Franklin Roosevelt, deliberately speaking over the heads of the fifteen thousand in the steaming hall to fifteen million radio listeners in the country, this time made his label "Happy Warrior" stick to Al in an apparently unified but unhappy convention. Dry Protestant Democrats, still distrustful of big-city politics, swallowed hard and took their medicine, easing the dose with a dry plank in the platform. They dispersed. Then many who had swallowed, choked. Smith repudiated the dry plank. He named Raskob, who had always been a Republican before, Democratic National Chairman. He did that, he said, because the Democratic Party, many of whose members had regarded themselves as members of the party of protest against Wall Street and the Money Power, could not win without the support of Big Business.

Even in this time of the adoration of the businessman as the stocks flew upward, Raskob arrived in the recognition of most Democrats almost like a rocket from outer space—and one with an unwelcome wet warhead on it. A pugnacious publicist whom he later hired for the harassment of Republicans described him as "the little magnate," referring to his physical size, not the dimensions of his portfolio. He was, of course, well known in the business community. Investment bankers, issuing a variety of new stocks for an eager public, often felt it wise to cut him in in advance at something below the price at which the stocks would be put on the market.

Still he was not quite the same kind of member of the Business Establishment as those in the traditions of the House of Morgan, whose financial affairs included vast market operations but also often passing the plate in Trinity Church. Like Smith, Raskob went to mass. And among the self-made he had not collected the popular affection of some who had fought their way upward, such as, for instance, smooth, genial Charles M. Schwab of Bethlehem Steel. Schwab that year seemed almost as much an American item as the flag-waving dancing man George M. Cohan or rope-swinging Will Rogers. He was suave and gracious even when at about this time to his dismay and denial he was suspected of hiring a loud lobbyist to disrupt naval disarmament discussions in Geneva. Armor maker or not, Mr. Schwab was to say he wished all battleships—well, nearly all—could disappear from the seas.

Raskob's rise had been explosive in connection with E. I. Du Pont de Nemours and Company which was finding that if it could not turn swords into plowshares, it could do something of the same sort in converting cellulose into rayon and cellophane as well as explosives. Raskob had gone to parochial school in Lockport, New York, on the Erie Canal which had typified earlier ideas of transportation. Also there shortly before he was born the art of advertising had been given impetus by the promotion of a gargling oil "good for man or beast." He had other education only sufficient to make him a stenographer but he went with his notebook into the employ of Pierre Du Pont at a time when the famous old Delaware family, which had been on the point of selling out, decided to reorganize its family company. A little over thirteen years later Raskob, at thirty-five, was treasurer of the company. Over strong opposition he urged the company to buy into the struggling, sprawling General Motors Corporation. His even greater contribution was in the development of the sale of cars on the installment plan, which contributed almost as much to the growth of the industry as the self-starter.

Setting up his own political headquarters in the General Motors Building in New York, where he could attend to his political and his market operations at the same time, the little and often domineering magnate discovered that getting votes was not quite the same as making money. He himself became a figure in a new triumvirate of rages: Rum, Romanism and Raskob. Amazingly, Hoover could make it seem that Smith, even though Raskob's candidate, was in his

power policies "'snuggling' up to socialism." Millions agreed with
the solemn Hoover that prohibition was an experiment "noble in
motive and far reaching in purpose." Certainly nobody laughed
scornfully as the market rose at the promise that the Republicans
"with the help of God" looked to the "abolition of poverty."
Prosperity seemed a Republican possession. In lesser but louder measure prejudice was, too. In a statement as mild as his Quaker af-
filiation, Hoover said that in the campaign "the lower rank and file
of party workers on both sides did not show the elevation of spirit
one could desire." That was a pious whisper after a whirlwind. But
bigots took more credit than they were entitled to for the overwhelming Hoover victory. And the defeated, in bitterness, needing
an explanation satisfying to themselves, gave pig-headed Protestants
and prohibitionists too much credit, too.

"Unpack!" wired Will Rogers in a pretended cable to the Pope
who sometimes somehow seemed to be running with Smith as his
proxy.

Still, Smith in his defeat lost only one more state in the Protestant,
dry and supposedly prejudiced South than Harry Truman did years
later when he won the Presidency in 1948. Indeed, the South gave
Smith all the votes he got except those of Massachusetts and Rhode
Island. The only Democratic crumb seemed Roosevelt's squeak-
through victory as governor of New York. He had reluctantly left
the hope of cure for his paralyzed legs to come up from Warm
Springs, Georgia, to run. To some it seemed less good fortune than
affront for this country squire, an Episcopalian moderate on the
liquor question, supposedly only a candidate to help Smith, to run
ahead of Al, whose brown derby they regarded as a crown.

Prosperity's part in the election was quickly demonstrated and
celebrated by the "Hoover bull market" on the stock exchange.
Prices rose to new record levels. Radio flew to 400. There was a
drop. Then, as in the previous June, the advance began again. The
Federal Reserve Board, set up in part to guard against speculation,
was disturbed but indecisive. Mr. Hoover, as President-elect, was
sailing confidently in South American waters on a battleship (Coolidge had suggested that a cruiser would be cheaper). But, however
battered and, as it turned out also, stubborn Raskob was as a politician, he was still businessman in the era of that figure's eminence.

At the year's end *Time* magazine, only four years old and some
felt an arrogant infant, put Walter P. Chrysler on its cover as its

Man of the Year. He was further evidence that the only American way was up. Son of a locomotive engineer and himself once a five-cents-an-hour apprentice in the Union Pacific shops, Chrysler in the motor industry had added the old Dodge Brothers properties to his own and was in full-scale competition with Ford and General Motors. Furthermore Chrysler announced that in this new year of 1929 he was building an eight-hundred-foot skyscraper of sixty-eight stories in New York just across the street from Grand Central Station. It would be, he said confidently, the tallest spire in the city of big buildings and high windows. On its ground floor in a special case would be displayed the mechanic's tools with which Chrysler began his climb. Obviously they would look more dramatic than Raskob's stenographic notebooks. Yet shortly afterward it was announced that Mr. Smith, who had moved as suddenly into business as Mr. Raskob had moved into politics, would as president of Empire State, Inc., backed again by Raskob, build a taller building still.

Such monumental construction was not unique. Indeed, a year before in Chicago Samuel Insull had already begun construction of a twenty-million-dollar-plus Civic Opera House. In its forty-two stories it would provide not only a thirteen-story stage for song; Mr. Insull would have a penthouse and office quarters in it which along with other rented quarters ultimately would pay for the building and provide an endowment for opera nowhere else equaled. Insull's employees and his agencies for selling stock in his proliferated utilities had easily disposed of bonds and preferred stocks for the building. It climbed as 1929 began, like the market and other aspects of life in America some of which seemed more explosive than elevated.

Nothing in Chicago seemed less related to Insull's rising culture palace on Wacker Drive than the nondescript one-story garage of the S.M.C. Cartage Company on Clark Street. Certainly not regarded as business news was the event which took place there on St. Valentine's Day, February 14, 1929, as the soaring year got under way. The garage looked like no set for drama. True, Clark Street ran not only north from the Loop; it also had been an Indian trail traveled long before the streetcar lines came. On this morning a light snow was falling along the humdrum thoroughfare when a dark Cadillac touring car drew up at the curb near the garage between taller neighboring buildings. Windows and doors along the street were closed against the 18-degree temperature. Three men in police uniforms and two in plain clothes entered the garage at 10:30 A.M. Neighbors heard muffled sounds like the backfire of trucks. Then the same men emerged, those in ordinary garb holding their hands high over their heads as the supposed police followed them, guns in hand. Only a short time afterward was the shocking discovery made that in the garage five men had been lined up against a whitewashed wall and sprayed between the head and thighs with machine gun bullets. Imaginative reporters and detectives reconstructed what had happened, some even supplying a dialogue of toughness and terror. The number of bullets poured into the doomed differed story to story from one hundred to one thousand bullets. The one man found still gasping on his way to death in gangster fashion would not talk.

Prohibition officials suggested that real police had done the job to shut up talk about their graft or to make it clear that protection had to be paid for—or else. But the generally accepted opinion was that the job was done to get George ("Bugs") Moran, who in an underworld dynastic fashion was undertaking to carry on the competition to Al Capone which had been interrupted but not ended five years before when Dion O'Banion had been shot down in his florist shop. This time Moran escaped by being late. The killers, supposed to be members of the Purple Gang of Detroit, apparently thought another man was Moran and moved in. So their butchery was a business mistake. It brought climax to clamor against crime in Chicago. But it did not bring the law's hand to businessman Capone. At the exact moment of the massacre, Capone was not only in Florida where he enjoyed a private island, he was in the office of the district attorney there, apparently just visiting. He would be back to attend to his Chicago interests which now included not only booze. He had an empire to guard, as did others in Chicago.

As fellow citizens of the city, both of foreign birth, Capone, at thirty, and Insull, already seventy, had strangely similar problems. It is not in the record that they ever met. Both made contributions to similar politicians, both for favor it was said. Capone's charities, if any, were as concealed as his operations. Austere, white-haired Insull was not quite accepted by Gold Coast society, which was ready to share in his profits. Its members, however, like everybody else, recognized him as the chief almoner of the arts and charities of the city from which his utility empire spread. The elegantly dressed Capone had extended his operations from booze to muscular activities in connection with lawful businesses ready to contribute for protection by him or from him. Nobody ever really measured the dimensions of his Chicago suzerainty in the underworld and the supposedly upperworld, too.

The utilities built and managed by Insull had around two billion dollars in assets. They produced a tenth of the nation's electricity and served five thousand communities in thirty-two states. That had taken elaborate financing. By sales of stock to employees and by complex corporate structures the British-born magnate, a cold creative man, had kept the control of his companies which great and exclusive Eastern banking interests and others covetously regarded.

Yet, to use a phrase usually restricted to the problems of Capone, Mr. Insull, who had come a long and complicated way from his days as Edison's secretary, felt that others were trying to muscle in on him. Specifically in 1928–1929 a group headed by Cyrus Eaton, of Cleveland, Ohio, a Nova Scotian who proudly recalled that he had begun his financial career "in a business position with John D. Rockefeller, Senior," was quietly buying large blocks of stock in Insull's companies. Eaton, of course, was no Bugs Moran. Insull's biographer described Eaton as "a creative capitalist in spite of his reputation as a financial buccaneer." He was a man of "vast ambition and wily talent." And now "swiftly, silently, sharklike," he was moving in. Insull, of course, was no innocent in dealing with other men. Though he seemed benefactor to some to whom he sold stocks and others whose cultural and charitable needs he met, perhaps he best described his attitude toward people in answer to a question about humanity and efficiency in his plants: "My answer is that the greatest aid to efficiency of labor is a long line of men waiting at the gate."

Certainly he did not want to lose his job. And it was evident that if Eaton's operations succeeded, he and his associates could demand that Insull pay them more than the market price for the securities they were accumulating or divest him of control. So beset, Insull had no such simple remedy as the St. Valentine's Day massacre had been expected to be. Instead, he undertook to insure continued Insull management by a reorganization concentrating ownership in two investment companies, seemingly safer from what he regarded as high-level hijacking.

These were holding companies, safe from such regulation as applied to operating companies, but providing a complex pyramid of stock holdings for their control. Insull made a maze baffling even to experts. But Will Rogers provided the best simple definition of a holding company as "a thing where you hand an accomplice the goods while the policeman searches you." Insull built not only in complexity but on confidence. Transferring employees, from department heads to meter readers, into stock jobbers, by the end of the twenties he had sold Insull stocks to a million customers, neighbors and friends, generally in small amounts. So safeguarded in control by complexity of structure and multiplicity of ownership, in 1929 he went on imperturbably building the great Civic Opera building which, viewed from a distance, it was said, looked like Insull's armchair.

Other businessmen wanted no intrusion from anybody, including the U. S. government. One such man was Clarence E. Mitchell, who, as Amherst graduate (four years behind Coolidge) and as president of the National City Bank of New York, belonged to the aristocracy of American finance. His background had been in the investment side of banking and he was not at all pleased when in March, the month of Hoover's inauguration, the often timid and indecisive Federal Reserve Board in Washington undertook to put some curbs upon what many regarded as runaway speculation on the New York Stock Exchange. In effect, it said that Federal Reserve funds should not be used for brokers' loans to buyers of stock on the margin. Money tightened. On March 26, the rate for call money jumped to 20 per cent, the highest since 1921, and the market slumped seriously. Thousands of speculators whose margins were wiped out by the fall were sold out. Some saw panic looming. Next day Mitchell, though a member of the governing board of the New York Federal Reserve Bank, came to the rescue. In what aging Senator Carter Glass, who had helped shape the Federal Reserve system, regarded as a slap in the federal board's face, Mitchell announced that his bank was prepared to lend twenty million dollars on call to stock buyers through brokers. His action pegged the call money rate at 15 per cent. Falling stocks began to rise again.

President Hoover had celebrated his entry into the White House by installing the first phone any President ever had on his desk. Afterward some said he could call anybody but hear nothing. There were rumblings to be heard. International finance had become like one of those machines designed by the popular cartoonist Rube (Reuben) Goldberg, creator of the syndicated Boob McNutt. Good-humored satirist of the advancing machine age, Goldberg drew complicated contraptions the end results of which might be swatting a fly or kicking yourself in the pants. Statesmen and bankers in striped pants saw no such fiscal foolishness in the financial situation. Behind rising tariff walls the United States only insisted on the payment of the World War I debts from its Allies. ("They hired the money, didn't they?" said Coolidge.) Allies could pay only on the basis of astronomical reparations payments by Germany to them. And the Germans had been able to pay only on the basis of German bonds sold by U. S. brokers to the same Americans to whom they were selling stocks. Now at home American farm surpluses grew. And it was confidently expected that more and more manufactured products could be sold to people who were getting a good deal less than a plush share of the profits of the boom. Somehow the contraption ran and, though great bankers tinkered with it, few apparently suspected that it could stop.

Other things were more apparent. In April the vulnerability of the self-confidently most efficiently operated and determinedly isolated country was demonstrated by two different, dramatic phenomena. The *Halterophera capitata* or Mediterranean fruit fly was discovered in the citrus groves of Florida. And in North Carolina there began a wave of Communist-inspired textile strikes. Both, of course, were foreign contagions come into the American stream. The orange crop was destroyed; banks failed. Communists (in the absence of ardor by other labor groups) moved in on mills, some of which for lower wages had moved South. Everybody was ready to fight the fruit fly. The strikers, most of whom had never heard of Marx, were more perplexing, and evidently more dangerous. Patriots formed mobs. State guardsmen were mobilized. Detectives and strikebreakers were hired. Also at a Congressional investigation in Washington strikers presented a fourteen-year-old girl who had been receiving $4.95 for sixty hours' work a week in a mill which had come South to avail itself of cheap Southern labor.

Not all were shocked at this and other such disclosures. Homer L. Ferguson, president of the Newport News Ship Building Company and a former president of the U. S. Chamber of Commerce, reassured the disturbed. As a stockholder in several textile mills, he declared that "the condition of the Southern cotton mill worker is very much better than it was a generation ago when he had no work at all." People who made such proposals as a twelve-dollar-a-week wage, he said, say nothing of free mill village houses, water, light and the good country food available to workers. If there was child labor, there was less "juvenile vagrancy." Unions would only drive the mills away. Many agreed. Few workers in the mills really hoped for any such millennial wage as twelve dollars a week. "Stretch-out" systems required more and more work in the same long old hours. In the face of the facts, people who had come from the hills to the mills turned to fantasy in their ballads. One ran:

> *Where the mills are made of marble,*
> *And the looms are made out of gold,*
> *Where nobody ever gets tired,*
> *And nobody ever grows old.*

Such longing for conditions only possible in heaven attracted less attention than other things. The South was outraged when the Hoovers included a Negro congressman from Chicago in a White House tea for members of Congress. And in the North, Raskob, Smith and others were more concerned about the evils of prohibition. The Negroes had even fewer friends than the Southern poor whites. Both prohibition's friends and its foes seemed more vociferous. Some hoped good might come from a Presidential commission, headed by former Attorney General George W. Wickersham, to investigate the whole crime and prohibition question. Most of those concerned for repeal, however, were getting what they wanted of adequate quality at reasonable prices.

Indeed, for the fortunate the year took on some of the air of the gay nineties. Certainly it was a nostalgic occasion in the gay twenties when Mr. Raskob and Mr. Smith, preparing to break ground for their Empire State Building on May 29, the day after the Wickersham Commission was named, held an auction sale of the furnishings of the old, long-loved Waldorf-Astoria. The hotel evoked not only memories of princes and Presidents but of old-time market speculators, too, like John W. ("Betcha-a-million") Gates, who was a leader of the "Waldorf crowd" of market operators and industrialists as America was entering the twentieth century. Charlie Schwab and others had done much of the talk which led to big steel mergers in its rooms and bars. Generations of plumed, jeweled and befurred loveliness lingered in the memories of lady-lined Peacock Alley. Some who shared or wanted to share the spirit of the place crowded to the sale. The bidding showed a lively market. When the last item was knocked down to the highest bidder the furnishings of the hotel brought $350,000—not much money on Wall Street then, but a lot for bric-a-brac, pictures, statuary, mementoes and ornate second-hand furniture.

There was almost continuous carnival that year at another, smaller, but already somehow antique-looking, hotel. At the Algonquin off Sixth Avenue in the Forties its famed Round Table was steadily crowded with members of the best-known literary group of the time. Most of them were better known than businessmen, some almost as well as movie stars. There peevish, impotent Alexander Woollcott pontificated, his words as sharp as his flesh was spongy. Changes in literary attitudes were marked by some like Robert Benchley, who as drama critic for *The New Yorker* was soon to say, "I am now definitely ready to announce that Sex, as a theatrical property, is as tiresome as the Old Mortgage." *The New Yorker*, which had set itself up in 1925 under the motto, "Not for the old lady from Dubuque," was satirizing with metropolitan wit and sophistication more things than sex—even overfed businessmen at play. Its brilliant founder Harold Ross, Woollcott declared, "looks like a dishonest Abe Lincoln." Also often at hand in the Algonquin were Marc Connelly, Deems Taylor, George S. Kaufman, Dorothy Parker, Robert E. Sherwood, Heywood Broun and Franklin P. Adams (F.P.A.), who with Broun enlivened the "op. ed." or opposite the editorial page in the famous old New York *World*. While much that was said at the Algonquin was ephemeral, none of the talkers then could have conceived that the gold-domed *World* would die two years later.

Undoubtedly wit, repartee, profound remarks sparkled the gathering of such folk, but their table constituted no island of immunity from the fevers of the now steadily mounting market. In his *World* column, "The Conning Tower," F.P.A. once a week surveyed the society about him in "The Diary of Our Own Samuel Pepys." And about this time it was of such a gathering of men in the arts which he wrote.

"I went to greet them," he said, "thinking to hear some news or comments of artistick matters, and they were in deep discussion of the Federal Reserve Bank, and were so engrossed in the subject that one of them did leave to telephone, in order to ascertain what had happened at the long session this afternoon, and he came back and said the rate had remained the same, and they all seemed to be delighted, and so they fell to talking of this and that stock."

So were taxicab drivers and shoe clerks, philosophers and barbers. There were jittery moments. There were some pessimists. Some doubted that the market could rise forever. Even Babe Ruth could not go on eternally, others said, though in this year when he was thirty-four he hit forty-six home runs and batted .345. Even Henry Mencken was seeming a little old-fashioned and frayed. The old advocates of ethics as the essential in letters, against whom the Baltimore Bombastes had inveighed early in the decade, were returning confidently to battle as the New Humanists, and finding agreement not merely among rustic Fundamentalists but city intellectuals in the idea that Mencken at his best was only "good intellectual vaudeville."

He was no longer the idol of companies like those which gathered at the Algonquin. Now he seemed a literary reactionary, too. He had damned Fitzgerald, quarreled with Dreiser. Hemingway, he said, ran away from his theme "to prove fatuously that he is a naughty fellow, and when he does so he almost invariably falls into banality and worse." Of William Faulkner, he announced, "I like clear sentences." And as for tall Thomas Wolfe, emerging this year, he couldn't even read him. Oddly, the books of both Wolfe and Hemingway appearing that year, *A Farewell to Arms* and *Look Homeward, Angel*, were titled in terms of loss and longing. Beside the rising market Faulkner's novel was perhaps more appropriately *The Sound and the Fury*.

Raskob, while his and Smith's preparations for their skyscraper advanced, had a literary message for the American people, too. In August, 1929, he gave his views to the *Ladies' Home Journal*, companion publication to the advertising rich and literarily reassuring *Saturday Evening Post*. The article was entitled, "Everybody Ought to Be Rich."

"I am firm in my belief that anyone not only can be rich, but ought to be rich," he said.

It was only necessary, he declared, to put fifteen dollars a month into good common stocks. At the end of twenty years that would amount in increment and dividends to an investment of eighty thousand dollars yielding an income of four hundred dollars a month. "That's rich," commented the *Gazette* of Little Rock in Arkansas where even this rich summer a great many hillbillies and black folk were not making fifteen dollars a month. In the Georgia around Warm Springs, where Franklin Roosevelt was spending as much time as his duties as governor would permit in hope that he might walk again, the net income of the average farmer was not more than three hundred dollars a year, only part in cash.

Still there was much to what Mr. Raskob said. Indeed, at the rate of the rise when he wrote he may have seemed conservative. Between March 3, 1928, and September 3, 1929, the value of stocks, including split-ups, rights, etc., had in general more than doubled. Some had made far greater gains. Radio, for instance, had gone up from 94½ to 505. But though hardly anyone appreciated it at the time, that was the golden peak. Stocks slumped. They rose. Averages as compiled by the New York *Times* were higher on September 19. But the slip beyond was at a more rapid rate. Still, there had been sagging times before. There was reassurance that buyers were not leaving the market in the rise of brokers' loans to speculators. On October 2, such loans to margin buyers who were borrowing to put up only 25 per cent to 50 per cent of the amount needed to buy shares of stock rose to $6,804,000,000. Obviously the storm of September was blowing over. This month Raskob's E. I. Du Pont de Nemours and Company let the world know that, due to its policy of diversification—into cellophane, rayon, etc., as well as G.M. stock—its income had increased by a million dollars a month.

There were promises not only of prosperity but of peace. On an early October inspection of Ohio River development projects, Mr. Hoover made it clear that he favored no such idea as a federal Tennessee Valley power system as advocated by the "socialist" Senator Norris of Nebraska. But he welcomed a visit from Ramsay MacDonald, Socialist Prime Minister of Great Britain. Late in August when Raskob was saying that everybody ought to be rich, there had been suggestions that some Americans were ready to get rich even at the price of building for war. A big, loud-voiced man named William B. Shearer then filed suit against American steel and shipbuilding companies for $275,655 which he said was still due him for lobbying efforts for a big navy that would bring them big profits. Included in his efforts, he indicated, were attacks made on the British admirals at the disarmament conference in Geneva two years before. That conference, not entirely due to Shearer's efforts, had ended in a failure. The U. S. Congress now seemed ready to embark upon a big navy program. Hoover wanted compromise with the British.

And on October 4, when Radio was going down from 114¾ to 82½, Socialist MacDonald arrived in America to a ticker tape welcome from still rambunctiously capitalistic New York. Such tumultuous greeting of great visitors and heroes returning home had been brought to a fine art by Grover Whalen, Wanamaker store executive turned police commissioner, who was the official greeter and parader of the metropolis. These were the prancing days when Tammany's play-around, song-writer, Mayor James J. ("Jimmy") Walker personalized New York as a gay city even if not a politically impeccable one. MacDonald went on from music and confetti storm to more serious business.

On October 6, as Hoover recalled later, he and the British leader at the President's Rapidan Camp in Virginia "went down the creek and on a log threshed out the points as yet unsettled in the naval agreement." They felt, he said, that Japan would go along. That country's demands then were regarded as rather foolish but troublesome. Most experts considered Japan only a second-class power. They assumed that there was no actual danger to the United States from that direction. The American naval base at Pearl Harbor in Hawaii, with its oil depots provided by Fall and Doheny, was both strategic and presumably impregnable. Mr. Hoover, however, was angered by the efforts Shearer had made to disrupt disarmament negotiations. Their exposure, he said, "left some of our shipbuilders explaining themselves to the American people for months."

Many Americans were too occupied with other things that month to be concerned with such explanations. Society had been pleased that on MacDonald's visit to Washington with his attractive daughter Ishbel there had been at least some intermission in the feud between Alice Longworth, as wife of the Speaker of the House, and Mrs. Dorothy Gann, as sister of Vice-President Curtis as to which should rank the other at dinner parties. It seemed fitting that when Socialist MacDonald came to New York from Washington he should be entertained at dinner by Thomas W. Lamont of the House of Morgan. Hoover went to see the World Series in which Connie Mack's Philadelphia Athletics beat the Chicago Cubs. Some felt sorry for old Secretary of the Interior Fall as his trial moved this month toward his conviction for bribery, but few took much stock in the testimony that he had leased Teapot Dome to Doheny with the patriotic purpose of providing oil depots to protect America at Pearl Harbor.

Sentimental attention turned to Dearborn, Michigan, where, as the market rose and spires were planned, America turned to its foundations and the folk heroes upon which so much of soaring prosperity depended. Hoover headed that way. In his Greenfield Village there, set up to prove that Ford did, too, care something about history, Henry Ford had restored the laboratory in Menlo Park, New Jersey, in which Edison had produced his incandescent light. Now on the fiftieth anniversary of that event Edison, at eighty-two, had come to Dearborn at the invitation of Ford who had pioneered, too, in the motor field to enrich his company and Chrysler and General Motors as well. Almost as a rite in the presence of worshipers, Edison re-enacted his invention from which had spread Insull's and other utility empires. The great day was drenched by rain and disturbed by the sudden, serious exhaustion of deaf old Edison who still looked somehow like a puzzled boy with a great mop of white hair. He was tended by Hoover's physician, Dr. Boone, who had been at the bedsides of Harding and the Coolidge boy. Edison recovered to live nearly two years more.

The fatal illness of the bull market was not to be so postponed. On October 17, as the distinguished company had started toward Dearborn, Dr. Irving Fisher, professor of political economy at Yale, whose *Who's Who* biography required a full column, was reported as saying that stock prices had reached "what looks like a permanent high plateau." Within a few months he expected the market to be "a good deal higher than it is today." On the day of the Edison-Ford banquet papers reported some trouble on the market but described it as the "dying spasms of a bear market." Mitchell of the National City Bank, who had defied the Federal Reserve Board, came home from Europe on October 22 with reassuring words: "I know of nothing fundamentally wrong with the stock market or with the underlying business and credit structure . . . the public is suffering from 'brokers' loanitis.' "

Next day the bottom seemed to be falling out. And the following day, October 24, became known as Black Thursday. Prices dropped in a flood of liquidations. In the enormous volume of selling the ticker lagged far behind. Then, a few minutes before noon, the banking Sanhedrin, including Mr. Mitchell, Albert H. Wiggin, head of the Chase National Bank, and others gathered in the offices of

J. P. Morgan and Company. Reporters waiting after the meeting were told by Mr. Lamont, of the Morgan firm, that "there has been a little distress selling on the Stock Exchange and we have held a meeting of the heads of several financial institutions to discuss the situation." The real news of the meeting, however, came when at half past one Richard Whitney, brother of a Morgan partner and himself the broker who handled much of that great firm's market business, came on the floor.

Whitney was then vice-president of the exchange, and its acting head. He began with dramatic unostentation to buy. Not only was he ready for the pool of great bankers behind him to buy twenty to thirty million dollars' worth of stock; he seemed then to carry in his person the presence of the financial aristocracy. Son of a Boston banker, schooled at Groton, stroke oar at Harvard and member of the Porcellian Club which F.D.R. did not make, he seemed the epitome of the top club of American finance, entry to which required more than mere money, though a lot of that. Hopeful newsmen then called him the "white knight" of this dark hour. Even people who disliked his arrogance had no doubt about his importance. All described him as impeccable. Only in aftermath did his picture as a tall man with his dark hair plastered to his head and parted in the middle seem to have a certain rodent quality about it.

The debonair way in which he met the selling flood was reassuring. The situation seemed better on Friday and Saturday. Hoover from the White House declared that "the fundamental business of the country, that is, production and distribution of commodities, is on a sound and prosperous basis." But on Monday the skids under the market seemed greased. And though Black Thursday was behind, Black Tuesday, October 29, was worse. Then the sell orders came in waves. Behind the lagging tickers all touch with price reality was lost. Gathering as unobtrusively as possible at noon that day the Governing Committee of the Exchange met in a small room under the Exchange floor. There, as Whitney reported later, "the feeling of those present was revealed by their habit of continually lighting cigarettes, taking a puff or two, putting them out and lighting new ones—a practice which soon made the narrow room blue with smoke." Smashed stubs gathered in high-piled ash trays like still-unexercised sell orders in baskets on the floor. The nervous men considered closing the Exchange but decided against it.

A closing could have created true panic in the dark. The decision to keep the Exchange open for limited hours seemed certainly right when Wednesday, October 30, showed less madness and some reassurance. U. S. Steel opportunely declared an extra dividend. American Can not only did the same but raised its regular dividend rate. More reassuring words came from governmental and financial powers. Aging John D. Rockefeller announced that he and his son were purchasing sound common stocks. And Raskob, undoubtedly still believing that everybody ought to be rich, said that he and his friends (perhaps including his new business associate Al Smith) were buying stocks at their present bargain level. Raskob and John D. Rockefeller, Jr., had more in common at that time. Raskob's Empire State Building was rising. And Rockefeller, having recently joined others in a long-term lease on properties on Fifth Avenue in the lower Fifties for a new home for the Metropolitan Opera Company, found himself after the crash holding the lease alone. In Chicago on November 4, less than a week after the torrent of Black Tuesday, at its opening performance Insull let Chicago operagoers see the dazzling interior of the great theater in his huge building for the first time. Many members of Gold Coast society, Insull's biographer thought, were astounded and chagrined because he had built an opera house without a single prominent box on a golden horseshoe. They "would have to sit in anonymous, proletarian darkness, just like people in the sixpenny gallery." There was some sort of simile made by the seating and Insull's preference for many customer stockholders over big banking ones.

This undoubtedly served some of Insull's almost secret resentments against "the club" of the elegant rich in New York and Chicago. He was undisputed manager for the many. As such he seemed to come safely through this crash. Also, though proletarian possibilities may have frightened some others who lost riches on the market, some of the New York bankers who undertook to save the market when all seemed lost, undertook to look out for themselves. It turned out later that Mr. Wiggin of the Chase Bank had made a lot of money by selling stock short while a member of the pool to keep prices up. Mitchell sold stocks to his wife at a loss to keep his income taxes down. Raskob and his partner and patron, Pierre Du Pont, sold stocks at losses to each other with the same end in view. Appealing from the Internal Revenue Bureau's disallowance of such dealing they went in vain all the way to the Supreme Court.

Not all the rich and powerful had made money on the market.

Jovial Charlie Schwab, who had built a fortune estimated at $200,-000,000 in his steel operations, had invested in stocks which afterward seemed only designed for smaller suckers. And even Richard Whitney, the "white knight," who had inside dope if anybody did, had so misguessed and overextended himself that he used for his own purposes stocks of others, including a yacht club in which he was a decorative social sailor. If he failed as hero, he kept his nerve. An admiring Stock Exchange elected him its president before disclosures sent him to jail for larceny in the 1930s. Also, before he fell like Lucifer, he was able to reassure President Hoover, who suspected that Raskob was selling short to beat the market down to hurt the Republicans.

For those outside the clamorous exchanges and smoke-blue conference rooms it had been a glorious autumn. Young Thomas Wolfe, whose first novel, *Look Homeward, Angel*, was published on October 18, felt that this October was the dividing line in his own life. Wolfe, who in his briefer lifetime had strode on as many metropolitan sidewalks as Al Smith knew, sometimes seemed obsessed with October. He kept its memory in rural Carolina metaphors as a time of sharp frost, bright leaf, of fields cut, granaries full, and when "the bee bores to the belly of the yellowed grape, the fly gets old and fat and blue, he buzzes loud, crawls slow, creeps heavily to death on sill and ceiling, the sun goes down in blood and pollen across the bronzed and mown fields of old October. . . ."

Not so poetically in this October, time seemed to fall apart for many men, some of whom did not realize it at all. There was a sense of change out in America, and not merely around stock tickers. Early in the month, when the Vermont countryside was as spectacular as sugar maples could make it, Sinclair Lewis left the place he and Dorothy Thompson had bought there not far from Calvin Coolidge's little empty Plymouth. He went down to Wolfe's North Carolina, colored then by angers as well as trees, looking for material for a labor novel he never wrote. At Marion, just down the abrupt rise of the red and gold mountains from Wolfe's Asheville, he regarded grim conditions in textile strikes which had spread from Gastonia.

He could hardly have come at a time when such material was richer or rawer. Three weeks before he arrived the trial of Communist strikers for the murder of the Gastonia sheriff in a raid on union headquarters had been interrupted when a juror went insane.

Madness seemed all around him. On September 14, Ella May Wiggins, mother of four children, had been shot and killed while she and others were fleeing in a truck from a mob of angry anti-Reds in Gastonia. Just before Lewis reached Marion, officers angrily undertaking to disperse a picket line had killed three workers and left a half dozen others seriously wounded. Two of the wounded were women. Mobs ranging the Carolinas were ready to whip or kill more. Mill owners were evicting strikers from the houses in their villages. Children stood beside cheap furniture before the houses on weed-grown streets.

Lewis wrote six articles for the Scripps-Howard newspapers, then not yet fattened (at the climax of their crusading character) by their purchase of the New York *World*. They seemed pallid beside the violence which provoked them. As put together in a pamphlet called *Cheap and Contented Labor*, his satire struck little fire. Nothing less than obscenity would serve his indignation as it did when, talking with some restless workers, he spoke of solemn, ineffectual William Green, head of the American Federation of Labor, as "a little shit." The pompous appeared more evil than the predatory. There was too little drama in the deflated. Certainly in Marion, in coal towns of Pennsylvania, in Boston, in Indiana steel centers, he saw too many men and women already down—long down—in slum, hovel, hopelessness. They were more tragically real, even before the crash, than any possible rain of ruined men from Madison Avenue offices.

Other writers were looking about them, some in bewilderment. Many of those who had gone abroad for spiritual sustenance were now finding lines of subsistence from America less secure. In more ways than in securities a surge had spent itself. Scott and Zelda Fitzgerald, already involved in his alcoholism and her approaching madness, moved toward Paris from the Riviera as the stocks fell. They spent the "night of the stock market crash" or one of them in the Hotel Beau Rivage at St. Raphael. They slept in the same room Ring Lardner had occupied when he had visited them in an earlier, happier year when his sardonic wit had about it no adequate quality of warning. More Americans had gone to Europe this year than ever before. And some who had been there longest were coming back.

They found no land changed by catastrophe. If confidence was shaken, humor survived. There were almost too many jokes about the crash, some of them grim. One went around about hotel clerks asking guests whether they wanted rooms "for sleeping or jumping."

Certainly more and more high windows were provided. The Chrysler and Empire State buildings rose almost in a race. Since 1913 the Woolworth Building, its sixty stories rising 792 feet, had been the highest peak in what Christopher Morley, whimsical novelist and critic of the era, had called the Downtown Dolomites. Now Chrysler's tower was pushing 1046 feet above Forty-second Street. Concerned more with space than height, Rockefeller on the land he had gotten by bad luck was planning his Center on Fifth Avenue in the Fifties where run-down brownstones served as almost wide open speakeasies. Raskob and Smith were not to be outdone. Up went their Empire State, disregarding market drops, its steel framework growing four and a half stories a week, up seventy stories to 1250 feet.

Lest that was not high enough to outsoar all, a higher tower was proposed above it. First it was said that one of the time's imaginative promoters proposed that the tower be built in the form of a huge simulated cigarette. After all, the consumption of cigarettes by men and more and more women soared in the twenties from 47 billion to 124 billion. Fortunately aesthetics intervened. It was proposed that the tower be made a mooring mast for dirigibles. No one, of course, imagined that at last this spike in the sky would become a 222-foot-tall television transmitter for the city's television stations. Yet from Washington, as Secretary of Commerce, Hoover had already been seen and heard over a telecast on April 7, 1927. Only electronics innovators were watching.

There had seemed at its birth in the boom an evident market for the Empire State's 2,158,000 square feet of rental space to which sixty-five passenger elevators would carry tourists and tenants. Nobody dreamed as it began to rise that when it opened, many of its 6400 windows might have been dark as night came on if lights had not been turned on, not for illumination within but for bold night-time appearance above a stricken city.

It was not built for jumping. Birds sometimes spattered themselves against its walls. Later a lost plane would crash against it. Actually neither from it nor any other of the city's skyscrapers was there any such leaping of bankrupt men in desperation as Sinclair Lewis had predicted the year before the crash. But legends grew in the pattern of his prophecy. Reporters took special note when some men whose wealth had been wiped out killed themselves. Such jokes grew as one about two men who jumped hand-in-hand because their failure had been in a joint account. Edwin P. Hoyt, in a study of the times made nearly a quarter of a century later, noted that one leading firm of advertisers in its war on pessimism purchased a full page in the New York *Times* to chide the man who "hurls himself from a high window with complete disregard for the busy people who are really going somewhere on the sidewalks below." But Joe Alex Morris, in his story of this startling year, dismissed the impression that Wall Street—or Madison Avenue—was a dangerous place to walk because of falling bodies. He found that there were only forty-four suicides in all Manhattan between mid-October and mid-November in 1929, as compared to fifty-three in the same period of 1928. There were, indeed, he found, more during the summer months of 1929 when the market was booming than during the months of the big break.

After all, as Frank Freidel said in evaluating Roosevelt's reaction to the situation, though everybody seemed to be playing the market only an exceedingly small percentage of Americans were. Before November was over, the New York Governor was off in Warm Springs again swimming for the hope of stronger legs. On December 1, he wrote to Louie Howe, who in his relationship with F.D.R. seemed not only to carry elections but parcels. The Governor was thinking about Christmas. He and his secretary, Marguerite ("Missy") LeHand, both had gifts to buy. He had a notice of a sale at the Anderson Galleries. He asked Howe to go to it.

"It is just possible," he wrote, "that the recent little Flurry downtown will make the prices comparatively low."

# XIII

## THE ROAD TO REVOLUTION

INAUGURATION DAY, March 4, 1929, was cold and rainy. American tradition, Herbert Hoover rather testily thought, insisted upon an outdoor ceremonial at the Capitol. Both he and Mrs. Hoover were soaked and chilled. Still he had every apparent reason to say to the crowd before him in the rain, "I have no fears about the future of our country. It is bright with hope."

He was ready to lead. The phone on his desk, not at a dignified distance as other Presidents had kept it, was the instrument of control and command. It gave him immediate personal connection with the government over which he had ranged as a Cabinet officer, by no means willing to confine his concerns to the Commerce Department. He was at wire—almost arm's—length from the whole wide and diverse nation. During his first days at his desk he demonstrated his readiness to use federal power to the full in dealing with serious local situations.

Two prominent Chicago citizens, much troubled, came to him for help. They said that their great, rich, sprawling city "was in the hands of gangsters, that the police and magistrates were completely under their control, that the governor of the state was futile, that the federal government was the only force by which the city's ability to govern itself could be restored."

Hoover did not hesitate. By this time the name of Al Capone was almost as well known as his own. If Capone was a public enemy, he was a public character. If he capitalized crime, he made good copy. At a time when many businesses were creating trade associations to regulate competition and maintain prices, no one, of course, knew the extent to which by intrusion or to meet another market for his services he had set himself up as "protector"-at-a-price of dry-cleaning shops, laundries, other businesses. Some of his methods and his men had come from the brass-knuck competition of the circulation departments of Chicago newspapers. Capone's operations were, of course, racket rule. But it provided the power of which some trade associations lamented the lack. Franklin Roosevelt found, for instance, that his efforts as head of the American Construction Council were rather futile. Hoover, as Secretary of Commerce, found his efforts to encourage trade associations discouraged by the possibility that critical courts might find in them violations of the antitrust laws. Capone was no more troubled by these than any other laws.

Hoover, however, while recognizing that federal authority was limited to the income tax and prohibition laws, "directed that all the Federal agencies concentrate upon Mr. Capone and his allies." Nothing seemed more characteristic of the good, energetic man of action Hoover had shown himself to be in his business and governmental career. He had had to be such a man. West Branch, Iowa, where he was born in 1874, was a Quaker-settled country but the sort of one chosen by old John Brown, ready in reform with gun and pike, for the training of some of his Harpers Ferry raiders. Herbert's birthplace was a one-story, two-room cottage across the lane from his father's blacksmith shop. He went as a working boy to Oregon and then managed by much labor to graduate as an engineer from the just-established Stanford University in Palo Alto.

There he met a tall California girl, Lou Henry, whom he later described as oversensitive and deeply religious. Also she was a companion and "a great lady." In 1899, as a young couple with little money but high hopes, they set out on "adventuring years" which took them in his engineering career in mining, railways and metallurgical works to Mexico, Mandalay, the Transvaal, Australia, China, Russia, almost everywhere. They alternated, he remembered later, between "the luxury of great cities and the primitive living of world frontiers." But his professional income earned in these far places, he said in 1914, "probably exceeded that of any other American engineer."

In that year at forty, settled comfortably and quietly at London, he was serving more for California than for income as European promoter of San Francisco's Panama-Pacific International Exposition. There he and Lou, in a prim house with a small garden at its rear, had time for such a pleasant joint job as translating Agricola's *De*

*Re Metallica.* Also, sometimes they moved in upper-class British company, where he was shocked to hear ladies and gentlemen declaring that talk of ameliorating the condition of the poor was "sheer wicked radicalism designed to destroy the Empire." Unexpectedly then he was catapulted to renown in the job of relieving a war-created poverty and distress hardly ever equaled. Suddenly in October, 1914, he became chairman of the Commission for Relief in cruelly conquered Belgium and as such convinced even the Kaiser's government of his neutrality in humanity. Spending millions in a combination of compassion and efficiency, he kept his overhead costs to about one half of 1 per cent. Then, with American entrance into the war, he became Federal Food Administrator, curbing consumption at home that the Allies might be fed. With the armistice he took on the task of helping the destitute populations of Central Europe, including regions overrun by the Bolsheviks. The demand for his services did not end with those labors. Six months before he became Secretary of Commerce in the Harding Cabinet, in 1921, the efficient engineer-almoner of the world, who insistently said that he wanted nothing so much as peace in a cottage on a hill above Palo Alto, was offered the certainty of great wealth as a partner in the vast mining and metallurgical interests of the Guggenheims.

In the Cabinet, by his own enthusiastic account, he ranged creatively over the whole governmental field. Labor was Commerce, too, he felt. Secretary of Labor James J. Davis, "a most amiable man," was glad to let him take the initiative and later the credit for pressing steel magnates, including Gary and Schwab, to end the "barbaric" twelve-hour day in the great, smoky plants. He brought order to the babel of conflicting radio waves even when decorative and piously petulant Aimee Semple McPherson, evangelist whose eyes were not always to stay heaven high, insisted that her broadcasts from her Angelus Temple in Los Angeles needed only to fit into God's wave reception. He helped build the infant industry of commercial airlines.

He was not yet done. Regarding increased exports for farm surpluses as within his personal province, he was ready to save the farmer. He might have been more helpful, he suggested, if Secretary of Agriculture Wallace had not objected in "the way of all bureaucratic flesh." Possibly Hoover's run-in with this "dour Scotsman" made him blind at the time to the faults of Secretary Fall, who had met similar resistance from Wallace when he wished to take national forest lands from Agriculture as he was taking oil reserves from the Navy. It was only in aftersight apparently that Hoover realized "what bugs crawled about under the paving stones of the Harding regime." Certainly no scandal touched the hem of his garments.

The Capone case showed Hoover acting swiftly in what Quakers called a "concern." He put that other, unrelated Hoover, J. Edgar (who, he said, had been named at his suggestion head of the still little-known FBI), to work. On the Chicago scene Elliott Ness, whose adventures in law inforcement later became part of the electronic folklore of America, moved in on stills and speakeasies. Capone, however, was always far beyond any prohibition net. Furthermore, he had never signed a check or kept a bank account in his own name. But a quiet lawyer, George E. Q. Johnson, Iowa-born like the President, as district attorney turned his attention to the mysteries and intricacies of Capone income.

The gangster was in more trouble than his increasing reputation as menace seemed to indicate. He had more to fear than even Herbert Hoover's agents. Almost without arraying his lawyers as usual, in 1929, he had taken a year in jail in Philadelphia for carrying a concealed weapon on a visit to that city. Some figured he was seeking sanctuary from pistol-ready competitors. But at the top Hoover's command, Ness, Johnson, and J. Edgar Hoover, worked on. In 1931, District Attorney Johnson filed a mass of charges of prohibition violations against Capone. In view of past experience there was small chance that they would stick. But in raids on various hide-outs the federal men had opened safes, found coded records, and cracked the code. Johnson charged that the gang chief had failed to pay six million dollars in taxes due on his past four years' income. Certainly that put him in a special class in a country in which in some of these years J. P. Morgan owed and paid no income tax at all and in a city where Colonel Robert R. McCormick, owner of the Chicago *Tribune* ("World's Greatest Newspaper") was paying about $1500 a year.

Capone offered to settle for four million dollars. Johnson, not quite sure of his case, recommended a settlement under which "Scarface" would pay his fines and taxes and spend two and a half years in prison. Capone was agreeable but he made the arrogant mistake of telling the press all the details. Then Judge James H. Wilkerson, famous earlier for granting the sweeping strike injunction asked by Attorney General Daugherty, could not admit any intent to "make a deal" with Capone. Instead of two and a half years, he gave the gangster eleven years, much of which, though only convicted as a tax dodger, he spent in Alcatraz.

The stock market crash during Hoover's first autumn in the White House could not be so simply faced. Neither guilt nor fault was so clear as in the case of Capone. Still, Hoover, while realizing that all Presidents "must be cheerful and optimistic," had his fingers crossed about some gentlemen in Wall Street and the situation they had helped create.

"Some of the so-called bankers in New York," he wrote, "were not bankers at all. They were stock promoters. . . . Their social instinct belonged to an early Egyptian period."

When the market did not recover and the Wall Street crash was followed by "the economic hurricane," he listened to counsels which increasingly seemed callous. He admired, though he was glad to get him out of his Cabinet and off to England as ambassador, small, unsmiling Secretary Mellon. Contrary to the oratory of Democrats and some Western Republicans and what seems now plain history, Hoover said that Mellon favored more taxes on the biggest incomes like his own. Still, he said the wispy Pennsylvania Croesus was a "leave it alone liquidationist."

"He held," the beset President recalled, "that even a panic was not altogether a bad thing. He said, 'It will purge the rottenness out of the system. High cost of living and high living will come down. People will work harder, live a more moral life. Values will be adjusted, and enterprising people will pick up the wrecks from less competent people.'"

Hoover was not ready to send the people of the United States through such a wringer. Yet he seemed little less expansive than Coolidge in his ideas as to governmental purposes for people as the depression deepened in 1931. "The sole function of government," he said that year, "is to bring about a condition of affairs favorable to the beneficial development of private enterprise." He pushed private enterprise and private charity to greater giving, though sums collected lagged steadily behind increasing need. But direct relief, wearing the dread British word, the "dole," seemed to him socialistic. He cut immigration to prevent competition for dwindling jobs. With six golden pens he signed the Smoot-Hawley Tariff Act which his Republican Senate leader said would put the nation "on the upgrade, financially, economically, commercially within thirty days."

Such protection instead only seemed to provoke foreign retaliation against U. S. goods, and that cut U. S. jobs. Farm prices sagged further. Reduction of the Federal Reserve rate did not stimulate credit. Building projects which he urged on business and governments at all levels did not materialize. Private outlays for construction fell off in 1930 by over $2,000,000,000. Public spending for such works rose only $400,000,000. Then in 1931 private expenditures dropped another $2,000,000,000—down almost to a fourth of the 1926 total. Federal contribution to construction works was inadequate. Hoover seemed more concerned with falling taxes than rising unemployment. The primary duty of government, he declared in thrifty Quaker faith, was "to hold expenditures within our income." And when Democrats proposed an increase in federal works he assailed their program as "the most gigantic pork barrel ever proposed to the American Congress." Yet there was work to be done and certainly available men to do it. In a nation with 3,100,000 miles of roads only 680,000 were paved.

Perhaps it was only his sense of waste of time and not a reluctance to confront people, but as early as New Year's, 1930, he was regarding public receptions as "preposterous." He and Mrs. Hoover managed to be out of town every New Year's Day after that. He resented small processions of visitors. Most of those who came to call on him, he said, "wanted something for themselves that they ought not to have." Young Herbert Hoover, Jr., married and the father of two babies, was ordered to spend a year in a tuberculosis sanitarium. As the depression deepened the President gave an impression of cool, evasive, high-collared lack of candor which alienated many of the reporters who covered his office. The telephone was on his desk but sometimes his lines to the country seemed more and more tenuous. Hoover began to believe that they were being deliberately snarled by Democrats who had set up machinery for smearing him.

That gave them too much political credit. The diminutive, militant John Raskob seemed throwing away the money he was amassing in the bull market early in the summer of 1929 when he set up an organization to hit Hoover harder and again for the benefit of Al Smith and repeal. Its efforts were pinpricks in the prosperity of that brief summer. Hoover concluded that the motor millionaire felt the 1928 defeat "more deeply than would a practicing politician." By this time evidently Hoover had decided he was one. But Raskob hired professionals. He made Jouett Shouse, native Kentuckian who had served in Congress from Kansas, where a Democrat had to fight to survive, full-time director of the Democratic National Committee. He promised political munitions around a million dollars over three years. And he and Shouse hired as party publicity man at $25,000 a year Charles Michelson, then head of the Washington bureau of the New York *World*. Born in the rough, rich mine town of Virginia City, Nevada, Michelson was a small, caustic, pixie-appearing man, reticent about his age and little else. He came in shooting but there seemed no reason for Hoover at first to dignify him by his later venomed opinion that the old *World* man "came out of the smear departments of yellow journalism."

Actually Michelson, with something of the skill of Virginia City gamblers, cashed in his chips at the *World* and took his place in political play with what afterward seemed excellent timing. The *World* then, as said his one-time greater colleague on that paper, Heywood Broun, was getting out of the yellow and into the red. It was already in trouble under Coolidge prosperity, as, it turned out, some other businesses were, too. The new "gutter journalism" of such tabloids as the *Daily News*, the *Graphic* and the *Mirror* cut into its circulation. In 1927, it skipped its customary Christmas bonus to employees. It lost prestige in 1928 when it fired Broun as a result of differences over his savage denunciations of eminent Massachusetts gentlemen who solemnly upheld the death sentences of Sacco and Vanzetti. Though the sale and death of the great old *World*, on February 27, 1931, was a year and a half away when Michelson left it, he was as lucky as a man who sold his stocks before the market crash. After the crash occurred, Raskob neither squealed nor welched on his promises to put up the political money.

Hoover, as unsympathetic Democrats would have put it, was squealing then. Certainly the thin-skinned President, sometimes seeing Mrs. Hoover in tears over unjust criticisms, began a cry of resentment which was still shrill a quarter of a century later.

"I did not say, 'Prosperity is around the corner,' " Hoover insisted.

But even if the phrase was manufactured by Michelson or was one of those he picked up from sharpening national satire and passed on, that and other anesthetic Hoover aphorisms have stuck in history or in the folklore which is often better remembered than history. And as the winds of the "economic hurricane" grew stronger, the repetition of reassurances from Washington provided a tragi-hilarious relief to the country which had lost much of its money but not all of its sense of humor. The dignified and deserving Hoover appeared like the impotent, pompous policeman nose-thumbed by such a little bum as Charlie Chaplin portrayed in his popular films.

It was not a role he liked. It was one he apparently could not escape. Drought in 1930 burned up farm regions which had been desperate enough before. Wheat which farmers sold in the fall of 1929 at $1.35 a bushel was now bringing only $0.76. New trouble was even more evident in the towns. Factory employment was down 20 per cent but payrolls were off nearly 30 per cent. It was a conservative guess that there were six million unemployed. Banks began closing as queues like bread lines formed at their doors. In Iowa City, just across the county line from Hoover's native West Branch, all five banks were shut.

The Hoovers became more and more glum. Ike Hoover (no kin but a long-time functionary at the White House) wrote, much to the greater Hoover's rage, in a book of backstairs memories, that the staff was delighted when they were absent. Mrs. Hoover departed "from sweet urbanity," her unhappy husband said, in outrage at criticism she regarded as unfair. It was piling in. Michelson did not have to manufacture criticism; at most he had to process it.

The President could not find the cause for the unhappiness of his country or himself in his philosophy of free enterprise, local initiative, individualism and thrift. They had served him from West Branch to Washington. They seemed to him the cornerstones of the republic. He stiffened in his faith. More and more he looked overseas for the causes and continuance of the depression. Taking advantage of world difficulties, the Japanese were moving aggressively in China. With only an observer sitting outside the League, Hoover could do little to stop Nipponese militarists. But the great problem in Hoover's eyes was the still festering European fiscal situation related to war debts and reparations. Repeatedly that situation had required repairs with American aid. The great industrialist, Owen D. Young, of the General Electric Company, had helped shape a Young Plan in the mid-twenties. A Dawes Plan had been worked out under the leadership of Charles G. Dawes, Chicago soldier, banker, politician, first director of the Bureau of the Budget and Vice-President under Coolidge. Ironically Dawes was to show that whatever foreign causes might exist, there were deep-seated troubles even in Chicago involving far more respectable men than Al Capone.

The world was shaking in 1931. From Germany came an appeal

from eighty-four-year-old President Paul von Hindenburg, senile and beset, that his land was suffering from "internal and external tensions caused by distress and despair." Behind Hindenburg then, Adolf Hitler seemed little more significant on the face of the world than Huey P. Long of Louisiana, who had not yet entered the Senate, appeared to be on the scene in the United States. Yet the economy of Germany and other nations, even their social orders, appeared threatened. And on June 20, 1931, Hoover came to the rescue with his moratorium for a year on international debt and reparations payments including $250,000,000 due the United States on war debts. It was a bold and necessary step though some murmured aloud at what seemed a generosity to foreigners while Americans, including veterans of the war with Germany, were left in need. Nevertheless, by January, 1932, about forty nations had gone off the gold standard, which Hoover identified with American fiscal security. As the black year 1932 began, it was evident that great financial institutions in America were tottering. Nearly 2300 banks had suspended in 1931. Some feared that in crisis revolution was at hand.

Chicago, escaping the managed malfeasance of Al Capone, had a more relentless hand at its throat in economic collapse. Even when the federal government was tightening the bonds on Capone hundreds of men had been seeking shelter on the lower level of Wacker Drive above which loomed the Insull offices in the Civic Opera House he had built. They warmed themselves at fires of scrap wood; they aimlessly, hopelessly watched the black river. Other men and women, too, began to crowd in the Insull offices. In a deeper market drop in September, 1931, the value of the Insull securities they had bought fell sharply. The old magnate was saying that he saw little in the situation to be disturbed about. But he soon surrounded himself with thirty-six personal bodyguards who protected him day and night. Then, in April, 1932, the top Insull companies went into receivership.

This was the shocking spring. On March 1, the infant son of Lindbergh was kidnaped from his crib at the famous aviator's home near Hopewell, New Jersey, northwest of Princeton. Despite Hoover's moves against Capone at least one chronicler of the times said that his "laissez-faire policy in law enforcement was shown to the public fully in this crime." Such a view only indicated the readiness to blame the President for everything. The case helped create a national state of shock. Then quickly came, almost offstage so far as Americans were concerned, the suicide in his regal apartment in Paris on March 12 of Ivar Kreuger, the Swedish match king. Death showed him a great rogue who had fooled American financiers. He had seemed a magnifico worthy of attention when two months before he had personally assured the President that Americans need not "become hysterical" about European problems.

To many there seemed much basis for hysteria at home. On March 7, a Communist-led company of three thousand unemployed men moved ominously in Detroit. There Ford, who years before had endeared himself to labor with a five-dollar-a-day minimum wage, had become a symbol of capitalistic capriciousness. He hated doctors, bankers, Jews, liquor, tobacco. As an old pacifist who now carried a gun, he insisted that government should "stick to the strict functioning of government." More and more people were angrily uncertain as to what that function was. Hoover did not seem to them to be sure. As early as 1930 Detroit was becoming a desperate city. That year the auto manufacturers made a million less cars than in 1925, though population had increased by eight million in that time. And by 1931 the city's auto workers, who had numbered 470,000 in 1929, were down to 257,000, most of them only working part time or on "share-the-work" plans. More than ever now such jobs as there were went to pets and stooges or men who set a pace few others could follow. Radicals or merely men with vague union ideas expected surveillance and dismissal slips. In the homes of many of the jobless, utilities had cut off light and water. An abortive strike in the Briggs body plant revealed men working fourteen hours a day for ten cents an hour. More stood hour after hour in long lines at the gates of companies hoping for a few hours' work, relief, even a handout. Gruff guards shooed them away. Tellers seemed nervous to the fewer people who had money left in the banks.

The motor city's socially concerned mayor, Frank Murphy, who, Hoover later said, was one of those who "interpreted liberalism as a sort of collectivism," was more and more helpless as misery mounted in cold, dark homes. Others saw the situation as a real Red chance. William Z. Foster, the tough-minded radical who had led the fruitless steel strike against the twelve-hour day a dozen years before, believed the city was ready for Communism. He had sent in organizers of an underground union called Auto, Aircraft and Vehicle Workers of America. Foster came to address a mass meeting they planned outside the Ford gates at River Rouge. There ostensibly they wanted to present a petition.

With Detroit police permission, the assembled unemployed moved from the heart of the city. Dearborn police, however, ordered them to turn back. But Foster and other leaders pressed the crowd on in the bitterly cold weather. Then Dearborn police and Ford guards, headed by Harry Bennett, whose rough methods made him a power in astringent old Ford's great organization, let loose with tear gas. The crowd of Red-led unemployed replied with a barrage of rocks, slag and frozen mud. The Ford fire department turned hoses of freezing water on the men. In the tumult, guards opened fire with guns and revolvers, finally machine guns. The supposed rally turned into a rout. Four dead and several wounded were left behind as the crowd scattered. At a great Communist-conducted funeral, attended by ten thousand people, bands played the funeral march of the Russian revolution of 1905. Huge red banners bore pictures of Lenin and were emblazoned with the words, "Ford Gave Bullets for Bread."

There was no evident correlation between Communism and crime. Together they suggest a violent, a downcast and an oppressive time. Red propagandists were only a few among those outraged by the case of the "Scottsboro boys" in the Tennessee Valley of Alabama which, a few years before, Ford had proposed to transform. Eight young Negroes had been sentenced to death there the year before for the rape of two young white women in a gondola car on a moving freight train. Now in 1932, after successful appeal to the Supreme Court, the "Scottsboro boys" had become figures in a *cause célèbre*. There were no eloquent Saccos and Vanzettis among them. No one spoke of the "Scottsboro girls." They were just tramps, it was said. Yet their gondola car travel revealed a poverty which deserved attention even among tramps. A New York defense attorney's description of the Scottsboro jury may have correctly portrayed tobacco-drooling bigots; he missed the degrading backwardness in which most of those concerned in this case were evidently caught.

A young Southerner, Erskine Caldwell, had just drawn portraits of similar people in *Tobacco Road* which, made into a play, seemed more amusing than pitiful to metropolitan audiences. Only later was both dignity and despair to be revealed in the faces of such people, more deeply lined than a depression could quickly make them, when Caldwell and Margaret Bourke-White in text and photograph produced *You Have Seen Their Faces*. Few had seen them until disaster made a mirror in which the faces of all, the new unemployed and the long neglected, might be seen startlingly side by side—the old and scorned *they* and the new and disturbed *us*.

More than the battling unemployed in Detroit or the submerged characters in the Scottsboro case, angry war veterans seemed to symbolize the American tragedy in 1932. In May they began to mobilize in the Pacific Northwest, a region in which the I.W.W. had once been troublesome to super-patriot employers. Men who had presumably served their country in war, they now asked its aid in need. With some humor they called themselves the Bonus Expeditionary Force. They felt that the time to pay the bonus Congress had voted them, despite Hoover's opposition, was now, not in distant 1945 as promised in the act. Choosing as their commander Walter W. Walters, a World War sergeant, they set out to ask it in person and en masse. Walters, a former cannery superintendent with a wife and two little girls, had been unemployed for eighteen months. He imposed upon his growing body of companions the principles of "no panhandling, no drinking, no radicalism." They moved east, becoming national news quickly when they collided with inhospitable railroad guards in southern Illinois. States provided trucks to get rid of them and pass them on to Washington.

The harassed Hoover watched the news of their approach. Nothing could be more revealing as to fears in the capital than a secret message he sent the Senate. Come what might, the budget, of course, had to be balanced. In order to accomplish it the Congress, with his approval, was working on a 10 per cent pay cut for all government employees. But Hoover requested that an exemption be made for enlisted personnel in the Army and Navy. In the event of internal troubles, he did not wish to have to depend upon soldiers disgruntled over pay cuts.

Impressively, ominously, the Bonus Expeditionary Force converged on Washington. Other veterans from other regions joined those from the Northwest. They made news as their numbers grew as a new kind of lobby. Some people, discounting any danger, recalled General Jacob Coxey's Army of the unemployed which had moved to Washington in the panic of the 1890s. Others thought of Mussolini's more recent "March on Rome." Some rather feared a march from Moscow.

The B.E.F. under Walters dispelled any notion of menace by respectful and decent behavior. Also, they were met with good will and good sense by General Pelham D. Glassford, superintendent of the capital's police. A West Point graduate from New Mexico, he had been a young brigadier general in the World War. He established himself as a veteran with veterans. He helped the bonus marchers settle on marshy flats beside the Anacostia River. He kept close to the marchers and the situation they created, often visiting their camp of tents and shacks on a big blue motorcycle.

Official patience with marchers, estimated by Hoover as eleven thousand "supposed veterans," was growing thin on June 17. That day the men gathered in the Capitol Plaza while the Senate voted on an immediate bonus payment plan. Hoover administration officials wanted to bring out machine guns. Such gun threat had been used effectively against some Communist hunger marchers in the December before. But Glassford won in argument against such a display of force. The marchers in the plaza got the bitter news that the bill for immediate payment had been defeated. But under Walters' discipline they moved quietly back to their camp on the flats. Some frustrated veterans departed. Others said they were going to stick around until 1945. And doubtful characters, eager to take advantage of the situation, moved in.

Hot sun poured down on the tents and shacks on the squalid shore. Tempers grew short. Walters seemed to grow dictatorial. Radicals questioned his leadership. It was not clear what the B.E.F. was waiting for, but women and children moved in to join men in the steaming, reeking camp from which they seemed to have no other place to go. The place was an eyesore and to Hoover it was at best an impertinence. His temper stiffened as such a commentator as Walter Lippmann wrote in wonder as to how he could "justify the fact that he never took the trouble to confer with the bonus marchers." The President only proposed that the Congress agree to lend the men the money with which to go home, the loans to be deducted from bonuses payable in 1945. He was evidently anxious and upset. Guards and Secret Service men were increased about the White House. Troops were stationed nearby. The President was firmly convinced that "the march was in considerable part organized by the Communists and included a large number of hoodlums and ex-convicts determined to raise a public disturbance."

"We're going to stay here until I see Hoover," Walters shouted to his men as they gathered again in the Capitol Plaza on the last day of the Congressional session. Hoover had announced that he would make the traditional Presidential appearance on that occasion. Then he did not choose to come. Once more the B.E.F. filed back to camp. Glassford had plans to move them to a site in the country. No such pastoral isolation of the problem was permitted.

On June 28, police were ordered to clear some abandoned buildings on Pennsylvania Avenue in which some marchers in overflow from the flats had taken shelter. Communists, it was said, saw the chance to create an incident. They rushed police lines and in the confusion an officer fired into the crowd, killing a man. In the rioting resentment another man was killed. Quickly the friendly police chief intervened and order was restored. But the President was militantly ready to move.

He received—or secured—a letter which he carefully preserved from the District commissioners. The area in which the trouble had occurred contained "thousands of brickbats." They were used, they said, against outnumbered police. Now they called for the assistance of federal troops in maintaining law and order. The letter was signed by a retired doctor whom Hoover had appointed chairman of the board of commissioners. The President sent his orders to General Douglas MacArthur, then at forty-eight Chief of Staff of the Army. With his second-in-command, Colonel Dwight D. Eisenhower, and other officers including George S. Patton, the top command of the military led the advance on the marchers.

Late in the afternoon they paraded in impressive force: four troops of cavalry with drawn sabers, six tanks with hooded machine guns and a column of infantry, with fixed bayonets, steel helmets, gas masks and blue tear-gas bombs. None of the enlisted men seemed disgruntled. Indeed, some apparently were more than necessarily enthusiastic. They cleared all buildings on the Avenue and evacuated the camp on the flats, which was left in flames. News accounts of the victory of the troops differed in sympathy and substance. One told of women and children weeping and lacking time to pack their pathetic belongings. It was reported that a seven-year-old child who turned back to a tent to get his pet rabbit was stopped by a soldier: "Get out of here, you little son-of-a-bitch." The child was sent flying with a bayonet wound in his leg. It was even suggested by the *B.E.F. News*, which somehow briefly survived the rout, that an eleven-week-old baby born in the camp should have as its epitaph:

"Gassed to death by order of President Hoover." This last certainly was overwrought exaggeration or outrageous smear. Nobody was killed. Only smoke like that over a trash dump remained in the morning.

Hoover extensively quoted in his memoirs the classic report on the Battle of Anacostia Flats made by General MacArthur. The General then was already a master of military prose. He wrote:

"We moved down Pennsylvania to the Avenue area. . . . That mob . . . was a bad looking mob. It was animated by the essence of revolution. . . . It is my opinion that had the President not acted today, had he permitted this thing to go for 24 hours more, he would have been faced with a grave situation which would have caused a real battle. Had he let it go on another week I believe that the institutions of our Government would have been severely threatened. . . .

"I have never seen greater relief on the part of the distressed populace than I saw today. I have released in my day more than one community which had been held in the grip of a foreign enemy. I have gone into villages that for three and one half years had been under the domination of the soldiers of a foreign nation. I know what gratitude means along that line. I have never seen, even in those days, such expression of gratitude as I heard from the crowds today. At least a dozen people told me, especially in the Negro section, that a regular system of tribute was being levied on them by this insurrectionist group; a reign of terror was being started which may have led to a system of Caponeism, and I believe later to insurgency and insurrection."

Perhaps the nation was saved and Washington relieved of a sense of enemy presence. General Glassford, who denied that he had asked for military aid and insisted publicly that he could have handled the situation without an army, was forced out of office. The President declined to see a group of writers, headed by Sherwood Anderson and Waldo Frank, who wished to protest the use of troops against unarmed civilians. Certainly among the populace, pleased, as MacArthur reported, by the event, none was more elated than Michelson at his Democratic desk. Hoover himself said that his "greatest coup of all was the distortion of the story of the Bonus March." Whether Michelson or the MacArthur versions should be accepted, so much suffering was real and present everywhere that almost any disregard of suffering people would be believed everywhere. So would be reports of Presidential impatience and unpopularity.

Michelson insisted that distortions were unnecessary. He had, he said, only to collect and disperse items of sharpening satire about Hoover. Some of them, he wrote, originated among Republicans in the Senate Cloakroom. One joker, he said, reported that Hoover asked Secretary Mellon for a nickel as he wished to phone a friend. (Calls did cost only a nickel then.) Mellon replied, "Here's a dime, telephone both of them." But angers rose above amusement.

As the long hot summer advanced, explosion came in the President's own state of Iowa. While the bonus marchers had been camped in Washington, Milo Reno, a big farm leader in his mid-sixties, was talking about a farmers' strike. As a former president of the Iowa Farmers' Union, Reno had been fighting agrarian battles since the days of the Populists. He was as American as his black Stetson hat. Even in days of Coolidge prosperity in 1927, which did not always reach the agricultural areas, he had come forward with a suggestion that if farmers could not secure help by law, they might well try "organized refusal to deliver the products of the farm at less than production costs." Such a radical idea had not secured adherents even among grumbling rural people then. But by the spring of 1932 others came angrily to the view that this might be the only way to curb the farm price collapse.

In August, the members of the Farmers' Holiday Association, armed with clubs, sticks and pitchforks, began to block roads. They laid spiked logs or threshing machine cables along the highways near Sioux City over which farm produce might pass. In apparent good humor but evident determination, they searched trucks and persuaded those bound for market to turn back. Then dairy farmers in Woodbury County took up the idea. They were receiving two cents a quart for milk which distributors sold for eight in Sioux City. On all ten highways into the town farmers' patrols barred the movement of any milk into the city except for hospitals. Their road-block plan spread to Council Bluffs, other Iowa communities and into adjoining states. The striking farmers ripped open cans and poured the milk into ditches. Besieged cities struck back. In the Council Bluffs area, the sheriff armed citizens with baseball bats for use on embattled countrymen. Then he arrested sixty farmer pickets. Only the threat of a mass farmer march on the jail secured their release.

Then, as on the Anacostia Flats, strange supporters began to appear. Some who arrived were dispersed bonus marchers headed home. Some others came just for the hell of it or the fun of a fight. Communists in New York dispatched agents to the scene. Leaders like Reno, though talking big, began to worry.

"You can no more stop this movement," he said, "than you could stop the revolution; I mean the revolution of 1776. I couldn't stop it if I tried."

Still, after a shotgun attack on the camp of some of his followers near the village of Cherokee, northeast of Sioux City, he found a pretext to call off the strike. It had done little apparent good. But it had dramatized the dilemma of the nation unable to put need and plenty together for the benefit of all. Communists who hung around after the strike got little farmer attention. And many in Washington felt with a sense of righteous frustration that farmers had only themselves to blame. Earlier efforts of the Farm Board to stiffen prices by the purchase of crop surpluses had only resulted in more production by farmers while demand was still declining. The Board and the Secretary of Agriculture urged farmers to reduce production but held back in horror from controls based on anything but voluntary action by the farmers themselves. As early as mid-1931, the Farm Board ended its price support efforts and began to liquidate the holdings it had acquired. The price sag swiftened. Milo Reno's strike had not stopped it.

Not much could be done for angry workers either. But in the March of so many shocking events, some friends of labor were active. Graying Senator Norris, of Nebraska, whom Hoover dismissed as a "socialist," and the fiery young Republican congressman from New York, Fiorello La Guardia, secured the adoption of their Anti-Injunction Act by Congress. This legislation made yellow-dog contracts unenforceable in federal courts. These so-called contracts were ones under which a worker had to promise not to join a union in return for the privilege of employment. Hoover's Secretary of Labor opposed the legislation. But when Hoover reluctantly signed it, one of the basic weapons of militant antiunion industry was taken away. Many regarded it as only a sop to labor at a time when vastly more men than jobs limited the real threat of unionism. And some felt that at this time, such a sop was required when gravy was being provided for industry and finance.

Hoover had only slowly come to approval of the policy involved in the creation of the Reconstruction Finance Corporation, an agency to bolster business with funds of two billion dollars. It became, however, the administration's chief tool in 1932 in efforts to end the depression. When it was first set up early in the year, Hoover called to its presidency Chicago soldier, banker, politician Dawes. A Nobel prize winner as a result of his European finance efforts, he was a pipe-smoking, tweedy, outspoken man who added public confidence to the corporation which the President sternly said was "not created for the aid of big businesses or banks."

There was an increasing American sensitiveness on this subject. Some continuing ostentation by the rich, such as a glittering debut party given in Washington not far from a bread line, had received front page publicity and not merely social page patter. And though its figures probably reflected little that was new, a Brookings Foundation report on the distribution of wealth in America had appeared especially appalling in this time. It indicated that 1 per cent of the people owned 59 per cent of the national wealth. At the other end of the scale 87 per cent of the people owned only 8 per cent of the wealth. The report did not indicate the number or percentage of the people who owned no part at all. There were plenty among sharecroppers and at the shut doors of industry.

The RFC went about its work to help all and not merely the big. But in June, suddenly Dawes resigned to return to Chicago to manage the affairs of his Central Republic Bank and Trust Company. Everything in Chicago needed attention then in the aftermath of the Insull receivership and possibly the Capone collapse. More idle men were gathering for shelter on the lower level of Wacker Drive. It was perhaps a necessity, certainly a coincidence, that a few weeks after Dawes departed, the RFC he had headed lent his bank $90,-000,000. At this point Central Republic had only $95,000,000 on deposit.

Certainly this was material for what Hoover regarded as the Democratic smear organization. Drawling John Nance Garner of Texas forced the RFC to report its loans to Congress. Garner had been elected Speaker of the House when the Republicans lost in the Congressional elections of 1930. He and other Democrats had not been impressed when Hoover said loan publicity would disclose shaky situations in banks which the loans were designed to cure. Hoover's later defense of the Central Republic loan may have made fiscal sense though it was heard by a skeptical country. He said that the

Dawes bank served 122,000 depositors and was associated with 755 other banks in fifteen states which had 6,500,000 depositors. Beyond them other related banks served 20,000,000 people.

Confidence in Dawes's character and capacity was such as to let him survive the storm. His bank did not. It was soon forced into reorganization, though later, after litigation, the RFC loan was repaid. Hoover was ready to make distinctions which seemed to him proper between what he saw as crime and what he regarded as smear. He had had no trouble in his decision about Capone. He stood squarely behind the loan to Dawes's bank. Now he faced the case of a man between them, a folk hero of American finance who had become a folk villain of depression. The President did not act with quite such dramatic directness as in the pursuit of Capone or the defense of Dawes. But said he, not amplifying the pronoun, "We ordered Insull's arrest."

The old magnate was seventy-two when his top companies had gone into receivership in the spring. The dimensions and complexity of his shattered empire was indicated by his resignation from eighty-five directorships, sixty-five chairmanships, and eight presidencies of companies. Thousands who had eagerly bought his stocks bitterly hated him as this old, arrogant man came faltering to his seventy-third birthday in July. As the receivership proceedings moved ahead he heard that he was to be indicted in the federal courts on charges of mail fraud in connection with the sale of his securities. He doubted that in the mounting mood of anger against him he could secure a fair trial. Suddenly he sailed for Europe, first to Paris, and then, beyond the possibility of extradition, to Greece. He became a bewildered ancient exile and the most sought-after American fugitive. It was anticlimax that when he was brought back after relentless pursuit he was found not guilty.

"What have I done," the old man had often asked in exile, "that every banker and business magnate has not done in the course of business?"

Nothing apparently, was the answer of Donald R. Richberg, who as labor lawyer in the politics of American reform, had often opposed Insull.

"The true significance of the career of Samuel Insull," he said, "lies in the fact that his sins were *not* exceptional, save in the sweep of his ambitions and the extent of the injuries he inflicted."

Hoover deserves no comparison with Insull. His failures were not exceptional in dealing with the disaster he confronted. Perhaps the America to which he had been called, however, resembled in comparison with its past the complicated web of his own making in which Insull was finally caught. Owen D. Young, who had not been fazed by the complexities of European finance, said that in Insull's organization of companies on companies it "was impossible for any one man, however able, really to grasp the whole situation." And he added: "I should like to say here that I believe Mr. Samuel Insull was very largely the victim of that complicated structure, which got beyond his power, competent as he was, to understand."

Hoover was a great American entitled by every expectation to make a great President. It was not so much fate which intervened to prevent it. Ironically perhaps he failed in the opinion of the people of his time because he clung by his lights to a faith which had seemed adequate to most Americans up to that time. Many then felt a revolution was required. Some, indeed, not only in rough crowds at factory gates or on run-down farms, were ready for Communist revolution. Such included some of the ablest writers and thinkers of the day not intimidated by fears of any lasting Red scar on their records—or their dossiers. Even Scott Fitzgerald, who had said that "it was characteristic of the Jazz Age that it had no interest in politics at all," now was reading Karl Marx and writing: "To bring on the revolution, it may be necessary to work inside the communist party." Actually there was no less likely revolutionary than he. He was facing revulsion, not revolution. A stronger spirit, Robert E. Sherwood, whose frivolous play *Reunion in Vienna* was produced in 1931, wrote in an apologetic preface to it that the generation since the war seemed to occupy a war-torn no man's land, a "limbo-like interlude between one age and another." Before it lay only "black doubt, punctured by brief flashes of ominous light, whose revelations are not comforting. Behind . . . nothing but the ghastly wreckage of burned bridges."

Hoover exaggerated the danger of Red revolution. But honest, able, devoted to his country, he was not ready with a creative alternative in terms of a truly American revolution. At the time such a revolution seemed not as much demanded as a scapegoat. That he became, not as a result of smears, though some were applied. His very name became the word for hoot and boo. Shantytowns, not all of which were new though tragically extended, became Hoovervilles. Far from Detroit, the powerless cadavers of old automobiles pulled by scrawny mules were Hoovercarts. Bone-tired, hurt and bewildered, the President grew angry, stubborn, rigid in confident rectitude. So did Mrs. Hoover. It was harder for him when she wept. He may have been wrong about many things but he came in pain to one unassailable opinion.

"Democracy," he said, "is not a polite employer."

Perhaps democracy's safety in America, when sometimes Hoover felt it was showing the manners if not the menace of the mob, lay in its impertinence. While he grew glum in the White House, the most popular musical on Broadway was *Of Thee I Sing*. It lampooned American politics up to and including the Presidency. People made queues as long as bread lines to get tickets to it. Thousands applauded its sparkling spoof with music by George Gershwin and lyrics by George Kaufman and others. They took to their hearts or their still undamaged risibilities the comic candidacies of romantic John P. Wintergreen for President and retiring little Alexander Throttlebottom for Vice-President. Not only did the people laugh at and with these caricatures in 1931, but also the pundits at Columbia University, in Hoover's dismal year of 1932, gave the play the Pulitzer prize provided by the builder of the New York *World* which had just gone down the depression drain. *Of Thee I Sing* may have been a monument as well as a musical. In a dark year it provided a sign not of American lapse but of American delight in the antics of its own democracy. It was not always polite but it planned to be permanent.

# XIV

## MAINSTREAM BRACKETED

An AMERICAN revolutionary came stomping (to use one of his favorite words) on the American scene early in 1928. Huey Long was not waiting—as, over in Georgia, Franklin Roosevelt was hoping to do—for a sense of the exactly right time for his personal appeal to people. At thirty-five the stub-nosed Louisianian with a face like a caricature of a cherub under unruly reddish hair came forward with an understanding that where he stood in America a revolution had long been required. He was prepared to provide it—and ride it. No one could consider Long was immobilized, as many thought Roosevelt would forever be. At a man-killing pace Long so moved about his state that his frustrated opponents felt that he was magically everywhere all the time—upstate, downstate, on both sides of the muddy Mississippi River. He used rougher language than customary in the languid elections of Louisiana, so long ultraconservative. He talked the crude vernacular and spoke the harsh protests of the poor. And he turned for political texts to William Jennings Bryan and, startlingly, to decorous and benign Henry Wadsworth Longfellow.

Neither Long nor Roosevelt was a literary man though Roosevelt later blandly said that he was offered Rudyard Kipling's place in the French Academy. Roosevelt had turned to William Wordsworth for his "Happy Warrior" accolade for Smith. Soon he was to attract the attention of Huey and others by his use of the phrase "the Forgotten Man," in exactly opposite meaning from that which its originator, William Graham Sumner, vigorous professor and philosopher of Yale, intended it. Both Long and Roosevelt picked up what they required and made it meet their requirements. If they were not literary men, they were characters for literature, almost enacting dramas which seemed made for them without their needing to bother to learn the lines.

Huey Long had begun stomping across Louisiana selling a shortening called Cottolene. Then after a quickly secured law license he moved at the same pounding pace into politics from the parish of Winn in the north central part of the Pelican State. His own people were not poor by the stunted standards of his scrawny hill parish. True, he was born in a log cabin, but a very substantial one. His father, as a result of a sale of land to the railroad which he hated, had been able to send six of his children, not including Huey, to college. The old man rasped the feeling from which his stomping boy came.

"There wants to be a revolution," he said. "I tell you. I seen this domination of capital, seen it for seventy years. What do these rich folks care for the poor man? They care nothing—not for his pain, nor his sickness, nor his death."

In Dixie he spoke of the rich in harsh memories of old times gone but not forgotten: "Why, their women didn't even comb their own hair. They'd sooner speak to a nigger than a poor white. They tried to pass a law saying that only them as owned land could vote. And when the war came, the man that owned ten slaves didn't have to fight. . . . Maybe you're surprised to hear talk like that. Well, it's just such talk that my boy was raised under, and that I was raised under."

So though Huey seemed only crudely grabbing for himself, he came from a country where the Populist and long pre-Populist protest had never stilled, where boom never touched and bust was the standard situation. He found that to be true not only in Winn but in the Cajun parishes along Bayou Teche in the south, to which long before, separating lovers and families, the British had exiled many French Acadians from Canada.

In this 1928 campaign, rough-talking Huey took his slogan from the smooth cadences with which Bryan had terrified the rich in his "Cross of Gold" speech in 1896. He made his own the Bryan phrase: "Every Man a King, but No Man Wears a Crown." Also slamming, swinging, moving with so little sleep that his eyes were bloodshot above his seldom closed mouth, he came to almost lyrical quietness when he turned to Longfellow for political support in a speech under the great oak in Martinville where, as the poet related, Evangeline had waited in vain in exile for her lost lover.

Herbert Hoover, as Secretary of Commerce, had been in Martin-ville on his flood relief expedition the year before Huey spoke there. He had brought needed aid but amidst distress he had found amusing things to remember. A Negro woman in one of his high-ground refugee camps had had triplets: Highwater, Flood and Inundation. And Evangeline, about whose grave the Cajuns seemed almost comi-cally concerned as the waters rose, he concluded, was probably a myth, only a name picked by the poet for rhythm, not out of history. Her name, Hoover said, might have been Gwendoline. Huey raised no such question, but he asked sadder ones.

"And it is here," he said to excited Cajuns crowded about him under the great oak, "that Evangeline waited for her lover Gabriel who never came. . . . But Evangeline is not the only one who has waited here in disappointment. Where are the schools that you have waited for your children to have that never come? Where are the roads and the highways that you spent your money to build, that are no nearer now than ever before? Where are the institutions to care for the sick and disabled? Evangeline wept bitter tears in her disappointment. But they lasted through only one lifetime. Your tears in this country, around this oak, have lasted for generations. Give me the chance to dry the tears of those who still weep here."

That language does not sound like the roar of the demagogue as reported by the politically dismayed then and since. It has been for-gotten in the tumult of the charges and the facts, too, about Huey's rough, often corrupt, regardless rule in office and power. Scornful charges were ready before Huey provided any facts to prove them. Before he took office and kicked others out of state jobs, before he corrupted political morals or damaged the dignity of the state, even as he arrived he looked like revolution to bourgeois Baton Rouge. Nice people watched from neatly painted porches and from behind drawn blinds as Huey's folk, gallused men and calicoed women, both with hard hands and hard memories, poured in for his inaugura-tion. In old Fords and mule-drawn wagons they came from the bayous and the burnt stump lands. They converged that summer day about the symbolic old gingerbread Capitol which long before Mark Twain had said derived "from too much Sir Walter Scott." Southern knighthood was in danger. Harnett Kane, then a cub reporter on the New Orleans *Item-Tribune*, later described the mood of the back-country march on Baton Rouge:

"We're a-going to get a look-in now. Things will be different, you watch, you young flibberty-gibbert, there, with your painted lips. And you watch, too, mister with your goddamned black chauffeur."

This was life, not literature. It was only coincidence that in adjoining Mississippi at Oxford, thirty-one-year-old William Faulkner was writing, in *Sartoris*, the beginning of his long, bitter comedy of the decadence of the representatives of the Old South and the emergence of the unscrupulous upstart Snopeses who displaced them. Gentle readers were no more shocked by the macabre violence and antic comedy of Faulkner than the easygoing and little-giving Old Order of Louisiana was by Long.

"The meek," wrote reporter Kane of the inauguration, "knew they were to come into their inheritance." Neither friend nor foe ever suggested there was anything meek about Huey—the self-styled "Kingfish." The poor, including many of his relatives, did get a look-in. Historian Arthur S. Link stated flatly that he "redeemed his promises to the common people." If there was extravagant spending some of it reached needs in the Cajun country. If there was corruption, it was scarcely new in this state which often had resembled a Caribbean republic. In Huey there was imagination, purpose and impertinence even to the point of calling such a dominant and often domineering industry as the Standard Oil an "octopus." That company threatened to leave the state if Huey persisted in his ideas about an "occupational" tax on oil refineries to pay for his promises made under the oak at Martinville and elsewhere. He secured a free textbook law and a thirty-million-dollar fund for highway improvement. For poor folks there was at least a look-in long overdue.

Publicity about other matters helped make Huey seem a national clown and political whipcracker. He dominated a reluctant legislature. Also he seemed to delight in flouting the formalities. He dressed for a flamboyant role—or undressed for it. He seemed almost to precipitate the threat of war between Louisiana and the then Republic of Germany when he received the formal call of the captain of one of its cruisers while wearing green pajamas. Sometimes his evident contempt for the proprieties pleased his bayou and back-country supporters. They could wait for fulfillment of all his promises while enjoying his impertinences toward a pompous society which had had little pity for them.

The "Kingfish" got national publicity when he loudly and argumentively insisted that corn pone was made to be dunked in pot-likker, not to be crumbled elegantly and eaten with a spoon. Roosevelt as part-time Georgian entered the debate. At that point he needed publicity, too. Certainly as one of the Dutchess County, Hudson River gentry he was no expert on potlikker and pone. He naturally joined the clean-fingered crumblers. At the time, many thought it would have been more characteristic of him if he had taken the view, "When in Rome, do as the Romans do," expressed by Emily Post (née Price). Her books on etiquette were produced for the twenties when so many who were supposed to be losing their morals indicated an eagerness to acquire manners as well as money.

Evidently, as Huey demonstrated when he stomped to his purposes in Louisiana, some roughness was required of Southern rebels, as shown by such widely diverse "demagogues" as Tom Watson of Georgia, Ben Tillman of South Carolina, James Vardaman of Mississippi and Huey's contemporaries Theodore Bilbo of Mississippi and Eugene Talmadge of Georgia. Beside them all, Huey was unique in both brilliance and bombast. Without both he could hardly have confronted the stuffed shirts which often substituted for shining armor in Louisiana.

Still there was in America, as more than Emily Post's publishers realized, a demand for smoothness. Nobody so well met it as Huey's corn pone and potlikker opponent Franklin Roosevelt. He was being sought the summer of Huey's inauguration as a candidate for governor in New York by Raskob and Al Smith not merely because he was a moderately dry Protestant with some nonmetropolitan appeal. Unconsciously, perhaps a little bitterly as time went on, Smith *et al.* recognized the need on the Democratic ticket of some genteel balance to the still gauche mannerisms and accents which Al had brought with him from the sidewalks of New York. Ladies and gentlemen in Roosevelt's background had only ridden in carriages past earlier Smiths sometimes spattering them on the sidewalks. There had been poor whites in city slums as well as rural counties. Prejudice had not just appeared in 1928 but neither had snobbishness disappeared. It applied not only to ascenders from sidewalks but to billies like Huey who had come down from gullied hills. And an inverse contempt like that of Huey's father could go up. Roosevelt later recorded that after he reluctantly agreed to run that summer of 1928, he was treated at Democratic headquarters

*Wide World*

15. DARROW AND BRYAN—ANTAGONISTIC GUARDIANS OF THE LOST GENERATION

6. WOMAN IN BLACK

*Wide World*

17. "DEMOCRACY IS NOT A
POLITE EMPLOYER"

19. THE BONUS MARCHERS

18. WALL STREET'S DARKEST DAY

20.   MR. MORGAN AND THE MIDGET

*Wide World*

21.   SALLY RAND: "THE FAN IS
QUICKER THAN THE EYE."

*Brown Brothers*

22. BARUCH AND BRANDEIS

by top Smith aides "as though I was one of those pieces of window dressing that had to be borne with because of a certain political value in non-New York City areas."

He was undoubtedly decorative—and in comparison with Huey as well as Al. Many saw and felt the difference but probably no one expressed it so clearly and so embarrassingly loudly as Franklin's mother, the dowager Sarah Delano Roosevelt. She might have come straight out of one of the novels of Edith Wharton. Mrs. Wharton, who had long been the friend of Roosevelts including the great Theodore, was this year finishing *Hudson River Bracketed*. Taking its name from the old-time architecture of Dutchess County, it presented the contrast of the culture of the Midwest with established New York society. In it were echoes of Mrs. Wharton's lifelong theme of an elegant society beset by change and of individuals captured within it. She had joined Theodore years before in writing the eulogies of Senator Lodge's boy Bay, rebellious poet who never quite escaped the bonds within which he was born.

Some had the feeling that Franklin's own escape was as doomed by his patrician place as by the polio. Later, when his flight from fixed caste and tradition seemed no longer in much doubt, to help make that certain he had Huey come to lunch at his mother's house above the majestic Hudson. Huey came, resplendent or repellent, in loud clothes including an orchid-colored shirt and a watermelon-pink tie. And suddenly in an unexpected lull in the conversation Madame Roosevelt blurted, "Who is that AWFUL man sitting on my son's right?" To many, including himself, Huey seemed far to the left of her son. Indeed, Roosevelt came in an odd coupling to regard Huey and Douglas MacArthur as "the two most dangerous men in the United States."

Roosevelt and Long were as different as Dutchess County and Winn Parish. The palaces of multimillionaires surrounded the substantial country house which was Franklin's birthplace. He was born eleven years before Huey. The only son of a doting mother married to a rich elderly widower, his education at Groton and Harvard ran like a red carpet across his youth. He was tied closer to a great name and his place was more firmly fixed in the society to which he was born by his marriage to Eleanor, the good, awkward, ugly duckling daughter of Theodore's tragic, alcoholic brother Elliott. The Rooseveltian name and a Rooseveltian manner helped his advance in politics even as a Democrat. Then, in 1920, when Long was only beginning his career as a rambunctious, news-making, public utilities commissioner, Franklin's political career seemed ended. Then, as Vice-Presidential candidate with Cox, he was buried in the Harding landslide. Yet in a sense he was set free from a sort of duty to be great, from the austere social expectations of his mother and from the improbable insistence of Louie Howe that he would be President of the United States.

Two years before this defeat, political ambition plus the mores of the sort of Wharton world in which he was born played their parts in terminating an affair which almost broke his marriage to Eleanor. Then, supposedly, he ended forever his relations with Lucy Mercer to whom actually he was to be attached by ties of deep and unbroken affection to the day he died. A lovely girl nine years younger than himself, she was a member of the famous Carroll family of Maryland. Her parents, who had been among the gayest of the leaders of Washington society, were impoverished and separated when the Roosevelts came to the capital with the Wilson administration. Lucy became Eleanor's social secretary who also sometimes supervised the cleaning of the house. Then, as world war came on with its tension on officials, tension grew too in the Roosevelt household.

Eleanor made no record of the situation. But Franklin's mother, in a still somewhat inscrutable, sometimes incoherent, letter, evidently saw threat to the standards of her family and society.

"I am sorry to feel that Franklin is tired and that my views are not his," she wrote, "but perhaps dear Franklin you may on second thoughts or third thoughts see that I am not so far wrong."

Her Wharton world seemed falling apart: "What with the trend to 'shirt sleeves,' and the ideas of what men should do in always being all things to all men and striving to give up the old fashioned traditions of family life, simple home pleasures and refinements, and the traditions some of us love best, of what use is it to keep up things, to hold on to dignity, and all I stood up for this evening."

Other evidences of the trouble then are more coherent. Eleanor put off the time of her usual departure for the Rooseveltian summer place on Campobello, and evidently, when she was gone, wrote of her sense of unwantedness. Franklin answered, "You were a goosy girl to think or even pretend to think that I don't want you here *all* the summer, because you know I do! But honestly *you* ought to have six weeks straight at Campo." And as a man who cavalierly had nothing to hide, he wrote her of outings with Lucy and others to Harpers Ferry, down the Potomac on a long weekend on the naval yacht *Sylph:* "such a funny party, but it worked out wonderfully!" He seemed in good spirits though he also wrote, "As you know I am unreasonable and touchy now." So were others. Reasonable or not, Eleanor was bitter and jealous of Lucy during all the years until the last when at Franklin's death in 1945 she found that Lucy, on one of her several trips to Warm Springs, had been with her husband when he died.

In February, 1920, five months before Franklin's nomination as Vice-President and at a time when he was low in finances and in spirit, Lucy was married in a very quiet ceremony to Winthrop Rutherfurd. Rutherfurd's first wife's family had been wealthy neighbors of the Hyde Park Roosevelts. He was old enough to have ridden after the hounds with Theodore Roosevelt before Lucy was born. Perhaps entirely without justification there was more talk about Franklin and Lucy after the election of 1920. Then, at Campobello in August, 1921, the swift, almost serpent strike of polio made him the captive of the crutch, the brace and the chair—and of those about him.

Then the story grew that the brush with death and the subsequent lameness changed the man almost as St. Paul was transformed by the sight of the burning bush on the road to Damascus. Roosevelt, as his image grew in office and in history, was evidently almost miraculously altered, enlarged and ennobled by suffering. Of course, the immobile man was changed. And certainly he who had been always exuberantly ready to seize life was the object of possession by others. However complete or incomplete had been the reconciliation between Eleanor and Franklin after their marriage was threatened, now he was hers to serve and to save. Her gallantry matched his. Yet there was a contest for both with his dominant, possessive mother who would have invested him with a kind of elegant invalidism.

It seemed incredible afterward that anyone, even such a protector of traditions as this Delano dowager, could have ever expected Franklin to become such a pitiful captured Wharton character then. Eleanor resisted. In her efforts she had the eager aid of the small, swarthy Louie Howe who like herself lacked some possibilities of fulfillment alone. A onetime newspaperman, Howe had been Franklin's first civilian and political assistant in the Navy Department.

Obsessed with politics, he was by personality and appearance incapable of advance in the field himself. So by 1912 he had decided that there was a career for him in making the charming New York assemblyman with the magic name President of the United States. He made himself Roosevelt's and Roosevelt his. Eleanor at first, as were so many others, had been repelled by Howe. Now their purposes met. When Franklin's acute illness was over they stirred his uncrippled political interests as occupational therapy. There was never a more enthusiastically cooperative patient. And Howe and Eleanor made him more than ever theirs, though sometimes, irritating them, he was impishly his own.

Neither of them advised him to bow to the pressures that he run for governor of New York in 1928 when Huey, requiring no urging from anybody, had stomped his way to the governorship of Louisiana. Howe felt strongly that 1928 was a year which might damn a Democrat, not advance him. Certainly when Roosevelt won by a patrician nose, no overturn in Albany was expected like that which had attended the arrival of Long in the old Capitol which he would soon replace with a skyscraper in Baton Rouge. Smith and Smith aides were prepared to write Roosevelt's inaugural address, select his appointees, and in general run the government while he swam in Warm Springs. Some were startled that Roosevelt wanted to be governor in full fact as well as in name.

He was. He and Huey divided publicity honors in 1929 as the hard times spread and stiffened. Values were falling and rising, too, in America—and not only in politics and finance. Few noticed that as Mrs. Wharton's gentle ironies of caste and tradition faded, the furies uncovered by Faulkner began to be read. But it came with a little start to Sinclair Lewis and the country in the week of the November, 1930, election when he was informed that he was to be awarded the Nobel prize for literature. Not everybody heard the news with elation. Some, like Theodore Dreiser, felt that they deserved it more. And some, including old-fashioned conservatives and the New Humanists, who believed that literature should purify and ennoble, were outraged. On November 28, Henry Van Dyke, clergyman, essayist, diplomat, preaching patriot and professor at Princeton, was quoted as telling one of those businessmen's luncheon clubs which Lewis had derided that the award to Lewis was "an insult to America." Two years before, Lewis had ostentatiously, and for publicity, some thought, declined the Pulitzer prize for his novel *Arrow-*

*smith*. He had sneered at the basis for the Pulitzer award as the book "best portraying the highest standards of American morals and manners." In his rejection he had taken a slap at the American Academy of Arts and Letters to which Van Dyke proudly belonged. It and such other organizations and agencies, he said, undertook to put compulsions on American writers "to become safe, polite, obedient and sterile."

The Nobel award shook conservative writers as the increasing outcries against the old order in economics and politics, as represented by Herbert Hoover, were shaking conservative businessmen and politicians. Van Dyke spoke for the thousands who had resented the caricatures which they felt Lewis had made of the American village, the bustling city, even evangelical religion. Van Dyke said he had been to a thousand American Main Streets. Of course, on them there were some mean, dull, slippery people. But there were interesting, generous folk, too, some of whom "deserve to be called sons and daughters of God." Lewis showed no trace of the latter. So his books in "addition to their dullness" present "a cock-eyed view of our country."

Lewis was hurt and mad. In his speech of acceptance in Stockholm he hit not only at Van Dyke but at most of his companions in the American Academy to which he belonged. Such men, he said, "like their literature clear and cold and pure and very dead." Then almost irrationally striking at the dead, he took out his grudge on the poet Huey had invoked in his promises by the Evangeline oak. The American Academy, Lewis told the Swedes, "does not represent literary America of today; it represents only Henry Wadsworth Longfellow."

Many Americans were proud that Lewis had brought the prize to his country. They approved his Stockholm snort at stuffed shirts. But guardians of genteel traditions shook their heads. The old guard New York *Herald Tribune*, the book review department of which had been earlier infiltrated by New Humanists, spoke sadly and ashamed of "Mr. Lewis in his hour of awful nakedness at Stockholm." It was almost as if he had received a German cruiser captain in his pajamas or even out of them. But Calvin Coolidge, now engaged in a profitable autobiographical literary career of his own, reflected most American opinion. "No necessity exists for becoming excited." America had other things on its mind, like the danger of not eating regularly.

No two governors were more concerned about that than Franklin and Huey. In New York Roosevelt was the first governor to call for state relief. Even he was evidently hoping that hard times would be brief as he set up his Temporary Emergency Relief Administration. To direct it he named forty-year-old Harry Hopkins, born like Hoover in Iowa but with very different notions about government and relief. Even in prosperous times he had been working in New York with the Association for Improving the Condition of the Poor. Also he had been a Red Cross director in New Orleans when Huey was reaching for power. Roosevelt also provided work for the unemployed in a variety of conservation projects.

Huey in Louisiana and particularly as a man from rural Winn was concerned for distressed farmers as well as unemployed town folk. His thirty-million-dollar road fund provided public works jobs. But he came forward most dramatically in his "Drop a Crop" plan for cotton farmers necessarily involving more states than his own.

"Back to the Bible" he proposed as the cotton price fell in 1931. In cotton as well as wheat, the Hoover administration had practically given up so far as huge and increasing surpluses were concerned. Huey cited Moses' sabbatical system whereby land was left idle every seven years. He proposed that the cotton states pass a cotton crop. Many approved. But in big-crop Texas, Governor Ross Shaw Sterling was apparently as opposed to anything resembling crop control compulsions as Hoover was in Washington. Texas, he allowed, was a little more democratic than Louisiana.

Other Texans spoke in raucous rebuke to Huey. He was "the arrogant jackass from Louisiana . . . ignoramus, buffoon, meddler and liar, who has the impudence to dictate to the people of Texas." Long replied that Sterling was a dirty oil millionaire in cahoots with cotton brokers. Sterling in fact was an oil millionaire who had been board chairman of Humble Oil and Refining Co., and may have gotten his opinions of the governor of Louisiana from Standard Oil associates across the state line. Some thought the plan might have saved the prostrate South. Maybe big tough Texas, maybe Huey's truculence prevented that. Certainly cotton came to be hardly worth the baling.

And on the national scene some conservatives were regarding the growing Roosevelt boom for President with almost the distaste shown by men like them for Huey in the South. Herbert Hoover in Washington was getting wan political satisfaction from his feeling that

Raskob, in his organization to smear him and elect Smith, was building a "Frankenstein." It would help the "enlarged left-wing" nominate "a leader of its own" in Roosevelt and make Smith seem "a reactionary"—as they were calling the President. Certainly Raskob, while encouraging his national committee in its attacks on Hoover, wanted no liberal or radical Democratic substitute for him. It was not the duty of the Democratic party, he said as its spokesman, "to engage in attacks upon business. . . . We should attempt to do everything to take the government out of business and relieve trade from unnecessary and unreasonable governmental restrictions." He wanted, however, high tariffs, which most Democrats had long opposed. He thought the Federal Trade Commission should have authority to suspend the antitrust laws.

Raskob's irritation with Roosevelt grew as more and more delegates, diligently collected by a big, glad-handed Irishman, James A. Farley, responded to the Roosevelt appeal. The governor from Hyde Park seemed no radical, though such Western Progressives as Senators Norris, Wheeler and young Bob La Follette early saw him as a man who would serve their views in the Presidency. Many liberals, however, dismissed him. Such journals as *The Nation* and *New Republic* regarded him as a man of no great intellectual force or moral stamina. And when Roosevelt formally announced his candidacy in January, 1932, Walter Lippmann, in a column designed to be devastating, wrote that Roosevelt was no crusader, no tribune of the people, no enemy of entrenched privilege: "He is a pleasant man who, without any important qualifications for the office, would very much like to be President."

Certainly he was no such "share the wealth" ripsnorter as Huey Long even if, which was not hard, he was to the left of Raskob. That last was made all too angrily clear to Raskob and Smith when Roosevelt in a radio speech in April invoked the phrase "the forgotten man" for the American "at the bottom of the economic pyramid." Few noticed then that the phrase had first been used fifty years before by the vigorous Sumner of Yale who deplored agitation against "big business," approved of trusts, opposed interference by government in the industrial field and doubted the wisdom of social panaceas and governmental experimentation. His "forgotten man" or men were not the destitute begging for bread but the sober, honest, industrious individuals "who attend no meetings, pass no resolutions, never go to the lobby, are never mentioned in the newspapers, but just work and save and pay."

In the "forgotten man's" name now Roosevelt minimized as just "a stopgap" the importance of some public works proposed by Smith (and so Raskob) and Bernard Baruch, also a rich contributor to the Democratic party.

"A real economic cure," he said, "must go to the killing of the bacteria in the system rather than to the treatment of external symptoms." Purchasing power must be restored to the farmer. Farms and homes must be saved from mortgage foreclosures. And finally and sharply he said the federal government should "provide at least as much assistance to the little fellow as it is now giving to the large banks and corporations."

The conservative answer was given in the same month by Smith who, after at first indicating reluctance to enter another race, had followed Roosevelt's announcement of candidacy with his own as evident leader of the Stop Roosevelt forces. He spoke at a Jefferson Day banquet in Washington arranged by the National Committee. Most of the sound, solid party leaders were there: John W. Davis, James M. Cox, Newton D. Baker, John Nance Garner, Harry Byrd of Virginia, Joe Robinson of Arkansas, who had run as Vice-Presidential candidate with Smith. Almost uniquely absent was the governor of New York. Obviously a Roosevelt rebuke was planned. Smith administered it.

"Oratory puts nobody to work," Smith declared in his best speaking style. He saw evil in appeals to "the forgotten man." He agreed that the purchasing power of the farmer must be restored, but how? Of course, public works were a "stopgap." Such projects were "at least better than nothing and infinitely better than a continuance of the disguised dole." He went on slugging with his target never in doubt.

"At a time like this, when millions of men and women and children are starving throughout the land, there is always the temptation to stir up class prejudice, to stir up the bitterness of the rich against the poor, and of the poor against the rich. . . . I protest against the endeavor to delude the poor people of this country to their ruin by trying to make them believe that they can get employment before the people who would ordinarily employ them are also again restored to conditions of normal prosperity."

He summed up in hard, threatening words: "I will take off my coat and fight to the end against any candidate who persists in any demagogic appeal to the masses of the working people of this country to destroy themselves by setting class against class and rich against poor!"

Even in the Raskob-arranged audience the New York *Times* reported there was no prolonged applause. Smith, some were already saying, had moved spiritually as well as physically from First to Fifth Avenue. Now he undertook to make Roosevelt in the nation seem what conservatives had long been saying about Huey in Louisiana. Down there Huey had already taken off his coat. If that was emblematic of fighting, he always had to keep it off. Had he not liked what Roosevelt said, he would have been pushed to his side anyhow.

Four years before, Long had discovered that the law did not require a state Democratic convention for the election of delegates to the national convention. So he had called a quick session of the state Democratic Central Committee which he controlled, and picked a delegation which left out his political opponents.

Now in 1932 his conservative opposition, which was anti-Roosevelt too, held a convention early and named delegates. Huey held a convention of his own, picked his delegates, and, arrayed in a temporarily immaculate pongee suit, set out for hot Chicago where Bryan had made the "Every Man a King" phrase thirty-six years before. No such oratorical miracle now seemed required for Roosevelt as that which then made Bryan the Democratic nominee and so, depending upon the point of view, the prophet of Protest or the wild agitator against the economic morality of Hard Money held by the few and the scared. In Chicago now before the convention began, Roosevelt forces had almost a certain majority of the delegates. They were uneasily aware, however, that they lacked the two-thirds vote required for nomination. They faced collision —and possibly another deadlock—with the Stop Roosevelt men.

Such details as rules never bothered Huey. As head of his contested delegation, he arrived to precipitate a quick row at a caucus of Roosevelt delegates. He moved to end the two-thirds rule. On its face that would have made the nomination of Roosevelt much easier. But some delegates who were for Roosevelt were against the change. Farley opposed the attempt to alter the rule but found that such leaders as Senator Wheeler, Cordell Hull of Tennessee, Josephus Daniels of North Carolina and Homer Cummings of Connecticut backed Huey's motion. Farley was bewildered by the enthusiasm. And before he could stop it, Huey's motion was carried, pledging the Roosevelt people to fight for the change.

The two-thirds rule might be, as a delegate from Mississippi cried, "a powerful weapon in the hands of the Wall Street element." To change it, however, cried small, irascible Senator Carter Glass of Virginia, would be a "gambler's trick." Solemnly Cox, Davis and Smith, the three living Presidential candidates of the party, opposed the change. Evidently a licking for Roosevelt on this question could hurt him in the race for the nomination. From New York Roosevelt issued a statement abandoning the fight. The Roosevelt strength was demonstrated instead when Alben Barkley of Kentucky was chosen as permanent chairman over Raskob's Shouse. It was also shown when after "a masterly, restrained presentation" by Huey, his much-needed Roosevelt delegation from Louisiana was seated.

On the first ballot Roosevelt showed his strength, 666¼ votes—far ahead, but 100 short of two thirds even with Huey's handpicked Louisiana delegates. Garner, backed by McAdoo and William Randolph Hearst, had 90¼ votes. Smith received 201¾. Seven other candidates had much smaller support. In that day before conventions felt it necessary to conform to television hours, this ballot was taken at 4:28 A.M. In the brightening dawn a second vote was taken. Before it, Long had Roosevelt on the phone begging him to come out for the immediate payment of the bonus, which would have been a crude form of "Share the Wealth." F.D.R. declined. "Well, you are a gone goose," said Long. But on the second ballot Roosevelt was up 11½, still short of two thirds. Smith was down 7½ votes. Garner's Texas and California held firm. A move by Roosevelt forces for an adjournment failed. The third ballot began with Mississippi and Arkansas wobbling among the Roosevelt states. Huey took on the job of holding them in line. While Farley, Howe and others bargained for the Texas and California votes, Huey, sweating in his pongee suit, as Arthur Schlesinger, Jr., reported, took on his Southern neighbors and "lectured, cajoled, pleaded, threatened, shook his fist in the face of Senators, employed all his arts of upcountry eloquence." They stayed fixed. As the light of full day came into the hall Roosevelt had gained 5 more votes. Smith had lost 4. But Garner had gained 11.

Then in the exhausted adjournment the deals were made. Mc-

Adoo and Hearst had old feuds to settle with Smith. Garner wanted no deadlock; also, he would accept the Vice-Presidency. McAdoo, enjoying the sweet taste of revenge on Smith for his 1924 defeat, cast California's votes for Roosevelt. Smith stubbornly to the end held on to 190¼ votes but the decision was made. The same sort of angry city crowds which had roared from the galleries in Madison Square Garden eight years before hooted the nomination. But the delegates on the floor shouted approval. Lacking full support in the convention of his own state of New York and its symbolic men of Tammany, the patrician Roosevelt had still somehow closed the old angry city-rural rift in the party. There was a sense that this was a time of destiny, not for deadlock. The Hudson River man had bracketed the Democratic mainstream.

Crushed between Roosevelt, whom he believed he had made, and McAdoo, who some felt he had destroyed, Al Smith left the hall in anger. Other conservatives were dismayed. When Raskob was asked if he would support the nominee, he turned his back on the questioner to inquire of a friend how the stock market was doing. Obviously he was returning to more familiar fields. But from Albany word came swiftly that Roosevelt, in an exciting break with tradition, was coming by airplane to accept the nomination in person and on the convention scene.

"I warn those nominal Democrats," he cried in his aristocratic accents, "who squint at the future with their faces turned toward the past, and who feel no responsibility to the demands of the new time, that they are out of step with their Party."

He outlined a program, exciting but by no means yet clear, of prohibition repeal, securities regulation, public works, a shorter work week, reforestation, planned agricultural production, reduction of the tariff and relief to all from the top to the bottom of the economic pyramid. Also, as he was not to be allowed to forget, he promised economy and retrenchment in Washington as an example for all. But what was remembered most and longest came in one sentence, even one phrase, which Samuel I. Rosenman, one of his chief aides, had supplied. Schlesinger thought that Rosenman had found it in the title of an article in *New Republic* by Stuart Chase, who had settled in both gaiety and concern in Washington at the beginning of the twenties when his frequent and often hilarious visitor, Sinclair Lewis, was writing *Main Street*. Chase's ar-

ticle had been called "A New Deal for America." Roosevelt shouted
to the Stadium:

"I pledge you—I pledge myself to a new deal for the American
people."

And the bands played, hardly heard among the cheers, the song
which was to become as much Roosevelt's as "The Sidewalks of
New York" belonged to Smith: "Happy Days Are Here Again."
Few noticed then or later that the song was written in the crash
year, 1929, by Jack Yellen and Newton Ager for use in the movie
*Chasing Rainbows* released by Metro-Goldwyn-Mayer in 1930.

Nobody was sure that the good days were at hand or what this
new deal would be to bring them back. Sometimes Roosevelt himself, surrounded by people who from their different philosophies
were struggling for the possession of his mind, seemed least sure.
Conservatives who had lost in his nomination now sought to shape
his campaign. Different varieties of liberals tried to push him to
their views. Sometimes members of his speech-writing "brain trust"
of professors and others he had organized differed among themselves. Garner from Washington sent him a message by a liberal
supporter, "Tell the Governor that he is the boss and we will all
follow him to hell if we have to, but if he goes too far with some
of these wild-eyed ideas we are going to have the shit kicked out of
us."

At the time "wild-eyed ideas" appeared least threatening to the
candidate. As governor as well as candidate, he seemed—or Republicans hoped that he was—caught in a much-publicized political
dilemma. Samuel Seabury, ambitious and implacable investigator of
civic corruption in New York City, had impaled gay Mayor "Jimmy"
Walker on carefully collected evidences of picking up a great deal
more questionable cash than his night-club checks required. Roosevelt was faced with the question of his removal. If he removed
Walker, he might almost dare already disgruntled Tammany to un-
dercut him in the election. If he did not, he would lose the regard
of many liberals in the nation. Roosevelt moved deftly, steadily. He
put sharper and sharper questions, always with evident fairness, to
the wilting mayoral blossom of New York's bistros. Then on September 1, while his friends were vigorously defending him before
the Governor, Walker resolved the whole matter by resignation.
"Still looking youthful if one did not peer too closely," as one
chronicler put it, the fifty-one-year-old Walker, though not yet di-

vorced, sailed away to Europe with the lovely movie actress Betty Compton. Roosevelt was left free to canvas at home without any such Tammany troubles.

Now in the field of ideas and not investigations, Roosevelt, dismissing Walker from mind, faced Huey Long as the most vociferous man pressing ultraliberal views on him. The Louisiana senator, as Arthur Schlesinger, Jr., wrote later, "regarded himself as the spokesman of radicals of both parties." He shouted his protests by telephone after Roosevelt had such a man as Owen D. Young, of the General Electric Company and the Radio Corporation of America, at lunch at Hyde Park. He warned Roosevelt against such men as Baker, Davis and Glass. Also Farley felt that Huey was eager to "steal the national spotlight" from Roosevelt in the campaign. At the outset, however, Huey had his doubts.

"I am so sincerely set," he wrote, "for the proposition that the rich and powerful must be scaled from their privilege and control over the finances of the country and our resources that along any other line I would be worthless."

He could not be wordless. He asked for a special train equipped with loudspeakers to carry him to the whole nation, promising, as Roosevelt had not, immediate cash payment of the bonus. The now wary Farley limited Long's activities, but he was astounded at how effective the Louisiana firebrand was, particularly in big cities far from his home state. Huey showed his power outside Louisiana also. He crossed the border into Arkansas to support in a tumultuous sound-truck tour Hattie Caraway. She had been named to succeed her husband in the U. S. Senate and was opposed for re-election by six men. There was a special zest for Huey in this campaign, since Arkansas was the state of the Senate leader Joe Robinson, who had shown less than sympathy for the "Share the Wealth" program. Huey made his invasion of Arkansas a crusade to "take the feet of six bullies off the neck of one, lone, little, defenseless woman" and a "widow woman" at that. But he got a "Share the Wealth" colleague in the Senate. He was not quite sure, even as he fought for him, of Franklin Roosevelt.

"When I talk to him," he complained, "he says 'Fine! Fine! Fine!' But Joe Robinson goes to see him the next day and again he says 'Fine! Fine! Fine!' Maybe he says 'Fine!' to everybody."

In a nation enthusiastically for Roosevelt as the campaign proceeded, only one man seemed absolutely sure of what he represented.

To the harassed Hoover the Democratic philosophy which he expressed was "the same philosophy of government which has poisoned all Europe . . . the fume of the witch's caldron which boiled in Russia."

In the possibilities of tariff changes, which had been the subject of political debate across the decades, Hoover saw the threat of doom as he moved trembling and white to the campaign's conclusion: "The grass will grow in the streets of a hundred cities, a thousand towns; the weeds will overrun the fields of millions of farms if that protection is taken away." Somberly and shaken he concluded, "This election is not a mere shift from the ins to the outs. It means deciding the directions our nation will take over a century to come."

Gaily Roosevelt went from the Biltmore where he had received the election returns to East Sixty-fifth Street where he and his mother had splendid town houses side by side. And the Dowager Sarah, meeting him at the door, was not disturbed by the notion that old-fashioned ideas, sternly guarded traditions, might be threatened. She kissed him.

"This is the greatest night of my life," she said.

Some, like herself reared in the traditions of a small, wealthy society, had long felt threatened by industrialism. They were not elated now. There was to be long debate as to whether her Franklin betrayed his class or escaped its confines. Persons of more recent and greater opulence were disturbed. Such a person was Raskob, and behind him with less money but more evident resentment was Al Smith. It seemed sad to some that Smith had somehow lately left his class and its concerns. He himself said, "After I left Albany, after living in a mansion for six years I couldn't see First Avenue very well, so I went over on Fifth Avenue. I signed a lease for $10,000 a year." And Mencken, adding a little sympathy to his customary scorn, reported, "The Al of today is no longer a politician of the first chop. His association with the rich has apparently wobbled him and changed him. He has become a golf player. . . . It is a sad spectacle."

Huey had not changed though he had amplified his arrogance and in the Senate seemed to dignified elders like Carter Glass and Joe Robinson to be making a fine art of impertinence. Sometimes he seemed ready for crude clowning just for the hell of it or for publicity profit in something of the spirit in which Faulkner said his sadistic horror story of this same time, *Sanctuary*, was "deliberately conceived to make money." The "Kingfish" was still talking like a blatant barefoot boy from Winn Parish about the poor and the need to "Share the Wealth." He and the country were hearing other voices along similar lines. There was the radio priest, Father Charles Coughlin, at the Shrine of the Little Flower near Detroit, who was preaching to thousands of eager listeners about Social Justice. Out on the West Coast, which had been crowding with retired old folks from the troubled farms, was Dr. Francis E. Townsend. He had come from medical practice in South Dakota, Wyoming and Nebraska to become physician to the indigent in Long Beach. Now he had a plan for two hundred dollars a month for citizens over sixty. Others in various ways were suggesting a sharing of the wealth. The babel of their voices might become a combined demand.

Huey cast his vote and only the angels knew how many others. He shared the triumph, more than willing to be regarded as one of a small number of men who had assured the choice of Roosevelt. He had continued as governor, over a year after his Senate term began, to keep an obstreperous lieutenant governor from taking over. But since January, 1932, his increasing interest was in Washington, though he had by no means removed his hand from Louisiana. He said, "I've done all I can for Louisiana. Now I want to help the rest of the country."

So did a lot of other people with varied and often odd ideas who saw a new chance in a new deal. Roosevelt seemed more than ever debonair in the tug and pull about him. He quietly arranged for special tickets and a special car for Lucy Mercer Rutherfurd at his inauguration. Huey was ready in the nation to demand greater promises than he had made under the oak where Evangeline waited in vain for her lover long ago.

# XV

## FIRE IN THE CAPITOL

I

THE *Nourmahal* came sparkling from an untroubled sea into Miami on February 15, 1933. She brought President-elect Franklin Roosevelt back to shore and responsibility after an eleven-day cruise of fishing and relaxation. His companions indicated the completeness of his brief escape. Neither politician nor brain-truster had accompanied him on this voyage on Vincent Astor's ocean-going motor yacht, the biggest and fastest ever built. Like Astor, his Dutchess County neighbor and distant relative, Roosevelt's other shipmates were men of the class to which he belonged and which some were already saying he had betrayed. Except for the status of his company, he had nothing to give them that they wanted. They neither asked for favor nor offered idea. All had been rich fishermen on a plush holiday. Indeed, the contrast between this company and the crowds which had clamored him to victory was such that the stalwartly Republican New York *Sun*, which expected no good of him, burst into tart verse:

> They were just good friends with no selfish ends
> To serve as they paced the decks;
> There were George and Fred and the son of Ted
> And Vincent (he signed the checks);
> On the splendid yacht in a climate hot
> To tropical seas they ran
> Among those behind they dismissed from mind
> Was the well-known Forgotten Man!

Certainly in its bright brass, gleaming paint, mahogany and teak-wood paneling, the *Nourmahal*, as its starched crew brought it into port, provided glittering contrast to the Florida city. None of the grass Mr. Hoover had predicted grew in its palm-lined streets. But unlike other cities, the Florida resort had known hard times for at least six years—since the big wind had blown away the boom. In the year of Roosevelt's election, building permits had reached a ten-year low. The wan hopes of real estate men were sustained only by paying off tax liens with the city's bonds, which were falling to fifty cents on the dollar. Assessed valuation of property was down to a fourth of what it had been when Bryan prayed to a crowded park and eloquently boomed real estate in a master suburb before he went off to Dayton to meet Darrow and death.

Now a park was full again. Thousands cheered in the late afternoon as Roosevelt's motorcade rolled toward a welcoming meeting in Bayfront Park. People had extravagantly spent their gasoline to drive distances to the meeting, many in well-worn vehicles. Some of those present looked neatly threadbare but gay children waved bright flags. All kinds of people filled the amphitheater. Some were old folks on dwindling pensions or inadequate relief—many of whom had come South to be warm if not otherwise secure. Politicians from great distances hoped to shake Roosevelt's hand or catch his eye. Not all had been his supporters in the election. One person present was the wife of an executive of power companies which had not cared for Roosevelt's ideas about utility regulation in New York State and dimly viewed reports about his plans to make public power on the Tennessee River. Among the ten thousand were veterans still hoping he might change his mind about paying the bonus. There were many of the curious and, as everywhere then, representatives of the country's unemployed. One of them had come with a stomach ache, a grudge and a gun.

In the second car behind Roosevelt's rode Raymond Moley, informed but self-confident head of the "brain trust" of the successful campaign. He had been running errands for his chief while he sailed and had now come to report. Traveling with F.D.R. as candidate he had seen bigger, noisier crowds. But now as an old student of crime among many other things, apparently only to make conversation he spoke to Astor of the risk of assassination in such gatherings. There seemed only good will in this one. In the park as the sun lowered there seemed, too, only good cheer.

The banking crisis, mounting to the danger of full financial collapse in Detroit, seemed far away. So did such a trouble-promising fellow as Senator Long in New Orleans arrogantly confronting Congressional investigation of charges of corruption in the election of his hand-picked Senate colleague. Even with Huey as chief actor this drew less attention than hearings in Washington at which recently reverenced financiers passed in a parade of admissions of wrongdoing or ineptitude. There down Pennsylvania Avenue in the White House, Herbert Hoover, who had been unsuccessfully seeking contact with his sailing successor, paced the last days of his tenure. Though stubborn in crisis, he seemed already part of the past in a present in which not only were bank doors slamming; but schoolteachers, in such a city as Chicago, were going without pay, and farmers, in the Middle West of rich lands and poor people, were threatening mortgage foreclosers with stick, gun and noose.

In balmy Miami Roosevelt was helped up to the back of his big touring car. He seemed no crippled man in a crippled country there. He was a man greeting friendly neighbors. He gave no talk about troubles. He spoke of his fishing luck. With mock ruefulness he reported that he had gained ten pounds which he would have to lose. With a great smile he waved his big hand. He slid back into his seat in the open car. And suddenly applause was interrupted by six pistol shots.

"I'm all right! I'm all right!" he cried.

But beside him Mayor Anton Cermak of bankrupt Chicago crumpled. The wife of the president of the Florida Power and Light Company was wounded, so were three others including a child. A menacing roar rose from the crowd. Only swift police efforts prevented the lynching of the small, dark, unemployed bricklayer, Giuseppe Zangara, who had fired the shots. His hostility, he later said, came from stomach ulcers rather than any certain radical philosophy. But he had bought a gun for eight dollars, gone to the park, waited Roosevelt's arrival.

"I sat in the park waiting, and my stomach kept aching more and more," he snarled at questioning police. "I do not hate Mr. Roosevelt personally. I hate all Presidents . . . and I hate all officials and everybody who is rich."

Increasingly many seemed to share that feeling. Guards were doubled about the incoming President and about Hoover in the White House. The President there wired Roosevelt congratulations on his escape. But he was more concerned about what he rigidly, self-righteously and honestly considered the need of escape for the country from what he all too clearly expected to befall it after March 4. By a Secret Service agent he sent Roosevelt a letter which he himself described as "unduly long." But he said he was sure Roosevelt "did not fully understand the situation." Hoover himself was fully confident that the crisis was not the result of mistakes in the past but fear of the future. What he asked Roosevelt to do, as he frankly explained to a Republican colleague but not to the President-elect, was a remarkable request. He wanted Roosevelt to issue a statement in which "he will have ratified the whole major program of the Republican administration; that is, it means abandonment of 90 per cent of the so-called new deal."

Roosevelt dismissed the letter as "cheeky." He was amazed at Hoover's arrogance in rejection. Possibly in his elation he could not understand the depths of Hoover's depression. It was a relief to both on Inauguration Day when Hoover, as soon as he decently could, scurried from the Capitol to the Union Station. There his secretaries were dismayed at the dismissal of their charge by the Secret Service. Behind the departing President were cheers for his successor's declaration that the nation had "nothing to fear but fear itself." Half sick, Hoover possibly felt a right to be most disturbed by the loudest applause when the new, tall, crippled President cried that if Congress failed to provide adequate remedies for the Depression, he would ask for "broad Executive power to wage a war against the emergency as great as the power that would be given to me if we were in fact invaded by a foreign foe." Hoover in a huff could be excused, but Hoover in history, writing in supposed objectivity years later, became hysterical. He saw dictatorship and doom in events at home and abroad and put the two together.

On February 27, twelve days after Zangara's shots missed Roosevelt and less than a week before he entered the White House, Adolf Hitler's move to dictatorship had been hastened. On that February night fire flamed in the ugly old Reichstag building in Berlin. Blame was put on the Communists. Hitler, damning the Versailles Treaty, Communists and Jews, advanced to absolute power in the last free election in the German Republic on March 5, the day after Roosevelt's inauguration. Long afterward these events seemed to Hoover to more than merely coincide.

As one of his first acts in office the new President ordered what newspapers described as a four-day, modified banking holiday. Actually it formalized a condition already existing on the day he arrived in office, when the Associated Press reported that banks in each of the forty-eight states were closed under holiday orders or were operating under restrictions. Then, the news account said, "financiers, economists and government leaders laid plans to bring America back to financial normalcy." Harding's word had stuck but Hoover insisted the holiday was unnecessary. It was a design, he wrote, to "project millions of people into hideous losses for a Roman holiday." The order, he declared, was "the American equivalent of the burning of the Reichstag to create 'an emergency.'"

Not many Americans took so ominous a view. Even in a chilly breeze under gray skies there seemed, as Roosevelt came to power, a new warmth in the country. There was exuberance in the parade led by General MacArthur whom Roosevelt had recently coupled with Huey Long as the two most dangerous men in the country. The handsome officer only looked pictorial now. So did Al Smith in the regalia of a Tammany sachem. Those who marched before the President's reviewing stand still felt the buoyant lift of his voice and a fresh power like the youthful tones which, with calculated pauses for emphasis, carried by amplifiers to the 100,000 faces lifted toward him and by radio to millions more Americans. He incarnated promise and he provided the expected sense of retribution in triumph when he cried that the "unscrupulous money changers" must be driven from the temple. The crowd stamped chill feet and clapped enthusiastic hands.

He set fire to no Reichstag. But there was in a fashion, different from Hoover's hard and long-held view, something similar. Will Rogers, chewing his gum in Santa Monica, described what had happened for his papers and his countrymen.

"America hasn't been so happy in three years . . . no money, no banks, no work, no nothing.

"But they know they got a man in there who is wise to Congress, wise to our big bankers, and wise to our so-called big men. The whole country is with him—even if what he does is wrong, just so he does something."

Unknowingly he humorously revised Hoover's Reichstag rap: "If he burned down the Capitol, we would cheer and say, 'Well, we at least got a fire started anyhow.'

"We have had years of 'don't rock the boat.' Go on and sink it if you want to. We just as well be swimming as like we are."

Behind the reviewing stand and after the parade, as observed the ever-eager-to-be-helpful Bernard Baruch, the glum White House was transformed as it filled with children and dogs, people and laughter. The new President did bring dogs as well as purpose. Children and grandchildren arrived. The sense of youth, change and confusion was symbolized when John Roosevelt, age seventeen, arriving late at night at the White House gate in a car definitely not Presidential in appearance, was denied admittance. He had to spend the night in the lobby of one of the hotels crowded with many who had come for the inauguration and others who needed jobs in the administration. Lights burned late in the White House and in the Treasury where brain-trusters and bankers eager to advise them labored on emergency banking legislation under the direction of rich, fragile, guitar-playing Secretary of the Treasury William Woodin. The President himself was keeping late hours, too, working on a legislative program for the special session of Congress he had called for the Thursday following his Saturday inauguration. Still in the emergency activity, remembered in terms of late-lit office windows and high-piled ash trays in smoke-filled rooms, F.D.R.'s days were ceremonially and emotionally packed too.

His administration had begun with impeccable Episcopal prayers said in St. John's Church on Jackson Square by the aristocratic schoolmaster Reverend Endicott Peabody of Groton. Across the street from the church of much Presidential tradition was the house of Henry Adams, the caustic friend of Senator Lodge and the devoted elder of the rebellious poet and imprisoned Brahmin Bay Lodge. Adams had told Eleanor Roosevelt years before that nothing men could do in the White House across the square would alter history a whit. On Monday the President attended funeral services in the Senate for Senator Walsh, the implacable investigator of the Harding scandals. Walsh, at seventy-three, was to have been F.D.R.'s Attorney General but instead, coming home with a handsome Cuban widow as his bride, had died in a Pullman passing through the Carolinas. This day, too, Roosevelt received the news that Cermak had succumbed in Miami to the bullet intended for him. Then touching a New England tradition as old as that of Adams and Lodge but vitally different, on Wednesday the President climbed the steep steps to the apartment of retired Justice Oliver Wendell

Holmes to join in the respects paid the great ninety-two-year-old liberal on his birthday. Though his visit was a gesture, the old judge seemed a source of strength. His visit had been suggested by Felix Frankfurter, protégé of seventy-seven-year-old Justice Louis D. Brandeis.

"We face grave times," F.D.R. said to the old justice. "What is your advice?"

In the language of a Civil War veteran, Holmes answered, "Form your ranks and fight!"

It was easier for Roosevelt, whom Holmes later described as "a second class intellect but a first class temperament," to fight than close his ranks. He himself was for both federal relief and federal retrenchment, a balanced budget and some currency inflation. He was willingly surrounded by a variety of advisers collectively described as New Dealers. Many of them became articulate autobiographers. They made their gathering seem an exciting migration of the intellectually elite to the capital which had still in some respects seemed a sleepy Southern town made more soporific by the long-napping Coolidge and what sometimes seemed the harassed sleep-walking of Hoover. Most who arrived came with a motive or a mission. Planners, philosophers, Ph.D.'s and schemers arrived. And some intellectuals came because law firms and universities were taking on no more hands than automobile factories. Not all were then or later impressed by the sudden assemblage. Mencken's friend Frank Kent of the Baltimore *Sun* wrote of "Boy Scouts in the White House . . . a government by Pink Pollyannas, first-name slingers, mothers' little helpers."

The crowding was soon to be emphasized by the quarters available to some of the chief actors in the New Deal drama. Such sound-money, fiscally traditional men as rich, easygoing Lewis W. Douglas as Director of the Budget and Undersecretary of the Treasury Dean G. Acheson, of course, found traditional quarters in the great old stone buildings flanking the White House. There was no such luck for the figures of the new administration's adventuring. When Harry Hopkins came down to take over emergency relief, he got only rooms with scaling paint and heat pipes running up outside the walls in a building where the necessary spraying for bugs gave it an institutional smell. General Hugh S. Johnson, arriving to direct and drive the National Recovery Administration under which industry freed of antitrust laws would supposedly regulate its operations for the common good, got quarters in the Commerce Building which had been Hoover's pride. But he proclaimed it the worst designed office building in the world. His offices like steel cells opening on a corridor, he said, resembled nothing so much as the men's room in the Union Station.

Ideas were as diverse as accommodations. Their complexity has been described by historians. Yet it seems both odd and clear that at a time when the survival of the Jewish people was put in doubt by Hitler in Germany, two great Jews embodied the chief philosophic differences as to American directions. In March, as the first hundred days of the Roosevelt administration began, in New York ten thousand Jews demanding boycott of Germany marched on City Hall mournfully chanting "El Mole Rachornim," the dirge of the dead. Not unconcerned with their fellows, in Washington Baruch and Brandeis offered divergent patterns for the fulfillment of American life.

At a time when young men were supposed to be remaking America Baruch was sixty-two, Brandeis an ancient seventy-seven. Both men had served Woodrow Wilson. His unpopular appointment to the Supreme Court of Brandeis as a Jew regarded as too liberal had marked his courage in peace. His selection of Baruch, then a Jewish speculator, as chairman of the War Industries Board helped his effectiveness in war. As lawyer, judge and writer, Brandeis had preached his crusade against bigness in American economic development. Baruch, who had mobilized industry for war, believed it could be safely mobilized against depression.

Neither Baruch nor Brandeis as the New Deal began took public positions of prominence. Brandeis was cloistered in his judicial office. Baruch always made his self-effacement part of an elaborate public relations apparatus. But both were active in New Deal recruitment. Both Hugh Johnson of NRA and George N. Peek of the Agricultural Adjustment Administration were Baruch protégés. Through Felix Frankfurter of the Harvard Law School, Justice Brandeis in effect brought many able men to Washington. The ideas of the two men were magnets. Baruch believed, as his biographer Margaret L. Coit wrote, that "bigness was inevitable." And "Power could destroy and power could build; power could not be conquered, but it could be controlled." Brandeis so distrusted bigness that Moley spoke derisively of his philosophy as one that America "could once more become a nation of small proprietors, of corner grocers and smithies under spreading chestnut trees." Roosevelt, "playing by ear," picked and chose almost indiscriminately at first from the philosophies of both. And Huey Long, who, many were trying to insist, was too insignificant for notice, chose Baruch as a target and made almost a caricature of Brandeis' faith for his own purposes.

On the surface, at least, in the blossoming spring of 1933, bigness seemed too routed to resist any rejection or regulation. The president of New York's great National City Bank had resigned just before he was put on trial for tax evasion. The administration was sharply examining the taxes paid even by such a personage as Andrew Mellon, until recently "the greatest Secretary of the Treasury since Alexander Hamilton." J. P. Morgan and all his partners had testified that they had paid no income taxes in the years immediately past. The respect for bigness was pictorially deflated when the unapproachable J. P. Morgan himself was photographed at a Congressional hearing with a pretty little circus midget, who had jumped there for publicity, seated in his ample lap. The country did not recoil at such an affront at bigness; it was grateful to the little lady for a guffaw.

First thunder at the ambivalent New Deal came like an impertinence from Long. At the outset of the Hundred Days he had been swept aside, only succeeding in infuriating the venerable Carter Glass of Virginia when Glass, who had been Wilson's Secretary of the Treasury, had been handling the administration's emergency banking legislation. The New Deal had been taken into camp by the goddamn bankers, Long insisted ineffectually then. But on April 11, he drew attention, if not blood. Then he hooted at the contradiction between Roosevelt's budget-balancing economy bill, passed overwhelmingly during the first two weeks of his administration, and the bill to create a Civilian Conservation Corps to take unemployed young men off the streets and put them creatively at work in the woods.

The President was a little sententious about his diverse directions. "For three long years," he had said on March 10, "the Federal government has been on the road to bankruptcy." As a budget balancer, he went to work under the economy bill cutting the pay of government employees and the payments to veterans. But some of his enthusiasms were costly. Along with other relief measures he had secured the CCC. Not only economizers but organized labor had opposed it at first. A labor committee headed by William Green saw the plan as a form of forced labor, the possible equivalent of black shirts and storm troopers, and so as "smacking of Fascism, Hitlerism, and a form of Sovietism." A surprised Roosevelt placated opponents by appointing a labor official as head of his corps. That did not satisfy Huey. He called the bill to create the CCC "a sapling bill, a sapsucker's bill."

"There are more men out of work than when he went into the White House," he said of Roosevelt on April 11, "and more banks are closed. We've swallowed enough of this stuff. We've swallowed this awful banking thing they brought in here hook, line and sinker.

"We took $400 million from the soldiers and spent $300 million to plant saplings."

Outraged Democratic Leader Joe Robinson protested the "unjust criticism."

"I'm not falling out with the President," said Long piously, "but to quote from the Bible, 'he who flattereth a friend his eyes should fall from his head.'"

His friendship seemed to Rooseveltians a good deal less than infallible. They declared that Huey's antipathy stemmed not merely from his indignation at the wickedness of financiers and his concern for the poor, including veterans and federal employees. He was also sore because of continuing income tax investigations of his friends and because he wasn't getting all the federal patronage he thought he was entitled to. Long was as complex in his clamor as in his personality. H. G. Wells described him as "a Winston Churchill who has never been at Harrow." Another observer spoke of him as "Tom Sawyer in a toga." He declined even to recognize the existence of protocol. Roosevelt that spring was receiving ceremonial and solicitous visits from European statesmen concerned for international economic stability, particularly since the United States had to a degree departed from the so-long, so-sacred gold standard. Pleasantness as well as protocol marked their visits. But when Long came to an arranged conference with the President he kept his bright-banded straw hat on in Roosevelt's office throughout the visit. Whatever else were his faults, Huey knew how to communicate by antics.

As the lilacs bloomed and faded, he seemed only an ugly little voice in Washington. There were ugly situations behind him in the country and the world. Crime in the nation was not abating with the approach of prohibition's end. It was pathetically pointed when

Lindbergh, at the trial of Gaston Means for cheating Evalyn Walsh McLean with a ransom hoax, had repeated the whole grim story of his child's loss. No one was yet concerned about thirty-one-year-old John Dillinger, who was paroled on May 22 by Governor Paul V. McNutt of Indiana though he had been judged incorrigible in prison. But all including the President were aware of the continuing operations in New York of such characters as Jack ("Legs") Diamond, Edward ("Fats") McCarthy, the Coll brothers, Vincent and Peter, and above all Arthur Flegenheimer, known everywhere as Dutch Schultz.

But now honest men were turning to violence—and with cause. As the Congress produced in alphabetical succession the AAA, the FERA, the NRA to deal with agriculture, relief aid, industrial recovery and such an adventure in regional planning as TVA, a country less docile than the Congress seemed to explode. Not depression but old prejudice necessitated the presence of the National Guard at a second trial of the "Scottsboro boys" in Alabama. It went on at a time when Richard B. Harrison was taking his first rest after 1300 performances in the role of de Lawd in the blackface modern miracle play *The Green Pastures*. Depression-born frustrations and angers, however, stirred in city and countryside.

In April as Roosevelt talked and sailed on the Potomac with tired, worried Prime Minister MacDonald of England, schoolteachers in Chicago roared in the streets. Five thousand who had received no pay since the beginning of the year descended on the financial districts demanding that the banks lend money to the city—funds which undoubtedly Cermak had been hoping to get from Roosevelt when he fell in Miami. As effectively as any run of depositors, they made the reopened banks close their doors. Foreshadowing later sit-ins, four teachers set up a table with the announced purpose of playing bridge until their demands were met. Others hooted at former Vice-President Dawes: "That's the man who borrowed $80 million from the government but won't lend any money to the teachers. He went along with Insull in cheating us." And of the government's action less than a week before in modifying the gold standard to push up commodity prices, a placard proclaimed, "We want food. What good is inflation when you are broke."

"To hell with troublemakers!" cried Dawes at his City National Bank. And apparently with the same idea some women were clubbed by police. Their cause was just, said Mayor Edward J. Kelly, appointed to succeed Cermak (teacher pay was to be ten months in arrears before it was paid), but in desperation they had been listening to Communists.

Three days later in Le Mars, Iowa, which had originally been founded by British gentlemen farmers who rode to hounds and dressed for dinner, the country equivalent occurred. There, Judge Charles C. Bradley had refused on demand to swear that he would sign no more mortgage foreclosures. So, the Associated Press reported, "A crowd of more than a hundred farmers dragged [him] from his courtroom, slapped him, carried him blindfolded in a truck to a cross roads a mile from here, choked him until he was only partially conscious, smeared grease on his face, and stole his pants."

In Washington nobody could be sure that a new bonus army on its way was not approaching in similar spirit. The capital remembered, as Eleanor Roosevelt wrote, the "feeling of horror" about how Hoover had dealt with the veterans the year before. Others remembered also, as Mrs. Roosevelt did, its effect—politically amplified, Hoover thought—on public opinion. Now in his place Roosevelt was not only opposed to payment of the bonus; also he had announced, as Huey Long had loudly emphasized, that he had cut $400,000,000 from the payments veterans had been getting even under Hoover. The situation was, to say the least, delicate, though the veterans this time were approaching only with the request that they be given the same lobbying rights as others—bankers, industrialists, trade association executives, farmers big enough to pay their way to Washington.

The business was put into the seemingly fragile hands of Louie Howe. In that period when others appeared to be soaring to greater prominence beside him he received as his chores problems involving the bonus marchers, Pearl Harbor and Huey Long.

2

Roosevelt's election was, of course, Howe's final, unique triumph. He was to be remembered as the long-time friend, the Warwick, the alter ego, l'éminence grise. But even before the election he had found himself no longer alone as the President-maker. Around the Governor and the candidate the company of aides thickened. Howe had helped create the increasing company close to F.D.R. He had first brought Ray Moley to Roosevelt's attention when, in 1924, they were working with an organization called the National Crime Commission. It provided a pay check for Howe which relieved Roosevelt's pocketbook. Also, like the American Construction Council, it helped keep Roosevelt in the public eye. Moley, then a relatively obscure associate professor at Columbia who had written several books on crime, was helpful. Crime did not subside as a result of the organization's efforts but Moley was available when the more effective Roosevelt movement to the Presidency began. His place close to Howe's was shown when in Chicago F.D.R. read to the convention the first page of an acceptance speech which tired Howe had written, then switched to the address Moley and others had prepared. Use of that first page alone seemed a bone kindly thrown to an old dog. Now in Washington, Howe's prestige was preserved as *the* Secretary to the President who lived in the White House. Still in a position of undefined powers as Assistant Secretary of State, Professor Moley's apparent power about the throne had so grown that the derisive were chanting: "Moley, Moley, Moley, Lord God Almighty."

Howe definitely, however, did not mean to be set aside. Ailing, asthmatic, ashen, he let no one forget his position in the White House. He had the appreciation of the President and the affection of Eleanor with whom he worked so long and whom he taught so well. He bought a tan Lincoln roadster as a sort of chariot of his triumph. If he seemed, as a newspaperman wrote, a "medieval gnome," he never forgot and meant to let no one else forget that he was the man behind Roosevelt. Even the old-time Progressive, Secretary of the Interior Harold L. Ickes, who bowed his neck to nobody, spoke almost obsequiously of Colonel Howe—a name not carelessly reminiscent of Wilson's Colonel House. Ickes brought to the Colonel seemingly a small problem but one close to America's security in the Pacific.

In his *Secret Diary*, kept so carefully for publication later, Ickes on March 30 made only a paragraph, subordinate to a description of a jubilant Press Club party for the President and the Cabinet, about a conference with Howe. He spent an hour with the swarthy little secretary, he wrote, considering the matter of a governor of the then territory of Hawaii administered by the Department of the Interior. Neither was satisfied that any of those proposed was the man "for what is a delicate situation." The delicacy of the situation there had been emphasized just six days before when Yosuke Matsuoka landed on the *Leviathan* in New York. At the time of inauguration in Washington, Japanese armies had overrun the province of Jehol beyond Manchuria and, as the press reported, were poised at the Great Wall of China for a march on Peiping. The United States had joined the League of Nations protest against this Japanese aggression. Matsuoka then had led the withdrawal of the Japanese delegation from the League. Now he was on his way home. But in New York, where his ship had been met by threatening Chinese, he talked to reporters in a carefully guarded suite in a Fifth Avenue hotel. His remarks did not seem guarded. Eight years later Roosevelt was to describe intercepted instructions which Matsuoka sent as foreign minister to the Japanese ambassador in Washington as "the product of a mind which is deeply disturbed and unable to think quietly or logically." In March, 1933, he seemed sternly logical from his own point of view and not quiet at all. He had no intention of appealing to the United States for support, he told reporters as he steadily puffed his pipe. He was a chunky little man with a thick mustache and yellow horn-rimmed spectacles. Also he evidently had a chip on his shoulder. Japan, he said, "is not a vassal state to America or any other nation." But his country was misunderstood in the United States.

"He also," said the Associated Press, "expressed the view that Japanese-American relations might be improved by the withdrawal of the U. S. Fleet from the Pacific."

Six days later Howe talked about the delicate situation in Hawaii where that fleet was based at Pearl Harbor. Then, on April 5, Roosevelt in a letter to Colonel House, mostly about domestic fiscal matters, spoke of Matsuoka who had gone on to Washington and lunched at the White House as "our Japanese friend." House, and perhaps Roosevelt, apparently had known the Japanese diplomat in Paris after World War I when his country was demanding Asiatic territories of defeated Germany and a League declaration on racial equality. Roosevelt did not seem disturbed, but he wrote that he thought "it inadvisable to converse more than formally—he has made the error of talking for quotation to newspapermen indiscriminately and his suggestions as to us in regard to where we should keep our fleet has brought me thousands of protests. I am wondering if he said this in order to ingratiate himself against assassination by the Junker crowd when he gets home."

The Junkers—Roosevelt called the militarists by the German term —had the year before indulged in a slaughter of the moderates in government. But what concerned Ickes and Howe when they talked again a month later was the situation pointed by a murder on the island of Oahu which was stirring racial antagonisms between the polytypic population of Honolulu and the Navy at Pearl Harbor. Sometimes Japanese concern about the U. S. Fleet at Pearl Harbor was equaled by American fears that sugar planters bringing in Japanese laborers were "orientalizing" the islands. Drunken sailors and Polynesian panderers sometimes had rowdy meetings. Even the many respectable Hawaiians who shared the profit of the trade sometimes felt that the Navy on liberty could be too free. The American press spoke of "underworld" Hawaiians and of corrupt police. Hawaiians resented the Navy's insistence on occasion that its people be tried in Navy courts. Rackets had grown in Hawaii as elsewhere under prohibition which, as a part of the Constitution, followed the flag. "Race hatred," the press said, had grown too. It exploded in the second of related crimes the year before Roosevelt came to the White House. It had been brought, the Associated Press reported, "to a fever pitch by the occurrences of the last six months." The danger of it persisted in 1933.

The "delicate situation" had begun in tragedy and crime. The young wife of an American naval officer, Mrs. Thalia Massie, had left a party at an inn to walk home alone through dark streets in the tropic night. On the way she had been seized, raped and badly beaten by five Hawaiians. The case had attracted attention not only because of its horror but because the girl was a grandniece of Alexander Graham Bell, the inventor of the telephone, and the daughter of Major Granville Roland Fortescue, a writer and retired army officer who had not only ridden with Theodore Roosevelt as one of his Rough Riders but had also served as his military aide at the White House.

Despite Thalia Massie's identification of her assailants in the civilian territorial courts, the case had resulted in a mistrial—to the fury of the naval establishment at Pearl Harbor. Then four months after the assault, police stopped a car speeding toward Koko Head and supposedly toward a geyser in which in the past bodies had fallen never to be recovered. In the automobile was found the sheet-wrapped body of one of Mrs. Massie's suspected assailants, Joe Kahahawai. A rope was tied around his throat, his skull was crushed, he had been shot through the heart. No mystery attended the murder. Mrs. Massie, her husband, Lieutenant Thomas H. Massie, her mother, Mrs. Fortescue and two sailors had kidnapped the Hawaiian by trick, taken him to the Massie house and, according to a police version, murdered him in a bathtub. They had not meant to kill him, they said, but only to force a confession from him. When it came in a brutal blurt, Massie could not restrain his trigger finger.

Quickly naval authorities took all but one sailor from the civil authorities and lodged them on an old cruiser beached in a mudbank at Pearl Harbor. In comfortable quarters, surrounded by friends and flowers, they were kept there, the Associated Press said, by a Navy "defending its honor . . . to prevent intrusion not escape." Marines were placed between those in the Navy's protective custody and civil authorities who wanted to question them. But in Honolulu angry crowds gathered about the funeral parlor where Kahahawai's mother sat "at the head of the casket, dry-eyed." If he had been a hoodlum, as Americans charged, he had been a popular, handsome athlete too. Native angers grew. A mob of three thousand had to be dispersed with tear gas. But at last the Navy, headed at Pearl Harbor by Admiral Yates Sterling, released the prisoners for trial in the territorial courts. Though they were defended by Clarence Darrow, who took the case because in the Depression he needed the fee, a jury of Chinese, Japanese, Hawaiians and mixed bloods found them guilty of manslaughter. Governor Lawrence M. Judd, later president of the Industrial Association of Hawaii, commuted their sentences to one hour. No one knew how long bitterness would last. Ickes moved slowly after his conferences with Howe. In 1934 he named as governor a retired judge, Joseph B. Poindexter, who was still, at seventy-two, holding the job in 1941.

The new bonus army presented a more readily seen danger in 1933. Howe handled that matter personally. He got word of their coming on April 29 while the National Guard was still on duty around Le Mars, Iowa, after the violence there. He tried to persuade the Veterans' Liaison Committee to cancel the march. They were coming. They asked no more than "any other group" of lobbyists except for one detail—they wanted to be housed and fed. Facing the inevitable or the explosive, that was agreed to. A camp for six thousand men was set up at Fort Hunt across the river in Virginia. Chow lines were provided. A Navy band played for them.

Not all agreed to accept this suburban sanctuary. A Democratic woman who had just come to Congress from an Indiana farm, Virginia Jenckes, was active in patching differences between Conservative and supposedly Communist marchers. She has been little remembered. The occasion has chiefly served to dramatize the entrance of Eleanor Roosevelt upon her career as itinerant humanitarian reporting to an immobilized husband.

Howe's strategy was both soft and stern. One drizzly afternoon he asked Mrs. Roosevelt to go for a drive with him. Unknown to her, their destination was the camp. There figuratively he pushed her from the car. He would stay and nap. "Very hesitatingly," Eleanor wrote, she got out. Some of the awkward shyness of her younger years remained. But she went in under the curious eyes of the veterans. She shared snack and song. She made a little speech. This version of Howe's victory ended with the quotation from the ragtag marchers: "Hoover sent the Army. Roosevelt sent his wife."

It was not quite that simple. A plan was devised to place the veterans in the new CCC. This took some legal revisions. The organization had been set up for young men between the ages of eighteen and twenty-five. No veterans of the war fifteen years before fell into that age group. No matter—and or else! The press at the time found no enthusiasm among the marchers for this plan. "Comfortably filled with army rations and snugly housed in army tents," said a dispatch from Washington, "the new Bonus Army tonight found the idea of going to work in Roosevelt's forest camps anything but a pleasant one."

But Howe was back this time without Mrs. Roosevelt and with younger, tougher Stephen Early, who handled the President's press and understood the good or bad story the bonus march could be in the papers. This time Howe did not snooze in weariness in his car. They inspected the camp. They stayed for chow. Also, certainly they prodded. Bonus marchers to the number of 2663 marched into the Civilian Conservation Corps. A third of them left it within five months. In a little over a year all but four hundred of them were out. But all the 1933 bonus marchers were out of the capital area, and when more bonus marchers appeared in the spring of 1934 the sting was removed from their threat.

Huey Long was not so easily handled. Early and late efforts were made to dismiss him as a parochial buffoon. But his clowning sharpened; his comedy made good newspaper copy. Even some conservatives, not sharing his views but not yet roaring themselves, enjoyed his discomfiture of the White House. Howe was not amused, though he rebuked his staff when at a swearing-in ceremony one added to an oath to defend the republic from its enemies "and Huey Long." Long roared at what he described as a phony war against the "money-changers." The only lions pulled out of the den, he said, were dead ones.

"First we prod them, kick them, poke them, and make sure they're dead. Then, once we're sure of that, we all shout together, 'Let's go after them,' and we do. They never went after Insull until he was in Greece."

To him the master of the New Deal became "Prince Franklin, Knight of the *Nourmahal*."

Roosevelt, with the protection of acclaim still around him, was as imperturbable as he was when he declined to notice that Huey did not take off his hat in his office. He was glad to say good-bye to the special session of Congress which, he was sure, would "go down in history as the one which, more than any other, boldly seized the opportunity to right great wrongs, to restore clearer thinking and more honest practices, to carry through its business with practical celerity and to set our feet on the upward path."

He hurried to Groton where Franklin, Jr., was graduating. Then with Franklin, James and John, he sailed in Maine waters to Campobello. Of his boys only Elliott was missing. He also was making history of a sort. As the Congress moved to adjournment news of his divorce came from Reno, the first in any family in the White House. But the skies were bright. The President handled his lines with his crew. And there was more luxurious sailing when from Campobello he moved south on the new cruiser *Indianapolis*.

He had a right to bask in the sun. Whatever might follow, from March to June, based on 1923–1925 averages as 100, manufacturing production had increased from 56 to 93. Employment had gone up from 58.8 to 66.9 and payrolls had risen from 37.1 to 47.2. There were other good signs. On May 27, only a month after unpaid teachers had rioted in the banks and at the City Hall, the thirty-million-dollar Century of Progress Exposition opened in Chicago with Dawes as chairman of its finance committee. Some were saying that the exposition covered continuing troubles in Chicago only about as much as the fan of one of its chief attractions, the dancer Sally Rand, covered Sally Rand.

Behind Roosevelt as he sailed, Hugh Johnson was launching the NRA with its blue eagle emblem, putting almost religious fervor along with governmental support into the kind of business self-regulation which had been impossible under the antitrust law when F.D.R. headed the American Construction Council. Mystical, mop-headed Secretary of Agriculture Henry Wallace, who had spoken of the vomit of capitalism, was hoping to make farmers happier, including those who almost lynched the judge in his own state two months before. But while they labored to control planting and pigs, he and George Peek, head of the Agricultural Adjustment Administration, were fearful of bounteous crops in a still-hungry land. It seemed odd to no one that in the effort to save farmers stifled under surpluses, Wallace had been the developer of more productive hybrid corn and Peek had come to his job as the manufacturer of agricultural machinery which would make fewer people necessary on the land.

The sea sparkled, and in the world beyond it, despite the Asian adventures of the Japanese, prospects of peace seemed to improve. Way off in India Mahatma Gandhi, a little man whose entire equipment seemed to be a loincloth and horn-rimmed glasses, finished a twenty-one-day fast on May 29. Less attention was paid to the final rejection of his German citizenship by Albert Einstein, a little fellow who some thought looked like Charlie Chaplin. After all, as one American said, he understood every word Einstein said but not a single sentence. Only theoretical physicists felt the necessity of understanding his theory, which seemed safely bound in scientific journals. France, England, Germany and Italy joined in a four-power pact sponsored by Mussolini. On the day the Hundred Days ended in Washington, Roosevelt wrote that he was "deeply impressed" by Il Duce's "evidenced honest purpose of restoring Italy and seeking to prevent general European trouble."

To some Europeans Roosevelt seemed to be the cause of trouble. As the President sailed, dignified Secretary of State Cordell Hull arrived in London as head of the American delegation at the World Economic Conference. A long-time member of Congress, Hull was a power in the politics which had put Roosevelt in the White House. Though he sometimes lisped (F.D.R. mocked his saying "Jesus Cwist"), his vocabulary included also the stronger barnyard language of Tennessee. His chief interest was in tariff reductions, but clearly what the Europeans, especially the British, wanted were assurances that a cheaper American dollar, off gold, would not disadvantage them in world trade.

Suddenly while the conference in London seemed bogged down in decorum, garden parties and other amenities, the mighty Moley roared by seaplane to the President's ship. His flight made drama and news. Off he went to London, accompanied, at F.D.R.'s request, by Herbert Swope, old New York *World* editor who was Baruch's public relations man. As a man apparently projected into the conference by the President, the Assistant Secretary of State then received in London the kind of attention that pushed Secretary Hull into the background. Into Hull's hands fell a supposedly secret code cable Moley had sent back reflecting on the qualifications of the delegation which had arrived before him. Moley undertook to placate Hull. But James P. Warburg, American financier there as an economic adviser, found the Secretary of State in a fury.

"That piss-ant Moley," he cried, "here he curled up at mah feet and let me stroke his head like a huntin' dog and then he goes and bites me in the ass."

Hull's Tennessee long knife was out. Also when Moley believed that a declaration on currency stabilization agreements had been shaped which the United States would approve, Louis Howe was with Roosevelt. Howe had been for Hull's appointment as Secretary of State; Moley had objected to it. Now from the President on the *Indianapolis* came a cable described as the "bombshell" message. It sternly, almost contemptuously rejected any idea that the United States should join in a declaration under which it would approve a prospect of stabilization of currencies on a gold basis. Europeans might think that Roosevelt's brusque insistence on a managed currency in the United States as a basis for domestic recovery was, as the *Manchester Guardian* said, "A Manifesto of Anarchy."

His insistence on freedom for inflation in the United States brought the clear deflation of Moley. To the shock of assembled statesmen and the surprise of his own delegation, Roosevelt had formed his ranks, ready to fight for recovery in economic isolation. His message came like a thunderclap at a garden party. And Hull's knife, and perhaps Howe's, were deep in the pretentious professor's back. In effect Hull told Moley so when the distressed Assistant Secretary came in consternation to him as the Secretary of State was leaving Claridge's to stay with Lady Astor at Cliveden.

When Moley returned, Roosevelt, evidently at the suggestion of Howe, proposed that the injured Assistant Secretary go to Hawaii to report on law enforcement there in connection with the delicate situation with which Ickes and Howe had been so much concerned.

The assignment seemed inadequate to his dignity to Moley, who was already contemplating journalism with Vincent Astor's aid. Hawaii seemed a dreamy distance off. Certainly crime there seemed insignificant compared with that at home. While Moley had been in London, Melvin Purvis of the FBI had finally brought down in Chicago thirty-two-year-old John Dillinger, whose roaring, murderous robberies and raids had made him seem an exciting new Jesse James to some and the Public Enemy No. 1 to the FBI.

At the summer's end the President sailed on Astor's *Nourmahal* again. Mrs. Roosevelt, on the kind of trip she would now never cease to make, had gone off with Lorena Hickok, an old newspaper friend who became one of the reporters on poverty for Harry Hopkins. At the suggestion of the Secret Service, passed on to her by Howe, she "religiously" carried a revolver, much to the amusement of her children. Also, she carried the kind of good will which had made her welcome in the camp of the bonus marchers. She collected tales of poverty in such areas as the coal mining country of West Virginia. There was, she reported, the little boy holding his cherished pet, a white rabbit, in his arms—and his scrawny, smirking sister who said, "He thinks we are not going to eat it, but we are."

Home from this *Nourmahal* cruise Roosevelt looked so well when he got back to Washington that Ickes complimented him on his appearance. He had had a good rest, the President told him, and one night with his elegant shipmates he had sat up until six in the morning playing poker and drinking beer. The Secretary of the Interior suggested that perhaps he ought to make that a regular practice. But more than such relaxation eased the Roosevelt mood. With many others he had enjoyed the recent melodramatic discomfiture of Senator Long.

Huey, whose companions were often as surprising as those of the President, had been taken to the Sands Point Bath Club on Long Island by Gene Buck, the chief song writer for the Ziegfeld Follies and Frolics. Long got drunk. One report was that he "picked up asparagus tips and other handy edibles from the plates of other guests, and made a remark to one of the women at another table which no Southern gentleman, not excluding a Senator, would make." The more accepted version was that he went into the men's room and found another guest ahead of him at the urinal: "Always the innovator, he stood back, took aim through the legs of the other, but missed his goal." The certainty was that he came staggering out of the toilet with a bloody gash above his eye. Huey's version was that four or five agents of Wall Street had attacked him. Few swallowed such a tale; more laughed. It was proposed that a medal be provided for the party—or parties—responsible for the widely welcomed blow. But at a convention of veterans for whom he wanted the bonus and more, his description of the mistreatment of the incident by the press so stirred his hearers that they moved with intent of mayhem on reporters.

With political troubles at home and hilarity in the nation, Long seemed to be on his way out. So did the Depression. There were, of course, some problems in Washington. Ickes, back home in Chicago, where he was welcomed with honors at the Century of Progress Exposition, ran into Harry Hopkins and mayors of some cities who were saying that the public works program handled by Ickes was entangled in red tape. Ickes himself was contemptuous of some of the propaganda Hugh Johnson was putting on for the NRA. The President was disturbed by the delay in shaping some industrial codes under NRA. Secretary of the Treasury Woodin was worried about stability of the dollar. So were such other fiscal sticklers as Dean Acheson and Lew Douglas. Early in October Mayor Kelly of Chicago sent word suggesting that the President should not come there to address the bonus-demanding American Legion Convention. He did not think he could protect him.

Autumn had come. The bright spring seemed far behind. ". . . The inevitable sniping has commenced," F.D.R. wrote to his ambassador in London, "led by what you and I would refer to as the Mellon-Mills influence in banking and certain controlled industries." But there was other sniping, too, from less opulent sources. "Dear Mama," he wrote to his redoubtable dowager mother in Hyde Park, "On the whole the situation is not good because so many people are getting their toes stepped on and cannot realize that the West is seething with unrest and must have higher values to pay off their debts." Others were murmuring on the right and the left and on the bottom as well as the top.

Yet the murmuring now was that of differences, not of despair.

There was a courage in complaint. People were somehow finding money to go to the World's Fair. More people talked about Sally Rand's dancing all but nude ("the fan is quicker than the eye") than about the gold standard or currency stabilization. And in the White House F.D.R. was still the buoyant spirit. His staff made jokes which easily stirred his roaring laughter. Howe wrote a comic poem about gold. His boss found relaxation in the animated cartoons of Mickey Mouse which Walt Disney had begun to produce shortly before the Depression began. Now Disney had come forward with his production of *The Three Little Pigs* (unrelated to the six million little pigs the Department of Agriculture had slaughtered to sustain pork prices in September). From the film came the melody the country was whistling, "Who's Afraid of the Big Bad Wolf?" Still there were more sounds than whistling in the land where some thought they still had more to fear than fear itself.

# XVI

## DIVERSE THUNDER

"IT's a choice between catalepsy and epilepsy," said George Creel of the California gubernatorial election in 1934. "Sinclair has a fantastic impossible plan and Merriam is as modern as the dinosaur age."

Often, between the no longer despairing but loudly debating left and right in America in 1934, that seemed the choice between Upton Sinclair, the Democratic nominee, and Frank Merriam, the Republican. Creel, who had been chief of Woodrow Wilson's wartime propaganda, undoubtedly spoke with some personal pique. In the Democratic primary he had confronted Sinclair, who only the fall before had left the Socialist Party to register as a Democrat. Both Creel and Sinclair had long been writing reformers. As newspaper editor and magazine contributor, Creel had collaborated with Edwin Markham in a work on child labor problems. Markham's poem, *The Man with the Hoe*, at the turn of the century had stirred the country with its grim portrayal of the exploited laborer on the land. In 1906 Sinclair had in his novel, *The Jungle*, exposed the ugly underside of American city life around the stockyards in the meat-packing industry.

Sinclair had become his own convert as a Socialist putting his fervor into a long succession of humorless exposés of almost every aspect of life in the United States. Personally, however, he was an amiable agitator well-liked by those who felt that his notions were nonsense. Now as a sudden Democrat, he stepped forward as candidate with a pamphlet, *I, Governor of California and How I Ended Poverty: A True Story of the Future*. His slogan, "End Poverty in California," provided his EPIC plan and campaign. At fifty-four he seemed to many only a frayed crackpot. His proposal that the

state take over idle land and factories and put idle people to producing for their needs was dismissed by many as plain foolishness.
Even Norman Thomas, perennial Socialist candidate for President,
called it "economically and politically absurd." Conservatives said
EPIC stood for "Empty Promises in California."

As an old-time, articulate, highly respectable Democrat who
wrote for *Collier's* and belonged to San Francisco's plush Bohemian
Club, Creel set out to slap down this upstart, almost instant Democrat. There were troubles in Creel's San Francisco. This year a long-
shoremen's strike in the beautiful port ended by involving all workers in a general work stoppage. Even violence in San Francisco,
however, seemed less appalling than the human, emotional and intellectual babel in the south below it. Oddly there Sinclair lived in
Pasadena, the richest city, per capita, in the United States.

"When I crossed the Tehachapi into Southern California," Creel
wrote later, "it was like plunging into darkest Africa without gun
bearers."

In the decade before 1930 California's population, much of it
around teeming, sprawling Los Angeles, had increased by 65 per
cent. Cults and ideas seemed to increase as much as people. Aimee
Semple McPherson, as a decorative evangelist of thirty-three, had
set up her Angelus Temple on January 1, 1923. In the years after,
she seemed to make a movie production out of Christianity, close
to the movie capital of Hollywood. Her following had not been
dispersed by a series of sensational stories about her behavior when
she was reported to have taken off her stunning white-and-blue
evangelical costume in one or more "love nests." Though more
bawdy jokes were circulated about her than about Mae West, who
was frankly then playing the role of the lady of easy virtue with a
heart of gold, the faithful welcomed Aimee back from a "kidnaping"
which sensational newspapers snickeringly suggested was an assigna-
tion. They sang:

> *Coming back, back, back,*
> *Coming back, back, back,*
> *Our sister in the Lord is coming back.*
> *There is shouting all around*
> *For our sister has been found;*
> *There is nothing now of joy or peace we lack.*

Coming back in 1934 had different connotations for Californians. Cults were desperately required in the economy, too. It was only necessary to look out of a window to see need. Dr. Francis Everett Townsend discovered that. He was not in very good shape himself. Born sixty-six years before in Illinois, from where so many retired farmers had come to Los Angeles, he had had to struggle to finish his medical education when he was thirty-six. From his office in Belle Fourche, South Dakota, he engaged in a wide-ranging rural practice in South Dakota, Wyoming and Montana. Then at fifty-two he came to California, as so many others did, because of his health. In Long Beach as the Depression began he was assistant health officer and physician to the indigent. In 1933, however, he lost his job in a change in the city administration. While shaving in late fall of that year he looked out of his bathroom window.

In the alley below where garbage cans were arrayed, he saw "three, haggard very old women . . . stooped with great age, bending over the barrels, clawing into the contents." Furiously then, he began screaming his message to be embodied in his organization, Old Age Revolving Pensions, Ltd., founded January 24, 1934. He proposed to provide pensions of two hundred dollars a month to unemployed U. S. citizens over sixty years of age. There was no indication of the origin of the three old women cadging garbage in his alley. Poverty had not just originated in Los Angeles. More were feeling it and more of the poor were coming.

It would be five years before John Steinbeck would dramatize the pitiful migration of the Okies in *The Grapes of Wrath*. But already the movement had begun. Rexford Tugwell, then the New Deal's Undersecretary of Agriculture, wrote: "In 1934 rainfall had been so short that severe damage had been done. Speaking nationally, that drought had been an ironic blessing—it had helped reduce embarrassing surpluses of wheat—but for the individuals and families involved it was disastrous."

Dust was already rising from the land. And already, too, under the acreage reduction program of the AAA, landlords were finding that they could get along with fewer tenants. Bulldozers pushed over cabins as jalopies hit the roads. And ahead of the migrants there were other folk already often long settled in California who had—and who desperately clung to—a vision like that of Steinbeck's Ma Joad: "I like to think how nice it's gonna be, maybe, in California. Never cold. An' fruit ever' place, and people just bein' in the nicest places, little white houses in among the orange trees. I wonder . . . maybe we can get one of them little white houses. An' the little fellas go out an' pick oranges right off the tree. They ain't gonna be able to stand it, they'll get to yellin' so."

It was some such vision that Sinclair with his EPIC program aroused among people already there and feeling perilously close to the garbage cans Dr. Townsend had seen in Long Beach. They were not migrants to be stopped by guards at the border. They were registered voters. In the Democratic primary in August, Creel, as Sinclair's principal opponent, had the support of now U. S. Senator McAdoo, who, in 1932, as he put it, had "cast the vote of California for Franklin D. Roosevelt on the 4th ballot, resulting in his nomination on that ballot." Creel also had the backing of the regular Democrats of the Los Angeles area. Yet Sinclair not only beat him; he got more votes than all his eight opponents put together.

Confidently Sinclair headed East. He saw Roosevelt and got what he thought was his blessing at Hyde Park. In New York Jim Farley was cordial. Leading writers and intellectuals lined up behind him, including Clarence Darrow, Archibald MacLeish, Theodore Dreiser. On his way back to California he stopped in Royal Oak, a suburb of Detroit, and received the approval of Father Charles E. Coughlin, whose radio voice was making his doctrine of Social Justice the gospel of millions.

But in California, as Schlesinger wrote, "the propertied classes saw in EPIC the threat of social revolution by a rabble of crazed bankrupts and paupers—a horrid upheaval from below, led by a Peter the Hermit, which could only end in driving all wealth and respectability from the State." A power in the Republican Party then was the movie magnate, Louis B. Mayer, of the Metro-Goldwyn-Mayer Corporation. Born in Minsk, Russia, educated in Canada, he had been a delegate to the convention which nominated Hoover in 1928, and now set himself up to save California from the Sinclair threat to its Americanism and safety. Sinclair, in his long writing life, had attacked practically everything from stockyards to schools, to the press, even organized religion. As a recently avowed Marxist he was a vulnerable candidate. But Mayer *et al.* went far beyond the record in manufacturing ammunition to shoot at him.

The big advertising firm of Lord and Thomas was called in to put on a campaign of venomous vilification. Fake movies were produced. One, indicating already existing fear of the Okies and Arkies, purported to show an invasion of the state by tramps and hoodlums attracted by Sinclair's promises. Pamphlets full of falsehoods were circulated. Mayer and other movie producers threatened to move the picture industry from the state if Sinclair were elected and raised half a million dollars to defeat him. Directors and stars were assessed one day's salary. Most actors and writers fell docilely into the line of attack. Aimee McPherson, presumably speaking as an expert, called the Democratic candidate "a red devil." Some writers and actors, however, rebelled against what they called the "Merriam tax." Notably one of those who declined to join in what reached the proportions of a political lynching was the Metro-Goldwyn-Mayer star, fragile twenty-three-year-old Jean Harlow, who to the public seemed only the first "platinum blonde" and the current leading exponent of sex appeal.

The result was a rout. Creel publicly repudiated Sinclair. Any support he had been expected to get from Roosevelt faded away. Indeed, an anti-Sinclair deal apparently was made by the administration. J. T. F. O'Connor of Los Angeles, former law partner of McAdoo and Comptroller of the Currency in the New Deal, came to California and got a secret pledge from Merriam that he would not say that his election could be interpreted as a New Deal defeat. Merriam came out for the Townsend plan which Sinclair had declined to support. By 250,000 votes California was saved from Communism and free love and a man described even as an enemy of the Boy Scouts. It was not saved from *The Grapes of Wrath*.

Obviously the California fight was part of a design not limited to that sunny state. Other men (not all of them so sweetly idealistic as Sinclair) were aware of the political possibilities in the explosive power of poverty. And opposite them better-known figures were prepared to save America after the fashion of Louie Mayer.

Like Mayer, Father Coughlin, who endorsed Sinclair, had been educated in Canada. Also, as his mammoth radio audience in 1934 indicated, he had a gift for public appeal not exceeded by the movies. A big, handsome man with an appealing personality in private contacts, he was, on the air, said *Fortune*, "just about the biggest thing that had ever happened to radio." His rise had been meteoric since he came in 1926 to take over the parish of the little frame church, the Shrine of the Little Flower, in Royal Oak. As hard times came to Detroit, his sermons became more and more tinted with politics. In the angry city he spoke up for the unemployed who had marched under Communist leadership into gunfire at the Ford factory in Dearborn. "The most dangerous Communist," he cried in 1931, "is the wolf in sheep's clothing of conservatism who is bent upon preserving the policies of greed." He hit hard at Hoover. Not indicating anti-Semitism so early, he only included the Rothschilds and the Kuhn-Loebs in his attack on bankers. Four financiers close to the Hoover administration, Morgan, Mellon, Secretary of the Treasury Mills, and Eugene Meyer were his Four Horsemen of the Apocalypse. In 1932 he preached that it was "Roosevelt or ruin."

He defied radio censorship. His mail became a mountain and crumpled dollar bills sent in it from the poor, who heard him as savior, in 1934 amounted to probably half a million dollars. In place of the little frame church he built a new edifice surmounted by a seven-story stone tower against which was spread a huge crucified Christ. In his tower, chain-smoking cigarettes and accompanied only by his Great Dane, Coughlin composed his sermons on Social Justice. Only slowly did he break with Roosevelt, though feeling like Long that the President was going too slowly, particularly in the field of inflation. Many sympathized with his criticism of the AAA crop-control procedures: "My dear Mr. President, there is no superfluity of either cotton or wheat until every naked back has been clothed, every empty stomach has been filled." Still, even in April, 1934, he said, "I will never change my philosophy that the New Deal is Christ's deal."

He was considerably less enthusiastic after the Treasury in Washington released a list of speculators in silver which included the name of his secretary. Still in the fall he said he would never fail to support the New Deal so long as he could speak. Almost immediately, however, he was describing both the Democratic and Republican parties as "putrefying carcasses," and already making plans for the formation of his own National Union of Social Justice.

It was the year of the founding of many such organizations. In January Senator Long had organized his Share-Our-Wealth Society, which proposed for every American family a homestead allowance of $6000 and a minimum annual income around $2500. While Coughlin's ideas about how to provide Social Justice to everybody were vague, Huey was ready to confiscate the wealth of the rich to provide for the poor. He was also in contact with people around Dr. Townsend who in January began forming local Townsend

Clubs. Huey expressed approval of Coughlin. He was even to seem ready for alliance with red-gallused Governor Eugene Talmadge who, though the idol of the wool-hat Georgians, did not want Share-the-Wealth but low wages and smaller relief payments. Increasingly Long appeared as the figure who might mobilize discontent behind a nativist dictatorship neither Communist nor Fascist but taking useful chunks from the philosophies of both. His chief Share-the-Wealth aide, a highly articulate fundamentalist preacher of Shreveport, Gerald H. K. Smith, had before he joined Long offered to join William Dudley Pelley, an anti-Semitic would-be Hitler of Asheville, North Carolina, offering to set up "the first Silver Shirt storm troop in America." From Mussolini's Italy, Ezra Pound, the poet, an exile who did not return, was writing Pelley about "the Nude eel." In Iowa, Milo Reno was calling it the "Jew Deal." Huey Long, whose mind Roosevelt did not put in a category with his manners, seemed the man who might combine those regarded in the White House as the crackpots into a cohesive, dangerous force.

Fortunately for Roosevelt, in the late summer a new different mobilization was being designed by those who regarded themselves as the keepers of sound economy and the traditions of true democracy. They constituted an increasing company and, as they were confident, an impressive one. Faults were appearing in the fabric of the original New Deal. Some original Rooseveltian enthusiasts had left in disillusion over his fiscal policies. Some who remained loyal pointed errors. Men as well as crops seemed to be being plowed up under AAA. Codes drawn under the NRA by trade associations were too often shaped by the biggest concerns, which dominated them.

Before the NRA was six months old such a loyal New Dealer as Harry Hopkins had told Hugh Johnson, "Your codes stink." Johnson himself had suggested that such an old warrior as Darrow be made chairman of a National Recovery Review Board, which the President had set up in the face of much discontent. Darrow's report sounded more like an indictment than a review. He mocked at the evidence he found of big business fairness in the codes. He had not realized before, he said sarcastically, how much the rich loved the poor: "They should do so. They have lived off them for many years." He called for a return to the antitrust laws to prevent "monopoly sustained by government."

Big business itself was not pleased by Section 7a of the National Recovery Act guaranteeing the right of collective bargaining. In

1934 the utilities had begun a determined legal campaign against the Tennessee Valley Authority. Hopkins, who was described by a friend as a man with "the purity of St. Francis of Assisi combined with the sharp shrewdness of a race track tout," was not content with relief payments, which in May, 1934, averaged only $24.53 per family per month. Many businessmen thought that was too much if the promise of a balanced budget was to be fulfilled.

It was already apparent that Johnson, as NRA chief, was coming to the end of his tumultuous tenure in August when dapper Jouett Shouse came to see Roosevelt. In a plush sense Shouse was one of the unemployed. When Farley took over after F.D.R.'s nomination, Shouse had retired from the job as chairman of the Democratic National Committee in which Raskob had placed him. He and Raskob, who had joined first to beat Hoover and then, as it seemed, to stop Roosevelt, moved their energies to the Association Against the Prohibition Amendment. It had been dissolved in December, 1933, its activities being no longer required after repeal. Now he and Raskob and some of their wealthy old associates, he told the President, were forming the American Liberty League—to teach respect for the rights of persons and property, and to teach the duty of government to encourage private enterprise and protect the ownership and use of property. The President declared he had no objection to the League as far as its statement of purposes went. It wasn't any of his business. It seemed to him just an organization to uphold a couple of the Ten Commandments while disregarding all the rest. Someone queried whether he had been asked to join. Roosevelt laughed and said he didn't think he was: "Must have been an oversight."

Former President Hoover indignantly declined to join up with the group which, he said, "financed the Democratic smearing campaign" against him. But the roll call of members included great names: Al Smith, John W. Davis, the Du Ponts of Delaware, Alfred P. Sloan and William S. Knudsen of their General Motors, Ernest T. Weir the steel man, Edward F. Hutton and Colby M. Chester of General Foods, J. Howard Pew of Sun Oil, Sewell L. Avery of Montgomery Ward.

"All the big guns have started shooting," Roosevelt wrote William C. Bullitt, whose appointment as the first ambassador to the Soviets had not pleased the fearful. "Their organization," he added, "has already been labeled the I CAN'T TAKE IT CLUB."

It was a time for listings. Elizabeth Dilling, of Chicago, who was to be active in Liberty League affairs, this year published her book, *The Red Network: A 'Who's Who' and Handbook of Radicalism for Patriots*. In it she labeled about five hundred organizations and 1300 individuals as involved in a Communist conspiracy to subvert America. Among those presented in her indictment were the now active public utility defender, Newton D. Baker; Senator Borah; Chiang Kai-shek; Monsignor John A. Ryan, director of the National Catholic Welfare Council; Donald Richberg, then general counsel of the NRA; Felix Frankfurter; Ambassador Bullitt; Mrs. Roosevelt; H. L. Mencken; Mahatma Gandhi; and Heywood Broun. Broun, then columnist on the New York *World-Telegram*, used his "dossier," set out in almost cryptic abbreviations in the book, as copy for his newspaper column. Of Mrs. Dilling's item that he was "pres. and org." of the just formed American Newspaper Guild, he said that it was true he was "pres." but he denied that he was its "org." He took occasion to make a list of his own, suggesting that guest privileges should be provided in the Society of Native Stuffed Shirts for William Randolph Hearst, Nicholas Murray Butler and Walter Lippmann. Evidently it was a name-calling time.

The Liberty League did not organize early enough to take much part in the election that fall. In the politics of its purposes it was already late. Its members undoubtedly shared the elation of conservatives in California when Sinclair was snowed under by 250,000 votes. They could hardly take heart from the fact that the year before they organized in New York City such an unfamiliar, ripsnorting Republican as the half-Jew, half-Italian Fiorello H. La Guardia became mayor with a plurality of a quarter of a million votes. His Democratic opponent said he was "a communist at heart." The people of New York, said this Little Flower (no kin of the shrine in Detroit), did not elect him for his looks; they chose him because they wanted action.

So evidently in 1934 did the American people. As the election approached, Roosevelt had expressed the idea that opposition to him and his program came largely "from about ten to fifteen per cent of the people whose mental slant is what might be described as being at the extreme right of modern philosophy and the rest of it is from ten to fifteen per cent of the mental slant that belongs to the extreme left." But not even he was so optimistic as the returns from the off-year Congressional elections justified. Democratic strength in the House rose from 313 to 322, while Republicans lost nine seats, leaving them only 103 votes. Democrats won 26 out of 35 senatorial contests. In the state capitals Republicans retained only seven governorships. It was, as Arthur Krock wrote in the New York *Times*, "the most overwhelming victory in the history of American politics."

New Dealers whooped. Harry Hopkins, who had been pressing for a strong work relief program, grinned at his staff in the Federal Emergency Relief Administration.

"Boys, this is our hour. We've got to get everything we want—a works program, social security, wages and hours, everything now or never. Get your minds to work on developing a complete ticket to provide security for all the folks of this country up and down and across the board."

That has seemed a cry to historians, who like neat periods, ushering in what they have called the Second New Deal. Undoubtedly the election gave a mandate to New Dealers. But the suggestion that the New Deal shaped in the first two years of Roosevelt was compounded of contradiction, experimentation, confusion and indecision has been overemphasized. Some have scoffed at F.D.R.'s declaration, "We planned it that way," seeing rather two years of extemporizing in the face of emergency. There were evidently conflicting directions. Relief and retrenchment did seem oddly equal aims. But before he came to office Roosevelt's budget-balancing promise had been made directly contingent upon the government's duty to provide for people.

If not so planned, the so-called Second New Deal grew implicitly out of the first. If there was not one consistent program, there grew a definite design. It was shaped step by step even if a destination was not always clear to those who clamored on the right or the left or those on the job in Washington either. Roosevelt's first duty was reassurance. It was essential to even the basis of recovery. Reconstruction was not possible without relief. And relief led inevitably to discovery of the need not only for reform but revision. On its way it took ideas from many, including such elder, apparently contending philosophers as Baruch and Brandeis—from the understanding for the need of a strong economy and the necessity that in it the small unit and "the little people" be protected.

Baruch and Brandeis were strangely similar men in their almost opposite philosophies. Both loved admiration. Both were almost ostentatiously unostentatious. Brandeis rejected as a place too grand for the work of justice the suite assigned to him in the glittering, marble new Supreme Court Building. Baruch as multimillionaire made almost a production of conducting his conferences on park benches.

As speculator whom Wilson had made a statesman, Baruch believed bigness was inevitable. Early in the Depression in Brandeis' Boston, Baruch had taken the machine tool industry as an example. In 1914, he said, 13,500 establishments used 1,256,000 primary horsepower to produce $1,000,600,000 worth of product. In 1925, 11,800 establishments used 2,714,000 horsepower and produced $5,000,000-000 worth. The old speculator did not translate the meaning of establishments and horsepower and product into people. It was there.

"It is a marvellous industrial system we are creating," he said, "but it exacts a dangerous price. It requires larger and larger units in every business and *it wipes out the little fellow*. Industry continues to combine in ever greater groupings until the trend seems to be toward an almost unitary national producing machine. . . . We are all, in some measure, parts of our great economic machine."

To cure this condition, his friend and admirer NRA Chief Johnson said, he recommended creation of NRA. The cure, many thought, turned out to be worse than the disease. Greed in the groupings was fed by the suspension of the antitrust laws. But the little fellow as a person and not a plant was reluctantly granted the right, never afterward to be effectually denied, of collective bargaining. Here, only dimly seen, was revolution where antiunionism had been called "the American Plan." Still, as Saul Alinsky said in a biography of intense, eloquent, mine workers' leader John L. Lewis, Detroit auto manufacturers regarded this right in the law with "bored indifference" even when the President tried to intervene. Even William Green, president of the American Federation of Labor, discouraged Lewis' eagerness in 1933 to organize the mass of workers in the auto and other industries. A paunchy man shaped in conservative craft union ideas, Green said, "Now, John, let's take it easy."

Justice Brandeis, who had made a fortune serving wealthy clients before he turned his great mind to nobler causes, regarded such an agency as the Baruch-inspired NRA, wrote Schlesinger, "as an administrative monstrosity suffering under the curse of bigness and dedicated to a policy of scarcity." The Justice did not accept the view that bigness was inevitable. While Baruch was helping shape

NRA in 1933, Wallace and Tugwell, working on legislation to be embodied in the Agricultural Adjustment Administration, called on Brandeis. Differences were clear. Tugwell insisted that bigness could be directed and subjected to discipline. Brandeis shook his big head. Bigness was always badness, he insisted.

Sometimes it seemed so, as crop control meant the dispossession of tenants and a program of organized scarcity chiefly benefiting the largest operators. As NRA pushed up industrial prices, farmers seemed more disadvantaged. Perhaps most important were conditions which the efforts to aid agriculture brought to light. On the farms as in the cities, it was clear that for many depression was the normal condition. The old crones whom Townsend saw at the garbage cans were not new in town or country. In Iowa, Milo Reno had been hollering since Populist days. The idyl of the family farm was for many an antique pastoral pretense. But concern for agriculture got down to the thousands of the inarticulate involved in it. If its situation was not saved it was exposed.

At the outset social protections had seemed simply the prevention of starvation in a land where thirteen million people were unemployed. "I'm here to see that people don't starve," said Hopkins, describing his duties as the head of the FERA in 1933. At that time a newspaper said, "What this relief business needs is less RFC and more PDQ." Careful Ickes in his extra job as head of the Public Works Administration saw to it that good projects were built with the government's money. Hopkins' idea was to see that it most quickly reached the people who needed sustenance. The word "boondoggle" had been coined by a scoutmaster in New York State in 1925 to describe a looped lanyard of plaited varicolored leather made by his scouts for use as a necktie slide or hatband. Now it was applied to some of Hopkins' projects, such as leaf-raking by relief workers. Working through the states, he got money as quickly as possible to the poor. In 1933, 60 per cent of all public relief money came from the federal government. But for the American future, almost as important as the relief which went down were the reports Hopkins brought to the capital and the country.

Whole states like South Carolina, Arkansas and Mississippi drew 99 per cent of all their relief from Washington, but five Northern industrial states required 42 per cent of the FERA's money. In west Tennessee, where previous yearly incomes of sharecroppers were said to be below $35 a year, they now mounted out of misery to $4.80-a-week opulence. Obviously emergency relief was touching standard destitution. And in insistence that it be distributed without discrimination, it reached the "last hired, first fired" lower depths even of black America. A North Carolina social worker reported, "While standards are still wretchedly low, they are better than many of these Negroes knew during the prosperity era." Something deeper, apt to be angrier, than the Depression was touched. In the same state a landlord complained, "I don't like this welfare business. I can't do a thing with my niggers. They aren't beholden to me anymore. They know you all won't let them perish." Perhaps more indicative of such feeling and less local and anonymous was a complaint made by a Du Pont son-in-law and executive, Robert R. M. Carpenter, to Raskob: "Five Negroes on my place in South Carolina refused work this spring . . . saying they had easy jobs with the government. . . . A cook on my houseboat at Fort Myers quit because the government was paying him a dollar an hour as a painter."

Hopkins had not only his social workers but his reporters, governmentally described as "field investigators." Two of the most perceptive of them were Martha Gellhorn, who later became a foreign correspondent and wife in turn of Ernest Hemingway and T. S. Matthews, and Lorena Hickok, who had known Hopkins and the Roosevelts as an Associated Press reporter in New York. Certainly Miss Hickok was a direct line between Hopkins and the White House. She steadily led or accompanied Mrs. Roosevelt on her visits to scenes of rural and urban destitution. What Mrs. Roosevelt saw with her and heard from her she passed on to the President. "My missus told me so and so," he often said. The lines from poverty to power and from Hopkins via Gellhorn–Hickok–Mrs. R. to F.D.R. were clear.

When the 1934 election returns came in Roosevelt was obviously as ready as Hopkins for the steps which seemed to shape the Second New Deal. In the June before he had set up his Committee on Economic Security, which began planning the New Deal social security policy. Now immediately after the election he not only went to work on plans for a vast work-relief program. Also two days after the election, in a letter to the one-time Wilsonian liberal Newton D. Baker, who had been employed by the utilities to fight the Tennessee Valley Authority, he suggested that the utilities not commit suicide. He stopped by TVA on his way to Warm Springs that month to emphasize the importance he attached to the Administration's multifaceted development. The utilities which he urged not to commit suicide might have feared murder, as they did later, had they known he was already planning the Public Utility Holding Company Act to restrict such Gargantuan groups as Insull had devised. Others, including particularly the more and more vocal Liberty Leaguers, were facing shock as the design for the Second New Deal developed in the anti-bigness Brandeis tradition. With his great head tossed back Roosevelt was ready to urge upon Congress not only the Social Security Act and the Holding Company bill, but also a tax bill and a $4.8 billion work-relief measure. In addition to providing funds for more schools, bridges, low cost housing, this measure set up such New Deal agencies as the National Youth Administration, the Resettlement Administration and the Rural Electrification Administration. Furthermore, though hesitant at first, Roosevelt was prepared to support the National Labor Relations Act, introduced by Senator Robert A. Wagner of New York, which would make the guarantee of collective bargaining stick as it had not done under Section 7a of the NRA.

Still, as the year began, he seemed indecisive or preoccupied. Soon after the election he had been much concerned about the increasing Japanese insistence on naval parity and Germany's creation of a large standing army. The Supreme Court was ominously considering the constitutionality of much New Deal legislation. There was debate as to directions in the coterie close to the President already becoming known as the Palace Guard. Some old faces, like those of Lew Douglas and Dean Acheson, were gone. The song about Moley as God Almighty was becoming muted.

A rising star was young Thomas G. Corcoran, who had been one of the brilliant boys in the succession of secretaries to Justice Holmes. He had also been offered the deanship of the Louisiana State University law school by Huey Long. He was a shrewd, boisterous operator who brought to his relationship with Roosevelt not only ideas but a guitar and a readiness for rollicking song. He had come into the New Deal in the Brandeis tradition through what was described as "the Frankfurter employment agency." There he found and made a team with the quieter, more reflective Benjamin V. Cohen. Irishman and Jew, they became coupled in the New Deal like Gallagher and Shean in popular song.

Much work was ahead of them in the preparation and passage of legislation. None of it was to be simple. Lopsided majorities on the

Hill could be at times unmanageable majorities too. As early as January, Roosevelt's efforts to buttress world peace threatened by militant nations was rebuffed when the Senate rejected his proposal for American entry into the World Court.

In domestic affairs the obvious, expected roar came from the right. Late in April, 1935, at the meeting of the United States Chamber of Commerce in its marble quarters a couple of blocks away from the White House, businessman after businessman rose to express indignant opposition to practically the entire New Deal program. Their fury was summed up by Silas H. Strawn, Chicago corporation lawyer and former president of both the U. S. Chamber of Commerce and the American Bar Association. He cried: "We have floundered along for two years without knowing whether we were going to be locked up or not. I think we have the right to know where we are going. Businessmen are tired of hearing promises to do constructive things, which turn out to be only attempts to Sovietize America."

The White House expected such cries from those whom Roosevelt described as "the ravens." But Huey Long, now strutting as a result of his part, with the aid of William Randolph Hearst and Father Coughlin, in defeating the World Court proposal, seemed a greater menace. For months his vindictive advance had been viewed with increasing alarm by the administration. Rex Tugwell wrote that in these days Franklin was "obviously apprehensive" about the Senator from Louisiana. Certainly early in February Louie Howe, though increasingly ill, was passing on his strong fears about Long to the President. At this time while the rich were complaining, Huey, ready with his book, *My First Days in the White House*, was crying that "the rich earn more, the common people less." Roosevelt suspected that in order to beat him some cynical Republicans were "flirting with Huey Long and probably financing him." As early as February the President was ready for all-out war against Long. Not only had his irritations grown; also he evidently already shared Howe's fears, later to be demonstrated by a poll made for Farley by Emil Hurja, that Long had real and dangerous strength in the nation.

Polls were really rudimentary then. The *Literary Digest* had already ventured into this business, to its later regret and disaster. Only three years before had George Gallup begun his work with samplings and statistics for the innovating advertising firm of Young & Rubicam. However, Hurja reported that Long had surprising support in the farm belt, in the Great Lakes region, on the Eastern seaboard. Even in rock-ribbed Republican Maine he had strength. Farley, a special subject of Long attack, added his fears to Howe's, reporting to Roosevelt that Long might poll three million votes in the 1936 election "and the result might spell disaster."

As early as February the President had given orders against the appointment or retention of any Long man in any government agency. Few federal funds were allowed to pass through Huey's hands. Publicly Roosevelt was silent, however, and it is not in the record that he had anything to do with the attack on a supposed Long-Coughlin axis launched by General ("Old Iron Pants") Johnson on March 4, the second anniversary of the coming of the New Deal. Johnson's explosiveness had helped end his usefulness as head of the NRA, from which he had resigned the fall before. It served now. At a banquet given him at the Waldorf-Astoria by the editors of *Redbook*, he let himself go. He had consulted no one in the administration, he said, before he went after the Michigan priest and the Louisiana politician as "the Pied Pipers." He roared:

"You can laugh at Father Coughlin—you can snort at Huey Long —but this country was never under a greater menace . . . Hitler couldn't hold a candle to Huey in the art of the old Barnum ballyhoo."

He mimicked the "Kingfish": " 'Ahm not against de Constitution. Ahm fo' de Constitution. Ahm not against p'ivate p'ope'ty. Ahm fo' p'ivate p'ope'ty.' "

The people should demonstrate, Johnson cried, that they are not in the market for this "magic financial hair tonic put up by partnership of a priest and a punchinello guaranteed to grow economic whiskers on a billiard ball overnight."

Then Secretary Ickes, inescapably a part of the administration, joined in the fray: "The trouble with Senator Long is that he is suffering from halitosis of the intellect. That's presuming Senator Long has an intellect."

Such speeches actually only gave Long and Coughlin greater audiences. Coughlin made the mistake of matching insults and lapsed into open anti-Semitism, coupling Johnson with Baruch, the Rothschilds, the Warburgs, the Kuhn-Loebs, the Morgans "and the rest of the wrecking crew whose God is gold and whose emblem is the red shield of exploitation." Long did better both in the Senate and on the radio. He added humor to threats. He recited his catalogue of New Dealers: Farley, "the Nabob of New York"; Ickes, "the Chinchbug of Chicago"; Wallace, "the Ignoramus of Iowa"; Johnson, "the Oo-la-la of Oklahoma"; and his favorite, Roosevelt, "Prince Franklin, Knight of the *Nourmahal*."

The exchanges were diverting to the country but disturbing, too. If Johnson had exaggerated the menace of the Coughlin-Long axis, he helped the building of what seemed a crackpot coalition. Not only were ties tightened between Detroit and Baton Rouge. Also now Long was in touch with tough old Talmadge of Georgia, who was to receive support from such Liberty Leaguers as the Du Ponts. He was talking to people high in the Townsend movement, which now numbered millions of old folks among the members of its clubs. Soon after his exchange with Johnson and Ickes, Long went by invitation from old, angry Milo Reno to the convention of the still growling Farmers' Holiday Association in Des Moines.

"The Lord has called America to barbecue," the "Kingfish" told the Middle Western farmers, "and fifty million people are starving."

Fortunately for Roosevelt, and possibly encouraged by him, Long was having his troubles in Louisiana where his puppet officials ruled. A year before, his candidate for mayor of New Orleans had been defeated by the Old Regulars there. So, threatened by a combination of the Old Regulars and the New Dealers, Long seemed headed for defeat and deflation at home. He was still the indefatigable Huey. There were thousands at home whom he had helped, not hurt. During 1934–1935 he called his legislature into eight sessions to reorganize the government of the state. At his bidding it created the most complete absolutism which ever existed in the United States. Local government was abolished. Long secured control of the appointment of every policeman, fireman and schoolteacher in Louisiana. He completely controlled the militia, the courts, election officials and tax-assessing bodies. All citizens were at his mercy, without redress, but not without resentment.

One of Long's last opponents in the Louisiana Legislature rose early in 1935 to issue a warning where his protests had not availed.

"I am not gifted with the second sight," he said. "Nor did I see a spot of blood on the moon last night.

"But I can see blood on the polished floor of this Capitol.

"For if you ride this thing through, you will travel with the white horse of death."

Huey was riding high. He was not worried about Hugh Johnson's statement that as an American Hitler on horseback "he knows what part of the horse he can be." He made politics even of supposed auguries of assassination. In the summer he rose on the floor of the Senate to charge that a plan to murder him had been uncovered. To his increasingly impatient colleagues, he presented what he said was a dictograph record of a conversation in Room 506 of the De-Soto Hotel in New Orleans. There was talk in the room, Long reported, of "one man, one gun, one bullet" being enough to dispose of him. Someone in the room declared, according to Long, "I haven't the slightest doubt but that Roosevelt would pardon anyone who killed Long." In Louisiana, it was said that while this was foolishness, a man might listen at a lot of rooms and hear somebody say, "I wish somebody would kill the son-of-a-bitch." Long had worn out his tales of plots to eliminate him. One, he said, had been arranged by the Standard Oil Company.

Though he increased the guards about himself, Senator Long did not seem concerned about his safety as Congress approached adjournment late in August. One of his sharpest critics, Ickes—the "Chinchbug of Chicago"—watched him with real, though grudging, approval on the evening of Saturday, August 24. The Senate seemed in mellow mood. Vice-President Garner, Ickes wrote in his diary, "had apparently had enough whisky to pep him up." But what impressed him most was Long delivering one of "his typical speeches."

"I had never seen him at his best, and he was at his best Saturday night. He waved his arms, he contorted, he swayed, and at all times he talked in a very loud voice. I must admit, however, that he was clever. Any Senator who ventured to cross swords with him was usually discomfited. He has a sharp, quick wit, even though he is a blatant and unconscionable demagogue."

Huey that night was just a couple of days short of his forty-second birthday. Certainly he showed no sign of weakening in Louisiana or in Washington either. Ickes, watching the ebullient Long, was himself an unhappy man. He was about ready to resign from the Cabinet, he confided to his diary, as a result of feud between him and Hopkins over spending in public works and work-relief—between his own "substantial, worth-while, and socially desirable public works" and Hopkins' "trivial, and, in many instances, make-believe, work that will not stimulate business, help infuse life into heavy industries, or add to the permanent assets of the country." On Wednesday, September 11, Ickes left Washington

for Hyde Park to argue with the President who, anxious for escape
from the harassments—about a possible break with Russia over Communist propaganda in the United States and neutrality problems in
connection with Mussolini's Ethiopian adventure—was about to set
off on another of his beloved cruises. The papers on the day Ickes
left Washington, he said, were filled with big stories about his fight
with Hopkins. Actually there was another, bigger story in them.

Huey Long had hurried from the Senate in Washington to the
tall Capitol he had built in Louisiana. There, at his call, another of
the special sessions of his legislature waited to ratify his recommendations. One item on his agenda was the gerrymandering out of office
of Judge Benjamin F. Pavy, who had held a place on a district
court bench for thirty years. He had held on longer than most of
Huey's critics. Now word spread that Long in his attack on Pavy
had made unfounded remarks, as he had made about others, that
there was Negro blood in Judge Pavy's veins. He might go on the
radio to repeat them. The charge reached Pavy's son-in-law, a quiet,
nonpolitical physician, Dr. Carl Austin Weiss. In Louisiana, as Harnett
Kane wrote, that would be "a stain that might mark the life" of
Weiss's child.

In the Capitol with its polished floors, Huey ended a smoothly
run night meeting. "Everybody be here in the morning," he ordered. Surrounded by his bodyguard, he swung out into the marble
halls. There, waiting behind a stone pillar, a small, bespectacled man
in white linen, was young Dr. Weiss. One bullet from the doctor's
.32 caliber pistol went into Huey's abdomen. Long's cry signaled a
fusillade from the guards. Afterward sixty-one bullet holes were
found in the body of the Senator's "putative assassin." Some always
believed that the bodyguard not only riddled the doctor, but shot
Huey, too.

"I wonder why he shot me?" the Senator said as he was hurried
to the hospital. There some thought he might have recovered if the
doctor in charge had not been one appointed to his post by Huey
for political rather than medical reasons.

"Oh Lord, don't let me die," he said, "I have a few more things
to do. . . . My work for America is not finished."

But he did die, thirty hours after he was shot, on September 10.
A hundred thousand persons, white and black, Cajuns and red-
necks, the curious and some of the satisfied, came for his burial on
the front lawn of the Capitol. Sonorously the Reverend Gerald L. K.

Smith spoke his elegy in weather so hot that two hundred persons fainted in the crowd. But a better man, a liberal Texas congressman whose name was a word for those not marked to run with the herd, Maury Maverick, later spoke most understandingly for his memory. In Long's blood and bones, he declared, there was hatred born of the oppression, undernourishment, sorrow, misery, ignorance and desperation of his people. Angrily he "slashed and cut and cursed the gods of oil and sulphur—then all the other gods across the national scene. He was like a violent Gargantua shouting his Rabelaisian song as he went. God rest his troubled soul in peace. There was much in him that was vicious but what he stirred up cannot be downed."

In the month after Long died, Roosevelt insisted that both his combative associates, Ickes and Hopkins, join him for a cruise on the U.S.S. *Houston*. At Los Angeles, where they went aboard, a million people greeted the President. In California then old furies of Upton Sinclair's EPIC campaign seemed far behind. Thanks to Social Security, which Congress had approved, the future might be free of such old women as Dr. Townsend had seen rifling garbage cans. It was a happy voyage of poker playing and fishing down to Panama and through the Caribbean and up the Atlantic to Charleston. Jim Farley came down to meet the President there. Ickes spoke of the situation in Louisiana. Farley said he was keeping hands off because whichever faction won it now would be friendly to the administration. Then he said, apparently boosting his estimates in the safety after Long's death, that if the Senator had lived he would have polled six million votes in 1936.

"I always laughed Huey off," Farley said, "but I did not feel that way about him. He was good for that many votes."

In Washington, a tanned, contented Roosevelt told his Cabinet, "We are going to win easily next year but we are going to make it a crusade."

It would be different with Long gone. Perhaps it would be different because he had lived. It was only coincidence, of course, that on the day he died Louie Howe, necessarily at last moved from the White House to the Naval Hospital, sent a message to the President through others nearer him. He was hurt: "he feels like he is on the outside, cut off." Seven months later the warning Howe, like the menacing Long, was dead.

# XVII

## DEFINITIONS OF LIBERTY

ANYTHING could happen in Akron. The Ohio city demonstrated by its former citizen Wendell Willkie, now utility magnate, the precious, unlimited possibility for the exceptional poor boy in America. Also, dull houses huddling together along the dirty snow on squalid streets suggested that escape was only for the exceptional—perhaps now for the explosive. There was no question about the quality of dark, beetle-browed, eloquent John L. Lewis, who arrived in town with a blizzard on January 19, 1936. Despite the weather, thousands of workers in rubber plants massed to hear this glowering head of the United Mine Workers now ejected from the American Federation of Labor because of his determination to build such industrial unions as rubber and other industries required.

"Partnership!" He sneered at the word which had been much bandied about in the now ended NRA experiment. "Partnership! Well, labor and capital may be partners in theory, but they are enemies in fact. . . ."

He made good sense to a man working on a tire machine in the mass processes that puckish and now pinkish Charlie Chaplin had recently satirized in his movie *Modern Times*.

"Organize!" Lewis shouted. "Organize!"

The Akron workers had tried and had been rebuffed not only by their employers but by the tradition-bound A.F. of L. That old organization had insisted upon splintering the rubber workers into craft groups. Lewis, one generation out of the stark, yet poetic poverty of the coal mine country of Wales, had rejected such foolishness. He had seen his own union's membership fall in the twenties from 400,000 to less, some said, than 100,000 in 1930. By 1931 the A.F. of L. had been losing seven thousand dues-paying members each week. Now new chance was at hand. Yet in it Lewis knew that not merely crafts but the mass of workers must be organized if any workers were to attain their goals.

In this understanding, he worked, among others, with Sidney Hillman, founder and president of the Amalgamated Clothing Workers, and David Dubinsky, head of the International Ladies Garment Workers Union. At the A.F. of L. convention in 1934 they secured reluctant permission to organize mass industries. A year later the reluctance of the craft union leaders had mounted to resistance. Striking back, the industrial union advocates organized the Committee for Industrial Organization. The division was to lead to creation under the same initials of the Congress for Industrial Organization as independent rival of the A.F. of L.

Anything might happen in Akron or in America—and from divergent aims to uncertain results. That was demonstrated in warmth and confidence in Washington six days after Lewis spoke in Akron. At a sumptuous feast of the Liberty League at the Mayflower Hotel, two thousand guests gathered. They represented, said the New York *Times*, "a large portion of the capitalistic wealth of the country." Twelve Du Ponts were there and, of course, their companion in the Du Pont and General Motors companies, Raskob, who had organized this plutocratic congregation. Others included such personages as Winthrop Aldrich of the Equitable Trust and Chase Bank of New York, Pittsburgh steel man Ernest Weir, and Elizabeth Dilling, who had provided the guide to *Radicalism for Patriots*. Also on hand were such disenchanted early New Dealers as James P. Warburg and Dean Acheson. Old Democratic leaders like John W. Davis and Maryland Governor Albert Ritchie were present in prominence. But gleaming above all in white tie and tails was the speaker, Al Smith.

"It is all right with me," the florid, one-time East Side boy said of the New Dealers, "if they want to disguise themselves as Karl Marx or Lenin or any of the rest of that bunch, but I won't stand for their allowing them to march under the banner of Jackson or Cleveland."

"It was perfect," said Pierre Du Pont of the occasion. But from the Capitol Senator Joe Robinson, who had run with Smith in 1928, made ripping reply to the "unhappy warrior." Smith had deserted to the "sanctimonious Tories," he cried, turning away from the East Side with its little shops and fish markets to the gilded towers and palaces of Park Avenue. John L. Lewis scornfully commented that Smith's speech was the act of "a gibbering political jackanapes." Sharper answer to arrayed wealth was quickly coming from his direction.

In Akron after midnight on January 29, an edgy foreman at Firestone Tire Plant No. 1 waited for something without knowing what. The big, plain clock on the south wall clicked to 2 A.M. Then a tire builder at the end of the line moved three paces to the master safety switch. Ruth McKenney reported that with this signal, in perfect synchronization with the rhythm they had learned in mass production industry, all tire builders stepped back from their machines. The whole room was as quiet as the snow-swept yard outside. Out of the silence came the voice of one big tire builder, "Jesus Christ, it's like the end of the world." Other voices were jubilant: "We done it! We stopped the belt! By God, we done it!" The first of the many coming sit-down strikes had begun. The tools had been put down by men who refused to leave the plants.

Within the same week the stopped belt in Akron and the banquet in Washington together dramatized the whole confused body of conflict in America as the Presidential election year began: conservatism against change; the old guard against the New Dealers; capital against labor and differences within labor, too; the rich against the wretched who had listened to Long and Coughlin. Many of the latter as industrial workers had recently come from troubled farms. They should not have found so strange the piecework stretch-out systems under which, as their pace swiftened, efficiency experts cut the pay per piece. That had been a pattern of American agriculture too. As surpluses pushed prices down, farmers, planting more in a race to raise income, built greater surpluses and so pushed prices further down. Both processes seemed compulsive. Farmers plowed lands which should have been left to grass. Workers found nothing funny in Chaplin's pantomime of a worker during a five-minute rest period in which for the first four minutes his hands continued the specific motions of their movement on the assembly line only slowing down in the last minute to permit him to grasp a glass of water.

Also involved, if cloistered, in the country's pattern of conflict was the Supreme Court. In this January it added the AAA to its constitutional casualties. Central in all the clashes, of course, was the man in the White House—already being called angrily "that man"

—who in the fall before had in response to business mutterings suggested a "breathing spell."

At the old year's end Roosevelt had been carrying on a merry correspondence with Baruch about the hunting exploits of some of their friends at Baruch's Hobcaw Barony in South Carolina. Of the comic charges and countercharges of the hunters, he wrote in "a Yuletide spirit," urging charity. He seemed an optimist in a tumult in January.

"Things are going well," he wrote, "in spite of Supreme Court majority opinion and Hearst and Alfred E. Smith, and an 85 per cent newspaper opposition. I still worry about world affairs more than domestic problems which includes election."

That letter went to the chief of the U. S. delegation at the Naval Conference in London on the day before the Japanese withdrew, demanding equality in warship building. Italy, despite wavering League economic sanctions, had established its power in conquered Ethiopia. Germany was preparing to march into the demilitarized Rhineland. There seemed only one item indicating the certain orderly transition of human events. Old, decorous King George V had died at his Sandringham estate, soon after the death of Rudyard Kipling. A recessional was in process in a world in which there seemed too few contrite hearts.

It brought to the British throne Edward, Prince of Wales, who still somehow seemed the young prince charming at forty-two, though he described himself as "middle aged." American society and readers of American society pages still saw him as he had been a dozen years before in America. Then, in the age of Coolidge and jazz, Clarence Mackay, telegraph and cable millionaire, had given a legendary dinner and dance for him at the $840,000 Mackay mansion at Roslyn, Long Island. Eight hundred guests had come to dinner and twelve hundred were welcomed to dance to the music of Paul Whiteman, who in the same year first presented Gershwin's *Rhapsody in Blue*. Much had happened since. Mackay's daughter Ellin had married not a prince but a Jewish troubador, Irving Berlin, born in Russia. Mackay had taken as his second wife Anna Case, once a Metropolitan Opera star. But Mackay's communications empire had been shattered in the 1929 crash. The British Empire was intact and Edward, ascending as its monarch, still appeared the unfaded Prince Charming. There were still—or already—tantalizingly around him whispers of a romance involving an American woman.

More serious concern in America was paid to old men. Before the New Dealers descended upon Washington, two contemporary muckrakers there, Drew Pearson and Robert S. Allen of the *Washington Merry-Go-Round*, had written of the Supreme Court as "the nine old men." They were elderly. In 1936 their average age was seventy-three. Oddly the one among them least catagorized in senility was the oldest among them, Brandeis, then seventy-nine. But as the most noted liberal on the court, on so-called Black Monday, May 27, 1935, he had not only joined in declaring NRA unconstitutional. Also, as he was being disrobed after the unanimous decision was rendered (looking, as Tommy Corcoran recalled, like a black-winged angel of destruction), he spoke sharply to the young Palace Guardsman.

"This is the end of this business of centralization, and I want you to go back and tell the President that we're not going to let the government centralize everything. It's come to an end. As for your young men, tell them to get out of Washington—tell them to go home, back to the states. That is where they must do their work."

So in his philosophy that bigness must be curbed he had joined those who most steadily upheld corporate over human rights on a court which had long delayed an income tax and such reforms as child labor regulation. Consistency had carried him, old admirers thought, into romantic reaction in an age in which predatory bigness was all too real. So he helped outlaw not only NRA but the labor-bargaining right of Section 7a which it contained. Some labor men watching the disregard of that section by industry had called the NRA the National Run Around. But it had at least set up a principle. Now they were dismayed. The brilliant Lithuanian Sidney Hillman, president of the Amalgamated Clothing Workers, who had been a disciple of Brandeis in the old man's earlier labor activities, was saddened. The Justice, he said, having devoted his great powers to closing the sweatshops, "has now cleared the way for their re-opening." Actually the decision cleared the way, if it did not lay down the paths, to the sit-down strikes. It made imperative the passage of the Wagner Labor Act early in July, 1935. John L. Lewis and men like him and with him began to cry "Organize! Organize!" in Akron, Detroit and cities and towns everywhere.

The great organizing force in 1936, however, and in reverse of its purposes, was the Liberty League. Its banquet backfired quickly. It had set up the very image of opposition which Roosevelt required. A safer people were not prepared to accept the arrogant leadership of the very *ancien régime* arrayed in all its ruffles which they felt had plunged them into disaster. Times were better for all, whether or not the New Deal was responsible. In 1936 the national income had risen 50 per cent since 1933—up from $39.6 billion to $64.7 billion. Unemployment had been cut in half. Only between six and eight million were unemployed compared to between twelve and thirteen million when Roosevelt arrived in office. But those now complaining most over sparkling silver and linen and crystal had benefited most—notably such chief organizers of the Liberty League as Raskob and his associated Du Ponts. The earnings of the Du Pont company in the first half of 1936 were up 72 per cent over the same period in the year before. General Motors, almost a Du Pont affiliate, was up 70 per cent. The auto industry, in which the CIO was at work, was looking forward to its best year since 1929. Steel was way up. So was the average of stock prices. Even so opulent a Liberty League banquet guest as Winthrop Aldrich was saying that the revival was such that inflation was now the danger.

The scene was set for the unveiling of the "economic royalists" by Roosevelt in the campaign ahead. In April, Lewis, Hillman and others announced the formation of Labor's Non-partisan League, which was to preach and pay in the campaign. Lewis' Mine Workers alone were to put up nearly half a million dollars, though Lewis never fully trusted F.D.R., saying that only "unprecedented" flattery kept him on labor's side. But his was the only side labor had. And labor included not only native cotton mill hands and tire builders but thousands of the still much ghettoed foreign-born. Three of the leaders in the Labor League had been born in Central Europe.

There was a mass move also to Roosevelt from the least organized, poorest Americans—the Negroes. Scorn for New Deal concern for them helped mobilize them behind him. That scorn had been bitterly pointed this year by a rich Hudson River neighbor of the President. To annoy Roosevelt, it was widely believed, he had given a five-hundred-acre estate near the Roosevelt place at Hyde Park for one of the "heavens" of Father Divine. This black cultist was the current organizer of and collector from the mass frustrations of poor Negroes, many of whom turned to him as others had turned to Garvey in the decade before.

Historically, colored people had voted for the Republican party of Lincoln, since nobody had done anything much for them since he set them free. Relief without discrimination helped them out of an ancient depression which had seemed their endless destiny. From Philadelphia, where the Democratic National Convention was held this year, had come Marian Anderson, making music beyond jazz and the blues. Others stirred black pride. There were setbacks, too. In the same month the convention met, Joe Louis, a brown boy out of the rural poverty of Alabama and the slums of Detroit, had been badly battered by Max Schmeling of Germany. Racists at home and abroad applauded—prematurely as it turned out when in 1938 the brown bomber came back to knock out Max and end the pretension of Aryan supremacy so far as the ring was concerned. Something similar happened at Philadelphia in 1936 when the powers in the Democratic party declined to be disturbed by the stomping walkout of Senator Ellison DuRant ("Cotton Ed") Smith of South Carolina when a Negro minister spoke the prayers. That made certain a mass black walkout from the Republican party which had promised in its platform to protect the Negro's economic status. That was exactly what he wanted to escape.

The big political swing, however, was in the great undefinable, even unadmitted, American middle class. Negroes and much of labor had been almost beyond greater injury when the Depression came. One of the paradoxes of the hard times was that many of the rich grew richer in them. Most quickly injured in pocket and pride were those whose jobs and savings had been wiped out in an order in which they thought they were secure. They took their places, often silently, in the ranks behind Roosevelt, but they would be there to be counted. Many who made the coalition—farmers and factory hands, the foreign-born and old Ku Kluxers—disliked and distrusted each other. It was a fragile-seeming, many-faceted alliance. Except in cheering crowds it made less noise than its opposition. Accident or angers, appeal to old fears might fragment it.

Accident occurred. Personal disaster to Roosevelt almost prevented what many then and later believed to be the President's greatest performance. When he arrived heralded by shouting and music at Franklin Field in the misty evening of June 27, he hailed in the crowd eighty-four-year-old Edwin Markham. The venerable poet, whose *Man with the Hoe* had nearly forty years before brought brief attention to men forgotten on the land, moved forward to accept Roosevelt's greeting. The multitude surged behind him. He was pushed into the crippled President. Roosevelt toppled, the pages of his speech went flying. But pale and shaken, he ordered as they raised him to his feet, "Clean me up" and "Watch those damn sheets."

"Okay, let's go," he cried.

Confidently he faced the vast, cheering crowd before him. The speech was filled with magnificent phrases, applauded then, remembered since. The assemblage roared when he impaled the "economic royalists." He was to amplify and alter that phrase later in the campaign when he declared that "we know now that government by organized money is just as dangerous as government by organized mob." But reporters found the crowd lifted beyond any "cheap political emotional pitch." This *was* crusade:

"Better the occasional faults of a Government that lives in a spirit of charity than the consistent omissions of a Government frozen in the ice of its own indifference."

Then he seemed to speak prophetically:

"There is a mysterious cycle in human events. To some generations much is given. Of other generations much is expected. This generation of Americans has a rendezvous with destiny."

And:

"We are fighting to save a great and precious form of government for ourselves and for the world."

He himself had not been so sure, as the year began, of his re-election. Five days after the Liberty League banquet he had estimated an electoral college victory of 325 to 206. His fears of the Townsend-Coughlin alliance had diminished with Huey's death. Old Socialists and Communists were hardly worth counting. But other furies surrounded him. Other well-known voices were added to the Smith tirade. Mencken, whose fulminations had grown a little familiar, still put his prejudices into roaring prose. The wizards of 1933, who had promised so much to so many, now had shown themselves to be "the sorriest mob of mountebanks ever gathered together at one time, even in Washington . . . vapid young pedagogues, out-of-work YMCA secretaries, third-rate journalists, briefless lawyers, and soaring chicken farmers." And of F.D.R. he said: "If he became convinced tomorrow that coming out for cannibalism would get him the votes he so sorely needs, he would begin fattening a missionary in the White House backyard come Wednesday." Now, he concluded, "they can beat him with a Chinaman or even with a Republican."

Delegates roared their approval when Hoover in savage sentences, at the Republican Convention in Cleveland, described the New Deal as the first phase of Fascism: "If there are any items in the march of European collectivism that the New Deal has not imitated it must have been an oversight. . . . If this is to continue the end result is the tears and anguish of universal bankruptcy. . . . For the first time in the history of America we have heard the gospel of class hatred preached from the White House. That is human poison far more deadly than fear."

His speech created, said the New York *Times*, "a wild and uncontrollable burst of frenzy." Evidently he stood ready to fight as candidate again. But over roaring romanticism reality prevailed. Hoover could be loved in his party but not elected in America. Alfred M. Landon was nominated on the first ballot. Born in Pennsylvania and educated as a lawyer, he had made his fortune in the oil business. No reactionary, he had worked with William Allen White in the liberal faction of the Republican Party in Kansas—even leaving the party to support White running independently in protest against the Ku Klux Klan. In 1932, he had been the only Republican elected governor west of the Mississippi River. He preached economy. He had, though some denied he was entitled to credit for it, kept the state's budget balanced. Others said he had done so at the expense of school children and the insane. Actually, though supported by loud reactionaries in press and politics, Landon was the amiable antithesis of the old guard which had cheered Hoover's bitter blasts but dared not nominate him.

Roosevelt boosted the forecast of his hopes: "FDR 340, AML 191." But he did not run in confidence that he was a shoo-in. He made the campaign, as he had promised, a crusade. He enjoyed it mightily. Two encounters in it must have pleased him much: his face-to-face meeting with Landon, and his confrontation of Liberty Leaguers in the Du Ponts' own feudal seat at Wilmington, Delaware.

Politicians cannot make the weather but the weather can effect politicians. Drought came again this year, searing the lands across Nebraska, Iowa, Kansas, Minnesota, the Dakotas, Montana, Wyoming, as far south as Missouri, Oklahoma and the Texas Panhandle. Tugwell, who had been put in charge of relief to farmers, had improvised measures to help in such cases. "But in 1936," he wrote, "when the rains did not come at all and when week after week the sun blazed down on the thousands of square miles once green but now dun-colored and grassless even where they were not covered with dunes of dust, many more families, discouraged and beaten, began to load their few possessions into trucks or trailers and go east or west, anywhere to escape the disaster."

Undoubtedly many of the farmers were at fault. As Tugwell said, "Much of the land effected by this terrible ordeal should never have been brought into cultivation, especially in the short-grass country." But for high prices in war or to try to keep income in line with falling prices in the long Depression, it had been plowed. The exodus from such lands grew. Californians who had once welcomed the poor farm families as low-priced, eager labor now set up "bum blockades" at their borders. Here en masse seemed to be the bankrupts and bums, paupers and radicals whom movie magnates had said Upton Sinclair was luring into California with his promises. Chamber of Commerce officials warned that the dispossessed at the state's doors would be "the finest pablum for subversive influence." One farmer told John Steinbeck, "A Communist is the guy who wants 25 cents an hour when we're paying 20 cents." Some of the folks who stayed home watched their cattle die and didn't make a dime.

Roosevelt, in August, decided to go to the drought country, including, as he told a press conference with a wink, Landon's Kansas. As he often did, on such a nonpolitical trip, he made much political hay grow on the scorched plains. He not only could say, with the burnt land as ally, "I hear the word 'planning' is not popular with some people, but one reason why the water table has sunk as low as it has is that we did not think about the future twenty years ago." Also, talking to crowds in little towns, he seemed by his very presence to bring rain. His train was followed by a welcome drizzle.

At a conference of Middle Western governors in Des Moines, he and Landon met. It was a test for both. Both met it well. Afterward a reporter asked Landon what he thought of Roosevelt. The Governor replied, "He's a very fine, charming gentleman." And Roosevelt, as he was leaving, told Landon, "Governor, however this comes out, we'll see more of each other. Either you come to see me or I'll come to see you." Senator Arthur Capper of Kansas said: "Harmony dripped so steadily from every rafter that I fully expected one candidate to withdraw."

No such amenity attended a brief visit Roosevelt, as a sort of aside in the campaign, made to the Delaware of Raskob and the Du

Ponts. The President in this Liberty League center spoke on Liberty. In it he quoted one of Abraham Lincoln's parables—the one about the sheep, the shepherd and the wolf:

The shepherd drives the wolf from the sheep's throat, for which the sheep thanks the shepherd as his liberator, while the wolf denounces him for the same act, as the destroyer of liberty. . . .

Plainly, the sheep and the wolf are not agreed upon a definition of the word liberty; and precisely the same difference prevails today among us human creatures. . . .

Recently, as it seems, the people . . . have been doing something to define liberty, and . . . the wolf's dictionary has been repudiated.

The opposition to Roosevelt grew shrill and strangely more confident as the election approached. Some desperate tricks were tried —such as stuffing the pay envelopes of some of the workers the CIO was trying to organize in Detroit with scare sheets about the coming wage deduction for social security. The *Literary Digest*, which on the basis of its direct-mail ballots had correctly forecast the 1932 result, predicted in October that Landon would easily win: thirty-two states with 370 electoral votes to sixteen with 161. A Harvard professor of statistics after scrutinizing the *Digest* poll assured Landon that he would certainly have 241 votes to Roosevelt's 99, with 91 votes in doubt. But other pollsters, Gallup and Elmo Roper, forecast a Democratic victory. Landon's friend, Emporia editor White, saw what was coming through the eyes of experience. Asked for an article to be published in the event of his friend Landon's election, he replied, "You have a quaint sense of humor. If Landon is elected I'll write you a book about him, bind it in platinum, illustrate it with apples of gold and pictures of silver, and won't charge you a cent."

Mr. White was not required to perform such a feat. Roosevelt carried every state but Maine and Vermont and won in the country by more than ten million popular votes. Delaware, of course, was in his column. No Presidential candidate had received so large a proportion of electoral votes since James Monroe. Less wise editors than Mr. White were surprised. The *Literary Digest*, which had a circulation of two million in the 1920s, was fatally wounded by its own poll. Its remains were purchased and absorbed by the newer, bouncing *Time*. Other publications suffered but survived. Ickes muttered to his diary that "the outstanding thing about the campaign was the lack of influence of the newspapers."

"Never have the newspapers in my recollection," he wrote, "conducted a more mendacious and venomous campaign against a candidate for President, and never have they been of so little influence. . . . The very bitterness of the assault upon the President by the newspapers reacted in his favor."

Newspapers in this same season were building circulation, if not influence, by one of the greatest stories of the century. It was a strange drama taking place in England beneath the noses of a silent British press but covered in romantic extension by U. S. papers. It involved an American girl, King Edward VIII, and in this year of Roosevelt's greatest acclaim a British literary man and politician who was then, according to the king he served, a "virtual outcast" even in his own Conservative party.

In 1931 Edward, then the thirty-seven-year-old Prince of Wales, had gone fox hunting in Leicester. There on a cold, damp, foggy week end he met an American couple, Mr. and Mrs. Ernest Simpson. The Simpsons were already members of that body of social expatriates or rich, decorative internationals called "cafe society." Newspapers used the phrase to describe those seen with the right people in the right night clubs from New York to London to Paris to the Côte d'Azur. Much of old society considered that its young were too often seen with the wrong people in the wrong places.

Edward wrote in his memoirs, *A King's Story*, that good and stimulating company was to be found outside the restricted confines bounded by the *Court Circular*. At the time much of such society seemed to the newspapers to be directed by a fat, ugly woman from Keokuk, Iowa, Elsa Maxwell, who helped build hotels and restaurants in Monte Carlo and organized parties in Paris and New York for people with more money or titles than imagination. Edward's society was not quite Elsa Maxwell's, though some credited him with inventing the "scavenger hunt," a lively race of the young rich to collect assorted odd items for a prize. Elsa claimed the invention of this diversion as a part of the opulent gaiety of hard times. Certainly the King's company was not Victorian. He had, indeed, in the twenties shocked Mrs. Cornelius Vanderbilt, who regarded herself as the queen of American society. Instead of seeking out her *Social Register* friends in New York, he had spent much time playing the ukelele with the Duncan sisters of current stage fame. The

London society of Edward and Wallis Simpson included such brighter stars as a wife of the novelist Somerset Maugham and Noel Coward, the playwright. Another member was Thelma, Lady Furness, one of the two beautiful Morgan twins, who danced much with both Edward and Aly Khan, a son of the fabulously wealthy Aga Khan. Edward feared the cocktail trays at his hospitable Fort Belvedere might have shocked his ancestors. He pleased the Scots and amused his friends by playing the bagpipes.

Soon Edward's attentions to Mrs. Simpson were the whispers of the world. One tale was that he gave the lady a million dollars in jewels and furs. Of Ernest Simpson, sharp tongues punned about "The Unimportance of Being Ernest." His wife was never one to be disregarded. She had been born Bessie Wallis Warfield in 1896 in the summer resort of Blue Ridge Summit, Pennsylvania. A casual historian referred to her as "the daughter of a Baltimore clerk of good family but small means." She had rich relatives—a railroad president, an insurance company executive. Certainly her mother, twice married after Wallis' father's death, was sufficiently prominent and lively to attract frequent mention in the old society gossip publication *Town Topics*, when Wallis was a girl. The girl, more sparkling than beautiful, was formally presented to Baltimore society at the Bachelors Cotillion in 1914. In 1917 she married well-to-do E. Warren Spencer, Jr., a lieutenant and flight instructor in the Navy. They were divorced in 1927 and a year later she married Simpson, the son of an American but born and bred in Britain. He was a member of the Coldstream Guards and had enough money for Wallis to contest with the Princess Marina, wife of the Duke of Kent, as to which was the best-dressed woman in London.

Within six months after Edward became king on his father's death, stories about his attentions to the forty-year-old Mrs. Simpson were appearing in the American but not the British press. And when Wallis filed a divorce petition, scheduled to be heard at the Ipswich Assizes on October 27, U. S. newspapers began to predict that she would marry the King as soon as she was free. As Edward wrote, Fleet Street's hand was restrained by its "long-standing reticence where the privacy of the Royal Family is concerned." But as the divorce hearing approached he also secured the help of British press lords in arranging a "gentlemen's agreement . . . to report the case without sensation." Actually it did not report it at all, while the gamin newsgatherers of U. S. papers played up the romance. The suppression was so complete that a Labor member of Parliament rose to inquire why so many paragraphs and pages were clipped out of U. S. papers and magazines arriving in England. The story got into British print only when a bishop in the Church of England made veiled references to it in a startling sermon. This bishop, Edward suggested later, was close to the Communists.

Prime Minister Stanley Baldwin, with the Archbishop of Canterbury behind him, moved in stern disapproval of the King's proposed marriage. Morality and religion seemed threatened in a regardless new world. The Empire and the constitution seemed shaken. As the struggle between the King and the Cabinet lengthened, the King heard that "Mr. Chamberlain . . . murmured that the continued uncertainty had already hurt the Christmas trade." (This was two years before Chamberlain flew to Munich.)

Edward felt that Baldwin had never quite approved of him. The Prime Minister was a big man who kept arriving on Edward's scene in a car much too small for his bulk. He had been a little fearful about the Prince back in 1929 when Edward planned a visit to coal mines in the North Country where much unemployment existed. Now, in the fall of 1936, as talk of his affairs mounted, Edward took a train for the coal-mining valleys of South Wales from which, long before in both bitterness and hope, John L. Lewis' father had come to America. There in the dreary towns among the jobless miners, Edward had said that "'something must be done' to repair the ravages of the dreadful inertia that had gripped the region." Some government circles were not pleased. The remark, they felt, suggested that the King had indicated that the government had neglected to do all that it might have done.

This truly would have been monarchical mischief. Edward denied any such intent. He was not, he said, as afterward charged, seeking to curry favor with Labor Party forces in opposition to Baldwin's Conservatives. However, in his memoirs he built the impression of the Prime Minister as representative of a puffy past and himself as unwilling to be captured by it. There was no fire in Edward's pity for the miners. His sympathy did not arouse his indignation. His duties galled him. He counted in weariness his paper work and ceremonial responsibilities. Unconsciously he described himself in *A King's Story* as more popular than perspicacious, not much more mature than he had been as a handsome boy. He loved fun and luxury. His grandfather, lusty old Edward VII, would have found

23.   THE KINGFISH

24.   SISTER AIMEE

25. THE KING AND THE
GIRL FROM BALTIMORE

26. WELLES WHO
BROUGHT THE MARTIANS

27. HARRY HOPKINS AT EASE

28. WENDELL WILLKIE
AT BAY

29. MR. INSULL COMES HOME

30. DAY OF INFAMY

a way to have had his woman and kept his crown. Edward VIII, of course, knew nothing of the story that Franklin Roosevelt, faced with a choice not unlike his, preferred the decorous, dutiful way because of either heritage or ambition or both. The present Edward's middle-aged infatuation was undoubtedly commanding. So may, in spite of his insistence, have been the woman, though from his story she emerges as something almost as unsubstantial as a well-dressed wraith on a royal week end.

In contrast to her, Prime Minister Baldwin, a huge, pipe-fuming man ready for a strong drink of whisky in the morning (Edward never touched it until 7 P.M., he wrote), was mentally and physically as solid and British as roast beef and Yorkshire pudding. Arrayed with him was not only Canterbury but Lords spiritual and temporal. The King had romantic followers among the people but some of the most sentimental and sporting among them were shocked when they belatedly learned that Edward's love was not only an American and a commoner but a twice-divorced woman too. Cinderella seemed a little smudged.

On the surface, while the press remained silent, affairs seemed to be moving smoothly. On October 30, the King received the new German ambassador, peaceful-talking Herr Joachim von Ribbentrop, of whom he noted that he had been among other things "a champagne salesman." Then on November 3, the day of the election in America, as new king he opened Parliament with the speech from the Throne in the House of Lords. Not yet crowned (the coronation was set for May, 1937), he wore an admiral's hat. His performance seemed eminently satisfactory to "the Lords Temporal in their scarlet and ermine robes; the Lords Spiritual in their episcopal gowns; the Diplomatic Corps in brilliant uniforms; the peeresses in decolleté, adorned with tiaras and parures." But in the hall his "senses were suddenly assailed by an almost suffocating odor of mothballs given off by the colorful robes removed from storage for this final airing." There seemed some such mothball atmosphere in the rigidities of constitutional monarchy which surrounded him as a man in love.

He needed a champion. He found one. It was too late. The position of pink, plump Winston Churchill then, as Edward wrote, "was regarded as anything but immortal." He was member for Epping. This year he was publishing the third volume of his biography of Marlborough. Even among fellow Conservatives he was "respected and even feared for his undoubted brilliance and audacity but distrusted by party leaders, who denied him a place in the government."

There was old affection between the King and this very patrician commoner. Churchill, as thirty-six-year-old Home Secretary a quarter of a century before, had invested Edward as Prince of Wales in that land of green hills and dark mines below poor villages. Also, Churchill's mother had been an American though her marriage had been attended by no such royal marital complications as attended the King's situation. A frequent visitor in America, Churchill had been almost killed there just a few years before. He narrowly missed death when he was knocked down by a taxicab on Fifth Avenue not long before Roosevelt escaped the assassin's bullet in Miami.

At sixty-two, Churchill came vigorously forward insisting that Edward should have both his lady and his crown. No constitutional issue had arisen, he insisted, between the king and the crown. None could arise until Wallis' divorce decree became absolute in April. Baldwin made the monarchy seem dry as bones; when Churchill spoke of it, Edward wrote, "it lived, it grew, it became suffused with life."

"I plead for time and patience," Churchill cried.

"Howsoever this matter may turn, it is pregnant with calamity and inseparable from inconvenience. But all the evil aspects will be aggravated beyond measure if the utmost chivalry and compassion is not shown, both by Ministers and by the British nation, toward a gifted and beloved King torn between private and public obligations of love and duty."

Yet when Churchill strode into the House of Commons, "undaunted and quite alone," to make his fight, he was howled down. "Hostility smote him like a great wave." People were getting tired of the conceited Churchill then. Not many shared Edward's feeling that Churchill was right in his campaign to rearm Britain. All he could do after he was hooted in the House was to help the King in the preparation of his broadcast after abdication, stating his cause which he could not constitutionally do as king. It became a legend, the now Duke of Windsor said, that Churchill wrote that speech. Churchill did generously supply "the final brush strokes." Those strokes went to the hearts of one of the greatest radio audiences of the world, crowding about sets not merely in Britain and the Dominions, but nowhere more sympathetically than in the United States.

People listening thought they heard a door symbolically slamming in Windsor Castle as the broadcast began. The words came clear:

"At long last I am able to say a few words of my own . . .

"You all know the reasons which have impelled me to renounce the Throne, but I want you to understand that in making up my mind I did not forget the Country or the Empire, which as Prince of Wales and lately as King, I have for twenty-five years tried to serve.

"But you must believe me when I tell you that I have found it impossible to carry the heavy burden of responsibility and to discharge my duties as King, as I wish to do, without the help and support of the woman I love. . . .

"And now we have a new King.

"I wish Him, and you, His people, happiness and prosperity with all my heart.

"God bless you all.

"God Save the King."

Momentarily America was sentimentally again a colony. The "brush strokes" and the beautiful voice brought a tale of the brave and the fair to men and women like listening weeping children whose hearts demanded that somehow for the world there must be the line added about living happily forever and ever after. On Fifth Avenue in New York taxicabs stopped while drivers and passengers together gave attention to the radio, some weeping as the words came.

Here were the materials of poetry and the stories for the tabloids. Wallis waited for her divorce in a rich villa at Cannes close to Mussolini's Italy. Edward found refuge with Rothschilds still safe and comfortable at their country home at Enzesfeld in Austria. The ex-King was speaking later not of his own life but Britain's lag in strength, despite the demands of Churchill, when he mentioned "'the locust years' of the 1930's." In Europe he danced and played the bagpipes for his bride and met many more interesting people "outside the more restricted confines bounded by the *Court Circular*."

President Roosevelt was again sailing on the U.S.S. *Indianapolis* on the day Edward said his farewell to his kingdom. Cheering crowds had greeted him everywhere on a twelve-thousand-mile good will and good neighbor trip to South America. Word of the abdication reached him just as he was about to land at Trinidad to be guest at lunch of the British governor. That created for him, he wrote home, an "awful dilemma." Should he or should he not propose the "health of the King"? Of one thing he was determined: "It is . . . to be solved by good manners and not by State Dept. diplomatic protocol." There would be other, tougher questions.

A year after the abdication, Roosevelt wrote Windsor his regret that "certain factors" were preventing him and the Duchess from visiting America. The certain factors were attacks made on him by labor and anti-Nazi groups. He had visited Germany under the guidance of Dr. Robert Ley, who had played a leading role in smashing the free German trade-union movement. His trip to the United States was to have been under the guidance of Charles E. Bedaux, an expert in stretch-out systems for labor.

Not even an abdicated king could be entirely free. There were problems of freedom in exalted place even for a re-elected President. At a Cabinet meeting soon after his unprecedented triumph at the polls, while Edward's dilemma of love and duty was not yet quite resolved, Roosevelt was exultant about the peoples' ratification of his rule. Now his cigarette holder seemed not merely a scepter but a wand. He had now, he said, an absolutely free hand without the danger of being charged with broken campaign promises. But he faced galling constitutional questions of directions and duty. Discussion turned to the Supreme Court and its "nine old men"—or at least the five-to-four majority of tough old anti-New Dealers on it. The President was obviously expecting the Court to knock down more New Deal legislation. He rather welcomed it. It was evident that he was looking forward, noted Ickes, "to that as a background for an appeal to the people over the heads of the Court." In America there would be no constitutional bar against his speaking—or acting—until after his cause was lost.

# XVIII

## FROM PIQUE TO PANIC

HARRY HOPKINS was still well enough to be merry. He had gained six pounds, which was a considerable addition to his cadaverous figure on which his clothes hung as if they had been flung. He thought he was "looking pretty well after all the things people have called me." So he exulted on election night in 1936. As he often did, he had chosen an odd place for a New Dealer to watch the returns. In the Iridium Room of the elegant St. Regis Hotel in New York much-dressed-up supper guests had come to watch the returns and dance in victory. But as the avalanching reports came in, while a Russian balalaika orchestra played, the watchers and dancers were not only overwhelmingly Republican but also Republicans overwhelmed. At Hopkins' table was Dorothy Thompson, who had watched as correspondent violent changes in European capitals. Her husband, Sinclair Lewis, had two years before published his novel, *It Can't Happen Here,* about a future fascist revolt in the United States. Now it had been dramatized for presentation by all units of the Federal Theater project of Hopkins' WPA, which was providing jobs for thirteen thousand actors and other stage workers.

Miss Thompson thought that in his jubilation among the disappointed Republicans Hopkins was almost "hilariously vindictive." Still as the lopsided returns came in, she threw away her Landon badge and proposed a toast to the re-elected President of the United States, Franklin D. Roosevelt. Louder music covered her unwelcome proposal. The disappointed danced in disdainful disregard. Harry chortled so that he spurted his champagne. Miss Thompson recalled that she was perturbed by the "rotten sportsmanship" of the Republicans in the room. And she felt that Hopkins "was delighted with imagining the further chagrins they would feel before the next administration was over."

Like Harry, the administration had a feeling of having put on a good deal of weight. And "that man" in the White House was evidently ready to throw it around. The country recognized that its face had been changed. The Public Works Administration under Hopkins' sometimes bristling competitor Ickes had backed thousands of projects from a $42,000,000 sewer tunnel for Chicago to hospitals, housing units, bridges, parks. Hopkins, as head of the Works Progress Administration, had provided jobs for the employable in infinitely varied projects. He provided jobs not only for much criticized slow-motion leaf-rakers and construction workers pictured as always leaning on their shovels. Also, and more outrageous to some, he had found jobs on his government works payroll for white-collar workers, artists, writers, teachers, even musicians and actors. Places in his program were found for out-of-work vaudeville troops, dancers. His Federal Theater Project among other productions presented a swing music *Mikado*, T. S. Eliot's *Murder in the Cathedral*, and an all-Negro company playing *Macbeth* with voodoo witch scenes. *The Army and Navy Register* later reported that in these years "when the regular appropriations for the armed services were so meager, it was the WPA worker who saved many Army posts and Naval stations from literal obsolescence."

"I have signed my name," said Hopkins about this time, "to $6 billion in the last three years and a half." His programs, originally set up as "small projects," would eventually represent an expenditure of over ten billion. Yet not all the WPA workers were content. Some demanded higher wages. The CIO's Lewis wanted to organize them, but to this Hopkins objected. Yet he was fiercely defensive of his workers against the criticism of people like the disappointed dancing guests at the St. Regis. He did propose more chagrins for such folk. And despite all projects his boss F.D.R. was not content. Harry's relatively few militant and perhaps, as often charged, Red workers were among demonstrators demanding more outside the White House, on January 15, when Roosevelt was preparing his Second Inaugural Address. It contained the both promising and perturbing sentence: "I see one-third of a nation ill-housed, ill-clad, ill-nourished."

Roosevelt himself needed shelter and scorned the need of it when he delivered that speech. Under the new Constitutional Amendment, eliminating the long hiatus such as had occurred after his election to succeed Hoover, inauguration came on chill January 20. Cabinet officers fortified themselves from a flask. A stiff wind blew sheets of rain on the bare-headed President, who insisted that if the people had to stand in the rain to hear him, he would stand in the wet to talk to them. There was more rough weather ahead.

The poor "one-third of a nation" still needed to be seen. In the land they were not all reached by the projects which extended from mammoth parkways to the subsistence homesteads to which Mrs. Roosevelt gave so much attention with Hopkins' help. Despite WPA, the Farm Security Administration, the National Youth Administration and related agencies, want remained real. Not all had even such facilities as gave Hopkins the derisive title of "privy builder without peer." But stronger forces demanded attention or, as some said, in the case of the Supreme Court, were impudently given it.

Fattened in confidence, Roosevelt saw the poor and remembered the Supreme Court which he felt was standing stubbornly between people and legislation to aid them. On February 4, the day before he sent his message to the Congress asking that the Court be reformed—or "packed"—he had been on the phone with CIO's Lewis in Detroit seeking settlement of the tensely mounting sit-in strike of the United Auto Workers in the General Motors plants. In massive proportions it followed the pattern set by rubber workers the year before in Akron. Both the CIO-backed strike and the court fight arrayed complicated antagonisms and brought strange alignments.

Roosevelt's friends and enemies in the big strike early in 1937 seemed clear. Lewis had brought half a million dollars to the Democratic campaign chest. Big owners of General Motors were the Du Ponts, who had spent at least as much trying to beat F.D.R. Compared to the billion-dollar company, the strikers in some motortown warrens were certainly the poor. Yet the sit-ins seemed, as Lewis' biographer later said, "illegal and revolutionary" not only to motor magnates and other capitalists; many top labor leaders had the same opinion. Green of the A.F. of L. still guarded old ideas of craft unions against the industrial organization the strikers sought. Coughlin cried Communism. So did less frayed flagellants of the American mind. Some left-wingers were, indeed, in commanding posts among the workers. Even Lewis was startled and disturbed at first by the sit-down tactics. Some left-wingers were much in evidence. Various degrees of militancy marked the local leaders in Michigan. The three Reuther brothers, Roy, Victor and Walter, were advancing in pressure to power. Reared by a Socialist father, they were suspect because of a recent stay of two of them in Russia. To their campaign such men brought the times' new trumpeters, sound trucks, blaring about big plants and in a war of nerves into the ears of motor magnates. Lewis was not deaf to the roar. He could lose the workers or lead them. As the year began he made his position clear: "The CIO stands squarely behind these sit-downs."

Charges of radicalism were not stopping the auto workers this time as they had smashed the big steel strike in 1920. And this time, too, the sit-in tactics left no places at machines for strikebreakers and prevented the old industrial practice of moving production to other plants while workers and their families about the struck plants were starved into submission. This time the workers sat in strategically at the plant in the big, fortress-like General Motors compound in Flint in which all the motors for the company's best-selling and money-making Chevrolet car were made. Chevrolet production stopped. The manufacture of other General Motors cars was slowed. And while G.M. dealers squealed, other motor manufacturers—Ford, Chrysler, Nash, Packard—instead of standing in antilabor solidarity, eagerly undertook to grab a share of the big General Motors market with their own cars. On February 7 (when Washington was adjusting it-self to the shock of Roosevelt's court plan), General Motors' di-rectors had to cut the company's dividend in half—at an estimated cost to Pierre Du Pont alone of $2,500,000.

Chagrin of such cash value may have pleased New Dealers of such hilarious vindictiveness as Miss Thompson thought she saw in Hop-kins. There was sympathy for the strikers among Democratic lead-ers in Washington and Michigan. But while such avowed New Deal enemies as the Du Ponts lost this crucial strike which so often threatened bloodshed in the snow, Roosevelt did not please all his friends. Rather crudely Lewis wanted a Presidential pay-off in the strike for his contributions in the campaign. But Roosevelt seemed to Lewis to be engaged in deceit, dishonesty and double-crossing. The CIO chief was sure of this at the end of May, when workers, march-ing through victories in rubber, glass, steel, were stopped short by gunfire at the gates of Republic Steel in Chicago. That became what labor called the Memorial Day Massacre. In it on a Sunday, police, firing on a crowd of strikers and their families already retreating before tear gas, shot down thirty people, of whom ten died—"all shot in the back." Almost as shocking seemed a Roosevelt remark at that time.

In a statement which he later tried to explain away as applying only to extremists on both sides, he quoted Shakespeare: "A plague on both your houses." Such extremists were involved. There were present, especially at Chicago, not only killer cops but hard-core Communists. Also, in the slums which were not much altered since the days when Upton Sinclair described them in *The Jungle*, there were native fascist movements, the more militant Coughlinites, the Silver Shirts, the American Vigilantes. Such groups drew support from various levels of society and from smelly stockyards to sky-scraper offices. Still the remark seemed to refer equally to the house-holds of John L. Lewis and Tom Girdler, to auto workers and the Du Ponts. Lewis found in it grounds for thunder.

"Labor, like Israel, has many sorrows," he intoned on a nationwide radio network. "Its women weep for their fallen, and they lament for the future of the children of the race. It ill behooves one who has supped at labor's table and who has been sheltered in labor's house to curse with equal fervor and fine impartiality both labor and its adversaries when they become locked in deadly embrace."

Other battles this year seemed more decorous than that at mill gates which set up new Big Labor against so long impregnable Big Business. Sometimes such conflict seemed almost as deadly, though it was remembered by participants in terms of piques as well as philosophies. Both are often present and side by side on the Potomac. Irritations did enter into some acts in Washington at this time. The New Deal's vast relief machinery had been put to test in emergency early this year by great floods in the valleys of the Ohio and Mississippi rivers. In times changed since Herbert Hoover in similar inundation depended on private charity, Hopkins, working with public funds, received much praise for his work in relief and rehabilitation. He did not win all hearts in Congress. Soon afterward, in an outburst of flooding spite, a combination of Republicans and conservative Democrats in the House cut his salary from twelve thousand to ten thousand, though Congress was providing nearly half a billion more for public aid.

Hopkins was authority for a story that a similar act of pique marked the beginning of the raging court fight. Obviously Roosevelt had been resentful of what he regarded as the judges' imposition of their own economic and social opinions upon the law of the land since the Court began knocking down the New Deal laws the year before. But Hopkins related that the President told him of a personal affront to him by the Court half a year after his crack at the judges that they were taking the country back to a "horse-and-buggy" definition of interstate commerce. It had long been the custom each year when the Court convened for the secretary of the Chief Justice to call the White House and announce that the Court was in session. Whereupon the President would invite the Court to call upon him. The traditional visits on such occasions were purely social and ceremonial.

But, said Roosevelt, though he noted the date and made it a point to be in Washington in the midst of his campaign, in 1936, no call came from the Court. After waiting three days the President had one of his staff make inquiries. He came back with word of a deliberate snub: "There will be no visit to the White House this year."

"And remember," Hopkins said Roosevelt told him, "this was six months before the Court fight started."

If true, this would have been a petty act receiving petty reaction. According to Merlo J. Pusey in his authorized biography of Chief Justice Hughes, however, no such incident occurred. Roosevelt, he related, was in Hyde Park on the day the Court convened. He concluded that in three days around this time which the President spent in Washington there was just no mutually convenient time for the Court to make its call. Evidently, however, there was rancor between the President and some members of the "horse and buggy" Court. If the President acted in "mounting anger," as Pusey said, or not, he moved with far less than his customary skill.

On the evening of February 3, the President and Mrs. Roosevelt gave their dinner for the judiciary. Among the eighty guest were all members of the Court except Brandeis and Harlan Stone—certainly not the most recalcitrant jurists. The four principal objects of Roosevelt's resentment—James McReynolds, Willis Van Devanter, George Sutherland and Pierce Butler—were among those present along with Hughes, Benjamin Cardozo and Owen Roberts. The President was unusually gay, perhaps treasuring the secret of the bombshell he was sending to Capitol Hill two days later. Only on the morning on which it was dispatched to Congress did he disclose even to a small group of Cabinet and Congressional leaders his "Plan for the Reorganization of the Judicial Branch of the Government."

They were "incredulous," wrote Pusey. The plan was, said Robert E. Sherwood, "the most startling—and to many the most alarming—development of Roosevelt's adventurous Administration." As the Congressional leaders rode back to the Capitol, Hatton Sumners of Texas, chairman of the House Judiciary Committee, blurted, "Boys, here's where I cash in." After the Presidential message was presented to the Senate, Vice-President Garner "vigorously shook a turned down thumb." But in that body, faithful Joe Robinson, whom Huey Long had denounced as a reactionary, assumed leadership to get the President's plan approved. Many assumed, remembering Roosevelt's thundering majority in the country, that Congress would pass anything he sent to it. Quickly, however, the plan became the "court packing" bill.

The proposal had been presented rather piously by the President—and with dissimulation some thought—as a means of reducing the heavy burden on the courts and of ending delays in justice by a "constant infusion of new blood." Divested of subterfuge, as many felt, its only purpose was to give the President power to appoint a new judge in any federal court when the incumbent did not retire at seventy. Pinpointed to his design it meant that with six justices on the Supreme Court over seventy, the President would be able to add six judges and so six votes in its decisions.

By a last-minute message to Brandeis, Roosevelt indicated his awareness of the paradox that the most liberal judge was the oldest judge, too. The great, old Justice was not placated. He appreciated the warning but opposed the plan. The furore created in the country was like that aroused against Brandeis' own confirmation when Wilson appointed him in 1916—and much of the protest came from the same conservative sources. But this time Brandeis was in opposition. In the fight in which the Justices never departed from an appearance of aloof dignity, they worked behind a brass-knucks battler who might have seemed the last man to oppose the plan—Senator Wheeler of Montana.

Roosevelt apparently had a right to his view; "the people are with me, I know it." Resentment of the interposition of the judges' opinions in the name of constitutional interpretation was almost as old as the republic. Jefferson, Jackson, Lincoln, Theodore Roosevelt had expressed it sharply. Old T.R. in 1912 had gone so far as to support not only recall of judges but also recall of judicial decisions on Constitutional questions. He put the problem vividly:

"We cannot permanently go on dancing in fetters." In his third-party campaign for the Presidency in 1924, in which Wheeler was his running mate, the elder La Follette had joined in the protest. When, in 1930, Senators Norris, Borah and Wheeler led a bitter fight against the confirmation of corporation lawyer Hughes as Chief Justice, Borah, who later completely changed his mind, spoke of the Court as an "economic dictator."

The resentment had sharpened as the Court struck at New Deal legislation. When the Court outlawed the AAA, six effigies of the judges who had voted against it were hanged near Ames, Iowa. Other decisions infuriated labor. Said John L. Lewis, "It is a sad commentary on our government when every decision of the Supreme Court seems designed to fatten capital and starve and destroy labor." And division seemed drawn also on more familiar lines. Conservatives felt that the Court had determined that the New Deal itself was unconstitutional. The chairman of the lawyers committee of the Liberty League proclaimed: "This is not a matter of opinion but of fact. The Supreme Court, the final and conclusive authority on such matters, has so determined." In such a fight Roosevelt threw off the wraps. In a fireside chat on March 4, he directly charged that the Court was usurping power and vetoing his program. He quoted Hughes—out of context, the Justice's biographer wrote—as saying, "We are under a Constitution, but the Constitution is what the judges say it is."

"We have, therefore," Roosevelt said, "reached the point as a Nation where we must take action to save the Constitution from the Court and the Court from itself. . . . We want a Supreme Court that will do justice under the Constitution—not over it. In our courts we want a government of laws and not of men."

Much of the opposition was expected. Its character was indicated in full-page newspaper advertisements by the so-called Constitutional Government Committee, headed by newspaper-chain-owner Frank Gannett, whose mounting riches had brought him to rising reaction. Cartoons showed a Supreme Court bench with six Roosevelts on it. The old dictator charge was loudly repeated. A roar was created in the country. The ark of the covenant seemed assailed. But the most effective opposition came startlingly from progressives, most of whom in general had supported the New Deal program—Borah, Hiram Johnson, Wheeler.

Their leader, Senator Wheeler, the nemesis of Harding's Daugherty, had been the first senator to come out for the nomination of Roosevelt in 1932. But somehow he and Franklin Roosevelt did not hit it off in Washington. Some said he felt he should have been named Vice-President with F.D.R. Certainly by 1934 the Senator felt left out. He and other progressives resented the President's failure to support for re-election in 1934 the ardent, able liberal Republican Senator Bronson Cutting of New Mexico. He had come from the same class and schools as Roosevelt. He had crossed party lines to support F.D.R. for President. Cutting was the only progressive the administration did not support that year. And when Cutting was killed in a plane crash, on a trip in connection with an election contest which the administration had approved, somehow his saddened friends in the Senate almost held Roosevelt responsible for his death. By 1935 Wheeler, feeling that Roosevelt had been taken over by the conservatives, was almost ready for participation in a Coughlin-Long-type third party. Also, already he was opposed to the United States mixing in the affairs of Europe. He seemed to Roosevelt a sorehead. He was able, well-liked by his colleagues, sometimes indolent in study, but a Rocky Mountain lion in action.

He was welcomed into the Court fight by Brandeis and Hughes. The elderly Brandeis, his biographer said, throughout the contest maintained his customary reticence. Not even his law clerk heard him express an opinion on the plan. Still he was evidently pleased by a visit at his California Street apartment from Wheeler who had long been one of those who sat seeking wisdom at the venerable judge's feet. Not troubled by any possible improprieties, as Wheeler had feared he might be, he sent the Senator to Hughes. The Chief Justice provided him with a very dignified, above-the-battle kind of letter demolishing Roosevelt's first pretentions that the plan was needed to protect elderly justices from burdens and justice from delays. The opposition was growing in the Congress but the Court itself demolished the bill's chances by sudden strategic retreat.

"A switch in time saves nine," said a wit of the action of the Court on March 29. This decision day was afterward called White Monday in remembrance of the New Deal's Black Monday two years before. Now the bewhiskered Hughes solemnly read an opinion which seemed to outmaneuver Roosevelt. With Justice Roberts shifting away from the intransigent anti-New Dealers on the Court, it reversed itself on liberal legislation it had held unconstitutional less than a year before. On April 12, the Court upheld the Wagner Labor

Relations Act, under which Lewis was operating. On May 12, it approved the Social Security Law, which some employers had told their hands would take money out of their pockets. Eleven days later Justice Van Devanter resigned. Roosevelt's plan was beaten, but he got what he wanted. Vacancies came so fast after 1937 that ultimately he was able to name the Chief Justice and the eight associate justices.

Still the fight had been a deadly one. As tension mounted in the Senate, overworked and overwrought Joe Robinson dropped dead. Senators on the other side now mourned him loudly. Baruch, who kept his Senate friendships well greased with campaign contributions, expressed the sentiments of many in the upper chamber when he urged the President to stop the fight and "not kill any more Senators." Ickes, who quoted Baruch, feared that feeling might run so high that the President's life would be in peril. The battle went on, but the bill, which such a White House operator as Tommy Corcoran had felt was "in the bag," was defeated. This came ten days after the death of Robinson, who, some said, made the fight after a Roosevelt promise that he would get the first court vacancy as a reward.

Wounds which never healed were left. Anger in the White House was hardened by statements like one by Wheeler that "a liberal cause was never won by stacking a deck of cards, by stuffing a ballot box, or packing a court." More bitterness and fear of retaliation was built in Congress when the President, working behind the scenes, intervened in the election of Robinson's successor as majority leader. Roosevelt's candidate, Alben Barkley of Kentucky, won only 38 to 37 over Pat Harrison of Mississippi, and that required White House pressure for the switch of votes earlier pledged to Harrison. After the vote it was agreed that "in the interests of harmony" Roosevelt better not attend a harmony dinner of Senate Democrats in Barkley's honor. Serenely he sent a message of congratulation through Vice-President Garner who, New Dealers had already heard, had arranged the final defeat of the Court bill on Robinson's funeral train. At the dinner a pigeon was loosed over the heads of the recently embattled Democratic senators to symbolize the dove of peace. It was not flying over F.D.R.

There was chagrin enough to go around even among the vindictive. It was startlingly disclosed that Hugo Black, the first appointee to the Court by the liberalizing President, had been a member of the Ku Klux Klan. (There had been nothing klannish about his Senate record as there was to be none about his decisions as a justice.) Also at this time came an event which might have been comic relief to some but which could not have been very comfortable for the President. He had been talking about apparent tax evasions of many rich men, including the Du Ponts. But in all Hudson River and White House family array he returned to Wilmington, Delaware, once the scene for the tale of the shepherd, the sheep and the wolf. There in formality and ritual took place the wedding of his twenty-three-year-old son, Franklin, Jr., who had just graduated from Harvard, to Ethel Du Pont, pretty princess of economic royalty.

This was an amazing occasion. In what the Associated Press described as the "packed" church, the bride's Juliet cap above her cloudlike gown emphasized that this was a sort of marriage of the Capulets and the Montagues. For once alignments seemed changed with "the DuPonts on the left side of the church and Roosevelts on the right." But even in the Du Ponts' Delaware Roosevelt's planning hand was suggested by the officiating presence of the Reverend Endicott Peabody, of Groton School. Peabody, as the AP noted, "has prayed at both of President Roosevelt's inaugurations." And: "President Roosevelt's famous smile was full of fatherly pride." Among the guests was Harry Hopkins.

If possibly stiff even at the reception for a thousand guests at the Du Pont estate Owl's Nest, this was an occasion of pomp and peace. Any moment of tranquillity was welcome anywhere that year. Abroad, but every day spread black and wide upon the newspapers of Americans, the so-called Civil War in tragic Spain had become the scene of the conflict of intervening Fascist and Communist powers. The term "fifth column" was invented by a Fascist-aided general who said he was leading four columns of troops against Madrid and had another "column" of secret sympathizers within it. Hopkins' "reporter" in early New Deal days, Martha Gellhorn, along with other correspondents, was reporting the situation, which seemed increasingly almost as close to American concern as poverty in the Depression. Ernest Hemingway there was already realizing that the bell tolled for more than dying Spaniards. Some ardent volunteers from America learned that, too, as they saw not only Fascist but Communist brutality. On the other side of the world Japan was pressing its all-out invasion of China, in evident determination to slam the "open door" of American policy there.

America had difficulties enough at home. In the administration, they seemed to be symbolized by Hopkins, who had been so gaily triumphant the year before. In a new budget-balancing mood the President had cut Harry's WPA rolls in half between January and August. That work-relief agency seemed as sickly lean as its chief was becoming. His wife, Barbara, who had earlier been troubled by tuberculosis, now was dying of cancer of the breast, for which she had been operated on before. He feared that he was suffering from a malignancy, too. In the summer he took her off on a final holiday at Saratoga Springs. Both pretended to be gay, but both felt the proximity of death. In the winter after Barbara died Harry went to the Mayo Clinic in Rochester, Minnesota. There a large part of his stomach which proved to be cancerous was removed.

The whole land seemed suddenly sick despite New Deal therapy —or because of it, some felt. Labor troubles which had begun with the year mounted to 4720 strikes and lockouts involving 1,950,000 workers, most of them over union recognition—but that as an approach to greater demands. Then, as September came, slump came also. Nine months before, *Time* had declared, "Last week with Depression vanishing into memory, the portents of Boom drummed excitingly throughout the land." Perhaps *Time*, like some others less willing to admit it, saw only its own prosperity in the mirror of its reporting. Its profits had grown from $325,412 in the crash year 1929 to $2,249,823 in 1935 and were still rising. In 1936 it had paid eighty-five thousand dollars just for the name of the dying old humor magazine *Life*.

Yet there were still seven million unemployed. Capital expenditures on industrial and commercial construction and equipment were far below the 1929 level. The WPA cuts between January and August had reduced the government's contribution to the country's buying power by over three billion dollars. The Federal Reserve system stiffened its reserve requirements on member banks and moved to prevent a supposed threatening monetary and credit inflation. In August Senator "Cotton Ed" Smith and other Southerners came to see the President about the fall in cotton prices. Then came what Secretary of the Treasury Henry Morgenthau, Jr., called "severe shocks" on the stock market. Other signs showed that a "recession" had set in. Advocates of government spending had warned of the danger of budget-cutting in the country where still so many were "ill-housed, ill-clad, ill-nourished."

The decline went on across the fall. By December stock prices would fall from a 1937 high of 120 to 81. Production would be down, too, and ten million people would be unemployed. The charge of some New Dealers that the fabulously wealthy "Sixty Families," including now F.D.R.'s in-laws, were responsible for the slump met the countercharge of New Deal interference with business. The President let his Cabinet know that he felt that the big money interests were in an "unconscious conspiracy" to force concessions in taxation, lightening of the regulations of the Securities and Exchange Commission, and a strong hand against the sit-down strikes. Business leaders were prepared to concede the need for controlled farm production, a wages and hours law and some kind of social security. They were not willing to advocate such things. The certain thing was that the "recession" was a fact. Democracy's ability to cope with problems at home and in the world seemed at best problematical.

"Democracy is sand driven by the wind," said Mussolini this year.

Certainly the winds were blowing when Roosevelt rolled over the reddening mountains early in October to speak in Chicago. There he stayed with Cardinal George William Mundelein, humanitarian cleric who approved many New Deal policies and was the first churchman of his rank to speak out against Fascism. His description of Hitler as "an Austrian paperhanger, and a poor one at that" had resulted in formal protests from Germany to the Vatican and to Washington where the Cardinal could expect approval, not rebuke. But now Ickes doubted the wisdom of the President staying with the Cardinal. In a time of quarrels about everything, he noted that religious controversy was running high. Actually the host, the occasion and the time were all suited to Roosevelt's purposes.

The occasion was the dedication of a PWA project, the Outer Link Bridge. It symbolized, or seemed to then, the wisdom of government's building for peace and people, not for arms and war. Mundelein represented the faith and hopes of Christians everywhere —and outrage at the increasing mistreatment of the Jews. From the belligerence of Germany, Italy and Japan, danger was already mounting, though many Americans insisted that it could be disregarded by the United States behind walls of strict neutrality. Chicago was already then the center of determined isolationism—or the focus of its infection.

Roosevelt dedicated the bridge. Also in bold words which afterward seemed only a testing sortie against isolationism he stirred hopes and angers.

"The peace-loving nations must make a concerted effort in opposition to those violations of treaties and those ignorings of humane instincts which today are creating a state of international anarchy and instability from which there is no escape through mere isolation or neutrality. . . . There is a solidarity and interdependence about the modern world, both technically and morally, which makes it impossible for any nation completely to isolate itself from economic and political upheavals in the rest of the world. . . . War is a contagion whether it be declared or not. It seems to be unfortunately true that the epidemic of world lawlessness is spreading. When an epidemic of physical disease starts to spread, the community approves and joins in a quarantine of the patients in order to protect the health of the community against the spread of the disease."

That "Quarantine Speech," as it was immediately called, drew not only applause but also a roar from those who demanded that America mind its own business, stay out of "foreign wars." They insisted that regardless of what happened elsewhere this country would be safe within its shores. The Hearst papers and the Chicago *Tribune* led a hue and cry. The demand mounted for an inflexible neutrality policy imposing embargoes on all belligerents, aggressor and victim alike. Roosevelt was not disturbed by charges of pacifist groups that he was leading the country down the same road that led to World War I. Almost in the language of a proper Grotonian he wrote his old schoolmaster describing the nations he would quarantine as those which "fail to maintain certain fundamental rules of conduct." He wrote Colonel House, who had played so great a role in the road to war before, that he enjoyed the "repercussions across the water." They had contained expressions of hope and fury. The beset Loyalist government in Spain and the overrun Chinese were briefly heartened. But Germany and Italy rattled their swords louder. Hitler intensified his persecution of the Jews.

A readiness, even an eagerness, to risk war with the United States seemed apparent when on December 12 Japanese bombers sank the American gunboat *Panay* and destroyed three Standard Oil tankers twenty miles up the Yangtze River from Nanking. In the attack three Americans were killed. Sharply Roosevelt, who had been suffering with an abscessed tooth, demanded compensation, apology and assurances for the future. This time Japan backed off, though it blandly contended that the attack on the plainly marked vessels was only an unfortunate mistake.

Roosevelt at this time had seemed to Ickes "to have the appearance of a man who had more or less given up." Certainly he had reasons for weariness and depression. His efforts to educate the country to awareness of dangers in his Chicago speech only seemed to have aroused greater determination by many to tell him to watch his words and actions in such matters. Announcement early in the new year that three light cruisers would be sent to the ceremonies at the opening of the new British naval base at Singapore brought charges of some sort of secret Anglo-American agreement about pooling naval resources. When he proposed an $800,000,000 naval building program the Federal Council of the Churches of Christ in America violently protested. It insisted that even if there were war in Europe there would be only the "remotest likelihood of its reaching our shores." Only by a vote of 209 to 188 in the House was a proposal defeated to amend the Constitution to require a national referendum on a declaration of war except in case of actual invasion.

However he may have looked to Ickes, the President had not given up on either the foreign or domestic fronts. It was at this time that he began to develop a strong right arm in Harry Hopkins. Both the time and the man seemed unlikely. Hopkins came from the Mayo Clinic as 1937 began with only two-to-one assurances from his doctors that his cancer would not recur. Whatever the danger of that, the operation left him with nutritional difficulties which plagued him and often floored him for the rest of his life. Like his health, his popularity did not seem improved. He was the target at which conservatives in Congress and in the country most frequently shot. Catholics had fears about him because some of his chief associates, as social workers, were "in favor of birth control and that sort of thing." He did have Catholic friends, however. This winter and early spring he was doing most of his work by telephone from the Palm Beach estate of Joseph P. Kennedy, soon to be ambassador to Great Britain. Not even friends, however, could protect him from reactions to his sometimes tart personality. He often spoke quickly and sharply and his mouth was regarded as a probable one in which to put manufactured misquotations. (He never said as a do-gooder at a race track, what some supposedly responsible journalists reported: "We shall tax and tax, spend and spend, elect and elect.")

Certainly while his almost secret charm appealed to many including Roosevelt, few felt that he possessed the qualities Roosevelt thought might make him a Presidential possibility and did make him a great diplomat and activator in crucial times. Mrs. Roosevelt, who was an early ally in his humanitarian purposes, rather disapproved of his association "with gay but more or less artificial society" at such places as the St. Regis and Florida estates. Roosevelt's ideas of Hopkins' possibilities seemed fantastic. He began trying to build the health and inflate the prestige of this man who looked like a dingy grasshopper. He was to set him up apparently as his proposed successor. Evidently with the Presidential "go sign" as candidate, Harry would make an almost comic pretense of re-establishing himself as bucolic citizen of corny Iowa, which he had left to tend city poor twenty-five years before. In this political enterprise, however, Hopkins was an obviously improbable instrument for the transfer of the Presidency from hand to hand. Could it have been that the master artist or Machiavellian in politics planned from the outset to put forward as heir one who could not take the inheritance that Roosevelt, even this early, had no real intention to relinquish? Roosevelt might have felt the need for some New Dealer to prevent default to conservative candidates, only too evidently on the scene, of the 1940 Democratic nomination. No one then or later could probe the mysteries of that sometimes mischievous majestic mind. Certainly rather than a hand-picked successor Hopkins seemed like a new Howe, chosen because, like Louie, Harry was really too frail and ungainly ever to be a competitor but would be, in part because of that, dependable in devotion.

Howe had picked Roosevelt when neither had much to lose. Roosevelt turned to Hopkins when the risks around Presidential preference were great. Aging Colonel House, who played and played out a similar role with Wilson, had demonstrated Presidential dangers in such relationships. Alter egos, as F.D.R. understood from his memories of Wilson and House, should preferably be figures so *alter* that independent egotism could not enter the relationship. In 1938, however, while he was swinging back to Harry's spending views in the recession, what he needed was a fighter in other causes as well. And looking like a wisp which a breath would blow over, Hopkins, then, as in greater affairs later, was a fighter when the chips were down—even when it looked to many as if the game was close to an end.

At this time Roosevelt was undertaking quarantine at home against senators who ran as Democrats but did not support the programs of the President and the platform. He flung aside the old notion that Presidents should take no part in primary contests in their parties. The liberal label now seemed to him more important than the party one. Already he had advanced from the time when he was ready to let Bronson Cutting fall, in 1934, to the support of such a progressive Republican as George Norris in 1936. Now he moved against the renomination of Democrats in the House and Senate who had been active in opposition to his measures. In the court fight he had appealed to Congress; now he went to the people behind it.

He put punch behind his preferences in what was quickly called the "purge." That was a word which had special dark connotations then in connection with the bloody elimination of dissenters by dictators in Germany and Russia. The American "dictator" only asked the masses behind him for political annihilation of opponents in his own party. On a transcontinental tour he undertook to liquidate by direct rejection, by significant silences instead of support. Also it was especially charged in Kentucky that the WPA was arrayed, not visibly by Hopkins but certainly under him, on the side Roosevelt wanted to win.

In Kentucky "Dear Alben" Barkley, as the President addressed him in a famous letter, was opposed for the Democratic nomination by popular Governor Albert B. ("Happy") Chandler. Early in the spring Roosevelt had told the Cabinet that "while the Administration could not take an active part in the Democratic primaries this year, we ought to do everything we could for Barkley in Kentucky." His opponent, he said, was "a dangerous person . . . of the Huey Long type, but with less ability." That suggestion was understood as a command. At a White House lunch F.D.R. even made a temporary truce with John L. Lewis who put his labor forces—and probably more money—behind Barkley. Still this was a fight made with transparent smoothness against "Happy," who was slick and thick-skinned, too. When Roosevelt went to Kentucky to a tremendously large meeting at the Latonia race track, Chandler as well as Barkley arrived riding with the President. Obviously, with Chandler boldly declining to be set aside in public, administration opposition to him had to move unostentatiously, even underground —another word coming more and more into the world's vocabulary.

Unfortunately for its operators the WPA did not operate underground. Thomas L. Stokes, columnist for the Scripps-Howard newspapers, went to Kentucky and came back with tales of operations in aid of Barkley, which won for him the Pulitzer prize. Hopkins later described as an indiscretion a statement at a relief conference during this campaign by his deputy, Aubrey Williams, that "we have got to stick together. We have got to keep our friends in power." Furore followed the Williams' remark and the Stokes articles. Robert E. Sherwood later wrote: "There were a great many Senators and Representatives who piously approved the Stokes articles, as slams at the hated Hopkins, and who secretly thanked heaven that this investigation had been conducted in Kentucky and not in their own states. I can say with assurance that there were not many members of Congress at that time who had never used W.P.A. in one way or another to shore up their own political fortunes."

Certainly Barkley needed it to shore up his. He won, but not all the administration's activities sufficed in other states. Walter George of Georgia, "Cotton Ed" Smith of South Carolina, Millard Tydings of Maryland, all won despite Roosevelt's opposition. His record in other states was not impressive. Also, already Louis Bean, the administration's own statistical forecaster in the Department of Agriculture, had calculated that in the fall election the Republicans would gain eighty seats in the House. To some it seemed that in two years the New Deal had come from sensational victory to political suicide. It looked as if Roosevelt had not picked Hopkins out of troubled seas to be a companion for a ride on a yacht like the *Nourmahal* but up from stormy seas to an awash raft to be an only possible survivor in a gale.

Frank Sullivan, in articles for subscribers still able to be amused, collected in *The New Yorker* the anti-Roosevelt clichés of the time:

The Madman in the White House.
That Fellow Down in Washington.
Trying to destroy the American way of life.
You can't spend your way out of a depression.
Our children's children will be paying.
Half these people on relief are foreigners anyhow. Let them go back where they came from.
Lewis has a key to the back door of the White House.

Sullivan repeated well-worn anti-Roosevelt jokes.

"Why is a WPA worker like King Solomon? . . . He takes his pick and goes to bed."

"There's only Six Dwarfs now. . . . Dopey's in the White House."

But not all even among *New Yorker* readers were easily amused. Not only those whose habit was to speak of Roosevelt with a hiss were disturbed. More were uneasy. There were shut-down factories by all too productive fields. The rich got richer and complained of taxes; the poor were still present in an abundant land. And gradually out of more than a corner of the eye Americans looked anxiously abroad. The war of nerves was already begun in Europe; its contagion was spreading in jitters to America.

On September 12, while Roosevelt was concerned about an operation, at the Mayo Clinic on his son, James, which it was feared might be like Harry's, Hitler at Nuremberg shouted that the right of self-determination must be given to the Sudeten Germans in Czechoslovakia. Rioting and martial law followed in that little country. On September 16, Neville Chamberlain, successor to Stanley Baldwin, who had saved the constitution and perhaps the Empire from Wallis Warfield, flew to see Hitler in Berchtesgaden. Believing he could appease the clamoring German, Chamberlain had rejected a disarmament proposal by Roosevelt earlier in the year. Now to satisfy the Führer, on September 21 Britain and France forced the Czechoslovakian government to cede to Germany the areas occupied by the Sudeten Germans. Then Hitler asked for more, threatening to invade the country. On September 22, almost a commuter carrying a famous umbrella, Chamberlain flew to another meeting with the clamoring German Chancellor, ready apparently to be sterner with this Nazi upstart. But Mussolini assured his Axis partner of support. Britain and France belatedly speeded the building of their defenses.

During the months before, F.D.R. had read the sidelined Churchill's book *While England Slept*. Sleep was full of nightmares now. On September 26, Roosevelt appealed to Hitler to negotiate. An "authoritative" statement in London said that Russia, Britain and France would defend Czechoslovakia. Hitler's demands were "unreasonable," Chamberlain said. Roosevelt sent a second appeal. The British fleet was prepared for action.

All this was not news of America but it was startling American

news. Even the possibility of war was, of course, far off, as isolationists and many more agreed. Still there was a sort of buzz of planes
in the ears even of safe Americans. More and more the jitters was a
transoceanic contagion not easily quarantined. And at this point
Orson Welles, a young radio actor-producer with a limping Sunday
night program which had not been able to secure a sponsor in competition to the popular ventriloquist's dummy Charlie McCarthy,
made plans for his weekly show.

Welles, born in Kenosha, Wisconsin, twenty-three years before,
had at sixteen begun his stage career at the Gate Theater in Dublin.
He had toured with the beloved actress, Katharine Cornell, and had
worked in Hopkins' Federal Theater directing the Negro *Macbeth*
with its voodoo scenes. Only recently had he turned from stage to
radio as maestro of the Mercury Theater of the Air. Switching from
Shakespeare, to whose work he was much addicted, he hoped to
attract a little attention with a dramatization of *The War of the
Worlds* by H. G. Wells. What he staged on the Columbia Broad-
casting System that Sunday night was not so much a dramatization
of the Wells novel as a translation of Wells into Welles. His agent
thought it was a pretty silly show.

Many of those who happened to be listening may have thought it
so as it began. The show started with a routine weather report.
A move to a New York hotel was announced and from it ostensibly
came some fairly commonplace swing band music. Then suddenly
came a "flash" interruption: An astronomer had just observed a
series of gas explosions on the planet Mars. Swiftly more simulated
news bulletins followed reporting the landing of a meteor near
Princeton, New Jersey, killing 1500 people. (Princeton, of course,
was just a charming college town then, not noted as the residence
of Albert Einstein, who, as a life member of the Institute of Advanced Study, already feared advanced ideas of annihilation.) Listeners had been shocked by the reported catastrophe. Others hearing of its reports tuned in on CBS. Suddenly came the shocking
"news bulletin" that no mere monster meteor had fallen. A great
metal cylinder containing Martians armed with death rays had
landed in an invasion of the Earth.

Incredulity seemed on a holiday. Panic stirred a mass hysteria
from coast to coast. Throughout New York City families fled from
their apartments following the broadcast's advice that cities be evacuated. In San Francisco the impression grew that New York was

being destroyed. It was being paralyzed by crowds in the streets. In Harlem groups rushed for help into police stations, firehouses. One man insisted that he had heard Roosevelt's voice telling people to leave the city and, indeed, a part of the realism of the broadcast was an actor imitating the President's voice in warning. Another actor cried, "Get gas masks!" People prayed hysterically in the Middle West. Credulity was not confined to the simple. Two Princeton professors of geology hurried into the night to find the meteor before multitudes heard of invasion.

Fortunately for Welles, four times during the broadcast CBS announced that this was only a play. So did most of the stations carrying the program. But alarmed people had not waited to hear reassurance. Before the broadcast was ended the studio control room filled with angry police. And after it was over the New York *Times* chastised already chastened radio executives on Madison Avenue: "Radio ought to act promptly to prevent a repetition of the wave of panic in which it inundated the nation Sunday night. . . . Thousands, from one end of the country to the other, were frightened out of their senses, starting an incipient flight of hysterical refugees from the designated area, taxing the police and hospitals, confusing traffic, and choking the usual means of communication. . . . Radio is new, but it has adult responsibilities. It has not mastered itself or the material it uses. . . ."

Some felt that way about the New World. And real fears increased in it when just thirty days after the broadcast Chamberlain flew again to Munich with Europe on the verge of war. In the world Hitler had shaken with his demands, he seemed to withdraw his taloned paw with something less than a roar if not a purr. He called for a four-power conference: Dictators and democracies both disregarded Russia. The world sat on the edge of its chair waiting for peace or panic to come like the dropping of the second shoe. With his ever present umbrella, Chamberlain, on September 30 in Munich, joined Edouard Daladier of France in the abandonment of Czechoslovakia to the Germans. On the Prime Minister's return to London, many hailed him as a man who had made a fine bargain. Little Czechoslovakia seemed a small price to pay for "peace in our time." But angry Churchill said, "Britain and France had to choose between war and dishonor. They chose dishonor. They will have war."

A week later Roosevelt wrote to his ambassador in Portugal: "The dictator threat from Europe is a good deal closer to the United States." But before he wrote that letter, on election day, November 8, the Republicans had made enormous gains in the Middle and Far West. They added to their Congressional strength seven seats in the Senate and eighty in the House. Though big Democratic majorities remained, a coalition of conservative Democrats and Republicans could have New Deal measures at their mercy. And the problem now was the effectiveness of democratic government in helping maintain the peace of the world. Obviously, however, Roosevelt held himself apart from blame in the serious setback when he wrote at the time that the Democrats lost in a good many states "because, frankly, our office holders and our candidates had not measured up."

He had no sense that he had not. He was irritated rather than disturbed when Martin Dies, roaring Red hunter from Texas and Chairman of the Committee for the Investigation of Un-American Activities, announced his determination to drive out of the government such subverters as Harold Ickes, Frances Perkins, Harry Hopkins and other "Communists and fellow-travelers." Imperturbably, in promotion Roosevelt prepared to name Hopkins Secretary of Commerce though a Gallup poll indicated the country was overwhelmingly against the appointment. But first he sent Hopkins to the Pacific Coast on "a secret survey" of "the capacity of airplane factories to build military airplanes." The President then, Hopkins noted later, "was sure that we were going to get into the war and he believed that air power would win it."

"About this time," he added, "the President made his startling statement that we should have 8,000 planes and everybody in the Army and Navy and all the newspapers in the country jumped on him."

Late in this 1938, Americans were more interested in an item which was brought up at a Cabinet meeting than in planes. The Du Pont Company had discovered a process for the making of artificial silk which could have important repercussions on the economy of Japan. It could be knit, the Cabinet heard, into stockings which would be more serviceable than those made from silk and have as good an appearance on women's legs. Apparently nothing in this top-level discussion of nylon related to parachutes.

# XIX

## THE PRICE OF PEACE

I

As THE dams rose in the 1930s the Tennessee Valley Authority more than any other thing made the New Deal visible to the naked, the admiring and sometimes the jaundiced eye. Here was valley where the forests had been cut, the lands eroded. Down it from the Appalachians to Paducah more flood was poured into the Ohio than from any other tributary. Freighted with the lost fertility of the land, its high waters swelled the Mississippi, creating catastrophe all the way down to the Louisiana Cajun country where Herbert Hoover had been both helpful and amused and Huey Long had been aroused and raging. On the often inundated river shores and on the hills beyond them, for most people, save in the cities, there was available in 1932 only hand labor and kerosene light. Power in the river was unharnessed and untamed.

But by 1939 the TVA was building in its dams the greatest monument of the years between the world wars. In comparison the development made a midget of Al Smith's Empire State Building. It dwarfed even such a fortress mass as the plants of General Motors which sit-down strikers besieged within. TVA's twenty-one dams, built or planned in 1939, comprised a magnitude a dozen times that of the pyramids of Egypt. And around them CCC boys in the woods, foresters, soil experts, agronomists, planners landscaped for use and enjoyment the massive project. Barges moved on the harnessed rivers. Power—public power—flowed from its falls to farms, towns, new factories. Its greatest dividend and the purpose of all its planning were, said David Lilienthal, who chiefly shaped this experiment in what he liked to call "grass roots democracy," an improved chance for people.

"Democracy is on the march in this valley," he wrote. He saw in that a demonstration that federal concern need not be remote, centralized control.

Not all regarded TVA with such panegyric attention. The Authority's growth was attended by bitter bureaucratic contention. Grabs at its regional authority were made from Washington by ambitious administrators and patronage-seeking politicians. Not all its friends were so idealistic as Senator Norris, whose dream it had been. One of its chief defenders was Congressman John E. Rankin of Mississippi who wanted its cheap power for his town of Tupelo, Mississippi, but remained a rampant racist after the river was tamed. Sometimes starry-eyed planners on TVA's own staff were ready to use brass knucks in defense of their different opinions of its purposes. It was big spending. It contained in terms of ideas long held by many people—not all of them alarmed utility executives—elements of creeping socialism.

Certainly it seemed the greatest single relief project, though it was not so regarded by its builders. No leaf-raking produced its great piles of enduring concrete. Not men leaning on shovels but mammoth earth-moving machines cleared the bottoms for its lakes. It was a project for the relief of an entire region and an impressive example, as armaments grew in the world, of how America could produce for power. As the most damned New Dealer, Harry Hopkins had little to do with its building, yet to some where you could see it, it loomed as the embodiment of his supposed philosophy "spend and spend, tax and tax, elect and elect." And perversely in its purpose to advance people, TVA chiefly put forward in 1939 its own chief antagonist, persuasive, driving articulate Wendell Willkie. So as TVA's power for people became an essential facility for defense in 1939, it dramatized Roosevelt's most dependable aid and greatest opponent, both of whom were shifting in their principle purposes, too.

Certainly no New Dealer, Willkie was listed in the 1938–1939 *Who's Who* as a Democrat. A democrat he clearly always was and a perfect product of democracy. Perhaps he was in a better sense than Ickes meant in a later barb about him "the barefoot boy from Wall Street." He never lost in the canyons of lower Manhattan the feel of the earth beneath his feet in his native town of Elwood, Indiana, small market center for a tomato-growing region. Of German descent (the family name had originally been Willcke), in 1939 Wendell Willkie looked at Nazi brutality as no incomprehensible surprise. His ancestors had been rebels against the despotic and military suppression of revolutionary ideas in 1848. His own father brought to America and kept here the memory of a beating given him as a boy by a Prussian officer.

There was more freedom of expression than money in the Willkie household in Elwood. The independence of the tribe was not only shown in its liberal political views. Also, Wendell's mother, practicing with his father, was both the first woman licensed as a lawyer in Indiana and the first woman to smoke cigarettes in Elwood. Perhaps along with devotion to freedom her son inherited his chain-smoking habit and personality from her. As a boy he acted *Hamlet* with his mother's petticoat as a cape. He began to debate as soon as he found a juvenile forum. At Indiana University, through which he worked his way to a law degree, his Class Day oration so sharply attacked the conservatism of the faculty and even the State Supreme Court that the degree he had earned was only given to him grudgingly and privately after the public graduation exercises.

After three years of practice with the family partnership, he moved to Akron to join a firm which served the Firestone Tire and Rubber Company. Harvey Firestone advised the young lawyer that he wouldn't amount to much if he stayed a Democrat. Mr. Firestone's advice was kindly given. Such warning seemed needed in 1929 when Willkie, then thirty-seven, took issue with the then apparently omnipotent seventy-year-old Insull, who denounced as "radical agitators" those who criticized Big Business. Willkie's evident ability was equal to his apparent brashness, however. In the same year in which he spoke up to Insull he moved to New York to join in corporate practice an older lawyer who was to become managing director of the Edison Electric Institute, top trade association of utility companies.

In January, 1933, after Insull had fallen and Roosevelt had been elected with the help of Willkie's vote, the barefoot boy from Elwood became president of the Commonwealth and Southern utility system, the biggest private utility in the Tennessee Valley area. In 1934, he joined in a legal opinion published by the Edison Electric Institute that TVA was "palpably unconstitutional." A year later, when the U. S. Chamber of Commerce at a famous meeting loudly broke with the New Deal, he joined the protest warning of the danger that a "great bureaucracy in Washington" was trying to "nationalize" the power business of the country.

At that time Congress, pressed by the President and impelled by revelations of high-handed holding company practices, had before it the utility holding company bill containing the so-called "death sentence" provision. The legislation proposed a voluntary simplification of holding companies and a reorganization of them to provide economic and geographical coordination. But after January 1, 1940, if voluntary action failed, the Securities and Exchange Commission could impose the "death sentence"—the dissolution of those holding companies which could not show the necessity of their existence to a geographically and economically integrated operation.

Since Willkie had come into the holding company system late, he had come in clean. He admitted past malfeasances in some systems: "There was a crazy period when men went crazy and did a lot of foolish things and I am not attempting to speak for that situation." But, he insisted, the whole system should not be destroyed because a minority had misbehaved. Still, when in a New York debate his TVA adversary Lilienthal described holding companies as vast tapeworms sucking the nourishment out of operating companies, Willkie even spoke up for Insull as a "forceful, dynamic and attractive figure." (Actually Insull was found not guilty in the federal courts in November, 1934; when he died of a heart attack in 1938 in a Paris subway newspapers concluded from his almost empty pockets that he was down to his last eight cents in francs. Better informed, his biographer, Forrest McDonald, was sure a thief had got to the pockets of the dead man who was by no means destitute, nor had those who invested in his companies suffered unusual losses. McDonald wrote: "And so in his death, as in his life, Samuel Insull was robbed, and nobody got the story straight.")

Willkie lost the holding company fight in part, perhaps, as a result of the backfire of undue pressures by some magnates who had not changed their ways. His efforts did not halt TVA in what Lilienthal called its march of democracy. He did get more for his properties there than TVA had wanted to pay. But most of all he gained enormously in prestige as a better and better known public figure: an anti-New Dealer but in a fresh new pattern, not a mere croaker though his voice was husky, a sort of positive conservative with tremendous human appeal. Younger Republicans, most of them amateurs, began a Presidential build-up which at first scarcely promised to become a boom. Willkie, with great gusto, was prepared to be built up. He spoke, he wrote, he moved about the country. Endorsements piled up. But to Republican regulars with Roosevelt facing a third-term hazard even in his own party, the articulate lawyer so recently a Democrat was an outsider.

After all, there were such available candidates as Thomas E. Dewey of New York and Robert A. Taft of Ohio. Dewey at thirty-eight then seemed a dramatic and popular figure. His freedom from old-time economic royalism was suggested by his prosecution as a special assistant to the U. S. Attorney General of tax proceedings against Mitchell, the big banker. Publicity had piled around him in his conduct of the case against Irving Wexler, alias Waxey Gordon, the gangster. He was a gang buster extraordinary even if Alice Longworth was devastatingly to describe him later as looking like the little man on the wedding cake. In 1938 he had come close to ending fifteen years of Democratic occupancy of the Governor's Mansion in Albany. Taft, wearing a great name, had in the same year been elected to the U. S. Senate. Beside them the so-recently-Democratic Willkie seemed a stranger at the Republican Convention which met in Philadelphia in June, 1940. Old regular Senator James E. Watson from Willkie's home state of Indiana, who had helped Lodge defeat the League of Nations, scornfully rejected Willkie's request for support. He wanted no recent Democrat. Didn't he believe in conversion? The old irreconcilable snorted:

"If a whore repented and wanted to join the church, I'd personally welcome her and lead her up the aisle to a pew, but by the Eternal, I'd not ask her to lead the choir the first night."

Old Jim's view did not prevail at that convention, which assembled in Philadelphia on an overcast Sunday at a time when Europe seemed falling apart and America endangered by the drive of Hitler, who had exploded out of the phony war, overrun the Low Countries and pushed a gallant but routed English army out of conquered France. Roosevelt seemed to move in a blitz, too. Suddenly the Republican party seemed rent by what the outraged regulars regarded as a new trick of the Machiavellian monster in the White House. On the eve of the convention, in what seemed a panzer thrust to conservative and isolationist Republicans, Roosevelt had brought into his Cabinet as Secretaries of War and Navy Henry L. Stimson and Frank Knox. Knox had run as Republican Vice-Presidential candidate in 1936.

Stimson had served in the Cabinets of both Taft and Hoover. Both now were strongly pro-Ally. Indeed, the dangers they saw for America had seemed real to Stimson when the belligerency of Japan mounted while he was Hoover's Secretary of State. They moved in patriotism but they threw the Republican Party into confusion.

Regardless of the feelings of old Jim Watson and others like him about an upstart newcomer in Republican ranks, the party desperately needed a new voice to lead its choir. There was plenty of evidence pouring in on the convention that Willkie was the public's favorite. Undoubtedly some zealots, whose faces were not familiar at Republican conclaves, had put on a blitzkrieg campaign for him. They blew up smoke-filled rooms with explosive enthusiasm—or seemed to. Suspicious Ickes thought their crusade was actually "a cunning masterful piece of work to make the people believe that it was an uprising on their part that resulted in Willkie's nomination when all of the time it was an ably managed and adequately financed campaign on the part of the big interests operating in the main through some of the ablest advertising executives in the country."

But Roscoe Drummond, then Washington correspondent of the *Christian Science Monitor*, wrote that Willkie, with his wide smile and lock of hair always unruly at his forehead, suddenly appeared as the most appealing figure who had come along to carry the Republican banner since Teddy Roosevelt. He was, Drummond said, "no more 'put over' on the Republican Convention than Babe Ruth was 'put over' on the New York Yankees." He was the exciting candidate required in explosive times. They were times of new divisions and alignments. If Willkie had moved from the Democratic to the Republican party in the New Deal years when others were moving the other way, now in the years of international violence shifts were being made not on conservative-liberal lines but on the basis of differences which later seemed like those between the ostrich and the eagle—the isolationists and those who felt that with democracy at stake in the world, the land almost of its origin could not stay safely, smugly uninvolved at home. The nomination of the strongly pro-Ally Willkie was a decisive American step against dictatorship even if both he and Roosevelt confused that issue in their campaigns.

An ugly mood remained. It had been evident even in the Democratic party which met in convention in Chicago in July. Nothing indicated it better than that Hopkins, who had once briefly seemed at Roosevelt's suggestion to be a possible Presidential candidate, had as a rank amateur to take charge of Roosevelt's fortunes. He had the direct phone line to the White House in his bathroom at the Blackstone. Not all professional politicians were as glumly angry as Jim Farley, still Democratic Chairman as well as candidate. He believed that the man he had "made" President had given him the go sign for the nomination, then reneged on it. Other conservatives had attempted to muster, for control of the party and an end to New Deal nonsense, behind the supposed barrier of the two-term tradition.

Roosevelt seemed to some almost deliberately to make it a doldrums convention. Often the galleries were only half filled. Opposition to him folded but his nomination was not unanimous. Reluctance almost became revolt when Hopkins passed the word that Roosevelt's choice as Vice-President to replace grumbling Garner on the ticket was Henry Wallace. One delegate got to the microphone with the cry, "Just because the Republicans have nominated an apostate Democrat, let us not for God's sake nominate an apostate Republican." Ickes, who would have liked the nomination himself, left the convention feeling that "if the President can retrieve this campaign after all the glaring blunders that he has made or been responsible for, then the god of elections is indeed on his side."

2

The danger that America would insistently stand aloof while all nations which shared its faith were destroyed remained. Roosevelt himself, as he first came to the Presidency, had placated those like Hearst who clung to the isolationist views which had kept America out of the League of Nations. Some felt that F.D.R.'s brusque assertion of economic nationalism to the London Economic Conference in 1933 struck a blow at international cooperation for order and peace. He had shown a will for international cooperation, however, in the Reciprocal Trade Agreements, aimed at tariff barriers, which Congress approved in June, 1934. But already in January of that year the notion that all "foreign wars" were promoted for private gain was mightily revived when the Senate set up a committee to investigate the munitions makers under the chairmanship of Senator Gerald P. Nye of North Dakota. A devil was sought; a devil was found. World War I was made a sort of case history proving that American entry into it had come as the result of a plot of the munitions manufacturers and the bankers who financed their trade. Many honest progressives, some in the tradition of opposition to American entry into the First World War, tied old distrust of Wall Street to new fears of war. They found a responsive audience.

Nye, a small-town newspaperman from Cooperstown, North Dakota, had first come to the Senate by a governor's appointment in 1925 when he was thirty-three. He was intense, honest, radical enough to try to embody Father Coughlin's not very clear views into legislation. He had been suggested as the candidate of the third party of the lunatic fringe in 1936. He was getting attention. Also, in his righteous pillorying of munitions makers—now "the merchants of death"—he had the aid of abler men. Such books as *One Hell of a Business* by H. C. Engelbrecht in 1934, and *Road to War* by Walter Millis in 1935, helped build the impression that the United States had been duped into "foreign war" before and might be again by those who would "jeopardize the peace of the world for the sake of private gain." Roosevelt himself unwittingly stiffened such indignation. Sweeping sentiment against the "merchants of death," as Engelbrecht called the armament magnates, and the "economic royalists" was aroused simultaneously. Few were impressed by the fact that in 1936 such an obvious target as the Bethlehem Steel Company was found guiltless of charges of taking outrageous profits on its World War I contracts. Fewer knew that when its old chief, Charlie Schwab, suspected even by Hoover of disrupting disarmament efforts, died in 1938 he was not swollen with war profits but insolvent instead.

The antiwar sentiment was fixed. It was made law by the Neutrality Acts of 1935–1937. Under it, as Allan Nevins and Henry Steele Commager wrote, Americans "disillusioned with the results of the last war, fearful of involvement in a new one, confident that any decision as to war or peace lay entirely in their own hands, . . . adopted a policy of peace at any price."

While Willkie was fighting his battle with TVA, the possible price was increasing rapidly. As the threat of war grew early in 1939, Roosevelt sent identical messages to Hitler and Mussolini asking them to assure the world that they would not "attack or invade the territory" of thirty-one nations, which he named. On April 28, Hitler scornfully replied in a speech before his relic of the Reichstag.

"Mr. Roosevelt! I fully understand that the vastness of your nation and the immense wealth of your country allow you to feel responsible for the history of the whole world and for the history of all nations. I, sir, am placed in a much more modest and smaller sphere. . . ." Then echoing American isolationist views he told the President to mind his own business.

"He asked for it," said Nye of Roosevelt.

Congress refused to modify the neutrality legislation under which the dictators could be sure that no intended victims could count on American help. Then, on July 18, Roosevelt with Secretary Hull called a conference in an upstairs study at the White House. Some who came were as stony-faced as the irreconcilables Wilson had asked to dine with him when he returned from Paris with the draft of the League early in 1919. One was the seventy-four-year-old but still powerful Borah, who had declined even to attend Wilson's dinner. Hull solemnly predicted that war would come by the end of the summer.

Borah shook his thinning mane. "There is not going to be any war in Europe. At least not soon. Germany is not ready for it. All this hysteria is manufactured and artificial."

"I wish Senator Borah," said Hull, flushing, "would come to my office and look over the cables coming in. I feel sure he would modify his views."

The Senator from Idaho disregarded Hull.

"I've listened to what the Secretary of State has to say about the information he has," he told Roosevelt, ". . . but I have my own sources of information in Europe that I regard as more reliable than those of the State Department, and I can say to you that there is not going to be any war."

Little more than a month later came the news that Russia and Germany had signed a ten-year nonaggression pact. Britain and France, which had disregarded Russia in some cynical wish that it might be destroyed, were now appalled at the Russian cynicism displayed in this abandonment of its pretense of a popular front against Fascism. Thousands of Americans, who had rejoiced in Russia's announced Popular Front policy against the Fascists, were dismayed. But Communists now joined German sympathizers in the Amerikadeutscher Volksbund in opposing any American effort to oppose Hitler's aggression. A week after the pact was signed, on September 1, 1939, German troops invaded Poland. Little time was required for its conquest between German and Russian divisions. Then followed the long, quiet winter in which Borah could take such satisfaction as he would from his phrase the "phoney war."

There was nothing "phoney" about the intensified struggle at home. Roosevelt had delivered a fireside chat in the flaming world on September 3: "When peace has been broken anywhere, the peace of all countries everywhere is in danger." But: "Let no man or woman thoughtlessly and falsely talk of America sending its armies to European fields. . . . I have said not once but many times that I have seen war and that I hate war."

In accordance with law he declared neutrality and imposed an embargo on all the belligerents. But he pressed, too, for a change in the neutrality law. He proposed the substitution for the embargo provisions of a requirement "that all purchases . . . be made in cash, and all cargoes . . . carried in the purchasers' own ships, at the purchasers' own risk." Stiff resistance rose to this "cash-and-carry" plan. The most dramatic resistance came in a radio speech, on September 15, by Colonel Charles A. Lindbergh. Some felt that he reflected Nazi racists' attitudes when he said, "This is not a question of banding together to defend the white race against foreign invasion." This was, he said, "a quarrel arising from the errors of the last war."

And who made the errors of the last war, he demanded. The "victors of that war."

In a following broadcast he said, "Our bond with Europe is a bond of race and not political ideology. . . . Racial strength is vital—politics a luxury. If the white race is ever seriously threatened, it may then be time for us to take our post for its protection."

Not only isolationists had their private-citizen spokesmen. On September 26, a committee to support the revision of the law was formed under the interminable name of the Non-Partisan Committee for Peace through the Revision of the Neutrality Law. Carefully chosen as its chairman was William Allen White, the old Republican from the central state of Kansas. Three years before he had been an original Landon man. No one could regard as a stooge of Roosevelt this editor who, in the 1936 campaign, had called F.D.R. "our old American smiler," a "slick old thimble rigger" whose logic was as "slick as goose grease and false as hell." Americans knew him as an editor of quips, courage and common sense. He had been at the Versailles Conference two decades before. He had shared Wilson's great vision of peace while saddened by what he regarded as his proud heart. Certainly no warmonger, active at seventy-one, he seemed the ideal choice to lead those who wanted aid for the embattled democracies.

Among the more ardent aides White found in the committee work was towering Robert E. Sherwood, the playwright, who had served in the Canadian Black Watch in the First World War. Twice a Pulitzer prize winner, as early as 1936 his play *Idiot's Delight* was a dramatic plea for world peace. He long remembered, as significant of feeling at the time the first White committee was formed, that the Kansas editor insisted that the group accept "no munitions-makers' money, no international bankers' money, no money from the steel interests." Such precautions were necessary at this time when the suspicions of isolationists erupted into slander. Father Coughlin was soon to write of the White committee: "Like thieves who operate under the cloak of night, there are in our midst those who operate beneath the cloak of protected auspices to steal our liberty, our peace and our autonomy. . . . Sneakingly, subversively and un-Americanly hiding behind a sanctimonious stuffed shirt named William Allen White, these men form the most dangerous fifth column that ever set foot upon neutral soil."

Such intemperate attacks probably helped the passage of Roosevelt's measure in November in the Senate by 55 to 24 and in the House by 243 to 172. It was hard to make traitors out of a group which included among many distinguished Republican and Democratic members President James B. Conant of Harvard; Henry R. Luce of *Time;* and Mrs. Dwight W. Morrow, Lindbergh's mother-in-law. Her daughter, Anne, was at the time writing in her book the argument that Germany was bound to win. The group's job was not completed with revision of the Neutrality Act. Inevitably it became, in 1940, the Committee to Defend America by Aiding the Allies.

The need for such a changed name and such continuing purpose had become desperately clear in the summer of 1940 when the Presidential contest began. Willkie had been nominated at a time when more than 300,000 Allied troops, caught at the end of Hitler's blasting drive, were escaping to England in an amazingly assorted, improvised armada of great ships and little ones. In that June, too, France fell. Hitler took its surrender in a ceremony of revenge in the Wood of the Eagle near Compiègne in the very same railway car in which bullet-shaped Matthias Erzberger had signed the armistice and, as it turned out, his own death warrant twenty-two years before. It was small wonder that in July the Democratic National Convention seemed uninspired. The shouts and cheers and band music of political conventions that summer were more than ever shrill, tinny and trivial compared to the great, sad, strong music from overseas. With Dunkirk just behind him, the round, jowled, sixty-five-year-old new Prime Minister of Great Britain, Churchill, began his magnificent campaign for survival. His words went to Englishmen and across the Atlantic, too:

We shall prove ourselves once again able to defend our island home, to ride out the storm of war, and to outlive the menace of tyranny, if necessary for years, if necessary alone. . . . Even though large tracts of Europe and many old and famous states have fallen or may fall into the grip of the Gestapo and all the odious apparatus of Nazi rule, we shall not flag or fail, we shall go on to the end, we shall fight in France, we shall fight on the seas and oceans, we shall fight with growing confidence and growing strength in the air, we shall defend our island, whatever the cost may be, we shall fight on the beaches, we shall fight on the landing grounds, we shall fight in the fields and in the streets, we shall fight in the hills; we shall never surrender, and even if, which I do not for a moment believe, this island or a large part of it were subjugated and starving, then our Empire beyond the seas, armed and guarded by the British fleet, would carry on the struggle, until, in God's good time, the New World, with all its power and might, steps forth to the rescue and liberation of the Old.

"In God's good time" seemed a more than ever indefinite term when catastrophe in Europe coincided with Presidential campaign in America. There were efforts to minimize the dangers which might come from political contention. White wrote: "In the summer of 1940, because I was chairman of the Committee to Defend America by Aiding the Allies, he (the President) talked in utmost confidence with me and let me talk in turn confidentially to Wendell Willkie, which I did and I hope with some effect. At least we kept the foreign issue out of the campaign as far as possible."

Excellent as was that purpose, the possibility was remote. In effect, it would have kept Willkie in his corner in his fight with his opponent whom he recognized as "the Champ." Yet as an honest man sharing views similar to those of the President, he tried. Willkie's hatred of Nazi-Fascist tyranny had come to him with his father's blood. Not even as a man seeking the Presidency did he mean to give even lip service to it. Without White's urging after confidential talks with Roosevelt, he was determined to say nothing that might stay American aid to Britain or in any way help Hitler's bloody hand. He backed the President's preparedness efforts requiring what seemed astronomical sums for the armed services and their air arms. Far from taking a demagogic advantage, he supported the first peacetime draft in American history which Roosevelt, dodging iso-lationist attacks, promised would send no boys "to take part in European wars."

On June 29, as the campaign was beginning, White conferred with the President on a plan to release some "overage" American de-stroyers to desperate Britain now standing alone against both Ger-many and Italy. Roosevelt asked White to talk to Willkie about it. It had been thought that legislation would be required and it was feared legislation would not be obtained. So the plan was devised to swap the destroyers for U. S. bases in British possessions in the Western Hemisphere. White talked to Willkie and sent word to Roosevelt that he was sure the Republican candidate would not attack the deal. When the exchange was announced on September 3, Willkie criticized the bypassing of Congress but publicly declared he favored this aid.

While such communications through White went on, Roosevelt practically ignored his opponent's existence. In his acceptance speech in Chicago the President solemnly spoke of his duties in the world emergency, adding, "I shall not have the time or the inclination to engage in a purely political debate." Willkie could take no such lofty position. In a flying campaign, making 560 speeches in fifty days, his voice was soon reduced to a rasping croak. Also immobi-lized by his own convictions on foreign policy, which involved so much hope and fear, he seemed to be whispering against the wind. On domestic issues he seemed so close to Roosevelt that Norman Thomas said, "He agreed with Roosevelt's entire program of social reforms—and said it was leading to disaster." He did seem in his liberalism only "the rich man's Roosevelt," as Ickes called him.

But if the President ignored him, other Democrats did not. In-deed, they undertook to make him seem the anti-aid isolationist can-didate which he had cooperatively shown himself not to be. Cried Henry Wallace, Roosevelt's new choice as Vice-Presidential candidate: "The Nazi support of Wendell Willkie is part of Adolf Hitler's plan to weaken and conquer the United States."

Such misrepresentation led to resentment. It helped those Republicans who urged him to strike at Roosevelt on the emotional issues rising from war in the world. But Willkie yielded to pulls and pressures only reluctantly. It was his duty to win the election; few men run for President who do not get the idea that on their election depends the safety of the Republic. The old guard professionals, as Sherwood wrote, begged him "to abandon this nonsense about a non-partisan foreign policy—to attack Roosevelt as a warmonger—to scare the American people with warnings that votes for Roosevelt meant wooden crosses for their sons and brothers and sweethearts." So, badgered and bruised, in late September, the boxed-in Republican candidate said in a half domestic, half foreign-war swipe at Roosevelt, "If his promise to keep our boys out of foreign wars is no better than his promise to balance the budget, they're already almost on the transports." The fat was in the fire. On October 30, he predicted that on the basis of Roosevelt's "past performance with pledges to the people, you may expect war by April, 1941, if he is elected."

Then the would-be-aloof Roosevelt, who in preoccupation with his great duties had suggested he would stay above the battle, was pushed to appeasement of those voters who wanted no aid to the Allies which involved the possible risk of war. Polls which showed the President leading by a safe margin in late September showed Willkie gaining sharply in October. Swiftly "the Champ" turned from the battle of Britain to the battle in America. He was at his swinging best in seriousness and satire. At a great rally in Madison Square Garden he rebuked Republicans for "playing politics with national defense." Then with a stroke of genius he brought rhythmic ridicule on conservative and isolationist Republicans. He chose for his dart Congressman Joseph Martin of Massachusetts, Bruce Barton, now a congressman who as advertising man in Coolidge days had written the life of Jesus as a master salesman, and Congressman Hamilton Fish of New York, from whose office it was later discovered German propagandists had operated. He rolled their names out in a scornful refrain, "Martin, Barton and Fish." His delighted audience chanted with him the catch phrase made of the euphonious combination of Republican names. In this speech, however, casting his net toward the fearful, he took credit for the very Neutrality Act which he had fought to repeal.

Evidently this bending to the winds of fear was not enough. Sherwood, whom Hopkins had brought to the President's aid as a ghost writer, described Roosevelt's unwillingness to take the political risks involved in his purpose to aid the free world. As his campaign train moved toward Boston, the deeply concerned playwright wrote, Democratic politicians were "becoming more and more jittery and attributing everything to the peace mania." Messages came from many campaign leaders demanding that "he provide absolute guarantee to the mothers of America that their sons would not fight." On the train even Sherwood, who was for all-out aid regardless of hazard, shared the political fear. Any danger of future embarrassment, he felt, was negligible as compared with the chance of losing the election.

"But how often do they expect me to say that?" Roosevelt demanded of the request that he reassure the mothers of America that their boys would not be sent to war. "I've repeated it a hundred times."

Sherwood spoke as the Boston speech was being finally shaped: "I know it, Mr. President, but they don't seem to have heard you the first time. Evidently you have got to say it again—and again—and again."

Those "agains" were put into his speech. They came out in the rising Roosevelt accent to serve him well in politics then but to plague him later. Sherwood, who invented them, said later that he burned inwardly whenever he thought of those words "again— and again—and again."

Possibly that promise that "your boys are not going to be sent into any foreign wars" was not necessary. Certainly Roosevelt understood then that events might not permit him to fulfill it if he was to fulfill his purpose to prevent Fascist victory in the world. It seemed necessary as transcribed Republican radio broadcasts, going far beyond anything Willkie said, blared: "When your boy is dying on some battlefield in Europe . . . and he's crying out, 'Mother! Mother!'—don't blame Franklin D. Roosevelt because he sent your boy to war—blame YOURSELF because YOU sent Franklin D. Roosevelt back to the White House!"

The race looked close as the campaign closed. Final high-level election eve Democratic speeches were made on a radio broadcast by Roosevelt, Hull, Carl Sandburg, Alexander Woollcott and Dorothy Thompson. Roosevelt, even before the campaign began, had sought for use this night a prayer for the nation which he remembered had been in a *Book of Common Prayer* in use when he was at Groton School. He read it:

"Bless our land with honourable industry, sound learning, and pure manners. Save us from violence, discord and confusion; from pride and arrogancy, and from every evil way. Defend our liberties, and fashion into one united people the multitudes brought hither out of many kindreds and tongues."

Such unity was much to pray for at that time. Roosevelt won no such sweep as in 1936. Yet he received 27,243,000 popular and 449 electoral votes while Willkie obtained 22,304,400 popular and 82 electoral votes. Even this year, however, his electoral margin was still greater than any other President had received in this century. But he had won it in an election in which both he and Willkie, in the pressures of politics, had thrown meat to the roaring lions of isolationism.

Now in the month following the election nothing was so clear as that less and not more neutrality was necessary if the dictators were to be stopped. Nazi planes were raining incendiary bombs on England, on two nights setting 1500 fires in London. "Cash-and-carry" could not save a Britain that was running out of cash. Out of their dollar resources of $6,500,000,000 at the beginning of the war the British had by the month of the American election spent $4,500,000,-000 in the United States. They stood alone under the bombs from the air and in the midst of submarines seeking to cut off their supply lines on the sea. Yet Roosevelt went off with only friends, including Harry Hopkins, on one of his beloved voyages on the cruiser *Tuscaloosa*. While supposedly fishing and relaxing Harry brought him a long letter which Churchill had written him shaped in the terms of "a partner in a common cause, not as a supplicant." Roosevelt responded, but Willkie, as much as any other man, made possible the response.

On December 17, the day after his return to Washington, the President talked to reporters like a country squire or a good suburbanite. He made a parable about a man whose house was on fire and a neighbor who lent his garden hose—without demanding payment for it—in order to put out the fire. Such simple language—indeed, oversimplification of the "lend-lease" program which meant lending not only the hose but the hydrant—seemed persuasive. It laid the ground for his fireside chat on December 29 when he explained his plan to the people. The British stood between the New World and Nazi aggression. They wanted materials, not men.

"We must," he said, "be the great arsenal of democracy."

Reaction was by no means universally favorable to the bill embodying the idea which was patriotically presented as House Bill 1776. To isolationists it was another step toward war. The Chicago *Tribune* said the lend-lease bill was one to "destroy the Republic." Senator Wheeler charged that the bill was a "triple-A foreign policy: it will plough under every fourth American boy." The America First Committee organized and financed opposition. And dramatically once again Colonel Lindbergh appeared. To great applause, he said the things which his fellow isolationists wished to hear. He was their hero. He had been presenting "inside facts" which he said he had learned while enjoying the hospitality of Nazi organizations of science and technology. These facts the Allies should recognize to avoid destruction. Now at a Congressional hearing on the bill he drew cheers from his admirers and fears from the bill's supporters that his testimony might delay action when time was running out for democracy.

A greater crowd pushed into the Senate Caucus Room on February 11 to hear Willkie as a witness supporting the bill. He came as a hero, too. He had not repined in defeat. Seeking to be useful, he had proposed that he visit London, then being bombed night after night. On the day before his third-term inauguration, Roosevelt, who approved Willkie's journey to battered Britain, welcomed him to the White House. On more counts than one it was an interesting occasion. In his oval office the President took pains to impress his visitor. He had more papers piled on his desk so that he might look very busy. Also in what seemed a spontaneous act, he wrote on a piece of his personal stationery a message for Willkie to take to Churchill. From memory he inscribed Longfellow's poem:

> *Sail on, O Ship of State!*
> *Sail on, O Union, strong and great!*
> *Humanity with all its fears,*
> *With all the hopes of future years,*
> *Is hanging breathless on thy fate!*

In less poetic fashion he suggested that Willkie in London see Hopkins, who had flown the Atlantic shortly before to observe the situation and assess the personality of Churchill for Roosevelt. Willkie showed no enthusiasm at this suggestion. Many at the time did not approve of the Hopkins trip. There were many who did not like the proximity to the President of this "left-wing Rasputin." His flight as Presidential emissary at this time recalled the European travels for Wilson of Colonel House, which some believed had turned out to be long steps toward war. Willkie disapproved apparently because he felt Hopkins might hurt rather than help any aid program.

Unintimidated by the piled desk and the President in poetic mood, he asked bluntly, "Why do you keep Hopkins so close to you? You surely must realize that people distrust him and they resent his influence."

Roosevelt did not resent the question. Speaking as in allusion to Harry's frail health, he replied, "I can understand that you wonder why I need that half man around me. But—someday you may well be sitting here where I am now as President of the United States. And when you are, you'll be looking at that door over there and knowing that practically everybody who walks through it wants something out of you. You'll learn what a lonely job this is, and you'll discover the need for somebody like Harry Hopkins who asks for nothing except to serve you."

Willkie himself then was facing lonely years. Already the Republican old guard, which had never liked him, was ready to class him with F.D.R. in the category of its hatreds. This flight to Britain itself was an evidence of his readiness to serve without the partisanship many opponents of Roosevelt demanded. Willkie set out on his self-chosen mission. Flight abroad then was no mere trans-Atlantic jaunt. Even in peacetime such travel was still the hazard which had made Lindbergh the hero. Under complicated wartime conditions it was an exhausting five-day trip to a dangerous destination where six months of blitz was increasing in intensity though the Battle of Britain seemed won. But the visit abroad added authority to what Willkie had to say at home. He spoke as a man who had seen the blows England had suffered. He had had three long private talks with Churchill.

In the packed caucus room his words on needed aid carried a sense of urgency. He urged openly more than Roosevelt had dared ask. He backed lend-lease. He proposed sending Britain all American bombers except those needed for training. He advocated a steady flow of more and more destroyers. He did not believe Britain would fall without our aid. Hitler would not make war on the United States while Britain stood. But if Britain should fall "we will be at war in a month" or at most "sixty days."

Now came questions. Senator Nye recalled the statement made by the witness as Republican candidate on October 30. He quoted Willkie's statement about Roosevelt then that "on the basis of his past performance with pledges to the people, you may expect war by April, 1941, if he is elected." Did Willkie believe that?

The husky man on the stand was not one to squirm. But he added another to his chain of cigarettes. Momentarily he parried. The pause lengthened, then he grinned. He shrugged.

"It was a bit of campaign oratory," he said.

A roar of laughter met his captivating candor. Nye and his like seemed swept aside in applause. If Willkie's lapses, like Roosevelt's, in the campaign had been on his conscience, it was cleansed. Isolationist righteousness was routed. Two days later the bill was favorably reported by the Senate Committee 15 to 8. Finally, despite all efforts to amend and delay by a vote of 60 to 31 in the Senate, 317 to 71 in the House, the bill was signed as law by the President. The garden hose was a river of rescue.

But as Willkie knew, when he spoke to Nye's questioning, to serve lend-lease he was selling himself down the river as a Republican politician with hopes for the future. White, while recognizing that his answer was indiscreet, wrote that he thought "one of the most courageous things any man ever said in public life was Willkie's 'campaign oratory' statement." It was characteristic of the man that his courage was expressed in humor, not solemnity. Certainly he understood as he spoke and grinned that he was arousing enmity as well as laughter and applause.

Churchill called the lend-lease victory "the Third Climacteric" of the Second World War. The first two were the fall of France and the Battle of Britain. The fourth came quickly, little more than three months after the flow of lend-lease began. On June 22, Hitler wheeled to the East and invaded Russia.

Much to the outrage of Republicans, Roosevelt designated Hopkins to "advise and assist" him on lend-lease. It seemed ridiculous to put a left-wing social worker on such a job even if he did not carry the title of administrator. Actually, as Sherwood wrote, his method of attack on the manifold problems at hand was essentially that of the New Deal days.

"Now, instead of breadlines, droughts, floods, or hurricanes, he was confronting the greatest disaster that had ever befallen the human race," Sherwood said. ". . . It was at this time that Secretary Stimson noted in his diary his thought that it is 'a Godsend that Harry Hopkins is at the White House.'"

On May 10, 1940, the day of the attack on the Low Countries, Hopkins, feeling miserable, had come to the White House for dinner. Roosevelt persuaded him to spend the night. Now he had lived there ever since. It was a joke among the staff that his long stay gave George S. Kaufman and Moss Hart the idea for their farce, *The Man Who Came to Dinner* and stayed interminably on. Hopkins was at Roosevelt's hand and at work, driving for results in the awkward production setup Roosevelt had arranged in sprawling new defense agencies. He pushed through bottlenecks. He would be ready, a man maintaining life with medicines, to fly again across the world to measure Joseph Stalin, Russian power, and help meet Russian needs. Loaded with war effort even before American entry, he was impatience personified—above all perhaps with those who wanted business-as-usual when Hopkins felt that the problem had changed from relief and reform to war for survival. One day the observant Sherwood found him at a moment of extreme irritability. One of his old WPA associates had asked him to influence the President about some matter.

"I'm getting sick and tired of having to listen to complaints from those goddam New Dealers!" he said.

Even those Republicans who thought that Wendell Willkie was too liberal would have been shocked by such a reaction from Hopkins. As a social worker in power he had seemed like a prodigal skeleton scattering taxes to the voting poor. Alteration appeared as striking in the anti-New Deal Willkie, now backing Roosevelt. Only death would save him from rejection by his party. Despite his robust appearance he was destined to die before Hopkins. But in their service of country both were as strong as the dams of TVA which held back the torrents for an ordered valley and would provide power to marshal the mysteries of the atom about which Professor Einstein had written the President on August 2, 1939—a month before Hitler threw the world into war.

# XX

## HURRICANE HOUSE

I

LIKE troopers on a one-night-stand tour, the three writers came, on June 22, 1941, to a Fight for Freedom rally at the Golden Gate Ballroom in Harlem. The ballroom had sounded with the jazz which had come saxophoning from the South. Amid the dark warrens of the slum, it was one place of shining floors. The ghetto had spread with the coming of more and more black folk, many of whom had been pushed from the land by the very farm programs designed to end farm poverty. Only a relatively few cared to listen to the well-worded warnings of foreign dangers brought by Robert E. Sherwood, Herbert Agar and Dorothy Parker. Harlem's concerns were at hand. Still many were ready to lead its people. The Fight for Freedom organization, Sherwood wrote, was as strongly interventionist as its antithesis, America First, was violently isolationist. Communists, more militant than either, pitched their appeal to poverty and for peace.

On their way into the ballroom, the three writers on a mission pushed through a picket line obviously organized by the Communists, who had put aside all their placating gestures of a popular Front against Fascism when Germany and Russia had signed their pact of amity two years before. White and black pickets now carried banners denouncing the Fight for Freedom people as the warmongering tools of British and Wall Street imperialism. They distributed pamphlets calling for an early march of fifty thousand people on Washington to demand equality for Negroes and peace for America.

Sherwood, Agar and Parker were odd warmongers. All were

products of the fine, fevered disillusionment of the twenties. Tall
Sherwood then had been editor of a humorous magazine. Though
months before he had brought his concern for the Allies into his
writing and action, his range as playwright had been from romantic
comedies about war to dramatic diatribes against dictators in his
*Idiot's Delight* and *There Shall Be No Night*. Agar, who had
begun as a rather elegant poet, was now editor of the Louisville
*Courier-Journal*, though he was often absent from Kentucky concerns in the campaign to aid the Allies. Dorothy Parker was no
longer the caustically cynical poet making lyrical lament about lovers
who sent her roses, not limousines. Now in a sense she had shaped
in blurted prose the epitaph of the earlier, lively literary years. Just
six months before this rally in Harlem, she had looked at the body
of Scott Fitzgerald laid out in a second-class undertaking parlor in
Hollywood. She repeated a line from his *Gatsby*. Quietly by his
coffin she said, "The poor son-of-a-bitch." The era of wonderful
nonsense was over. Comedy seemed about to be succeeded by catastrophe.

The rally lasted an hour and a half in a sweltering room innocent
then, of course, of air conditioning. The speaker-writers came out
into the only less stifling street—and to startling change there. The
picket lines had disappeared. The pamphlets had been thrown into
the gutters. In the brief interval word had come that Hitler in
swift turn had invaded the Soviet Union. By lightning transmission
word had also come to shift the Communist party line. Isolationist
pickets had suddenly become for the first time in two years almost
over-ardent interventionists. The *Daily Worker* was preparing its
praise of Roosevelt, who the year before had been the devil. And,
said Sherwood, the monster march on already crowded Washington
had been canceled. Certainly three days later, not impelled by sudden love of Communists, but perhaps appalled by the prospect of
something like earlier bonus armies in blackface, Roosevelt by executive order set up a Fair Employment Practices Committee assuring
Negroes against job discrimination in the complex defense organization.

This order was only an item from an apparently confused capital
in a clamorous year. It was to seem to many, who attached their
hates and hopes to it, only more of the wordy and generally unin-
telligible governmental jargon soon to be christened "gobbledygook" by militant Maury Maverick of Texas. The voice of America

seemed no more clear. Aging journalist Mark Sullivan, who had made himself a chronicler of the period, described the confusion. Much of the nation, he wrote, was suffering from "split personality— mass schizophrenia" in the conflicting convictions that Hitler's defeat had become a matter of life and death for America, but that under no circumstances should the United States go to war. Not only was the noise of debate loud in the land; also, confusion was on wheels. People were moving everywhere in Defense, which seemed to many most important as the first real release from Depression.

Production lines lengthened. In pine forests where cantonments rose, the sound of hammer and saw came from workers, some of them innocent of carpentry before. Okies and Arkies found goals other than California in the mounting production drive. Facilities were overwhelmed beside camps in the Carolinas, shipyards in Maine, aircraft plants in California, everywhere. Towns spread where there had been only fields before. About them houseless but well-heeled workers slept in their cars, cooked in cans beside them. With cash in hand, some of them overwhelmed restaurants, bars. A typical scene was a once generally half-empty, cocktail lounge in a small-town Louisiana hotel. Now nightly it was packed to the doors with construction workers. Cute, costumed waitresses, who had once had time for light chitchat with leisurely drinkers, wearily brought the booze without blandishments on a pay-as-you-get-it basis to men whose eyes indicated that they regarded the waitresses in swift passage as items definitely in short supply in the defense effort.

Other changes crowded the time. Though not welcome in the bar, a Negro down the street (possibly aided by FEPC) received wages unlike any he had ever seen before. He cried in astonishment, "Thank God for Hitler!" The Führer, indeed, had transformed America even if at the moment he only seemed in brutality to have thrust a golden cane into an anthill—or a hornet's nest! The old economic order, not yet quite regreased, rattled at an accelerated pace. Social problems grew as plants rose. A variety of agents from Washington came to the swarming boom towns of Defense. A local official snarled, "We have coordinators, cooperators and cohabitators and we don't know which does the most harm." Still, as a poet put it at the time, "Paul Bunyan is back!" He was working miracles even if he sometimes seemed a quarrelsome giant.

The biggest boom town, of course, was Washington. Into it had poured and was pouring still a greater, more varied swarm than had confronted Depression crisis eight years before. Its more elegant bars were filled, too. In them old New Dealers rubbed shoulders with new dollar-a-year men with whom at the time they were also often knocking heads. In the big planning and spending for production, Roosevelt, as many had felt he had done in shaping the original New Deal eight years before, seemed to make himself the uncertain commander of men with conflicting ideas. Early he turned to the General Motors of his old adversaries, the Du Ponts, and brought that company's president and production genius, the big Dane, William S. Knudsen, to town. But he set beside him with equal powers the Lithuanian-born labor leader, Sidney Hillman. Knudsen brought in so many Republicans as dollar-a-year aides that Roosevelt in mock surprise told him that he must have made a mistake: One among the twenty on a list was a Democrat. Grinning, Knudsen reassured him, Yes, but the Democrat had voted for Willkie.

Other New Dealers were less easily placated or amused than their boss. Rex Tugwell, of the original "brain trust," spoke skeptically of a new "business brains trust," members of which Roosevelt not long before had characterized as "economic royalists." Tugwell sneered at the suggestion that now "practical men" were close to power instead of "theorists." Certainly the businessman was rising from his fall in the crash. Still, many of them, though rehabilitated in popular regard, expressed dismay in the maze of bureaucracy. Others felt they were less perplexed than they pretended. Some pre-Defense officials felt that the big men of the big companies were doing entirely too well. Bigness certainly seemed no bugaboo, as contracts flowed to the biggest companies. Thurman Arnold, who had been brought in as trust buster, sensed a moderation in the administration's attitude toward monopoly.

Businessmen, like colored folks, could expect increasing attention. Yet a *Fortune* poll in the midst of the defense effort found that 75 per cent of the business leaders interviewed felt that the President was using the emergency as a means of "pushing still further the more radical social and economic aims of the New Deal." Some New Dealers felt that many new arrivals, seeking contracts and granting contracts, were still as concerned for private profits as for military power. Some certainly were fearful that the explosive expansion of facilities might, after the need passed, result in the remembered procession from boom to bust. And some of Knudsen's men felt that when cigar-chomping Leon Henderson, old-time New Deal economist now dealing with price control and civilian supply, proposed a 50 per cent cutback in automobile production, he was talking about something that was none of his business. A cynic pointed out that the telephone number of the chief war production agency was Republic 5050. Some feared that the republic might get an even smaller break.

There were patriots on all sides of the contentions. Also, as Baruch's biographer said, the town filled with the "self-appointed purveyors of advice." Many rooms in such hotels as the Carlton and the Mayflower were hoarded by corporations for both their executives who had gone into government service and those seeking contracts in the defense flood. Old Georgetown houses and apartments on obscure streets bulged with New Dealers determined to maintain their places, prestige and programs beside the now more glamorous business newcomers called to office and arms. The Battle of Washington was begun. As in the first days of the New Deal, offices were found in old buildings; new, drab "temporaries" rose on Constitution Avenue. In them all were "go slowers," who argued still that actual war might be avoided, and "all outers," eager to go headlong in readiness for it.

Beside the workers in camps and the capital, the real combatants seemed the bristlingly arrayed forces of Fight for Freedom and America First. More persons as ardent as Sherwood, Agar and Parker were ranging the land. The Martins, Bartons and Fishes in the House and Wheeler, Nye and others in the Senate opposed any element of intervention. Roosevelt in the White House, though committed to aid, recognized, as he felt some around him failed to do, the necessity for "realism" in the politics of Defense. He was, as Sherwood said, "haunted" by the memory of the mistakes and failures of Woodrow Wilson who let himself and his goals be damaged in debate.

That earlier President's portrait hung above the mantle in the Cabinet Room where, at the long oval table, many of Roosevelt's speeches in his efforts to lead and unify the country were shaped this year. While his determination on aid for the democracies never lagged, as the country was torn, so was he. Under the portrait of Wilson, who had been pulled from his New Freedom purposes at home, Roosevelt shaped in advance of American entry into war a sort of proposal for a New Deal for the world. His Four Freedoms, listed in a message to Congress but directed over the shoulders of the senators and representatives to the world, contained the familiar liberties of expression and religion. But he added startling, perhaps starry-eyed, proposals for freedom from want and fear. The earlier President in his Fourteen Points, effective as propaganda in war and made the basis for charges of betrayals in the peace, had set up a code of conduct for nations even in victory. The Four Freedoms were promises to help people—and not only for people like unhappy Negroes in America but people "everywhere in the world."

F.D.R. took his Freedoms with him when in August almost gaily he wrote his mother, now not only old but also seriously ailing, that he was off on a "cruise away from all newspapermen & photographers." He sailed out of New London on the small Navy yacht the *Potomac*, which earlier had seemed to landlubber Ickes a very small ship for traveling in troubled waters. At sea he transferred to the U.S.S. *Augusta*. What had appeared to be only one of his beloved voyages of relaxation took him, on August 10, to his meeting with Churchill on H.M.S. *Prince of Wales* in the Newfoundland Bight. There, in a meeting of ceremony and comradeship, the two statesmen and their commanders considered the problems of the Grand Alliance, now containing embattled Russia. They discussed the problems of the Pacific and Japan. And along with more elaborate expression of war aims, they embodied in the dramatic but wholly unofficial Atlantic Charter the two great new freedoms from want and fear—for people "everywhere in the world."

Even the pretension to such promises seemed presumptuous then. At one point in their talks Churchill told Roosevelt that there were 150,000 men on guard at Britain's vital air bases armed only with "pikes, maces and grenades." Roosevelt promised rifles. But on August 12, the last day of their conference, word came that Roosevelt could count only precariously on being armed for strength in the United States.

Not only was the roar of the isolationists still mounting. Now America's reluctance to sacrifice in aid was demonstrated to the nation's friends and its enemies, too. Young men drafted into the Army for a year's service saw civilians drawing big wages. They were disgusted with a training which still depended often upon broomsticks instead of rifles, on trucks masquerading as tanks. They listened to the isolationist assurances: Japan seemed slowed down in China. Germany had run into more trouble than it expected in Russia.

The initials O.H.I.O. began to appear on the walls of training camps. They did not refer to the State from which Harding had come but cryptically proclaimed that if drafted men were not released after their year of service called for by law ended, they meant in desertion to go "Over the Hill in October." (This was a long time before the proud scrawl in the world, "Kilroy was here." Some who sympathized with grumbling draftees then also were those most sure that the New Deal had coddled the country into softness.) Beyond the initials, letters poured in on Congress protesting the extension of service beyond which the boys had been called. The prospect loomed of camps deserted as they were completed, of an army disintegrated before it was trained.

Roosevelt had recognized the fight the proposal for extended service would bring. He had hesitated to risk it. He made it. And on August 12, on the perilous margin of a single vote in the House, the extension was approved. Isolationists hailed the close vote as a victory. Cried Senator Wheeler, "This vote indicates clearly that the Administration could not get a resolution through the Congress for a declaration of war. . . . It is also notice that the Congress does not take seriously the cry of the Administration that the so-called emergency is greater now than it was a year ago." A month later, on September 11, at an America First rally in Des Moines, Lindbergh seemed almost to take the straight Nazi line. The emergency, he suggested, did not exist or was only made by that man in the White House. Then he added that "the three most important groups who have been pressing this country toward war are the British, the Jewish and the Roosevelt Administration." Warmongering Jews, he said, were "a danger to the country" chiefly because of their "large ownership and influence in our motion pictures, our press, our radio and our government."

Even such an isolationist as Hearst thought that went too far. But with the aid of Wheeler, Nye, "Martin, Barton and Fish," the Chicago *Tribune*, America First, some German Bundists and many patriotic but misguided Americans, the Allies were rebuffed and the Axis reassured. When that month the destroyer U.S.S. *Greer*, aiding in guarding British supply lines, was attacked, the country was not aroused, though Roosevelt in a broadcast about it used the words, "When you see a rattlesnake poised to strike, you do not wait before you crush him."

It seemed only a ripe and a richer October to many in America. More had more, and hoped to keep it without sacrifices. In Congress there was bitter opposition to the President's proposal that the old troublesome neutrality law be amended to permit the arming of merchant ships and to give them the right to carry trade into the war zones. During the debate the Germans were driving hard against Moscow. Also in October, the so-called "moderate" Japanese government of Prince Fumimaro Konoye was replaced by the openly militaristic cabinet of General Hideki Tojo. Back of Tojo, as foreign minister, was Yosuke Matsuoka, who in the first hundred days of the New Deal in 1933 had been in America complaining about the presence of the U. S. Fleet at Pearl Harbor. Now he had made a firm pact with the Axis and had told Hitler that "sooner or later a war with the United States would be unavoidable . . . in his opinion this conflict would happen sooner rather than later."

From the State Department, concerned with problems in the Pacific and so many other areas, Dean Acheson went on October 7 on a sad errand unrelated to explosion in the world. In the Washington swarm he was neither old New Dealer nor new plutocrat in bureaucracy. More than twenty years before he had come to Washington as ex-ensign and brilliant Harvard Law student to be one in a selected succession of law secretaries to Justice Brandeis. He had been Assistant Secretary of the Treasury in the first days of the New Deal but had left—apparently just before he was fired—in an early disagreement over Roosevelt's gold program. Now he was Assistant Secretary of State, having left an opulent law practice to aid in the mounting problems in the overornamented department building where Secretary Hull was already engaged in apparently interminable conversations with Japanese diplomats.

Acheson's errand now was one of farewell and remembrance. The occasion was little noticed then by people concerned with an all-too-ominous future. Yet, almost as much as explosive events, it may have marked the end of an era. The impeccable Acheson, under the red and gold of shade trees above all downtown contentions, moved up the hill from Connecticut Avenue to California Street where the great old Brandeis lay in his long coffin. The tall Assistant Secretary knew the quiet neighborhood well. At the end of World War I he had tramped the area with such friends as

Sinclair Lewis, Stuart Chase, Elinor Wylie, all looking, in their various ways as novelist, statistician, poet, at the America around them and before them. Promise had seemed all about them. That had been soon after Justice Brandeis at the war's end had hailed Wilson in triumph with a quotation from Euripides containing the phrase, "to stand from fear set free."

Even the possibility of such a phrase seemed far behind now. In the world the great old Jew had loved so much, a charnel house, not a homeland, loomed for his people. The Bigness which he had feared seemed suddenly the defense of freedom. In the tumultuous expansion of business and industry in Defense no one bothered to ridicule his philosophy as a faith that "America could once more become a nation of small proprietors, of corner grocers and smithies under spreading chestnut trees." In the Defense effort Bigness exemplified America's patriotic muscle. Most contracts were going to the largest companies with a specially big share for General Motors. There was no more furiously frustrated man in the teeming town than Maury Maverick who, as chief of the Smaller War Plants Corporation, substituted crystal-clear Texas profanity for gobbledygook.

Brandeis had died at a time when not even he could have spoken in clarity of change. The capital was serene only about his bier. The funeral in the small apartment on the hilltop was private. Only a little company—of old friends, of comrades on the Court and in great causes, of the successful, middle-aging men who had once been in their turn his law clerks—gathered by invitation. A violin quartet played the music of Beethoven which Brandeis had much loved. Then, in the muted room by the quieted violins, Acheson spoke of the great man—and perhaps out of his own dark mood.

"We are the fortunate ones," he said. But he did not stress good fortune. He looked back that October day upon "these years of retreat from reason," a "time of moral and intellectual anarchy and frustration." Sadly he described the era from armistice, 1918, to the all-too-possible prospect of Armageddon. He did not need to know as he spoke that for Americans that period would be finally punctuated with disaster exactly two months after his eulogy—almost to the hour.

"We are the generation," he told the company in the silent room, "which has lived during and between two wars."

And he named their time: "We have lived in the desert years of the human spirit."

Even in an ominous autumn "the desert years" seemed an unlikely label for the period. Such tags were always apt to be unlikely. The world had not stood after 1918 "from fear set free" but in the midst of angers loosed. The return of "normalcy" had meant the advent of unprecedented scandal. Just as old William Jennings Bryan had been forgotten (even by people who now, as he once had done, opposed entrance into a foreign war), so few recalled that he had hailed as a millennial time the arrival of woman suffrage and prohibition: the "passover from the old era to the new." Perversely that new era had been quickly called the Jazz Age though it was also marked by the surge of puritan angers. The years had contained the "lost generation" and coincidentally businessmen apparently fit to be put into a theology by Bruce Barton. The same years included boom and bust, the "Happy Warrior" and the "Forgotten Man," the Okies and the economic royalists. Maybe once—no longer—it had been the time of an America which had nothing to fear but fear itself. There had come the age of anxiety—the "locust years." There were many now prepared to say that while the goose-stepping ants of the Axis had laid in their store of arms, America had made the period a grasshopper's winter of dancing materialism and profligate self-pity. Now it seemed only certain, though some denied that still, that the years between the wars led Americans to a rendezvous with destiny.

Acheson hurried back to his duties in the now always late-lit State Department. Across the narrow, tree-lined street, lights were burning in the White House offices, too. "That man" there would never have agreed that only "desert years" lay between the wars. Yet this October seemed a sort of desert time in the American spirit. The rendezvous had come but the response was less than needed. Roosevelt himself in a divided country seemed more the captive than the commander.

He undertook to assert leadership now as before. Most difficult for him, he took steps to untangle the complicated and often contentious arrangement of new defense agencies which some believed he had almost designed to keep more decisions in his hands than he could wisely make. Despite a siege of sinus he was in good voice. In his rhetoric he was not waiting for the rattlesnake to strike. Boldly he declared that "we shall do everything in our power to crush Hitler and his Nazi forces." Presuming a unity which he knew was lacking in the country and the Congress, he announced, "We Americans have cleared our decks and taken our battle stations."

On November 27, he received a report of a committee of outstanding physicists of the National Academy of Science that a sufficient mass of U-235 could produce a bomb of unprecedented power. Concerned scientists were told on December 6 that Roosevelt approved an "all-out" effort toward the possible atomic bomb with funds assigned for use at the President's discretion. On the same day Roosevelt declared, "The American people have made an unlimited commitment that there shall be a free world."

In a divided country he felt far from free. Sometimes as he edged toward great and greater aid to the Allies and tightened the tether by which he was "babying" Japan along to keep it at peace, he murmured half in amusement about the possibility of his impeachment. There were some who would have liked to have seen that done. Earlier in the year his long-time personal secretary, "Missy" LeHand, had said that his persistent cold was "a case of sheer exasperation." Then "Missy" had suffered a stroke. His mother, the great old dowager Sarah, died on September 7, soon after he returned from the Atlantic Charter meeting.

Behind the essential façade of his leadership he sought escape. He turned often from oppressive news to his stamp albums. He was much pleased with a gift to him of a cigar which had belonged to Garibaldi. His irritation ran to rebuke of the White House housekeeper who provided a notoriously poor table: "Feathered game should never be plucked until just before it is eaten. Taking off the feathers dries up the meat." He began taking time to dictate anecdotes and amusing recollections from happier years: experiences in the Wilson days, boyhood memories like that of the sinking of his father's yacht, the first *Half Moon*. Sherwood wrote: "In the midst of the uncertainty and hair-trigger danger of the months before Pearl Harbor, Roosevelt expended a great deal of time on a project for a fishing retreat for Hopkins and himself." The records about his concern for this plan for a place on a storm-swept Florida key relate to mid-November, 1941. The President took time to draw a plan for a house which he believed would be hurricane-proof.

Then Hopkins, who had come to the Atlantic Charter meeting after a strenuous flight to Russia, was again ill. Early in November he had gone to the Naval Hospital in Washington. There he remained for four weeks, though tending to business by phone and occasionally coming to the White House for dinner. Perhaps it was to divert Hopkins as well as himself that Roosevelt spent "a great deal of time" this month on this design for relaxation and escape. He sent a memo to Hopkins about it on November 15, ten days after the military leaders in Japan won the Emperor's consent to war if negotiations with the United States were unsuccessful.

"Perhaps," the President wrote, "if we can go to Warm Springs within a week, you could run down . . . for a week and look it over."

There was not going to be any such free week before hurricane in the world.

2

The sinister timing or the perfect execution of the Japanese brought the planes with the symbol of the sun on their wings over Hawaii while sailors and soldiers still slept, and the same timing meant that the news in America cut the day into halves. The afternoon was war, but the morning lay in the years between wars. The news of disaster came at 1:50 P.M. Eastern Standard Time. The whole portrait of a period about to be ended lay between cockcrow and catastrophe.

It was a beautiful morning in America. Along the Atlantic seaboard the sunshine was warm for December; the winds only began to whip gray clouds about the sun in the afternoon. It was Ham Fish's birthday and Senator Nye was confidently on his way to address an isolationist mass meeting in Pittsburgh. To loud applause in New York, Myron Taylor, the President's personal representative at the Vatican, praised the peace efforts of the Pope and the President at the annual communion breakfast of the Notre Dame Club of New York. But at the Riverside Church, Dr. Harry Emerson Fosdick saw a sickness in democracy.

"The world splits up," he said, "dictatorships naturally emphasizing loyalty but not liberty, democracy naturally emphasizing liberty but not loyalty. Somehow we must get these two indispensable qualities together."

They were not together at twelve o'clock when Fosdick's congregation poured out into the sun. And not everybody had been to church even to contemplate the fission. In New York and Raleigh, North Carolina and Washington, D.C., many people slept late in the American celebration of Sunday morning. Some who on December 6 had enjoyed a gay American Saturday night slept still later. And some others, like Donald M. Nelson, who was soon to have the responsibility for American production for war, got up early out of habit rather than apprehension. A man who had devoted most of the period behind him to providing low-priced plenty to his countrymen as official of the big mail-order house of Sears, Roebuck and Company, he seemed the antithesis of austerity. Kenneth S. Davis, historian of war to come, felt that in appearance Nelson might have been a model for Sinclair Lewis' Middle Western booster and businessman George F. Babbitt. Nelson was much more than that but this morning as merchandiser as well as one who had come to Washington in the first emergency of May, 1940, he gave long, lazy reading to the Sunday papers.

There were the big headlines which afterward were warnings in the record. But there were also big advertisements of new automobiles. The Matson Line was advertising vacation cruises to Hawaii. The upsweep hairdo was receiving early attention. Traffic accidents in the country were already up 16 per cent above "the lamentable record" of 1940. John L. Lewis was about to win a decision in his contention that miners in the captive coal mines of the steel companies must join his United Mine Workers of America. A New York gambling house had been raided in which "prosperous businessmen" were robbed of many thousands of dollars with dice which had only twos, fours and sixes on them. An editor wondered how such businessmen got "prosperous" or stayed so. Department stores advertised white shirts at two dollars (regular two-fifty and three-dollar values—and plenty of them). The Tecla Pearl people were preparing an annual bargain sale at which five-thousand-dollar necklaces might be snapped up for $2500. Americans were urged to say, "Merry Christmas with fragrant whimsies by Coty." People were reading The Keys to the Kingdom, by A. J. Cronin, and—in a sort of undeciphered code of coincidence—The Sun Is My Undoing, by Marguerite Steen and Reveille in Washington, by Margaret Leach.

Like a lot of Americans that morning, Donald Nelson was in no great hurry. He dressed slowly to go to a Sunday luncheon at the

Headwaters Farm of old Harold Ickes and his pretty, young, red-headed wife at Olney, Maryland. He drove out in the sun to find good company and good talk. Behind the fat columns of the Ickes' country house, surrounded by the fat Ickes pigs and cattle and the hundreds of cackling Ickes hens, Ickes and Nelson, Supreme Court Justice Hugo Black and Senator Tom Connally, chairman of the Senate Foreign Relations Committee, talked about the Japs with whom old Secretary of State Cordell Hull was still talking in special conversations that had begun twenty days before. Ickes, back in June, had proposed cutting off shipments of oil to Japan. But then the President felt that it was "terribly important for the control of the Atlantic for us to help keep peace in the Pacific. I simply have not got enough Navy to go round—and every little episode in the Pacific means fewer ships in the Atlantic." Now at Olney the representatives of the Court and the Cabinet and the Congress agreed (Nelson remembered) that there would be no war with Japan—not, at least, in the foreseeable future. While they talked there was already other noises in the Pacific, but at Headwaters Farm they could only hear the Ickes hens.

It was very quiet at the White House that morning. In the middle of Washington it was still an unguarded mansion with no sign of soldiers about it. Mrs. Charles Hamlin, of Albany, an old Hudson Valley friend of the Roosevelts, woke up in the Lincoln bed. Across the north lawn she could see the warm sun casting the shadow of the portico toward the fountain. She got up quietly, as a familiar and considerate guest. Across the long corridor the doors to the President's bedroom and to his oval study were shut. She went off alone across Lafayette Square to old St. John's Church, whose bells ring into the White House on such quiet mornings. She found her old seat in the church. She met "the Conrad girls and Susie Stone from Milton." A gentleman named Russell Sard, of Albany, walked back with her to the portico of the White House through unguarded gates. And there she met a long line of people coming upstairs from the East Entrance for luncheon.

There were thirty people for lunch and they lined up alphabetically in the Blue Parlor. The President did not join them, but that seemed natural enough to those guests familiar with his habits. There were no guests who would have attracted him from his Sunday rest and seclusion. It was, indeed, a casual sort of company, some Roosevelt relatives and friends, a couple of New Dealers, some minor government officials, some Army Medical Corps people, some of the sort of people who for one reason or another (and there were always many reasons) had to be invited to the White House.

"It looks as if Mrs. Roosevelt's secretary has been cleaning up around the edges of the list," said one guest who had been there often. He was Lowell Mellett, Presidential assistant who had set up a preliminary office of defense information in a temporary building erected in a one-time small park on Pennsylvania Avenue. Already the press was calling it "Mellet's Madhouse."

The luncheon company went into the dining room at about 1:30. Mrs. Roosevelt told them good-bye at about 2:45, though, at her request, one guest stayed a little later to talk to her about one of the many matters with which she was concerned. Beyond the big entrance hall the sun was still very bright outside, but there was already a little sharpness in the wind. About the same time the party at the Ickes farm broke up, too. Nelson, driving along slowly on the road back to Washington, turned on his radio to hear the regular Sunday afternoon concert of the New York Philharmonic-Symphony Orchestra. It began soon after three in Carnegie Hall and on the Maryland highway. Also listening in Norris, Tennessee, David Lilienthal, content because rains had fallen the day before to fill the dams and assure full power and production, remembered that the orchestra played a Brahms concerto. As Nelson drove along, a voice suddenly interrupted, saying, "More news from Pearl Harbor." Even earlier, one of the White House luncheon guests had gotten across Lafayette Square to the Cosmos Club to find a body of its gray-haired habitués clustered about a radio eagerly hoping for amplification of the news which the President had announced at 2:25 P.M. from his oval study—while the luncheon party was still in progress and in ignorance in the dining room below.

In the serious business of history the day began perhaps when Cordell Hull came at 10:15 into the empty, echoing halls of the old baroque State Department. Hull had got to be seventy years old that fall on the very day on which Hitler, in an order of the day to German forces in Russia, announced the beginning of the last great decisive battle of the year. The day before that, Charles Lindbergh, in Fort Wayne, had suggested that a warmongering administration might not permit Congressional elections in 1942: Roosevelt's progress toward war was a march to tyranny. And on Thursday, December 4, the Chicago *Tribune*, undertaking to prove that the President was planning to involve the country in war, published the top-secret plans, like those all war offices regularly produce, of a hypothetical invasion of Germany by five million Americans in 1943. Ickes and others in the Cabinet wanted indictment for treason. Certainly it emphasized that lack of loyalty in democracy about which Dr. Fosdick lamented.

In such an atmosphere of division at home and danger abroad Hull, since November 17, had been talking with increasing fears and suspicions to the special Japanese "peace" envoy and his reluctant companion, the regular ambassador. Subsequent disclosures indicate that a curious game was being played on both sides. Clearly the special envoy was sent to lull and delay while militarists behind him prepared their movements. But Hull, in effect and in part, was able to look into his opponent's hands. Army and Navy cipher experts had been able to break the most secret of the Japanese communication codes. The Secretary came to conversations knowing in advance what the Japanese were going to say. But he and others in the American government were perhaps deluded by their advantage. They did not know what the Japanese warily did not put into any code. It was increasingly clear that the Japanese, moving impressive forces into Indochina, were ready to strike. Yet if they struck, as seemed probable, at Singapore, Siam—at British or Dutch possessions—America's course could still be confused in the raging home debate about "foreign" war. As late as November 27, when final "war warnings" were dispatched to military and naval commanders at Hawaii and other posts in the Pacific, it was stated that if war became inevitable "the United States desires that Japan commit the first overt act."

That was emphasized on the night of December 6 when a young naval commander brought to Roosevelt the first thirteen parts of an intercept of the message meant to be delivered by the Japanese emissaries to Hull the following day. Roosevelt read the text brusquely rejecting American proposals for peace in the Pacific. He handed it to Hopkins.

"This means war," Roosevelt said.

As a junior officer to be trusted but not consulted the young commander stood listening, surprised at the President's conviction. Senior officers who had seen the decoded message had reached no such conclusion. The President and Hopkins discussed the deployment of Japanese forces. Indochina, about which the President had written in a final peace appeal just dispatched to Emperor Hirohito, was particularly mentioned. There was no mention of time.

Then Hopkins said, "It's too bad we can't strike first and prevent a surprise."

The young officer quoted later the answer of the President.

"No, we can't do that. We are a democracy of peaceful people. We have a good record. We must stand on it."

Evidently, despite the exchange, the two men had no sense of imminent danger to the United States. When the startling news came next day they, as Hopkins said, "were talking about things far removed from war," conceivably of the Florida hideaway and the hurricane-proof house Roosevelt had designed.

Hull at the State Department then was awaiting the last, most belligerent section of the intercepted message, the first thirteen sections of which the President had seen the night before. He was joined by Secretary of War Stimson and Secretary of the Navy Knox to discuss the situation. They had been kept informed of developments. Stimson, concerned but not unduly excited, went home afterward to the old estate of Woodley, where Francis Scott Key had stayed long before. Knox drove down to the Navy Department. Hull remained in conference with his Far Eastern experts. And at 1:10 there was a call from the beautiful Japanese Embassy (one of the architects of which had been a Delano) asking for an appointment with the Secretary to deliver the answer to the American proposals. (Already then at 12:32 P.M., Washington time, 7:02 A.M., Hawaiian time, a U. S. Army private, listening on a radio plane detector in Hawaii, had reported a large flight of planes to the north, but the careless assumption was made that they were American.) The Japanese envoys asked for an appointment at 2:00, but the hour set was 1:45. They arrived, nevertheless, at 2:05, and were kept waiting for fifteen minutes in the Secretary's anteroom, which looked like a parlor in a conservative undertaking establishment. Those were the fifteen minutes in which an American period came to an end.

Other people also had gone to work in Washington that day. Watch No. 3 (about thirty-five men and a watch officer) was on duty at Radio Central in the Navy Department handling the usual flow of Sunday traffic on Radio Washington, the Navy's biggest communications station. The clocks above them turned in precision. At about 1848 G.C.T. (1:48 P.M. E.S.T.) the traffic chief of the

watch, Chief Radioman Frank A. Ackerson, U.S.N., was summoned
to the Washington-Honolulu circuit by the operator, E. E. Harris,
Radioman First Class, U.S.N., in response to an alert to stand by
for an urgent message by the Honolulu operator. At 1850 (1:50
P.M. E.S.T.) Harris gave the Honolulu operator his receipt for the
following message:

NPM 1516
Z ØF2 183Ø ØF3 ØF4 Ø2FØ O

From: CINCPAC
ACTION: CINCLANT CINCAF OPNAV

AIR RAID ON PEARL HARBOR THIS IS NOT A DRILL

The message moved from Harris to Ackerson to the communication watch officer, Lieutenant William L. Tagg, U.S.N., to Admiral Harold R. Stark, Chief of Naval Operations. Quickly it was
taken to Secretary Knox. Soon after the event good reporters recorded the conversation which took place when Knox got through
to the President. Roosevelt, who had looked worn the night before
at a large White House dinner, was lunching from a tray in his
study with Harry Hopkins. His incredulous "No," in response to
Knox's report, has been set down. There is also the record of his
immediate commands about acts and safeguards to be taken. The
sinuses from which he had been suffering were forgotten. The room
became a conning tower. He began the process of direction by a
call to Hull.

Some confusion has slipped into the first historical efforts to fix
the exact timing of that first afternoon of war. It has been reported
that when the President received the news, the brass hands of the
ship's clock on his desk stood at 1:47 P.M. What happened, however,
is precisely timed by the receipt of the message by Radio Washington
at 1:50 P.M., and the flash of the news, which Roosevelt personally
dictated, at 2:25 P.M. It was stark and incomplete. Clearly the surprise at Pearl Harbor had been absolute. Military and naval commanders in divided authority there had obviously been remiss in
precautions. Both services seemed to have been as imprudent in the
face of warnings as Thalia Massie had been ten years before when
in a crime-plagued Hawaii she had left a party at an inn to walk,
unescorted, in the tropic night. Talk grew early around American

radio sets that there must have been much liberty and Saturday-night frolicking.

That was spilt milk and spilled blood now. The slowly developing facts had to be faced. Of eight great battleships at Pearl, the power force of the Pacific Fleet, not one was left capable of sea duty. The *Arizona* and the *Oklahoma* were completely destroyed. The *California*, the *West Virginia* and the *Nevada* were beached or sunk. Less severely damaged, the *Maryland* could be repaired in a few weeks, but the *Tennessee* was jammed against massive blocks of concrete. The *Pennsylvania* had been hit in dry dock where its restoration to service could proceed. Three destroyers, a target ship, three cruisers and three auxiliary vessels had been more or less seriously damaged. A hundred and eighty-eight Army and Navy planes had been demolished, 158 more damaged. Two thousand four hundred and three American lives had been lost.

The Japanese diplomats were coming into the State Department while Roosevelt talked to Hull. The President directed that they be received formally and coolly. Apparently that was an order disregarded. Old Cordell let the two Japs sweat before he saw them. And when the Secretary reported their reception later, Hopkins gathered that he had "used some pretty strong Tennessee mountain language to the two Japanese emissaries." Evidently Hull, whose dignity was never damaged by an occasional lisp, had given the first American characterization of the sneak infamy of such liars in governmental power as the old man had not before believed could exist on this planet. The news had been flashed to the country before they left the Secretary's office running before news cameramen down the dim marble halls. The morning was gone; the afternoon was of a different time in a wholly altered world.

The President's phone summoned staff and Cabinet. The radio broke the beginnings of a lazy afternoon. Crowds began to gather about the Japanese Embassy, where a little gray spiral of burning diplomatic papers rose above the neoclassic building and men and women in the street stood as ominously quiet (as one woman witness remembered) "as a lynch mob I once saw in Valdosta, Georgia." Two Japanese drove up in a taxicab and scurried across the pavement and the brief lawn to the chancellery. The only actual violence reported was that some anonymous idiots chopped down one of the capital's Japanese cherry trees. In general, there was an amazing mass calm which was all flamboyant little Fiorello

La Guardia, as chief of Civilian Defense, could have wanted while he cried in New York for "Calm! Calm! Calm!" after a flight in a sirening police car to a radio station to announce that "we are not out of the danger zone by any means." Before sunset people looked not only at the White House and the Japanese Embassy, but fearfully, if a little apologetically, at the sky. There was a steady and spontaneous mobilization in the War, Navy and State Departments, and the War Production Board, of men who poured in, called only by the news.

The calmest place in town and the most exciting was the White House. Hull came from across the street. Stimson and General George Marshall arrived together. Knox led his admirals. Other Cabinet members arrived. Vice-President Henry Wallace in New York phoned that he was coming by the next plane. Among them all the Commander in Chief wore a turtle-neck sweater. Not since the first days of his arrival in the White House, when the national economy had seemed to be collapsing, had he seemed so clearly the genius of leadership in crisis. Swiftly and easily plans were made for the meeting of the Cabinet and the Congressional leaders. An address to the Congress had to be prepared. The report to the nation itself began to shape up. It was not, however, a time of great leadership merely. Before the day was over, among plain people and politicians, Republicans and Democrats, the emphasis on loyalty had swung neatly into place beside the emphasis on liberty in the defense of democracy.

The passage from era to era was not quite so plain. Pearl Harbor was a scene of disaster. It was also, as Churchill said, the fifth climacteric of the war on the way to Allied victory. Those turning points in his mind were the fall of France, the Battle of Britain, the adoption of lend-lease, the invasion of Russia—and the swift, stunning Japanese attack in the Pacific. They were easily counted in aftermath. What was not visible to the yellow flyers in the planes with the mark of the sun on their wings, which came out of the dawn over Diamond Head, was the growth of American power in apparent American confusion. The planes which came so swiftly came too slowly. In December, 1939, America had produced no tanks; in December, 1941, it built nine hundred. Military plane production from 1939 to 1941 was up from 2100 to 19,500. The Army had grown from 174,000 enlisted men on July 1, 1939, to more than a million and a half when the bombs fell at Pearl. Plants were already built; yards were already producing ships. The mechanism of victory, though still inadequate, was in being. More was needed. The Japanese provided it. They struck with unexpected boldness and power. Yet in the blow, dictatorship struck with almost incredible misunderstanding of the cohesiveness of democracy under stress.

It is not so simple to count the climacterics of America's way toward Pearl Harbor in the years between the wars: the joyousness of armistice, the defeat of the League, the oscillations and obscenities of normalcy, the boom and the crash, the Hundred Days, the packing and the purge. Some had seen not climax but catastrophe in the debonair disposal of the two-term Presidential tradition by That Man who was feared or praised as a possible dictator whose baton or scepter was a tilted cigarette. He had seemed to many too much and too long battle ready in the naval cape he liked to wear. Yet sometimes in a democracy frustrated by divisions and fears, the blue cloak had long only seemed to hide his crippled powers before the spread of stomping aggression.

Certainly the era had often seemed uncertain. Many had not agreed on the role prepared for America at its beginning. There had been roaring differences as to the direction in which it was—or should be—heading. Not only had the meaning of liberty been obscured in the varying attitudes toward it expressed in the fable of the wolf, the sheep and the shepherd. The nation in the years had built Bigness and shown concern for "little people," more of whom had escaped docility than had certainly been rescued from depression. The New Deal, which would not be modified, was certainly not universally approved. Advertising and refrigeration had changed food habits. Science was saving more lives and motors were killing more people. On the eve of Pearl Harbor government production managers crying in confusion for more of everything were involved in a battle of zipper manufacturers. And almost like its breeches, the American period was suddenly zipped closed.

Certainly the era at its completion fitted into no neat frame save as a sort of interlude in Armageddon. In the aftermath of attack, the years behind seemed to many a sort of prodigal period for the nation which had strayed from great vision and was, with destiny thrust upon it, recalled to the vision's fulfillment. Orators, exhorting America to the rescue of the world, looked back to Woodrow Wilson. They remembered the day when on the verge of collapse he urged that no future wars leave "dear ghosts" deployed on battle-scarred fields. Time had come round circle to his warning. Men must be deployed to die. American idealism must not collapse again. Yet Pearl Harbor stirred little martial music. There was less of a sense of parades than of a tough job to be well done.

Roosevelt with his great gift for phrase named the era's final day as "a date that will live in infamy." Yet perhaps it was a day of glory, too. Not only did people fall into ranks together; it was evident that there was a mysterious gathering together, too, of factors and forces only dimly seen before. That made possible—made inevitable even—the new world leadership of the United States.

Roosevelt undertook to put the period into unity. With his genius for gesture, he arranged for the presence at the historic joint session of Congress of Mrs. Wilson, a well-preserved, still elegantly dressed widow of sixty-nine. She was handsome as she applauded the President with white-gloved hands. But she seemed more a period piece than a symbol for the continuity of times and causes. This lady of Wilson's crusade beamed as a relic of remote and irrelevant greatness emphasizing the unpredictable pace of change. Despite orators—even Roosevelt—she chiefly seemed to prove only that the end and the beginning of the era of the years between the wars were as different as the morning and the evening of its final day. America was ready to fight again. But it was wary about millennial dreaming.

# SOURCES AND
# ACKNOWLEDGMENTS

Basically my "bibliography" of these years between the wars was the fact of being one of the Americans in them. A friendly Congressional leader slipped me into the House chamber in 1917 to hear Woodrow Wilson call for a declaration of war. Too young for service, I went drilling on the campus of the University of North Carolina where a tall boy in the ranks beside me was Thomas Wolfe. I studied more liveliness than law in the New York of the early twenties. Also there then a great lady asked me to bring my roommates to Sunday supper with her crippled husband. One of them, on his way to fortune as a stockbroker, declined. He just didn't have time, he said, for a has-been. The crippled has-been was Franklin D. Roosevelt.

As a young newspaperman I covered the roaring Democratic National Convention in New York in 1924, but I remember less the row of the wets and the drys around William Jennings Bryan than the privilege of drinking beer with Heywood Broun. In Washington I listened as correspondent to Coolidge making a parable for economy about the pencils on his big desk. Before my scornful eyes the Ku Klux paraded down Pennsylvania Avenue. I died a little when Al Smith was defeated. Just after the stock market crash I got a job on *Fortune*, the brand new magazine of American munificence. Then on a Guggenheim fellowship I went to France where the last of the expatriates were drinking at the Coupole and the Dôme. I was a confident New Dealer in the South where that revolution was most required. On the night before Pearl Harbor I was dancing with good friends on the Starlight Roof in Mr. Rockefeller's Center.

Many as there are above, there are no personal pronouns in the story I have tried to write of these times, but they were my years as well as my country's. Writing this book has been a business of remembrance but also one of revision of opinions. I have not found in history the absolute heroes and the certain villains I once knew in life. Even old Henry Cabot Lodge appears to me now a figure more sad than satanic. Certainly Hoover, in his torn term, was more than the caricature economic catastrophe made him seem. Franklin Roosevelt's halo seems in history as rakishly tilted as his cigarette holder was in life. In retrospect and from research he appears less a man who remade America than one for whom American events fell into precise pattern for his needs.

My study has been, I suspect, as random as my recollections. The books piled up across the years in an accumulation which my wife condemned as rooms-bulging clutter. The sources are infinite. I have certainly not consumed them. There were the old standbys of documentation: the *Dictionary of American Biography*, the *American Guide Series*, old *Who's Whos*. Because it sits by my desk, I turned with steady profit to a bright new set of *Collier's Encyclopedia*.

People helped most: David Mearns, Lodwick Hartley, Admiral Joel T. Boone, Stuart Chase, Dean Acheson, Leon M. Little, William D. Hassett, Clyde Smith, Willis Harrison, Admiral E. M. Eller, Joyce and H. E. Howard, Frank Freidel, Philip Wagner, Sam Ragan, Thad Stem, Jr., Lucy Daniels Inman. Also as always, this book was written almost as much by my wife, Lucy, as by me. Its faults are mine. What merit it may possess is due to her as an aid, editor, critic, typist and above all as a patient woman lugging books and papers back and forth between writing places at Raleigh and Hilton Head in the two Carolinas. I list below, with thanks to their authors, some of the books which helped me most.

Adams, Henry. *The Life of George Cabot Lodge* (published anonymously). Boston, 1911.

Adams, Samuel Hopkins. *Incredible Era: The Life and Times of Warren Gamaliel Harding*. New York, 1939.

Alinsky, Saul. *John L. Lewis—An Unauthorized Biography*. New York, 1949.

Allen, Frederick Lewis. *Only Yesterday*. New York, 1931.

———. *The Big Change*. New York, 1952.

American Heritage. *History of Flight*. New York, 1962.

Anderson, Isabel. *Larz Anderson*. New York, 1940.

Anonymous. *The Mirrors of Washington*. New York, 1921.

Baker, Ray Stannard. *The Life and Letters of Woodrow Wilson—Armistice*, Vol. VIII. New York, 1939.

Barrett, Marvin. *The Jazz Age*. New York, 1959.

———. *The Years Between: A Dramatic View of the Twenties and Thirties*. Boston, 1962.

Baruch, Bernard M. *Baruch: The Public Years*. New York, 1960.

———. *Baruch: My Own Story*. New York, 1957.

Bates, J. Leonard. *The Origins of Teapot Dome*. Urbana, Ill., 1963.

Beach, Sylvia. *Shakespeare and Company*. New York, 1959.

Bright, John. *Hizzoner Big Bill Thompson*. New York, 1930.

Britton, Nan. *The President's Daughter*. New York, 1927.

Broun, Heywood. *Collected Edition of Heywood Broun*. New York, 1941.

Bryan, William Jennings and Mary Baird. *Memoirs of William Jennings Bryan*. Philadelphia, 1925.

Burlingame, Roger. *Of Making Many Books*. New York, 1946.

Childs, Marquis W. *I Write from Washington*. New York, 1942.

Churchill, Allen. *The Improper Bohemians*. New York, 1959.

Coit, Margaret. *Mr. Baruch—the Man, the Myth, the Eighty Years*. Boston, 1957.

Cowley, Malcolm. *Exile's Return: A Literary Odyssey of the 1920's*. New York, 1951.

Crane, Milton, ed. *The Roosevelt Era*. New York, 1947.

Cronon, E. David. *The Cabinet Diaries of Josephus Daniels, 1913–1921*. Lincoln, Neb., 1963.

Daniels, Josephus. *The Wilson Era—1917–1923*. Chapel Hill, N.C., 1946.

Darrow, Clarence. *The Story of My Life*. New York, 1932.

Daugherty, Harry M., and Dixon, Thomas. *The Inside Story of the Harding Tragedy*. New York, 1932.

Davenport, Walter. *Power and Glory—Life of Boies Penrose*. New York, 1931.

Davis, Kenneth S. *Experience of War—The United States in World War II*. Garden City, N.Y., 1965.

Dos Passos, John. *Mr. Wilson's War*. Garden City, N.Y., 1962.

Dunn, Gordon E., and Miller, Banner I. *Atlantic Hurricanes*. Baton Rouge, La., 1960.

Edward, Duke of Windsor. *A King's Story—The Memoirs of the Duke of Windsor*. New York, 1947.

Farley, James A. *Behind the Ballots*. New York, 1938.

Fleming, Denna Frank. *The United States and the League of Nations, 1918–20*. New York, 1932.

Foch, Ferdinand. *The Memoirs of Marshal Foch*, trans. by Col. T. Bentley Mott. Garden City, N.Y., 1931.

Ford, Worthington Chauncey, ed. *Letters of Henry Adams, 1892–1918*. Boston, 1938.

Freidel, Frank. *America in the Twentieth Century*. New York, 1946.

———. *Franklin D. Roosevelt—The Ordeal*. Boston, 1954.

———. *Franklin D. Roosevelt—The Triumph*. Boston, 1956.

Gellhorn, Martha. *The Trouble I've Seen*. New York, 1936.

Gibbs, Wolcott. *A Bed of Neuroses*. New York, 1936.

Goldman, Eric F. *Rendezvous with Destiny*. New York, 1952.

Gurko, Leo. *The Angry Decade*. New York, 1947.

Hagedorn, Hermann. *The Roosevelt Family of Sagamore Hill*. New York, 1954.

Harris, Rex. *Jazz*. London, 1952.

Hart, James D. *The Oxford Companion to American Literature*. New York, 1956.

Harvard College Class of 1910—25th Anniversary Report. Cambridge, Mass., 1935.

Harvey, George. *Henry Clay Frick*. New York, 1928.

Hemingway, Ernest. *The Sun Also Rises*. New York, 1926.

———. *For Whom the Bell Tolls*. New York, 1940.

Hibben, Paxton. *The Peerless Leader—William Jennings Bryan*. New York, 1929.

Hicks, Granville. *John Reed, The Making of a Revolutionary*. New York, 1936.

Hoover, Herbert. *The Memoirs of Herbert Hoover*, 3 vols. New York, 1951, 1952.

———. *The Ordeal of Woodrow Wilson*. New York, 1958.

Hoover, Irwin Hood (Ike). *Forty-two Years in the White House*. Cambridge, Mass., 1934.

Hoyt, Edwin P. *The Tempering Years*. New York, 1963.

Hutchens, John K., ed. *The American Twenties*. New York, 1952.

Ickes, Harold L. *The Secret Diaries of Harold L. Ickes—The First Thousand Days, 1933–1936*, Vol. I. New York, 1953.

———. *The Secret Diaries of Harold L. Ickes—The Inside Struggle*, Vol. II. New York, 1954.

Irwin, Will. *Herbert Hoover*. New York, 1928.

Johnson, Gerald W. *Incredible Tale*. New York, 1950.

Johnson, Hugh S. *The Blue Eagle from Egg to Earth*. New York, 1935.

Johnson, Walter. *1600 Pennsylvania Avenue—Presidents and the People, 1929–1959*. Boston, 1960.

Kane, Harnett. *Louisiana Hayride—The American Rehearsal for Dictatorship, 1928–1940*. New York, 1941.

Kent, Frank R. *The Democratic Party*. New York, 1928.

La Follette, Belle Case and Fola. *Robert M. La Follette*, 2 vols. New York, 1953.

Leighton, Isabel, ed. *The Aspirin Age*. New York, 1949.

Lewis, Sinclair. *Main Street*. New York, 1920.

Lilienthal, David E. *TVA: Democracy on the March*. New York, 1944.

Link, Arthur S., with the collaboration of William B. Catton. *American Epoch: A History of the United States since the 1890's*. New York, 1963.

Lodge, George Cabot, intro. by Theodore Roosevelt. *Poems and Dramas of George Cabot Lodge*. Boston, 1911.

Lodge, Henry Cabot. *Early Memories*. New York, 1913.

———. *The Senate and The League of Nations*. New York, 1925.

Longworth, Alice Roosevelt. *Crowded Hours*. New York, 1933.

Lowry, Edward G. *Washington Close-Ups*. Boston, 1921.

Lyons, Eugene. *Herbert Hoover: A Biography*. Garden City, N.Y., 1964.

McDonald, Forrest. *Insull*. Chicago, 1962.

McPhaul, John J. *Deadlines and Monkeyshines*. New York, 1962.

Manchester, William. *H. L. Mencken: Disturber of the Peace*. New York, 1950.

Mason, Alpheus Thomas. *Brandeis: A Free Man's Life*. New York, 1946.

Means, Gaston B. (and Mrs. May Dixon Thacker). *The Strange Death of President Harding*. New York, 1930.

Michelson, Charles. *The Ghost Talks*. New York, 1944.

Millay, Edna St. Vincent. *The Buck in the Snow*. New York, 1928.

———. *Letters*, ed. by Allan Ross Macdougall. New York, 1952.

Millis, Walter. *Why Europe Fights*. New York, 1940.

Mizener, Arthur. *The Far Side of Paradise: Biography of F. Scott Fitzgerald*. Boston, Mass., 1949.

Morris, Joe Alex. *What a Year!* New York, 1956.

Myers, William Starr. *The Republican Party*. New York, 1928.

Nelson, Donald M. *The Arsenal of Democracy*. New York, 1946.

O'Connor, Richard. *Hell's Kitchen*. New York, 1958.

*Official Report of the Proceedings of the Democratic National Convention, 1924*. Indianapolis, 1924.

Parry, Albert. *Garrets and Pretenders*. New York, 1933.

Pasley, Fred. D. *Al Capone—The Biography of a Self-Made Man*. Garden City, N.Y., 1930.

Patrick, Walton R. *Ring Lardner*. New York, 1963.

Pearson, Drew, and Allen, Robert S. *More Merry-Go-Round* by the authors of *Washington Merry-Go-Round*. New York, 1932.

Pollard, James E. *The Presidents and the Press*. New York, 1947.

Pringle, Henry F. *Alfred E. Smith*. New York, 1927.

Pusey, Merlo J. *Charles Evans Hughes*, 2 vols. New York, 1951.

Rice, Arnold S. *The Ku Klux Klan in American Politics*. Washington, D.C., 1962.

Robinson, Corinne Roosevelt. *My Brother Theodore Roosevelt*. New York, 1921.

Rodman, Selden, ed. *A New Anthology of Modern Poetry*. New York, 1938.

Rollins, Alfred B., Jr. *Roosevelt and Howe*. New York, 1962.

Roosevelt, Eleanor. *This Is My Story*. New York, 1937.

———. *This I Remember*. New York, 1949.

Roosevelt, Elliott, ed. *F.D.R. His Personal Letters—1905–1928*. New York, 1948.

———. *F.D.R. His Personal Letters—1928–1945*. New York, 1950.

Roosevelt, James, and Shalett, Sidney. *Affectionately, F.D.R.* New York, 1959.

Russell, Francis. *Tragedy in Dedham: The Story of the Sacco-Vanzetti Case*. New York, 1962.

———. *The Great Interlude*. New York, 1964.

Schlesinger, Arthur, Jr. *The Age of Roosevelt—The Crisis of the Old Order, 1919–1933*. Boston, 1957.

———. *The Age of Roosevelt—The Coming of the New Deal*. Boston, 1959.

———. *The Age of Roosevelt—The Politics of Upheaval*. Boston, 1960.

Schorer, Mark. *Sinclair Lewis: An American Life*. New York, 1961.

Schriftgiesser, Karl. *The Gentleman from Massachusetts*. Boston, 1944.

Shapiro, Nat, and Hentoff, Nat, eds. *Hear Me Talkin to Ya—The Story of Jazz by the Men Who Made It*. New York, 1955.

Sherwood, Robert E. *Roosevelt and Hopkins*. New York, 1948.

Sinclair, Andrew. *The Available Man: The Life Behind the Masks of Warren Gamaliel Harding*. New York, 1965.

Slayden, Ellen Maury. *Washington Wife—Journal of Ellen Maury Slayden, 1897–1919*, intro. by Walter Prescott Webb. New York, 1962.

Smith, Gene. *When the Cheering Stopped; the Last Years of Woodrow Wilson*. New York, 1964.

Smith, Webster. *The Kingfish—A Biography of Huey P. Long*. New York, 1933.

Starling, Edmund W. *Starling of the White House*. New York, 1946.

Stearns, Harold, ed. *Civilization in the United States*. New York, 1922.

Steinbeck, John. *The Grapes of Wrath*. New York, 1939.

Steinberg, Alfred. *Mrs. R: The Life of Eleanor Roosevelt*. New York, 1958.

Sullivan, Edward D. *Rattling the Cup*. New York, 1929.

Sullivan, Frank. *A Pearl in Every Oyster*. Boston, 1938.

Sullivan, Mark. *Our Times—The Twenties*, Vol. VI. New York, 1935.

Tugwell, Rexford G. *The Democratic Roosevelt*. New York, 1957.

Unofficial Observer. *The New Dealers*. New York, 1934.

Van Dyke, Tertius. *Henry Van Dyke*. New York, 1935.

Villard, Oswald Garrison. *Fighting Years—The Memoirs of a Liberal Editor*. New York, 1939.

Walker, Stanley. *The Night Club Era*. New York, 1933.

Watson, James E. *As I Knew Them*. Indianapolis, 1936.

Wecter, Dixon. *When Johnny Comes Marching Home*. Boston, 1944.

Werner, M. R. *Tammany Hall*. New York, 1928.

———. *Privileged Characters*. New York, 1935.

———. and John Starr. *Teapot Dome*. New York, 1959.

Wharton, Edith. *Hudson River Bracketed*. New York, 1929.

White, William Allen. *Masks in a Pageant*. New York, 1928.

———. *A Puritan in Babylon*. New York, 1938.

———. *The Autobiography of William Allen White*. New York, 1946.

Williamson, Jefferson. *The American Hotel*. New York, 1930.

Wilson, Edith Bolling. *My Memoir*. Indianapolis, 1938.

# INDEX

## DATE DUE